Kenneth and John B. Rayner
and the Limits
of Southern Dissent

Kenneth and John B. Rayner and the Limits of Southern Dissent

Gregg Cantrell

University of Illinois Press

Urbana and Chicago

Library of Congress Cataloging-in-Publication Data

Cantrell, Gregg, 1958–
    Kenneth and John B. Rayner and the limits of southern dissent /
Gregg Cantrell.
        p.   cm.—(Blacks in the New World)
    Includes bibliographical references and index.
    ISBN 0-252-01937-7 (cl)
        1. Rayner, Kenneth, 1808–1884. 2. Rayner, John B., 1850–1918.
3. Politicians—Southern States—Biography. 4. Southern States—
Politics and government—1775–1865. 5. Southern States—Politics
and government—1865–1950. 6. Racism—Southern States—History.
7. Southern States—Race relations. 8. Afro-Americans—Southern
States—History.   I. Title.   II. Series.
F213.R38C36   1993
975'.00496073—dc20   92-14168
                                                           CIP

for my parents,
Jimmie and Mary Lynn Cantrell

Contents

Acknowledgments

This book has been a long time in the making, but it would not have been written at all without the help of a large number of friends, colleagues, and family members. I owe my greatest academic debt to Dale T. Knobel of Texas A&M University. He rendered indispensible advice, criticism, and moral support from the beginning of the project to its end. Despite a demanding schedule as a professor and university administrator, his door was always open to me. He fielded my thousands of questions with unfailing good cheer and set an example as a teacher, scholar, and friend that I will do well to imitate.

My editor, August Meier of Kent State University, has helped untangle dense prose, sharpen interpretations, and identify errors. Whatever is good in this book owes much to his extraordinary knowledge and professionalism.

Others both in and out of academe have provided welcome assistance. I am particularly indebted to Walter L. Buenger, Robert A. Calvert, Dale Baum, and Kenneth Price of Texas A&M University for their expert advice and criticism. As department chairs, Henry C. Dethloff and Larry D. Hill placed unwarranted faith in me. Lawrence Goodwyn of Duke University gave generously of his time and furnished valuable ideas when the study was in its formative stage. Worth Robert Miller of Southeast Missouri State University shared freely of his encyclopedic knowledge of Texas Populism. B. T. Bonner of Wallis, Texas, provided unique insights into black history in Texas. D. Scott Barton was a fellow-traveler in my analysis of Texas Populism and listened patiently to my endless stories about the Rayners' exploits. Shannon L. Smith and Maggy Shannon read and expertly critiqued portions of the manuscript. DiAnne C. Smith of Clarksdale, Mississippi, Janet Coryell of Western Michigan University, and Mark Fernandez of the College of William and Mary took time from their busy schedules to help me track down hard-to-get sources. Jack Abramowitz of Ft. Lauderdale, Florida, and Thomas Appleton of the Kentucky Historical Society provided much-needed encouragement. Barbara Coleman proofread the entire manuscript. My colleagues at Sam Houston State University helped in innumerable ways, and the support given by Lori Key can never be repaid. None of the people mentioned here will agree with everything I have written, and the errors are my own.

Dozens of able librarians and archivists have gone beyond the call of duty in making this book a reality. Paul Scott of the Texas State Library, Bill Page of the Texas A&M Evans Library, Ralph Elder of the Barker Texas History Center, John White and Richard Schraeder of the Southern Historical Collection, and Howard Beeth of the Houston Metropolitan Research Center have put letters and documents into my hands that I never would have found on my own. The efficient staffs at the following archives performed indispensable research and duplication services by mail: the Huntington Library, the Rutherford B. Hayes Presidential Center, the Massachusetts Historical Society, the University of Rochester Library, the National Archives Atlanta Branch, the New-York Historical Society, the New York Public Library, and the Penfield Library at SUNY-Oswego. The entire staff of the microtext department at the Texas A&M Evans Library deserves special commendation.

A number of friends and relatives provided material assistance in completing my research. My parents, Jimmie and Mary Lynn Cantrell, and my grandmother, Vera Wiman, were generous beyond expectations in their financial support during six years of graduate school. Bill and Janet Wiman, Fran and Ron Hattin, Jacquidon and Charlie Gallardo, Craig and Roxie Strain, Dal and Karen Payne, Lawrence and Nell Goodwyn, Brian Hurst, Kip Patterson, Richard Brandes, and Clark Jernigan put roofs over my head and hot meals in my stomach in the course of my research-related travels.

An Ottis Lock Grant from the East Texas Historical Society helped to defray travel expenses during the research stage. The Texas A&M University College of Liberal Arts provided a generous fellowship and a fine office that proved invaluable during the writing phase.

Finally, I owe a special thanks to the several Rayner descendants who shared their thoughts, memories, family traditions, and keepsakes with a prying stranger. Kenneth Rayner's white descendants, Kenneth R. Glennan, Jr., Kenneth R. Hyman, Hyman Kirkpatrick, Sallie Savage, and their spouses graciously talked with me and showed me portraits, photographs, family heirlooms, and one important 1866 letter. Arlene Carrington enlightened me as to the black Rayners' genealogy and shared related stories about Kenneth's black daughter, Cornelia. Ann Rayner Childs not only told what she could remember of her grandfather John B. Rayner, but she also fed and housed me for three days while I interviewed her father, A. A. Rayner. A. A. Rayner, of course, told me things about his populist father that no one else could know. Other members of the Rayner family in Chicago helped me put bits and pieces of the puzzle together from stories their parents had told them. Special thanks, however, must go to the grandson of the Texas populist, Sammie Rayner. He invited me to Chicago to meet him and the rest of the family and treated me like royalty while I was there; tickets for the Bears-Redskins playoff game were hot items in 1987, but one had my name on it. He shared not only his family's history with me, but also his own fascinating political career. In politics, Sammie was a first-rate dissenter in the Rayner tradition. He is also a first-rate person.

Introduction

This book is an inquiry into the power of white supremacy and its impact on public life in the southern United States. The vehicle for this inquiry is the biography of two men, Kenneth Rayner (1808–84) and his son, John B. Rayner (1850–1918), whose careers spanned a period of American history from the presidency of Andrew Jackson to that of Woodrow Wilson. Both men sought to lead constructive public careers in the midst of a political culture grounded in racism. As political leaders they attempted to eliminate racial issues as the dominant force in their region's politics and replace them with a variety of other social and economic themes. In doing so they tested, and eventually exceeded, the permissible limits of southern dissent.

The story of the Rayners, like so much of southern history, is steeped in irony. Kenneth Rayner was a member of the southern slaveholding aristocracy; his mulatto son, John B. Rayner, came into the world as his father's human chattel. In 1861 the father supported the South's war to preserve slavery; four years later that war brought freedom to the son. The elder Rayner's life was marked by luxury and high social standing; the younger Rayner struggled against the racism of his father's people as well as the suspicion of many of his mother's race.

If differences in skin color, wealth, and social status made their lives a study in contrasts, the similarities between the two Rayners are even more striking. At the most basic level, kinship was evident from their shared physical characteristics. In addition, both men were well-educated and throughout their lives were eager students of history, literature, and the sciences. They both entered politics as young men and earned the confidence of their constituents. In their times, father and son became transcendent orators whose behind-the-scenes political skills rivaled their unsurpassed talents on the stump.

Yet the resemblance between Kenneth and John B. Rayner extends even beyond these relatively superficial similarities, for the two men also possessed strikingly kindred political philosophies that shaped their actions—actions suggestively illuminated by the recent historiography that has distinguished between the "republican" and "liberal" tendencies in Americans' worldview during the eighteenth and nineteenth centuries. Although these distinctions can be, and often have been, taken too far, in the case of the Rayners it is useful to note the differences between Revolutionary-era republicanism and the liberalism that increasingly prevailed by the Jacksonian period.

Long after the United States had embraced liberalism, both men continued to adhere to many of the more orthodox tenets of classical republicanism as promulgated by the Revolutionary generation. Their attachment to republican ideals long after the majority of Americans had abandoned them repeatedly placed the Rayners politically at odds with their peers. Among the republican principles to which they clung were the ideas that concentrated power corrupts and that America's success depended upon an intelligent and virtuous electorate deferring to enlightened and disinterested leaders chosen from among the elite. The interests of the individual were important but not to be placed above the overall welfare of the community. Likewise, strictly sectional issues were not to take precedence over national considerations. This Jeffersonian conception of government and society neither discouraged commerce and manufacturing nor forbade positive action on the part of government to promote economic development. However, it did demand that equality of opportunity be preserved and that the people control economic and governmental institutions instead of being controlled by them.

While the Rayners based their public actions on their belief in Revolutionary republican ideology, they also embodied the tensions inherent in that ideology. Bernard Bailyn, Gordon Wood, and others have firmly established the direct influence of the British Whig or "country party" tradition—communal values, suspicion of power, fear of corruption—in republican thought. Other scholars such as Joyce Appleby and Drew McCoy have examined the beliefs of the Founders and reaffirmed the seemingly contradictory presence, particularly by the 1780s and 1790s, of Lockean liberalism with its emphasis on natural rights and economic freedom. Whatever nuances of the various historiographical interpretations one wishes to emphasize, it is clear from recent scholarship that the ideology of Jefferson and other leaders of the Revolutionary generation was based upon traditional republicanism tempered with a distinctive strain of Lockean liberalism. The Constitution and the Bill of Rights in particular represented an effort to develop these Lockean elements while maintaining the more traditional precepts of republicanism. Much of the political history of nineteenth-century America represents a working-out of this conflict with the result being the triumph of liberalism at the expense of republicanism. The Rayners, like their professed idols Washington, Jefferson, Madison, and Monroe, rarely denied the liberal positions on individual liberty, broad suffrage, and pursuit of economic self-interest. But unlike most Americans in the post-Jeffersonian era, they continued to be motivated by the Revolutionary fear of corrupting power, the need for virtue and intelligence in government, and the reconciliation of community, state, and national interests with those of the individual. Their stubborn attachment to these beliefs often flew in the face of Americans' growing liberalism as well as competing liberal strains within their own outlooks.[1]

Adherence to older notions of republicanism brought both Rayners into conflict with the dominant political parties of their eras. It made them dissenters. Both men began their public careers believing that one of the major parties—in Kenneth's case the Whigs, and in John B.'s case the Republicans—stood for republican values.[2] When it became apparent that each party had abandoned republican principles, both father and son left their parties and joined organizations that seemed to promise a restoration of republicanism. Through these third parties—the Know-Nothings of the 1850s and Populists of the 1890s—they registered their dissatisfaction with the liberal orthodoxy of the two major parties.

Moreover, the Rayners were not just politicians but *southern* politicians, and racial attitudes were bound to play a crucial part in defining their roles as dissenters. It was on issues relating to blacks that the differences between the Rayners and their peers were most apparent and most damaging. Although they shared the Jeffersonian belief in traditional republicanism, the Rayners also accepted certain liberal positions born of Enlightenment rationalism. Paradoxically, one such tenet was the liberal position on race. This was paradoxical because the theory of natural rights was one of the few liberal concepts that most nineteenth-century southerners rejected out of hand. Even slaveholding Founding Fathers such as Jefferson had admitted that slavery was at best a necessary evil and that in some theoretical place and time blacks might be able to share in the rights and duties of free citizens. But as southern slaveholders in the early nineteenth century increasingly embraced liberalism, they came to emphasize personal property rights, explicitly denying that natural rights extended to blacks and regarding slavery as a "positive good." This denial of blacks' inherent equality continued beyond the Civil War and Reconstruction and was actually reinforced at the end of the century when Populism was defeated. Thus Kenneth Rayner in the mid-nineteenth century found himself outside the southern mainstream in affirming the essential humanity of blacks and pronouncing slavery a necessary evil, and John B. Rayner was equally out of step in the late 1800s when he worked to bring equal political and economic opportunity to blacks. Their attachment to traditional republican principles estranged the Rayners from the major political parties in the South, but in the end it was their adherence to an unacceptably liberal position on race that destroyed their political careers. The South could tolerate and occasionally even embrace idiosyncratic views about the relationships between government and society or labor and capital; unorthodox attitudes about race were another matter. As Kenneth and John B. Rayner learned, this was the limit of southern dissent.

This study, covering nearly a century of American history, necessarily encompasses a wide variety of political events, parties, and movements. Kenneth Rayner was, by turns, a Whig, Know-Nothing, secessionist, peace advocate, Redeemer, and Republican. John B. Rayner at one time or another identified himself as a Republican, Prohibitionist, Populist, Independent, and Anti-prohibitionist. The basic contention of this work—that the South's demand for racial consensus quashed dissent—is hardly a revolutionary idea. What the story of Kenneth and John B. Rayner provides is a working-out of this theme at the personal level. More specifically, this study examines the various parties and movements in which the Rayners operated, considers them in the framework of ideology, and analyzes the effects of ideology on practical politics.

Kenneth Rayner entered public life as a Whig, deeply devoted to the nationalistic vision of Henry Clay. The roots of the elder Rayner's brand of Whiggery are clearly traceable to his belief in republican ideology. Growing up as the son of a Revolutionary veteran on a tidewater plantation near the North Carolina-Virginia line, he accepted unquestioningly the dictum that the survival of the Republic depended upon a virtuous and intelligent citizenry who would choose enlightened and disinterested leaders. Sovereignty, he believed, rested not primarily in the states nor in the federal government but in the people. According to this view, people should delegate their power sparingly and for short periods to elected officials. Too much power, especially when vested in an executive, surely would corrupt. Such a philosophy, however, did not lead Rayner to embrace the idea of a rigidly negative government, as did many nineteenth-century Americans. To the contrary, he was quite anxious to see federal and state governments intervene actively, if such intervention were consistent with public interest and could be reconciled with the Constitution. To this end he championed enlarged powers for state and federal legislative bodies (who after all reflected the will of their constituents) at the expense of the corruption-prone executive branches.

Jacksonian-era Whiggery, as expounded by Clay, thus provided for Rayner the ideal means of expressing his beliefs. The anti-partyism, Unionism, and fear of corruption (personified by "King Andrew the First") so often attributed to Whigs comes into sharper focus by tracing Rayner's rise to national leadership within the party. This set of beliefs also helps to account for his break with the Whigs in the early 1850s, before it was at all certain that the party's day as a viable political force had passed.

Republican values likewise aid in explaining Rayner's subsequent role in the founding of the American, or Know-Nothing, party. Southern Know-Nothingism has been variously written off as simple bigotry, Unionism, or Whiggery in disguise. But Rayner's experience in the party belies these simplistic labels. The republican concern about corruption, the dedication to the rule of intelligence and virtue, the respect for constitutional law—in short, the same Revolutionary-era worldview that drew Kenneth Rayner to Whiggery—also made him a Know-Nothing. Immigrants, Catholics, and the Democratic and Republican parties all represented corruption, placing the Republic in imminent peril. Rayner's prominence as a major national Know-Nothing spokesman suggests that he was not alone in holding such beliefs. Behind the nativist rhetoric lay a deeply felt devotion to republican ideology, a devotion that struck a responsive note in thousands of average Americans who flocked to Know-Nothing lodges and voted for the party's candidates. Unthinking hatred of foreigners and Catholics did not represent the be-all and end-all of the American party that Rayner envisioned; republicanism did. Catholics and immigrants (along with the corrupt sectional parties) simply numbered among the most serious contemporary threats to a republican form of government—threats that virtuous and patriotic Americans were duty-bound to oppose.

The American party was destroyed by its inability or unwillingness to follow Rayner's advice and hold itself aloof from the slavery controversy. Sacrificed on the altar of corruption and sectionalism, in Rayner's mind it constituted the last hope of the nation. By 1861, a southern planter clinging to republican ideals had no place to turn politically. This lack of options resulted in a course that can only be described as irrational. Swept along with the tide of events, Rayner deserted the Union he had defended for twenty-five years and lent his support to the secession movement. Later, while publicly urging more vigorous prosecution of the war effort, he privately entered

into discussions with other North Carolinians about how to bring about an
early peace under the best terms possible. After the war he wrote a laudatory
campaign biography of Andrew Johnson, only to endorse the Grant administration and black suffrage a few years later. Political frustration and a failed
planting venture resulted in bankruptcy and a bout of severe depression that
almost ended his life. Recovering, and faced with the need to support his
family, Rayner threw himself upon old political friends in the Grant administration and secured positions as judge of the Court of Alabama Claims
and solicitor of the Treasury. He spent his last years a tragicomic figure in
the nation's capital, bewildered and enraged by the lack of principles in the
administration and the party on which he depended for his livelihood.

The younger Rayner's career displays many of the same themes: a reverence for outdated Revolutionary republicanism, opposition to the alleged
corruption of the two major parties, a belief in the sovereignty of the people,
advocacy of the positive state acting in the public interest, and a conviction
that American politics must be organized around principles other than race.
Growing up as a privileged house servant and openly recognized as Kenneth
Rayner's offspring, John B. clearly inherited his father's abilities as well as
many of his beliefs. How much of this inheritance came from personal obser-
vation, how much was purposefully taught him by his father, and how much
lay in his genetic makeup remains uncertain. But Kenneth cared enough to
see that John received a college education before the two parted ways.

His abilities, education, and family name propelled John into local Republican politics during the 1870s in North Carolina. Serving in a variety of
municipal offices during the most idealistic days of Reconstruction, he saw
his early hopes dashed as the Democrats regained control of the state government and stripped blacks of their offices and political power, while the
national Republican administration watched apathetically. For the next fifteen years the younger Rayner witnessed the Republican party relinquish the
liberal position on race and apotheosize the individualistic values of liberal
capitalism. After moving to Texas in 1880, he followed the example of his
father thirty years earlier and cast loose from his party in order to pursue
an independent political course. In 1892, that meant allying himself with the
Populist party. Then, in a rather remarkable parallel to his father's career in
the American party, John B. Rayner rapidly rose to a position as the leading black Populist in Texas and a major ideological spokesman, taking his
place on the party's state executive committee in one of Populism's greatest
strongholds.

The economic issues had changed since his father's time; *sharecroppers, furnishing merchants,* and *crop lien* were terms with little salience for ante-bellum southerners. But while the People's party was created primarily to alleviate the desperate agricultural depression of the late-nineteenth century, for John B. Rayner and those who responded to his brand of Populism it had an even greater significance. American politics remained a sectional affair, with big business and government in a lucrative partnership and southern blacks as pawns in the game. Entering the Populist party, Rayner sought the same goals for which his father had worked in the 1850s: the creation of a truly national party, organized around principles other than race and sectionalism. His ideological conception of the party was also reminiscent of his father's vision of the American party. Populism, for John B. Rayner, would purify the body politic, taking the reins of power away from corrupt politicians and greedy capitalists and placing the nation in the hands of virtuous and intelligent freemen. The Farmers' Alliance chapters that provided the grass-roots organizational structure for the Populist party represented the same kind of popular voice for American voters as did the Know-Nothing lodges of the 1850s.

Throughout his years as a Populist spokesman, the younger Rayner voiced the same critique of the sectional political system that his father had articulated in the antebellum period: preoccupation with racial issues prevented the South and the nation from dealing with other pressing problems. In the 1840s, Kenneth Rayner had complained bitterly of the way in which the never-ending slavery controversy obstructed the business of Congress, when that body should have been spending its time stabilizing the country's erratic finances, developing national resources, and promoting commerce, manufacturing, and agriculture. In the 1850s, he had warned even more vigorously about the manner in which a country obsessed with the slavery question was ignoring the threat posed by political corruption and massive foreign immigration. Thirty years later, with the slaves technically freed and ostensibly possessing the right to vote, John B. Rayner complained just as vociferously about a government that would let its producing farmers, both black and white, starve while politicians endlessly harped about the threat of "Negro domination." And, like his father, Rayner saw racially charged sectionalism prevent the triumph of his genuinely national political alternative.

His experiences in the Populist party suggest that the agrarian revolt was more than just a program for economic reform. Rayner and the Populists who placed him in a leadership position envisioned neither a socialist nor a classically liberal America. Instead, they carried with them into the movement an attitude toward government and society that harkened back to Jeffersonian republicanism leavened with the liberal outlook on race. Like the Revolutionary fathers, John B. Rayner and the Populists sought not to restrict individual economic opportunity but to broaden and equalize it. To accomplish this they advocated sweeping political reforms designed to return sovereignty to the people, restore respect for the Constitution, and reinvigorate the communal and national values that unbridled individualism had destroyed.

Southern Populism, with its Jeffersonian foundation and tentative experiment in racial liberalism, foundered on the same rock of racially inspired conflict and unrestrained individualism that crippled Kenneth Rayner's attempt at building a national reform party in the 1850s. When considered from the perspective of its most important black spokesman, the divided mind of Texas Populism is apparent. Among the party's upper echelon was a group of white leaders sincerely interested in the material betterment of the poor of both races. Achieving this meant organizing southern politics along economic rather than racial lines. It also meant defeating the Democrats, which could only be accomplished with the help of black votes freely cast and fairly counted. A large cross-section of the party's white rank and file welcomed black votes, but their commitment to seeing blacks receive justice was tenuous at best. In 1896, faced with probable defeat, Populist leaders in Texas took the fateful step of proposing a fusion deal with black Republicans. The white rank and file rebeled against this overt blow at the region's racial orthodoxy and returned to the party of white supremacy, the Democrats. Populism was destroyed, and many white Populists blamed blacks for its downfall. Some Populists dropped out of politics altogether, while others took out their frustration by disfranchising and segregating their erstwhile black allies.

The defeat of Populism brought John B. Rayner to a political and personal crisis similar to that which Kenneth had experienced after the downfall of the American party. The institutionalization of Jim Crow devastated the younger Rayner's way of life in much the same way that Civil War and Reconstruction had brought disaster to his father. With no acceptable political alternative available, he pursued an increasingly checkered and irrational course. At times he claimed to be an Independent who would support "the best man" for elective office. At other times he counseled his people to stay out of politics altogether. As the father had cast his lot with the corrupt Grant administration, so the son went to work for the Texas beer oligopoly as a paid political organizer in the battle against prohibition. He attached himself to the ultra-conservative lumber baron John Henry Kirby and was labeled an Uncle Tom by some of his own people. At the same time, he labored tirelessly as a fund-raiser for black education. Like his father, he died an embittered and forgotten man.

A study of this type requires a minor caveat. It is clear from the preceding sketch of the Rayners' lives and careers that this is not a heroic story. Although each of the Rayners was capable of remarkable political courage, they were not always dissenters in the sense of the virtuous hero who bravely speaks out against wrong despite the certainty of retribution. Neither man desired to be a martyr, and they certainly lacked many of the qualities needed to make them admirable figures in the eyes of most late-twentieth-century Americans. While their racial views were unpopular for the times and places in which they lived, both the white father and his black son fell far short of being true egalitarians. Like the Revolutionary heroes they so venerated, the Rayners could be elitists, believing that voters should defer to leaders such as themselves who possessed superior virtue and intelligence. Their attitudes toward foreigners and women were usually consistent with those held by the mass of American males. They possessed large egos, and the causes they spent their best years defending—Know-Nothingism and Populism—were in their own particular ways chauvinistic and out of step with the political realities of their times. Late in life, each man compromised his principles and personal dignity in futile efforts to salvage a way of life that his earlier actions had jeopardized.

I harbor no illusions about the place of my subjects in history; Kenneth and John B. Rayner clearly failed in their efforts to change the societies in which they lived. But it is perhaps for this very reason that their lives are of interest today. Their story opens a unique window onto what the historian Carl N. Degler termed "the other South"—that set of nineteenth-century southerners who, in his words, "stood out against the prevailing views and values of their region while remaining there."[3] Of the many views and values that set the nineteenth-century South apart from the rest of the nation, one characteristic has always stood out above the rest: the presence of the black southerner. Take away the slaves and their descendants, and the South likely would have differed little from the North. Without the presence of blacks there would be no sectional conflict, no Civil War, no need for Reconstruction, nothing to be "redeemed" in the 1870s, no racial minority to disfranchise, and no meaning to the words *Jim Crow*. Thus it is not surprising that the region's politics revolved around racial questions, often to the exclusion of other vital issues. From the 1830s well into the 1900s, questions associated with slavery and race played so central a role in the southern polity that to dissent from the prevailing view placed the dissenter's political credibility—and sometimes his life and property—in danger. Southern society drew a fine line between the racial attitudes and approaches tolerated under this polity and those not tolerated. That line marked the limits of southern dissent. What follows is the story of two men who ventured too near it.

I

Kenneth Rayner
1808–84

Deeply as I sympathize with the people of the South in our common sufferings, and highly as I admire their noble and manly traits of character, yet, it has been my lot to differ with a large majority of them.

Kenneth Rayner, 1874

CHAPTER I

"A Man for the Times"

On a spring morning in 1835, carriages began arriving at the stately Greek revival governor's palace on Fayetteville Street in Raleigh, North Carolina. One by one they stopped in the circular drive before the white-columned portico, as liveried slaves steadied the horses and assisted their masters in climbing from the carriages. Although the arrivals included the cream of North Carolina society, it was not a social occasion. This impressive-looking assemblage was meeting to draft a new constitution for the state—one that would replace the charter under which North Carolinians had been governed since 1776.

Surveying the delegates, one would have found many of the names prominent in the previous half-century of North Carolina history. Among the many recognizable personalities were the venerable Nathaniel Macon, a life-long leader of his people and a veteran of both branches of the national Congress; William Gaston, a state supreme court justice and perhaps the North State's most distinguished jurist; John Branch, former governor and navy secretary in Jackson's first administration; and David Lowry Swain, the current governor. Also present was a large number of legislators, past, current, and future. As the notables continued to arrive, one particular delegate attracted little attention, for he had never held elective office and possessed neither great wealth nor a distinguished family name. He would have attracted even less had it not been for his striking good looks and the fact that, at age twenty-six, he was the youngest of the 130 delegates.[1]

As he took his place in the convention, Kenneth Rayner must have felt a certain degree of trepidation. The very idea of constitutional revision struck more than one North Carolinian as unwise tampering with the hallowed principles of the Founding Fathers. But beyond this widely shared source of doubt were several additional concerns specific to Rayner. One was his family background. In a region where familial connections and reputation counted for much, Rayner came from a relatively unassuming home. His father, Amos, had served as a mere private in the Revolutionary War and became a Baptist minister in Bertie County, in the tidewater country bordering Albemarle Sound. Amos later married Hannah Williams, who brought into the marriage a modest fortune—enough to enable him to purchase a plantation and a few slaves in neighboring Hertford County. Over the years, the elder Rayner's estate grew sufficiently for him to provide adequately for his three sons and one daughter. As they reached adulthood, Amos divided his assets among the children. He gave Kenneth the Hertford plantation known as Little Town, consisting of about a thousand acres of land along the Chowan River near Winton. The size of the plantation is deceptive, however, because the land was of mediocre quality, much of it being swampy and unsuitable for agriculture. As late as 1840 only eighteen slaves lived on Little Town.[2]

Amos's status as a middling planter from an undistinguished background made his son's entry into the ruling elite of North Carolina quite unlikely. Kenneth also lacked the advantage of having attended the acknowledged training ground for the state's leaders, the University of North Carolina at Chapel Hill. But the nearby town of Tarboro in Edgecombe County boasted one of North Carolina's best and largest country academies, and there Kenneth had received an education surprisingly thorough in the basics of reading, writing, arithmetic, and spelling, as well as in Latin and Greek, natural and moral philosophy, history, astronomy, mathematics, and English. The principal of Tarboro Academy during his time there was Eugene Farnan, a native of Ireland and a classical scholar of considerable repute. Farnan was known as a master of the "dead languages," as well as Spanish, French, and English, and he was said to have been "without a superior in North Carolina" as a linguist. Surviving volumes from Rayner's library indicate the breadth of his training; the works of Homer, Tacitus, Virgil, Plutarch, and numerous other classics abound. In addition to the literary works—many of which were in the original Latin—Rayner's school books included a large number of scientific and mathematics texts, historical works, and treatises on religion and theology. The evidence of his education clearly indicates the continuing influence in the early-nineteenth-century South of the Enlightenment, with its emphasis on reason, the importance it placed on understanding the natural world, and its veneration of classical antiquity.[3]

Rayner thus compensated for his lack of opportunity to receive a prestigious university education by attending the best possible local academy and applying himself studiously. Apparently he anticipated a professional career beyond that of the gentleman planter, for he soon began preparing himself for the next step. Then, as now, lawyers largely ruled the political domain. Rayner, upon completing his studies at the academy, sought out a local attorney in Tarboro and began reading Blackstone and the other basics of legal education. Realizing that studying under a country lawyer would not by itself secure the ambitious young planter the training that he desired, Rayner made the acquaintance of state legislator Louis D. Wilson, a man with statewide political connections whose endorsement could provide the stepping-stone to a more advantageous arrangement.[4]

In 1830, learning that the newly elected chief justice of the North Carolina supreme court, Thomas Ruffin, was considering accepting a limited number of students to read law under his tutelage, Rayner persuaded Wilson to mention his name to Ruffin. Rayner himself then wrote a letter proposing to the distinguished judge that he consider taking him as a student. Ruffin accepted him, and Rayner spent the next year studying under the watchful eye of the man who, in more than twenty years on the state's highest court, would gain a reputation as one of North Carolina's finest legal minds. It was excellent training for an aspiring politician.[5]

Although the 1835 constitutional convention marked Rayner's first appearance upon the statewide political stage, he was no stranger to politics. Upon completing his education he had moved back to Hertford County to pursue what would become his two lifelong passions, agriculture and politics. On one hand, he was ready to assume a larger share in managing the family plantation because Amos was nearing eighty. On the other hand, the political arena beckoned, for at no time in the young American republic's history had national politics intruded more upon local affairs. In Hertford County, as in many other parts of the United States, the personality and policies of Andrew Jackson were creating new political alignments by 1835. The county had long been a Jackson stronghold, and in 1832 Jackson outpolled Henry Clay by a 173–15 margin. Consensus, however, would soon break down, and the youthful Kenneth Rayner would side with the opposition.[6]

Sketchy evidence suggests that Rayner may have broken with the Jacksonian Democrats over the president's opposition to internal improvements, his war on the Bank of the United States, and perhaps over Old Hickory's handling of the nullification crisis. An early biographer portrayed Rayner as a disciple not of Jackson but of John C. Calhoun. Although there is no way to assess Rayner's prenullification opinion of the famous South Carolinian, it is possible that Calhoun's early nationalism and his break with Jackson in 1830–31 did hold appeal. It appears that Rayner's first attempt at elective office came in 1833, when he sought a seat in the North Carolina House of Commons (the lower house of the state legislature). Virtually no sources survive to tell the story of that race except Rayner's own brief statement years later, when he was in the U.S. House of Representatives. Speaking in 1842, he explained that he was defeated in his first race for the legislature because he "dared to combat the Federal heresies" of Jackson's 1833 antinullification proclamation. "General Jackson's popularity," explained Rayner, "resting as it then did upon the very basis of Federalism . . . consigned me to private life." Yet if strong states' rights beliefs led Rayner to fear Jackson, they apparently did not bring him to favor nullification. By 1835, at least, he had repudiated both Calhoun and nullification and for the rest of his political career treated the South Carolinian and his disunionist doctrines with contempt.[7]

Further indication of Rayner's early anti-Jackson sentiments can be found in his friendship with former North Carolina governor John Branch. Jackson had named Branch secretary of the navy during his first administration, but when Old Hickory purged his cabinet of Calhoun supporters in 1831, Branch was one of those asked to resign. Rayner became Branch's political ally and promised to keep him updated on county political developments. In July 1834, as state elections were in full swing, Rayner reported to his friend that his county's campaign for state legislature was going to be a close one. "The contest seems to be one of principle entirely—it is decidedly Jackson & anti-Jackson," he wrote to Branch, adding that "there has been a great falling off from the Administration." Rayner explained that he had again considered running for the legislature himself but believed it to be in the best interests of the anti-administration forces for him sit out. Perhaps he feared that a second loss to a pro-Jackson opponent would brand him a loser. He chose to bide his time.[8]

Rayner's earliest recorded political activities, therefore, coincided directly with the creation of the Second Party System in America. In his county, as elsewhere, the overriding issue was Andrew Jackson and his "high-handed measures" (to use Rayner's phrase). Over the course of the Jackson administration, as the Old Hero had taken strong stands on issues such as executive authority, state's rights, internal improvements, and banks, politicians at all levels of American government had succeeded in creating two competing political cultures or "persuasions." Although Rayner himself had chosen not to run for office in the 1834 elections, he was deeply involved in the anti-Jackson campaign in Hertford County. When neither of the aspirants for the local legislative seat declared their position on Jackson, Rayner explained how they were to be dealt with: "We are trying to keep Carter & Smith silent, our object is to prevent them from pledging in favour of the administration. Whichever of them succeeds, will, I think, by proper management be induced to go with us." Rayner's "management" evidently proved astute, because after the 1834 elections neither Carter nor Smith was ever heard from again in North Carolina politics, and for the next two decades Kenneth Rayner dominated his county's political scene.[9]

Hertford County men like Rayner who took a stand for or against Jackson in the early 1830s created a dynamic local two-party system that reflected national political divisions. Those who fought Jackson's measures soon began calling themselves Whigs, taking the name from the patriots of the Revolutionary era who had opposed George III. Although until the 1850s the Whigs usually won in Hertford County, the Democratic, or Jackson, party offered lively opposition. Both parties normally fielded strong candidates and campaigned vigorously on clearly defined platforms. Rayner set the tone in 1834 for the party battles that were to come. "We may *perhaps* fail," he confidently admitted, "but our cause is prospering, and cheered by the reflection that revolutions never go backwards, we shall in case of defeat only prepare for a more vigorous exertion next year. In fact, we will never give up the contest till we have them in our power."[10]

The coalescence of an anti-Jackson party in Hertford County was thus accomplished by 1834. But national issues, important as they were, were not sufficient to create a stable, statewide opposition, or Whig, party in North Carolina. Because state and local governments in the antebellum period affected the average American's life far more than they do today, the anti-administration forces needed to reach consensus on state issues. This process of consensus-forming was well under way in North Carolina by 1834, but it was not yet complete. The constitutional convention of 1835 and Rayner's role in it demonstrate the degree to which consensus among the Whigs was still lacking.

North Carolinians voted to revise their state's constitution in 1835 because of geographic, rather than partisan, divisions. The 1776 constitution gave eastern counties such as Rayner's disproportionate representation in the legislature, but over the half-century since the constitution was adopted the state's population had steadily shifted westward into the piedmont and mountains. Westerners longed for state aid to internal improvements in order to improve their poor transportation networks. As long as the east controlled the legislature, that aid would not be forthcoming. Accordingly, it also comes as no surprise that the west would be the stronghold of the Whig party, which was on record as favoring internal improvements.[11]

Despite their party allegiance, eastern Whigs like Kenneth Rayner felt themselves compelled for reasons of sectional interests to join forces with eastern Democrats and vote against their western Whig brethren. In fact, party lines seemed to count for little in this situation. Hertford County voted against holding a convention by a lopsided margin of 436–16. Despite this almost unanimous opposition to the convention, the county's citizens of course had to send representatives to the Raleigh meeting. They elected as their delegates two anti-Jackson men: the wealthy, aristocratic, and rather colorless Dr. Isaac Pipkin and the young, fiery, handsome Kenneth Rayner.[12]

Rayner's early biographer explained that Rayner "had opposed the call of a convention, believing that it was a dangerous precedent to set, and preferring that the constitution as handed down from the Revolutionary fathers should remain for all time." This characterization rings true for a number of reasons. Hertford County had been "strongly on the patriot side" in the Revolution and had supported the ratification of the U.S. Constitution. Rayner's father had seen combat duty in the Revolutionary War. If ever a delegate had reason to venerate the 1776 constitution and suspect the wisdom of drafting a new one, it was Kenneth Rayner. Still, Rayner must have felt some reluctance to vote against the western Whigs, for, like them, he favored state aid to internal improvements. The barrier islands of the northeastern North Carolina coast made the fine waterways of Hertford County largely useless as conduits to the ocean, a problem railroads and canals could remedy. But Whigs such as Rayner could not afford to gamble away their section's political power on the mere chance of internal improvements. They had to oppose the calling of a constitutional convention.[13]

As it turned out, the convention was something of an anticlimax. The real battle over changing the basis of representation had been fought in the 1834 legislature, which in authorizing the convention in effect required that the new constitution give control of the lower house to the more populous west. But while the sectional redistribution of power was a fait accompli before the convention met, the delegates would still have jurisdiction over such issues as the rules governing suffrage in the state. A study of two of these suffrage debates, one concerning free people of color and the other concerning Catholics, helps to shed light on Rayner's beliefs in 1835 and explain his actions during the next fifty years of a stormy political career.[14]

North Carolina was unique among southern states in continuing to allow free blacks to vote for state legislators subject to the same restrictions as whites (a simple taxpaying requirement to vote for house members and a fifty-acre freehold requirement to vote for senators). By the 1830s, however, racial attitudes—especially among southern slaveholders—were changing. Many of the delegates who assembled in Raleigh in June 1835 evidently had decided already that taking the vote away from blacks would be a progressive measure.

Delegate Hugh McQueen stated the basic position of those who supported black disfranchisement. The Negro, he claimed, "came here debased, he is yet debased, and there is no sort of polish which education or circumstance can give him, which ever will reconcile the whites to an extension of the right of suffrage." Judge Joseph Daniel spoke for Rayner and the other delegates who wished to preserve the free blacks' franchise. Allowing blacks the continued right to vote, Daniel argued, would "conciliate the most respectable portion of the colored population" and "give them standing distinct from the slave population." Daniel reminded his fellow delegates that blacks had fought honorably in the Revolution, and that good relations between whites and free blacks might help deflect the growing criticism leveled at slaveholders by northern abolitionists. In a final attempt to preserve at least a limited vote for blacks, the pro-suffrage delegates suggested a one-hundred acre property requirement for free Negroes. Rayner and sixty-one other delegates voted for the compromise, but the disfranchisers held fast. The convention ultimately denied suffrage to all free blacks and mulattos. Later during the convention Rayner would bitterly complain that taxpaying free blacks, "an unfortunate, though degraded race of beings," were being "deprived of all participation in the selection of those who administer that Government, thereby compromising that cardinal principle in free governments, that representation and taxation should never be separated!" He clearly felt that the original intent of the Constitution's framers should not be sacrificed on purely racial grounds. Hertford's sizable population of free blacks in some respects might be "degraded," but he was not about to deny the wisdom of the Founding Fathers or betray his black constituents. It was the first time—but not the last—that Rayner would publicly oppose the southern majority who took the hard line on issues concerning blacks.[15]

In regard to Catholics, the 1776 constitution had officially barred from officeholding anyone who denied "the being of God, or the truth of the Protestant religion." While North Carolinians had ignored this provision for decades and allowed a few prominent Catholics to hold office, a new spirit of nativism in the state now brought the issue into open and acrimonious debate. Rayner took a bold stand in favor of repeal and rose to make his only formal speech of the convention. Calling religious freedom "a principle of the greatest magnitude that has ever agitated society," the young orator argued that in revising the constitution but retaining the religious test, the convention would "mutilate the most sacred provisions of that venerated instrument, and retain the only one which is at least a century behind the improvement of the age." Insisting that he was no apologist for Catholicism, Rayner explained that he was "opposed to making this a Catholic question," trying instead to "view it upon the broad and general principle of religious toleration." But if the convention retained the religious test and the state began to enforce it, "the Catholic and the Jew will be placed under the ban of proscription, no matter how great may be his merit." When the vote to abolish the religious test was tallied, Rayner and only thirty-five other delegates voted for repeal. The convention ultimately struck the word *Protestant* from the constitution and inserted the word *Christian*. While this compromise fell short of completely removing the religious test, Rayner at least had the satisfaction of knowing that he had helped preserve the political rights of Catholics.[16]

When the convention concluded its deliberations in mid-July, Rayner traveled back to Hertford County, content that he had handled well his first appearance in the public spotlight. In the convention he had taken controversial but liberal positions on two issues: the status of blacks and the rights of Catholics, two questions that in various forms would give shape and meaning to much of his subsequent political career. In championing the rights of free blacks, the youthful North Carolinian was giving voice to his belief that under some circumstances blacks were capable of exercising the responsibilities of American citizenship. The black voters of Hertford County, after all, had possessed the patriotism and good sense to help elect him to the convention. Similarly, Rayner's outspokenness on the religious test underscores the seriousness of his belief in Jeffersonian pronouncements about religious toleration. From his study of the Revolutionary era and his heritage as the son of a veteran of the war for independence, he was committed to the idea that artificial distinctions such as one's religious faith should not be the test of one's ability to participate in government. Intelligence and virtue alone dictated such fitness, and the respectable, native-born Catholics of North Carolina had repeatedly demonstrated their fitness. The following November Rayner's constituents voiced their approval of his course by electing him to a seat in the state house of commons.

Rayner took his first seat in the legislature in November 1835. It was a time of great upheaval in both national and state politics. On the national scene, with Jackson's second term as president drawing to a close, his domineering personality and controversial leadership had polarized the country as never before. Some of the burning issues on which Jackson had taken strong stands, such as government aid to internal improvements, affected state politics in much the same way they did national politics. Party lines in North Carolina had taken shape around such issues. Whigs, for example, optimistically envisioned the day when a far-reaching network of state-assisted railroads and canals would knit together the far-flung, isolated mountain settlements with the plantation country of the coastal plain, easing intrastate sectional tensions, opening distant markets to farmers in all sections, attracting immigrants to the state, and reversing the ongoing exodus of North Carolinians to greener pastures in the southwest. Many Whigs also longed to see the legislature create a network of state-supported free public schools which, in Rayner's words, "would carry the blessings of education to every poor man's door, and thereby foster, and bring to the service of the State, native genius, which must otherwise remain in obscurity forever." If only the citizens of North Carolina would awaken to the possibilities inherent in a more active government, they could put the state on the path to a new golden age. Whig majorities at both the state and national levels would enable them to put their plans in motion.[17]

Although a freshman legislator, Rayner soon threw himself into the fray of partisan politics, where his Whiggish ideology soon became evident. In debates over land policy and internal improvements, he passionately supported a plan that would have the federal government periodically distribute the proceeds of public land sales to the states, reserving for the federal government the "ultimate control" of the fund in order to meet national emergencies. Rayner always went to great lengths to show that such a distribution was entirely consistent with republican principles as promulgated by the Founding Fathers. In striking such a compromise between states' rights and federal authority, Rayner's solution displayed the sense of balance that Whigs so often sought. Distribution of the proceeds would enable the individual states to pursue their own projects of internal improvements and education, but it arguably safeguarded states' rights better than the Democratic alternative of a one-time distribution, which in the future might concentrate too much corrupting power in Washington. "Shall they [the proceeds] accumulate in the Treasury to a gigantic fund, subject to the disposition of Congress, or to the control of a corrupt Executive?" he asked. The specter of King Andrew the First hovered in the Whigs' collective consciousness. If future proceeds were allowed to accrue entirely to the federal government, the young orator predicted that "we should see one great, consolidated Government, which would prostrate every barrier of Constitutional restraint, and wave its golden sceptre in triumph over the land." [18]

Rayner's position on land policy illustrates well the Whig mindset, in which there need not be a conflict between states' rights and positive government. As devoted as Whigs like Rayner were to the anti-centralization impulses of the Revolution, they held even dearer the wise balance between state and federal powers achieved by the framers of the U.S. Constitution. Like their ideological forebears of 1787, antebellum Whigs deplored the chaos that resulted from too weak a government as much as they dreaded the tyranny of one too strong. They feared anarchy as much as monarchy. Rayner and his Whig contemporaries were largely accurate when they described themselves as true conservatives, because they sought to *conserve* the delicate balance of a government that protected individual liberties to the fullest extent possible without sacrificing the collective good. Invoking the Madisonian conception of federalism, the Whigs of 1835 held individual and states' rights precious, but not at the expense of a more perfect union. A mix of suspicious republicanism and optimistic liberalism, antebellum Whig ideology harkened back to a supposedly purer era of American politics, all the while reserving for the government the right to legislate creatively in the interest of national progress. It was a vision that contrasted starkly with the Jacksonians' apparent desire for a strictly negative government, presided over by a powerful and arbitrary executive.

One other critical factor shaped Rayner's opinions on land policy, internal improvements, and most other issues: all public questions must take into account the overriding need to preserve the Union. For example, in the case of the debate over distribution of public land proceeds, Rayner noted that a proposed plan to grant the public lands to the states in which they were located would disrupt vital national harmony by shifting too much power to the newer states. "It would lay the foundation for the most bitter heart-burnings and collisions between the States, which would not only sow the seeds of dissention, and mar the bright prospects of our country's future destiny, but would inevitably rend the Union into fragments." But using the proceeds to fund internal improvements would strengthen the ties that held the Union together, much as improvements within North Carolina would help unite the tidewater with the mountains. And in Rayner's mind, any measure that strengthened the bonds of Union without materially infringing upon individual liberties fully justified the prudent use of federal authority. [19]

The freshman legislator's outspoken eloquence in support of Whig measures won him reelection to a second term in the legislature by a two-to-one margin. After taking his seat in the house of commons, Rayner spoke out publicly on another national issue that periodically agitated state politics, the issue of slavery. During Jackson's presidency a small but vocal minority in the North had increasingly criticized the institution of slavery, while southerners were discovering that defending human bondage as a "necessary evil" was increasingly difficult in a nation founded on the concept of natural rights, particularly when slavery was spreading rapidly westward. In the 1830s the issue manifested itself in a congressional debate over the reception of petitions in Congress calling for the abolition of slavery in the District of Columbia.

In a series of resolutions he introduced in the legislature in December 1836, Rayner argued against Congress's reception of these petitions. At first glance, there was little in the resolutions to mark their author as a dissenter. Congress, Rayner suggested, was under no constitutional obligation to accept petitions that violated the Constitution or might "be highly detrimental to the public interest." This legalistic proslavery argument, however, did not constitute the main thrust of the resolutions. Instead, Rayner's central contention argued that slavery agitation posed a threat to the survival of the Union: "We cherish a warm and devoted attachment to the Union of these States, and do therefore deprecate the measures of the Northern abolitionists, as tending to weaken its bonds, and to produce a state of sectional disaffection, which, if not checked, must inevitably end in disunion." Significantly, these are the only proslavery arguments Rayner ever employed in his public career. One argument defended the peculiar institution on constitutional grounds and suggested that slavery could only be defended by constitutional means; the other appealed emotionally to Americans to preserve the Union by leaving slavery where the Founding Fathers had placed it. Neither defended slavery as an abstract proposition. Rayner unquestionably was well versed in the militant proslavery argument. His personal library contained a number of the pseudoscientific texts of the antebellum period that purportedly established the inherent inferiority of blacks. As early as 1836 he corresponded with James Henry Hammond, the South Carolina proslavery propagandist, requesting a copy of Hammond's writings on slavery. But nowhere in his public or private writings did he ever sanction the notion of inherent biological inferiority of blacks.[20]

The legislature failed to pass Rayner's slavery resolutions, and the state's attention was soon absorbed by party politics. Rayner participated enthusiastically in the presidential election of 1836, helping organize anti-Van Buren committees of vigilance and campaigning for Whig idol Hugh Lawson White of Tennessee. The Democrats succeeded in electing Martin Van Buren, but Rayner's increasingly high profile in Whig politics won him an easy third term in the statehouse in 1838. The Whigs posted clear majorities in both houses of the legislature and elected Edward B. Dudley governor. Rayner was now the undisputed leader of the party in Hertford County, and he was anxious to plunge headlong into one of the most ferocious party battles in North Carolina's history.[21]

The Whig triumph of 1838 in North Carolina promised exceptional excitement because of the unusual circumstances surrounding the state's two U.S. senators. In 1834 the Democratic majority in the state legislature had sent formal instructions to the state's Whig senator, Willie P. Mangum, directing him to vote for a pro-Jackson measure. Whigs claimed to support the concept of instruction as long as it was used legitimately and constitutionally, and eventually Mangum reluctantly resigned his seat and was replaced by a Jackson man. When Rayner took his seat in the 1838 legislature, he and the new Whig majority determined that the Democrats should be given a taste of their own medicine, in the form of Whig instructions to the two Democratic senators, Robert Strange and Bedford Brown. On December 4 Rayner himself introduced the long-awaited resolutions of instruction. In language one might have found in the 1760s, he protested the "extravagance" and "corruption" of the Van Buren administration, decried the "alarming" increase in executive power and patronage, and ordered the two Democratic senators either to vote for the national Whig legislative agenda or resign their seats.[22]

The resolutions caused a furor in the state. Rayner took the floor in the house of commons on December 14, speaking "with great animation" for two hours in their defense and concluding his speech the following day. The Raleigh *Register* praised the young legislator's actions: "Every man, whatever may be his party predilections, must accord to this gentleman a character for honesty, independence and fearlessness. He is, unquestionably, one of the first young men in the State, and is destined, we predict, to shine on a broader theatre than in the Legislative Halls of his native State." The resolutions passed both houses of the legislature by nearly a straight party vote. Another year was to pass before Strange and Brown actually resigned, but finally they did, and the triumphant Whigs elected Mangum and William A. Graham to fill their unexpired terms.[23]

Rayner's successful generalship of the resolutions of instruction propelled him to a position of leadership in the state Whig party. His efforts in the battle to depose the two senators, according to the Raleigh *Register*, "will place Mr. R. in public estimation where he deserves to stand, among the most prominent young men of the State. Let him but cherish and cultivate the fame he has already acquired, and he cannot fail to rise to enviable distinction. He is a man for the times—firm and fearless—and the noble, manly, bold and independent views advanced in his speech, cannot fail to be read with satisfaction by every true-hearted Whig." These were heady accolades for an intensely ambitious young politician, coming as they did from the state's leading Whig paper. But the praise did not overstate Rayner's meteoric rise in North Carolina politics. Soon after the legislature adjourned in January 1839, the Whigs of the First Congressional District nominated their thirty-year-old hero for a seat in the U.S. House of Representatives.[24]

Rayner's campaign took him through a succession of debates, rallies, and militia musters in the summer of 1839. His opponent, Major S. T. Sawyer, was the incumbent congressman. A personally popular man in the counties bordering Albemarle Sound, Sawyer had won election to the House as a Whig but earned his party's enmity by siding with the Democratic administration's financial policies. The district contained only one heavily Democratic county, Currituck, and Rayner's chances of success depended on his ability to persuade the rest of the district's Whig majority, which had elected Sawyer, to desert the incumbent and rally around a true national Whig. When the two candidates faced each other in debate, Rayner championed internal improvements, the Bank of the United States, and the Whig agenda from start to finish. He told pro-Sawyer audiences that if "you are determined to be *politically d—d*, you shall incur the penalty with your eyes open." According to the partisan Raleigh *Register*, Rayner so eloquently exposed Democratic iniquities in a Currituck County speech that "many who went to the gathering, violently opposed to him, were so struck with the manliness of his deportment, that they determined to vote for him."[25]

In August the voters of the First Congressional District went to the polls and gave Rayner a sweeping majority of more than six hundred votes. The thirty-one-year-old congressman-elect would take his beliefs in limited executive power, legislative dominance, and positive government to the nation's capital, where he intended to continue battling against Democratic corruption and championing what he saw as the hallowed principles of the Founding Fathers. Holding beliefs that for the most part were shared by a large body of his fellow Whigs, Rayner's was not yet a truly dissenting voice. His exceptionally strong views concerning the separation of church and state and his old-fashioned description of slavery as a necessary evil did not automatically stigmatize him as a politician outside the political mainstream. Applauding the Hertford planter's victory, the *Register* summarized what his election meant for North Carolina and the nation: If the voters would continue to maintain the principles that Rayner represented, wrote the Whig editor, then "the end at which they so nobly aim—the restoration of the Federal Government to its original purity and simplicity—will surely be attained." [26]

CHAPTER 2

"High National Considerations"

December 1839 was cold and disagreeable in the nation's capital, but heated battles were raging on the floor of the House of Representatives. Rayner arrived in Washington and took his place in a legislative body torn asunder by partisan strife. From the very beginning of his congressional career, the North Carolinian disapproved of what he saw happening in the United States government. In time that disapproval would turn into bitter disillusionment.

So intense were animosities between congressional Whigs and Democrats that the House of Representatives took more than two weeks just to organize itself for business. The first major conflict occurred when competing delegations from New Jersey each claimed seats in the House. Although the Whig delegation held official certification from the governor, Democratic congressmen denied them their seats. Rayner, perceiving this as blatant partisanship, with his usual assertiveness immediately took the floor to make a long speech against the Democrats' underhandedness. Describing his first speech before the House, John Quincy Adams pronounced his young colleague's argument to be "sound, his impressions fervid, his delivery vehement."[1]

Not surprisingly, Rayner based his argument in favor of seating the Whig delegation on republican principles as he interpreted them. He argued the case from his usual standpoint of constitutionality, the original intent of the Founding Fathers, and the dangers posed to the survival of the Republic. Rayner was convinced that Democrats were trying to defeat the will of the people in a crass effort to gain five more Democratic seats in Congress. This "band of partisans," he complained, had refused to be "fettered by precedent, or trammelled by the forms and technicalities of the law," and Rayner, "for one, was sorry to hear that doctrine avowed" on the floor of the House.

Again echoing a theme common in republican rhetoric, he admitted that such ideas found support among the "wretched rabble that infest our Northern cities," but he had hoped the House of Representatives still stood as "an ark to preserve inviolate the Constitution." Believing that the concept of a law higher than the Constitution would "sap the foundations of our free institutions," he stated his logic forcefully: "When the Constitution and the laws are dethroned, violence and faction must usurp their places."[2]

The youthful representative also criticized the Democrats from the vantage point of states' rights. Jackson's and Van Buren's disciples, he complained, had always made a great deal of noise about their devotion to states' rights, but they did so only when politically expedient. Because the New Jersey congressmen who carried with them the governor's certificate had been denied their seats, Democrats in Congress had trampled on the rights of the state of New Jersey. Rayner clearly believed that Jackson, who had repeatedly used executive power in ways unimaginable to earlier presidents, had perverted the *constitutional* doctrine of states' rights. Whigs such as himself, Rayner maintained, were the true "state Rights men" because they insisted that the will of the states—as expressed by the states' elected representatives in congress—be respected by the executive. Indeed, the expansion of executive power under Jackson was the principal reason why a Whig party existed. To true believers like Rayner, the need to curtail the executive's reckless use of power took precedence over any specific economic policies. It came as no surprise to such Whigs that in 1824 the elderly Jefferson had frowned on Jackson's candidacy and that Madison and Albert Gallatin, still alive in 1832, had favored Henry Clay. Therefore, he took pride in the fact that he was "one of those who stood firm and steadfast by their principles and the Constitution, when our great leader and captain went over to the enemy." That great leader and captain, of course, was Andrew Jackson, and the enemy was the "band of partisans"—Democrats—who used government to further selfish ends."[3]

Rayner laid low for most of the remainder of the session. Yet as the session proceeded, he grew more and more disillusioned with the conduct of his fellow legislators. "The scenes of violence and disorder that prevail in our house, are much more befitting a bear-garden [*sic*], than the legislative Council of a great and (self-styled) free nation," he complained. Rayner declared that he had never before seen such "disorder, such indecorous conduct, such want of independence, such servile subjection to party leaders, . . . such dearth of character and talent" as he was then witnessing in the House of Representatives. But despite his deprecation of the disorder and partisanship that marred the dignity of the House, in May 1840 Rayner himself contributed to the problem. The incident began with a March 25 speech made by fellow North Carolina representative William Montgomery, a staunch Jacksonian Democrat. Aiming to defend the economic policies of the administration, specifically with regard to a treasury note bill then under consideration, Montgomery repeatedly made the rather dubious claim that the nation's current economic distress had been brought on by the Whig "majority" in the previous Congress. Everyone, of course, knew that Democrats had controlled that Congress and had defeated the Whigs' principal measure for relief, the Bank of the United States. Virginia Whig Henry A. Wise interrupted Montgomery, asking if the North Carolinian really intended on publishing to the world the "ridiculous statement" that the Whigs had been a majority in the last House. Rayner followed with a similar denunciation, and some debate between the two North Carolinians ensued, with Rayner insisting that if Whigs had indeed been in the majority they would have passed a bill reestablishing the national bank.[4]

When Montgomery submitted his speech for publication in the *Congressional Globe,* his version of the brief debate with Rayner differed considerably from Rayner's version of events. The Democrat portrayed his Whig opponent as leaping to his feat "greatly excited," amid cries of order "from all parts of the hall." Denying all this, Rayner published his own account of the debate, referring to Montgomery's speech as "a tirade of nonsense" and "a tissue of misrepresentations." This inaugurated a petty war of words in the Washington press that soon outstripped the importance of the original misunderstanding. The language used by both combatants grew increasingly intemperate, with Rayner accusing Montgomery of "detestable hypocrisy" and Montgomery calling Rayner "low," "ill-natured," and "ungentlemanly."[5]

Conflicting versions of what followed render it difficult to ascertain the exact facts, but this much is clear. On May 30, after the most recent of Montgomery's letters appeared in the newspapers, the two men encountered one another in a corridor of the House of Representatives. In the Whig accounts, Rayner walked directly up to Montgomery and slapped his face. The Democrat responded by breaking his cane over his assailant's shoulder, and Rayner, carrying a cane with a concealed sword in it, then struck Montgomery several blows on the head. In the process the sword flew out of the cane and went clattering down the hall. The altercation degenerated into a fistfight before bystanders separated the two congressmen. Neither party suffered appreciable injury. At one point in the affray, Rayner was heard to say, "Damn you I only wanted to show you that I would resent your calling me a liar."

Montgomery claimed that Rayner unexpectedly seized him by the arm and struck the first blow without announcing his intention, that his own cane was small and harmless, and that his attacker's sword-cane was large and heavy. He charged that Rayner had lain in wait in a "cowardly attempt at assassination" and had "acted the part of a base coward and an unprincipled scoundrel." Worst of all, Montgomery suggested that Rayner had intended to use the sword.[6]

District of Columbia police arrested Rayner for the assault, and in the trial he was found guilty and fined $50. The actual evidence, according to a disgruntled Rayner, justified his actions and contradicted Montgomery "point blank." He insisted that he "was tried before a rabid Loco foco [i.e., Democratic] judge, presided by a loco foco foreman of the grand jury (whether upon the instance of Montgomery or not I can not ascertain)—and prosecuted by a loco foco attorney." Rayner planned to publish a transcription of the trial and distribute it to both his and Montgomery's constituents. "It must disgrace him, if the people of his district have any sense of morality left there," huffed Rayner.[7]

This rather comic episode illustrates several things about the fiery congressman from Hertford County. First, he adhered to the strict standards of the southern code of honor. Why did the affair not result in a duel? Because duels were the way in which *gentlemen* settled their differences and, according to Rayner, William Montgomery was no gentleman. If, on the other hand, a gentleman were offended by a coward or scoundrel, the proper course for the gentleman was to slap or cane the scoundrel. In terms of the code (and depending upon his own version of the actual events), Rayner had behaved precisely as a gentleman was supposed to act; he had treated Montgomery like a dog. Rayner's North Carolina neighbor, William Valentine, concisely summed up the Whig attitude toward the assault. "Honorable men say this was his only proper course in the present State of things," wrote the diarist. "It is to be regretted; but perhaps he ought to do it again." The affray also shows the deadly seriousness with which both men held their partisan loyalties. Finally, the altercation provides a clear example of Rayner's hot temper and impulsive nature—characteristics that would mark his public life for the next forty years. Although he usually controlled his temper, he would always feel a burning need to vindicate whatever course of action he took. Thus, a month after the incident Rayner reported to Governor Dudley that "Montgomery has behaved himself very well since he got his whipping—all my friends here justify my course—even the most prudent."[8]

Rayner avoided the spotlight for the rest of the session. The highest single priority on his legislative agenda was securing federal assistance in opening a navigable passage through the barrier islands of coastal northeast North Carolina. The absence of a passage to the ocean clearly crippled the economy of a large section of North Carolina. Furthermore, the lack of a harbor along such a long stretch of dangerous coastline over the years had exacted an enormous toll in sunken ships and lost lives, and a safe port also would be of strategic military importance in time of war. Indeed, the pressing need for this inlet was the single largest reason why the First Congressional District was a Whig stronghold. It would, of course, be a large and costly undertaking, and Rayner had to fight the impression that it was a project of strictly local significance. To this end he spent considerable time and effort marshaling the testimony of experts as to the importance and feasibility of the project and trying to get the legislation to a vote in the House.[9]

Not surprisingly, Rayner almost always voted the party line. The Whigs, however, could achieve little against the Democratic majority in Congress and a Democratic president. Rayner was especially aggravated that North Carolina's two embattled Democratic senators (who at this point had not yet resigned) refused to aid with the plan to open the coastal inlet. "There is no chance of getting the work done by the genl. gov. as long as these two *delectable articles* occupy seats in the Senate," he noted bitterly. The Whigs' legislative impotence frustrated Rayner tremendously. "Congress is still 'Dragging its slow length along,'" he complained in April 1840, "doing little (in fact, nothing) for the benefit of the Country, but sinking itself more and more every day in the estimation of the sober and reflecting portion of the Community." An increasingly disillusioned Rayner would repeat this lament countless times before his tenure in the House came to an end.[10]

According to Whigs, eight years of Jacksonian dictatorship and four of Van Buren's weakness and corruption had nearly ruined the Republic. Rayner deeply believed that the long period of Democratic dominance had been "revolutionary" in character. "The people must come to the relief of our free institutions, through the peac[e]ful medium of the ballot box," he told William A. Graham, "or else we have the alternative of revolution on the one hand, or the yoke of bondage on the other. For a more practical despotism never existed in any age or country, than that which represses all the talent and energies in our house, and weighs down the prosperity and commerce of this *once* free people." He was convinced, however, that a great wave of reform would sweep the nation in 1840, when William Henry Harrison, "Old Tippecanoe," would be elected to the presidency and a "corrupt dynasty will be hurled from the high place of power, which they have so long desecrated, and *honest men* will occupy their places."[11]

A weary Rayner departed from the national capital in late July, bound for

home. He traveled by sea, accompanied by fellow Whig congressman Edward
Stanly in the circuitous coastal water route rendered necessary by the lack of
a direct opening to the ocean. The firing of cannons signaled his arrival in
Winton, Hertford's county seat. As the boat touched shore, a crowd with "a
splendid Tippecanoe flag" that bore stars and stripes and was emblazoned
with Rayner's and Stanly's names greeted the Whig heroes. It was a heady
and triumphant homecoming for the thirty-two-year-old politician.[12]

Although Rayner had been plagued with near-chronic ill health of an
unspecified nature during most of the recent congressional session, the campaign for Old Tippecanoe would not wait. The day following his arrival,
Rayner attended a militia muster at nearby Bethel. According to William
Valentine, a normally moody and introspective neighbor of Rayner's who
attended, it was "a glorious day." A local Democratic leader, Godwin C.
Moore, spoke on behalf of the Van Buren administration, followed by various
Whig leaders from the area. Speechmaking occupied the entire afternoon,
but the crowd had come to hear Rayner. Valentine described Rayner's "fiery
eloquence," paying particular attention to "one flash of genuine oratory that
thrilled the feelings of all by a sudden as it were effective shock." In this
passage, which so enthralled the audience, Rayner painted a verbal portrait
of the Revolutionary fathers turning over in their graves and refusing to look
up "lest they countenance the wicked measures" of the Democrats. "This
shock of eloquence elated and raptured to the highest," observed Valentine.
"The locos appeared converted. The truth is there was no resisting Whiggery today."[13]

Valentine's observations rang true as this scene was repeated throughout the late summer and fall. At the small town of Coleraine, near Rayner's
birthplace in Bertie County, six hundred people turned out for a dinner in
his honor, even though Bertie was not in his congressional district. In Gates
County, three militia companies carrying Whig banners marched in a procession that was followed by Rayner's speech before a throng of some four
thousand. From Raleigh to the coast the dashing young lawmaker thrilled
crowds who had assembled in specially constructed "log cabins" in honor
of Harrison's alleged humble origins. The various "Tippecanoe Clubs" vied
with each other to see who could throw the grandest celebration and concoct
the most outrageous feast; in Scotland Neck, the dinner following Rayner's
speech included a 114-pound apple dumpling. At Boon's Mills in Northamp-
ton County, Whig partisans constructed a log cabin that would hold four
hundred people. Unfortunately, on the day of Rayner's speech, it poured rain
without ceasing all day. Still, five or six hundred Whigs showed up, filling

the structure beyond capacity and as a result engaging in "more drunkenness and ugly behavior" than was usual for a Whig meeting.[14]

In the final weeks before the fall election, Rayner traveled to a different rally or convention almost every day, met always by huge crowds, brass bands, silk banners, admiring women, and the ubiquitous log cabins drawn by mules and decorated with raccoon skins (representing the Whigs) or foxes in traps (representing Van Buren). In his speeches, which could last more than three hours, Rayner concentrated almost wholly on national politics. He typically began with a denunciation of congressional Democrats, referring at length to their refusal to seat the New Jersey Whigs. He not only exposed the extravagance and corruption of the Van Buren administration, citing in detail instances of wasteful government spending, especially in the military, but he also attacked the president's qualifications, noting that all the presidents from Washington to John Quincy Adams "had well established merits on which to found their elevation, but Mr. Van Buren had *none, none.*" Rayner trusted that a wise Providence would see to Old Tippecanoe's election "and thereby bring back the Administration of its affairs to that order and purity which distinguished it till within the last 12 years of disorder and embarrassment." According to Valentine, a Whig rally with Rayner as featured speaker was "something of a feast of reason and flow of soul." On election day, Americans in every state of the union flocked to the polls in unprecedented numbers. In North Carolina, voter turnout topped 83 percent, far exceeding any election of the preceding twenty years. Harrison carried forty-four of the state's sixty-six counties with a popular majority of 13,141.[15]

The great groundswell of political participation that resulted in Harrison's election encouraged most Whigs, who felt that the Republic had been redeemed at the last possible moment. As lawmakers made their way back to Washington for the lame-duck session beginning in December 1840, "mutual gratulation at the downfall of the Jackson Van Buren Administration," in the words of John Quincy Adams, was "the universal theme of conversation." But Adams, the venerable senior statesman of the U.S. Congress, felt uneasy. "No one knows what is to come," he confided in his diary. "Harrison comes in upon a hurricane; God grant he may not go out upon a wreck!"[16] Although Rayner was more optimistic about Harrison's abilities than was Adams, he clearly would have preferred to see Henry Clay, the unequaled champion of Whig doctrines, occupy the White House.

Legislators assembled on December 7, 1840, in the midst of a bitter Washington blizzard. Congress had been in session only two weeks when Rayner voiced what was becoming his usual complaint about the nation's legislative halls. "We are doing literally nothing in Congress," he confided to Governor Dudley. The outgoing Van Buren administration would block all constructive legislation, he predicted, and an extra session in the summer seemed inevitable. More significantly, the depression then plaguing the nation had thrown the government's finances into disarray. Rayner, like Adams, knew that the new administration would inherit the financial difficulties brought on (as Whigs believed) by years of Democratic misrule and did all in his power to prevent further damage until Harrison could take office.[17]

Democrats were seeking to issue $5 million in treasury notes to tide the government over, a measure that Rayner, in a lengthy February speech, branded as corrupt and "deceptive in its character, and calculated to conceal from the knowledge of the country the embarrassed and ruinous condition of the National Treasury." Printing more money, Rayner explained, "in fact, entails upon the Government a debt—a national debt, in every sense of the word." He urged Democrats to "confess that the Treasury is empty, that the country is in debt," and authorize an honest loan. With its impressive array of statistics and projected expenditures, the speech displayed the powers of analysis and argument that were becoming a Rayner trademark. Moreover, it resounded with the traditional Whig warning about corruption, which republican ideology had always identified as the greatest threat to liberty. Rayner complained not so much about the amount that the Democrats had spent, but rather how it had been spent: "paying $450 a day for steamboats, $20 a cord for wood, purchasing splendid furniture and silver spoons for mud boats, paying high salaries to crowds of loungers attached to your customhouses, giving high and expensive jobs and contracts to political favorites, &c."[18] As he had predicted, however, Whig-inspired reform would have to wait for the new administration. After Harrison died a month later, Henry Clay disciples like Rayner anxiously bided their time, waiting to see if Tyler would prove true to the principles of the party that elected him.

The freshman congressman's stern opposition to the Van Buren administration had earned him immense popularity at home, as evidenced by the fact that the Democrats of the First Congressional District mounted no organized challenge when Rayner stood for reelection in May 1841. "Rayner is elected by so large a majority, that nobody seems to think it worth while to communicate the vote," reported the Raleigh *Register* shortly after election day. When the returns finally came in, the citizens of the Albemarle district gave their representative a huge majority of nearly 1,500 votes.[19]

Congress convened in special session on May 31, with Whigs anxious to begin dismantling Van Buren's economic program and enacting their own.

But as usual, the public business had to wait as Congress debated endlessly on the question of abolition petitions and whether the gag rule barring the reception of such petitions would be readopted. Rayner entered the fray two weeks into the acrimonious debate, rising on the floor of the House to propose that the rules of the previous session—including the gag rule—be adopted temporarily until the committee on rules could report and that report be acted upon. This would at least get the session under way. He also added one extra provision: that the House consider *no* subjects other than those embraced in the president's recent message. On the petition question, Rayner clearly was willing to abide by whatever the House decided; the important thing was that it be put to a vote so more important matters could be addressed.[20]

Significantly, in his three-hour speech Rayner refused to "argue slavery as an abstract question." He did not want the issue to be discussed in Congress at all. Rayner claimed that he and his friends were simply "anxious to go to work, and not to fan the fire between the North and the South." Invoking the traditional republican ideal that dictated that patriots should put the common good ahead of selfish private interests, Rayner warned that it was the duty of Congress to "forget all sectional feelings, and make a sacrifice of them upon the holy altar of their country's good." He was trying to make Adams and the other northerners understand that discussing abolition outraged the feelings of southern men. It was "a question on which the South could yield nothing." If the issue was to be debated in the Congress, he wanted it understood that the southerners must force the northerners to be the aggressors, "if aggression there must be."[21]

Largely reiterating his North Carolina resolutions of 1836–37, Rayner elaborated on his argument. He considered the reception of abolition petitions unconstitutional because the object sought in the petitions was unconstitutional. He held dear the constitutional right of Americans to petition their government for redress of grievances. "But whose grievances?" Rayner asked, "The grievances of the petitioners, or those of other people?" Common sense dictated that if the people of a slaveholding state felt aggrieved by slavery in their midst, then they might have a right to present a petition protesting it, but northerners possessed no such right. Moreover, Rayner openly acknowledged something that few southern representatives would admit: If a vote had been taken on a recent petition seeking a constitutional amendment abolishing slavery, he would have voted for it because such a petition sought abolition "by constitutional means, viz: an alteration of the instrument." What he comprehended so much better than most other southerners was that attempts by the South to force the slavery question upon the North would only lend encouragement to the abolitionists. Once southerners made it clear that they would oppose even constitutional efforts to interfere with the peculiar institution, they passed the torch of legitimacy and righteousness to the antislavery forces. The key weapon for combating the abolitionists, as Rayner understood it, was exploitation of the reverence that virtually all white Americans held for the Constitution and the set of compromises that the Founding Fathers had constructed to keep slavery from destroying the Union.

In the course of his speech, Rayner became involved in an entertaining debate with the great opponent of the gag rule, John Quincy Adams, who repeatedly tried to steer the discussion away from constitutional questions and focus instead on the immorality of slavery. With considerable aplomb, the young southerner eagerly responded to the elder statesman's points. If Adams wished to make this a debate on morality, then what about the "moral issue of plighted faith and reciprocal confidence that prevents this world from becoming a social chaos," Rayner asked? "Destroy confidence and you dissolve this Union." A few days earlier, Adams had suggested that in the event of a servile insurrection, God would side with the slaves. Unwilling to defend slavery as a divinely sanctioned institution, Rayner replied by pointing out that the doctrine of a "Divine law" higher than the Constitution "sweeps away every thing like human compact and rests the mutual rights of men on what the imagination of fanaticism may picture to itself as a Divine requirement." The ultimate outcome of such a belief was plain: "It is a doctrine of blood—to that it leads."

Rayner repeatedly reminded Adams that the Constitution, which left the issue of slavery largely in the hands of the states, was framed by the same men who had fought the American Revolution. "Could they entertain the idea that faction and fanaticism would one day shake this Union to its centre," he asked, "and that the provision they made to guard the rights of the citizen would be attempted, itself to be converted into an instrument of tyranny?" In the ideology of republicanism, fanaticism was incompatible with the spirit of civic virtue, which often required compromise. Southerners had entered into the compact that created the United States with assurances that slavery would never be interfered with where it existed. At the same time, northerners trusted the South to abide by the constitutional exercise of federal authority. If southerners, in their zeal to protect slavery, violated that trust and defended slavery on grounds other than the Constitution, they were just as guilty of endangering the Union as were northerners who sought unconstitutionally to abolish slavery.

Constitutional considerations aside, Rayner appealed to his northern colleagues to "count well the cost" of continuing antislavery agitation. "I can tell them that before they reach their purpose they must march over hecatombs of bodies, we will convert all our smiling fields into a camp; we will beat every ploughshare into a sword, and long before they reach the banks of the Roanoke, every plain and every hill shall be whitened with our bleaching bones." Rayner spoke these seemingly extreme words not as a threat to the North but rather with the hope of impressing upon the antislavery advocates the indisputable consequences of their actions. "It was time," he told the House, "that the North and the South should understand each other on this subject."

Rayner's analysis displayed a remarkable comprehension of the political realities inherent in the deepening sectional crisis. While he continued ostensibly to deprecate partisanship, he was coming to understand what at least one modern scholar has made clear: The perpetuation of the Union depended upon two parties, with national constituencies, which staked out clearly defined opposing positions on a wide range of socioeconomic issues around which voters could rally. "Now, if this was a question between the North and the South, and a question of liberty and slavery, and if we were to be eternally annoyed on the subject, and if all political and party differences were to be merged in one great question," Rayner suggested, "the sooner it was decided the better." The great danger, as he saw it, was that "it mattered not what might be the political differences which existed heretofore on other subjects; they [the South], at least, upon this presented one undivided front." Rayner despised the fact that slavery-related issues compelled southern Whigs and southern Democrats to cooperate. This only contributed to the estrangement between the northern and southern members within each party, making it increasingly difficult to maintain national party cohesiveness on other issues.[22]

The conclusion of Rayner's speech echoed a nationalistic theme that he would often repeat during the next two decades of his political career. Appealing to his northern Whig colleagues "in the name of justice not to interfere with the constitutional rights of the Southern States," he beseeched them "not to continue to give the unoffending descendants of our common ancestry and the participants in the blessings of our glorious Constitution any further trouble in relation to this question." "Above all," Rayner appealed to his northern allies "in the name of this glorious, this blessed Union—this Union which is the terror of tyrants—this Union which mounts the star-spangled banner as its glory—this Union which is the first of free Governments . . . to stop the march of fanaticism before it is too late—before it destroys the foundations of this Republic, and before this fair fabric shall be crumbled in the dust." He ended this emotional speech with a prophecy that he would reflect upon many times in later years, when the Union had been torn asunder by civil war: "We can never know the value of this Union until we have lost it. But when passion and fanaticism shall have stalked across the land—when fanaticism and the horrors of civil war shall pervade our country—when the brother's hand shall be reeking with the brother's blood, and the sun of freedom has gone down in blood, then shall we only appreciate the value of this glorious confederacy. I ask, then, of the Northern and Southern Whigs to come to the rescue, and that before it be too late."[23]

Even Adams, whom Rayner criticized so severely during the course of the petition debate, admitted in his diary that it had been "a splendid speech." The next day, the House finally readopted the gag rule in a form similar to that which Rayner had advocated. With this "vexed question" (in Rayner's words) for the moment resolved, and with a Whig president and Whig Congress at last in power, perhaps the country might now set about returning the nation to the republican principles of the Founding Fathers.[24]

To Rayner's enormous relief, as the session got under way Henry Clay framed the Whigs' legislative agenda, which featured as its centerpiece the reestablishment of the Bank of the United States. Realizing the president's misgivings about an institution with the sweeping powers of the old Bank, Tyler's allies in Congress sought compromise. But nationalistic Whigs like Rayner held firm to Clay's proposal. Having been denied the presidential nomination in 1840, Clay clearly intended to act as the power behind the throne, but Tyler had no intention of being a puppet. After two successful votes on the bank bill and two vetoes from Tyler, at Clay's urging the entire cabinet resigned, with the exception of Secretary of State Daniel Webster, who was in the midst of important negotiations with the British. Six months after the Whigs' triumphant accession to power, the party lay in shambles.[25]

Rayner played a central role in what became American history's most traumatic rupture between a president and his own party. As Congress prepared to adjourn, Rayner and four other Whig leaders composed an address reading Tyler out of the party. On September 13, some seventy Whig senators and representatives caucused in Capitol Square to hear novelist-congressman John Pendleton Kennedy recite the address, which presented a solemn recitation of the events of the special session leading up to Tyler's two bank vetoes. The striking thing about the document is its clear statement of Whiggery's overriding aims. Despite the party's earnest commitment to the positive state—programs like a national bank and internal improvements—one idea stood "conspicuously and pre-eminently above all others": the Whigs' fervent republican conviction that executive power must be curtailed. Specific policy questions might come and go over the years, but the issue in 1841, as in most of the previous twelve years, was whether the president would be allowed to frustrate the will of Congress. In listing the "duties which remain for the Whigs" following Tyler's apostasy, Rayner's committee called for strict limits on the veto power, adoption of a single term for presidents, and restrictions on the president's control over patronage.[26]

For Rayner, the remaining three-and-a-half years of Tyler's presidency were like a replay of the Jackson-Van Buren nightmare. Tyler employed the veto to defeat Whig legislation with the same infuriating stubbornness as his Democratic predecessors, earning him the derisive nickname of "Old Veto." Indeed, most of Tyler's cabinet officers, as well as his unofficial advisers, were former Jackson men. Lacking a significant base of support in Congress, Tyler increasingly found that he had to bypass traditional channels of government and appeal directly to the masses for support.[27]

It is impossible to exaggerate the contempt that Rayner felt for John Tyler. His public and private writings from the period bristle with stinging terms of denunciation against the president. He described Tyler's actions as "the most shameless treachery that ever disgraced our civil annals." "In the very moment of victory," he complained, "we were unexpectedly robbed of the fruits of twelve years of toil, by the most heartless duplicity and barefaced treason." Tyler's treachery "not only stalked forth at noon day with unblushing front, but actually boasted in the face of its victims, of its disgraceful triumph." Rayner's bitter complaints about the president became a litany over the next three years. The very thought of Tyler upset him, and the once-optimistic Whig grew increasingly disillusioned about politics.[28]

When in early 1842 it became clear that Tyler entertained ideas of creating a third party out of those Whigs and Democrats who adhered to his strict-construction, states'-rights philosophy, Rayner took two hours of the House's time to make a strictly partisan speech, something he had rarely done. His ostensible purpose was to defend himself against the rather vicious attacks that had been mounted against him as one of the authors of the congressional Whigs' anti-Tyler manifesto, but Rayner used the occasion to vent his growing frustration with the course of American politics. "I, for one, am tired of the present state of things," he confessed. "The forbearance of the Whig party will work their ruin. The long cherished principles of that party are not the principles of John Tyler." Future events would prove him correct. If Whigs sacrificed the set of programs and principles that united the party's adherents in all parts of the Union—as they had when they chose John Tyler as Harrison's running mate—their party's viability as a national organization would be destroyed. If, as Rayner told the House,

> this great and mighty party is to become merged in a mere junto of Virginia politicians—I, for one, wish to know it. If this is to be the consummation of the Whig promises, Whig hopes, and Whig prospects, I wish to know it as soon as possible, that I may take leave of that party forever. I may be asked, Where will I go? I will not go to the Loco focos, for there I should expect to meet John Tyler again. I will go first to my constituents, and tell them that the hope of our country's deliverance is past; that the anger of Heaven, followed by the treachery of man, has blasted all our prospects, and destroyed the fruits of twelve long years of toil, that virtue and patriotism have been unable to resist the onward march of faction and corruption; that the stern political honesty, and bold resistance to tyranny, which we inherited from our fathers, have yielded to the lures and temptations of power; and that, if they wish me to represent them longer, I must come here free from all ties or connections with any party, but prepared to make war on the corruptions of all.[29]

Leaving the Whig party was one course of action Rayner was considering; retiring from Congress was another. The prospect of losing their young representative positively distressed the Whigs of the Albemarle district. "I hope it is not so," wrote an alarmed constituent to Whig leader William A. Graham. "Tell him it *must not* be. . . . we have no other man to depend on. He is our main-stay." Rayner appears at one point to have decided against seeking a third term, but the North Carolina legislature—with its new Democratic majority—had recently gerrymandered the state's congressional districts with an eye to defeating several Whig incumbents. The changes in Rayner's own district threatened to reduce the normally large Whig majority there to a very narrow margin, although most analysts thought he could still win. In April 1843 the district's Whigs met in convention and unanimously renominated their representative for a third term. Penning a gracious acceptance letter, Rayner affirmed his desire not to serve another two years, but he claimed that the gerrymander had caused him to reconsider. The "principal author" of the redistricting plan was now the Democratic nominee for Rayner's congressional seat, and the young incumbent had been forced to recognize what everyone else seemingly knew—that the Whigs had no other candidate who could carry the new district.[30]

In accepting his district's call to run for a third term, Rayner announced his public position in a way that left no doubt about where he stood on the issues. "I hardly deem it necessary to refer to my political principles," he told his constituents. He then reiterated his support for rechartering the Bank of the United States, distributing the public land proceeds to the states, limiting executive power, and enacting a protective tariff. "I need not say," he concluded, "that of all men living, I prefer HENRY CLAY for President of the United States." [31]

The August election in Rayner's district was an exceedingly bitter one. The Democratic nominee, Godwin C. Moore, was also a native of Rayner's own Hertford County and had been elected to the state legislature two years earlier, a fact that must have irked Rayner. Early in the campaign Rayner "found the tide setting strongly against me," but after the opponents met in two debates, Moore refused to make any more joint appearances. Rayner and the Whig press accused the Democrat of cowardice, a charge that could be costly in North Carolina politics. The contest quickly degenerated into name-calling and accusation, with Moore harping on Rayner's numerous absences from the House. Rayner indeed had missed a considerable number of roll calls due to his near-chronic ill health, but it was not considered gentlemanly to attack a political opponent on those grounds. The race was further complicated by the fact that Moore, as moderator of the Chowan Baptist Association, was considered "a great favorite with his church brethren." With his "immense Baptist connection" he apparently tried to appeal to Rayner's constituents on religious grounds, but the strategy bore little fruit. After the election, Rayner described Moore as "one of the meanest dogs that ever barked. . . . one of your psalm-singing pharisees . . . who went whining through the district begging his brethren to vote for him on considerations of church membership." After Moore's refusal to debate, Rayner reported that he "put the lash to him so severely, that he would not meet me again, and went whimpering through the district with the cry of persecution. He will not forget me for the balance of his life." [32]

Rayner's 840-vote majority surprised even him. Statewide, the Whig party eked out a narrow four thousand-vote majority, although the Democratic gerrymander took its toll by giving the Democrats five of the state's nine congressional districts. Nevertheless, while he may have entertained fears about the viability of the national Whig party, in North Carolina the two-party system was alive and well.[33]

Despite his decision to run for reelection, Rayner's pessimism about the future of his party and nation had continued to grow. "I have, till very lately, indulged in the full faith that the Whig party was only undergoing a purification—that they were passing through an ordeal of trial, from which they would emerge 'redeemed, regenerated, and disenthralled,' " he told the House in early 1843, but those hopes were now dimmer than ever. Drawing from his classical education and his upbringing as the son of a Revolutionary veteran, Rayner adhered to an interpretation of human history common to the Founding Fathers' generation. According to this view, all of history's great civilizations had experienced a rise to prominence, a golden age, and an inevitable "degeneracy, decline, and ruin." "But I have consoled myself with the hope that this period was in the far, far distant future," Rayner stated. Now he had been forced to reconsider that assessment. He saw numerous parallels between the decline and fall of the Roman Empire and the events of the past dozen years in the United States. "How times must have changed!" he exclaimed, "how the public mind must have degenerated!" [34]

Holding these opinions, Rayner viewed the national elections of 1844 as the probable last chance for the Whig party and perhaps for America's republican experiment. At last Tyler and his followers appeared finally to have given up all pretense of being Whigs, and the old party lines, so badly muddled by the Virginian's treachery, might once again be clearly drawn. The Whigs now could regroup and rally around a true Whig patriot in the upcoming 1844 presidential election.

As a fervent champion of Henry Clay, Rayner had complained bitterly about Whig leaders who, looking for a less outspoken candidate, had refused to endorse Clay for the nomination. Their "want of nerve and decision" and "shrinking from responsibility," Rayner claimed, had led to the Tyler disaster. By 1844, with the Tyler wing of the party ostracized, Clay and his supporters finally had the prize within their grasp. "To whom ought we to look," Rayner had asked publicly as early as July 1842, "to whom *can* we look but to HENRY CLAY?" If Clay were not electable, as many suggested, then Whig principles were not destined to triumph in America, and Rayner believed that the party might as well be abandoned. To those Whigs "whose timidity and indecision would suggest delay" in endorsing Clay, Rayner could only administer a sarcastic rebuke, telling them to "take your own time and come up to the struggle whenever you may think it *safe and convenient* to do so." [35]

To Rayner's great satisfaction, Clay's nomination and eventual victory in the general election seemed assured in the spring of 1844. The only potential stumbling block was the troubling question of Texas annexation, an explosive issue that could sabotage a candidate's hopes if not handled wisely. In April, during a triumphant campaign tour of the South, Clay visited Raleigh, where he intended to clarify his position on Texas. Tradition in Raleigh holds that during his visit Clay was Rayner's houseguest at the Polk-Rayner mansion a few blocks from the state capitol. According to the legend, it was a warm afternoon on the seventeenth when Clay requested that a small writing table and chair be carried from the house and placed under a massive oak tree in Rayner's yard. The letter that the candidate then wrote to the *National Intelligencer* presented his views on the Texas question in great detail. In short, while Clay did not rule out eventual annexation—especially with Mexico's assent—he opposed it for the time being, counseling moderation and patience regarding the Lone Star Republic. Van Buren's announcement of a nearly identical position seemingly put Texas on the political shelf until after the fall election.[36]

While Rayner approved of Clay's position on Texas, the quaint story of Clay's writing the Raleigh Letter while at Rayner's house appears to be apocryphal. In fact, Rayner in all likelihood was not even in Raleigh during Clay's time there. Despite his status as Clay's staunchest ally in North Carolina, Rayner was never mentioned in the detailed press coverage of Clay's visit, and all indications suggest that he was confined to his sickbed in Washington for a prolonged period in the spring of 1844. Two weeks after Clay wrote the Raleigh Letter, North Carolina newspapers reported that Rayner's health, which had been "very bad through the winter," had "undergone no improvement." The Whig press felt compelled to defend their champion from Democratic charges that he had neglected his duties in the House, explaining that he had been "suffering under a disease which has thus far baffled all medical skill."[37]

While he fought ill health through the spring and summer of 1844, Rayner's spirits improved when he contemplated Clay's anticipated victory in the fall. "All we have to fear," he wrote in March, "is from the abolitionists—and their constant increase from year to year, is really becoming to be alarming." As it turned out, Rayner had more to fear than just antislavery sentiment in the North. Indeed, it was southern Democrats who dashed Whig hopes by nominating pro-annexation dark horse James K. Polk instead of Van Buren. In the fall election, Polk defeated Clay by a razor-thin margin. Polk's unabashed expansionist stance, a late-in-the-campaign equivocation by Clay on the annexation question, and the heavy support given to Polk by thousands of recently naturalized immigrants, led to the Whig defeat.[38]

For Rayner and many other Whigs, immigrants in the northeastern cities were the most obvious immediate cause of the 1844 defeat. Although he would never forgive the immigrants, in Rayner's mind Clay's defeat was not entirely due to the immigrant vote or even to the Kentuckian's mishandling of the annexation question. For several years Rayner had feared that the party's stands had not been bold enough on a broad range of issues and principles. Those principles differentiated Whigs from Democrats and kept the country's attention focused on national rather than sectional issues. Only by doing so could the parties keep slavery out of the nation's political dialogue.[39] Thus, while the Democrats had corruptly exploited the sectional issue of annexation and manipulated the immigrant vote, the Whigs had to shoulder their share of the blame. A party more dedicated to principles never would have given the 1840 nominations to Harrison and Tyler, the one an undeserving war hero and the other a Democrat in Whigs' clothing.

Rayner's disillusionment with politics received reinforcement during the stormy debate over Texas annexation in the first weeks of 1845. Because the Senate had rejected an annexation treaty, the lame-duck president interpreted Polk's election as a mandate from the people in favor of annexation by any means. It would also be the only concrete achievement of his administration. In December, Tyler had put forth the highly questionable proposition that Texas could be legally annexed by means of a joint resolution instead of a treaty. The debate raged in the House through most of January, with Rayner attending the session only sporadically, probably on account of his nagging health problems. Of course, nothing short of total incapacitation could have kept him from attending at the crucial moment when the House was to vote upon the annexation resolution. On the twenty-fifth, it became apparent that the vote would soon be taken, and Rayner borrowed time from a colleague to complain that "by some system of management . . . no Southern Whig had been suffered to open his mouth" on the Texas question. The chair called him to order, and the representatives proceeded to pass the resolution by a 120–98 vote. During the first week of February, Rayner clung to hopes that the "outrageous measure" would die in the Senate, where it was now being debated. Foiled in his attempts to speak publicly prior to the vote in the House, he determined to state his case before the final Senate vote. Thus in two major speeches ten days apart, Rayner presented the arguments against annexation. It was to be his valedictory in the United States Congress.[40]

Rayner's Texas speech placed the annexation debate in the proper context by stating that "the tone of the debate and the peculiar sectional feelings" aroused by the Texas issue "involved remote consequences, that might hereafter jeopard[ize] our institutions, and shake this Union to its centre." He believed that annexation by any means other than a Senate-ratified treaty was patently unconstitutional. But constitutional questions notwithstanding, he cautioned his fellow congressmen to look beyond the present to the future. Annexation would prove an "apple of discord . . . it would prove a fruitful source of jealousy and heart-burning between different sections and interests; . . . it would prove an enduring element of mischief to the reckless and turbulent in every section; . . . it would ultimately sever those ties and associations of fraternal feeling which are the only sure bond of our Union and guaranty of our freedom." Rayner expressed grave doubts about "whether the contemplated advantages to be derived from annexation could outweigh the danger to the stability of the Union with which the subject is fraught." Thus his opposition to annexation, like virtually every other public question that he had dealt with in public life, rested on the twin pillars of constitutionality and the survival of the Union.[41]

Rayner's dire warnings about the danger of annexation went beyond vague predictions of increased sectional tension. In a remarkable prediction of events, he contended that "if Texas is admitted with her present definition of boundary, this government will at no very distant day be placed in the attitude of committing a manifest outrage upon Mexico, by despoiling her of a portion of her acknowledged territory." Experience had shown "that the insatiate rapacity of western enterprise for land, will not stop to reason about the technical principles of international right." Rayner not only accurately foresaw the illegal land grab that would result from annexation, but he also had no doubt that acquiring Texas would involve the United States in a war with Mexico. He was "surprised, as well as pained," to witness how readily some of his fellow legislators endorsed such a war. It was easy, Rayner argued, for politicians and poets to rhapsodize on the glories of battle. "Unfortunately for mankind, the duty of waging and conducting war rarely falls to the lot of those whose passions and indiscretion plunge nations into it." Although Rayner disliked war, he firmly believed in a very Whiggish version of manifest destiny:

The march of Anglo-Saxon improvement and Anglo-Saxon institutions must and will sweep on, not by the agency of this government, but in despite of it even. The principles of freedom, to be sure and permanent in their establishment, must depend on moral causes, which are slow and progressive in their operation. . . . We shall lose our moral influence as a nation, excite the enmity and suspicion of the christian world, and thus, in fact, injure the cause of freedom, when we deliberately avow it as one of the leading objects of our policy to disseminate the principles of our system over other countries.[42]

Having shown annexation by joint resolution to be unconstitutional, dangerous to the Union, and imperialistic, Rayner focused his attack on those who sought to use it as a weapon in the war over slavery. "I know not which to consider most reprehensible," he complained, "northern gentlemen who oppose, or southern gentlemen who advocate, the annexation of Texas on the avowedly leading consideration of slavery." He believed that experience should have taught Americans that "the introduction of this exciting subject must prove fatal to anything like calm and dispassionate deliberation." This was the same viewpoint that Rayner had always taken with regard to the peculiar institution: Slavery must remain strictly a state issue, with Congress neither interfering with it nor fostering its advancement. He severely criticized Secretaries of State Abel P. Upshur and John C. Calhoun for basing their support of annexation on the grounds that it would provide protection for slavery. Citing Calhoun's letter to the English foreign minister, in which the South Carolinian argued that "slavery is a great moral as well as political blessing," Rayner exclaimed, "Deplorable humiliation of our diplomatic character in the eyes of the world! Every man of enlarged views must admit that Texas should not be annexed except upon high national considerations, appealing to the patriotism of all sections and to all interests."

Rayner had exposed the fatal flaw in the proslavery justification for annexation. Those who championed the joint resolution primarily as a proslavery measure were in effect admitting that Congress could legislate on slavery-related considerations. Such views, according to Rayner,

> would take from us of the South the impregnable position which we have heretofore maintained on this question. Our argument has ever been, that with slavery as an institution neither Congress nor the people of the North can constitutionally interfere. If we admit that this general government can interpose to extend slavery as a blessing, we must also admit that it can interfere to arrest it as an evil. If the people of the North can be called on to extend the area of slavery, as a precautionary measure for the protection of southern interests, may not the people of the South be called on to extend the area of non-slavery, as a precautionary measure for the protection of northern interests? I do not choose to yield this our strong ground. We ask no favors, no protection, no encouragement for our institutions, except those which we claim under the solemn guaranties of the constitution.

Referring to Upshur and Calhoun, he suggested that "if it had been the especial object and design of those two gentlemen to forever prevent the peaceable annexation of Texas, to arouse against it all the angry feelings of fanaticism, and to destroy this union in the conflict, it seems to me that they could not have taken a course better calculated to answer their purpose." Time would prove Rayner absolutely correct in this entire line of reasoning.

As if violating the Constitution, plunging the nation into a foreign war, and dividing the nation were not enough evils to come from annexation, Rayner identified one additional dangerous consequence: The annexation of Texas and the resulting Mexican war would destroy his beloved Whig party. This "wild crusade for foreign territory" would divert the party from its real mission in domestic politics by absorbing Whigs in the slavery controversy. Then what would become of the National Bank, distribution of the public land proceeds, a protective tariff, curtailment of executive power, and internal improvements? "Above all," he asked, what would happen to "the great principle which lies at the foundation of whig policy, the elevation of intellect and virtue in the political and social scale?" Rayner called for Americans to "purify our own altars" before attempting "new plans of conquest." With revealing candor, he placed much of the blame upon the Whigs themselves. "By the united action of the whigs, we could have preserved the constitution and the integrity of the Union inviolate. Defeat is bad enough; but its disasters are aggravated when our reflection is that of the dying eagle, that the arrow which pierced our hearts was feathered from our own wing." The party's refusal to stand by its own principles had worked its own undoing.

Rayner's last words in the House of Representatives were a mixture of defeat and quixotic hope. "This is, in all probability, the last speech I shall ever make on this floor," he told his colleagues. "Experience has taught me that the strife and turmoil of political contention bring no substantial joys, and that, after all, true happiness is only to be found in the quiet and repose of domestic life." But in what was almost an afterthought, he added, "We have been defeated, but not conquered."

The next day Rayner composed an emotional letter to his constituents announcing his retirement and recapitulating his six-year career in Congress. He claimed that his refusal to seek another term resulted from private and domestic considerations that required no explanation, but the letter suggested the frustration he felt after six years of futile effort spent trying to combat Democratic corruption, enact Whig programs, and preserve the Union. He referred to the victory of 1840 and spoke of the "sad disappointment" caused when Tyler "betrayed us into the hands of our enemies." Alluding to Clay and the 1844 campaign, he expressed sadness that "the ablest statesman and purest patriot of the age" had been denied the presidency. But Rayner paid special attention to the cause of Clay's defeat. "It is one consolation to know, however, that our defeat was not effected by the native born sons of America, not by the descendants of Revolutionary patriots, not by those who have an abiding interest in the preservation of our free institutions. A large majority of these cast their votes for HENRY CLAY. But this result, so disastrous to our country, was brought about by foreign aid, fresh from distant lands, who cannot appreciate the nature of our institutions, or estimate the theory of our glorious Constitution." As a result, he explained, the country was just where it was eight years earlier: "The people are suffering, our country's honor is sullied, our Constitution lies trampled in the dust, and our only hope is in the recuperative energies of the nation, and a returning sense of duty to themselves, on the part of the people."[43]

Thus Kenneth Rayner stepped from the national political stage, convinced that self-serving politicians, ignorant immigrants, and reckless sectional agitators were endangering the Union. "Shall we ground our arms in despair of the Republic?" he asked. "Shall we surrender the contest, because wrong has temporarily triumphed over right?" He hoped that the battle was not finished. "The Whigs are yet unconquered, unterrified, and undismayed," he contended, although in reality he retained few illusions that the party would ever reclaim the high ground of principle and purify the body politic. He knew that Whigs—especially southern Whigs—were partly to blame, for they had allowed the unpatriotic sectional issue of Texas to tarnish their enthusiasm for Clay. Resigning his congressional seat was a sign of Rayner's frustration, but it was also an act of protest; the voice of dissent within him was growing louder. Although no one who read the closing lines of his letter could have predicted the direction in which the rising tide of dissent would take Rayner, few believed that he was through with politics. "In the struggles which await us," he wrote, "although I shall not be an actor on the busy theatre here, yet, as a private in the ranks, who has enlisted for life, I shall ever be found ready to do service where the calls of duty demand my humble aid." Those calls were not long in coming and would ultimately bring him face to face with the reality that he no longer represented the mainstream of southern opinion.

CHAPTER 3

"We Live in the
Age of Improvement"

Kenneth Rayner departed the nation's capital in 1845, his faith in politics shaken. Six years of struggle had seen him and his party meet one defeat after another. In his final session in the House of Representatives, Rayner at last had succeeded in getting Congress to appropriate $50,000 to begin the work of opening the Roanoke Inlet that would connect Albemarle Sound with the ocean, only to have President Tyler pocket-veto the bill containing the appropriation. North Carolina Whigs expressed dismay at Rayner's refusal to seek a fourth term. Commenting on his service, the Raleigh *Register* stated that "if ever constituents had a faithful representative, Kenneth Rayner has been one." The editor predicted that the citizens of North Carolina would not allow the retiring congressman to remain long out of public office, and during the first few months of 1845 the Whig press repeatedly called for him to reconsider.[1]

Rayner, however, remained adamant. Not only had political considerations and poor health persuaded him to retire, but his private affairs had also undergone a dramatic change. In 1841 he had become interested in a young woman from Raleigh, Susan Spratt Polk, no ordinary southern belle. The youngest of fifteen children, Susan belonged to a family that was about the closest thing North Carolina had to aristocracy. The Polks were one of the wealthiest families in the state, if not the South. Susan's grandfather, General Thomas Polk, and her father, Colonel William Polk, both had compiled distinguished records in the Continental Army during the Revolution. Following the war, William embarked upon a fabulously successful career as a western land speculator, and by the time of Susan's birth in 1821 he owned more than a hundred thousand acres. When he died in 1834, Susan's father left behind a dynasty.[2]

Susan received the upbringing and education expected of the youngest daughter of an immensely wealthy family. Her mother, Sarah Hawkins Polk, ruled commandingly as matriarch of Raleigh society and manager of the family fortune after William Polk's death. The large brood of children loved, respected, and perhaps feared her a bit. Like her colonel husband, Sarah delegated responsibility to the troops—her grown sons—who assumed much of the task of making sure the younger children were properly educated and selected appropriate marriage partners. In Susan's case, this responsibility fell largely upon her brother Leonidas, who would later earn fame as an Episcopal bishop and lieutenant general in the Confederate army. When Susan was fourteen or fifteen, she was sent to an exclusive boarding school in Philadelphia. At the time, Leonidas was living in the city and could keep a close eye on her. The girl's letters to her mother reveal a homesick teenager little interested in chemistry or Latin and somewhat bewildered at not being pampered as she had been at home. However, with Leonidas's wise guidance and Sarah's stern attention from Raleigh, Susan completed her studies and returned home to the parties, balls, teas, and excursions that occupied the days of a young, single socialite in the antebellum South. The ultimate objective of these activities, of course, was to identify and snare a suitable husband.[3]

Kenneth and Susan no doubt met—or at least became aware of each other—during Rayner's four years in the state legislature. Even though it was the state capital, Raleigh was still a small town in the late 1830s, and the Polk mansion stood only a few blocks from the capitol grounds. Next to soldiers, politicians were the heroes of the day, and plenty of both could be found in the halls of the legislature. A hot debate in the senate or house of commons was as much a social occasion as a lawmaking exercise, and admiring women often filled the galleries to witness the gallant orators. Rayner's oratorical skills, rugged build, sad, dark eyes, and unruly shock of brown hair would have attracted the attention of more than one of Raleigh's belles. His election to Congress at age thirty made him one of the state's most eligible bachelors and helped compensate for the fact that he did not hail from one of North Carolina's first families.

By the summer of 1841, insiders in Raleigh and Washington knew that Kenneth had his eye on Susan. In August of that year, Susan traveled with her best friend Ellen Mordecai and a large party of other people from Raleigh on an extended vacation that included a stop in Washington. Rayner's colleague William A. Graham told his wife that Kenneth was "quite devoted" to Susan, but when the Carolinians reached the national capital, Rayner was grieving over the death of his brother Henry and would not socialize. However, two weeks later he had recovered sufficiently to accompany Susan and her friends to the next stop on their itinerary, Baltimore. Graham professed not to know what Rayner's "prospects of success" were with Susan; marrying into the Polk family was not an easy accomplishment, and the very rich and pretty Susan could afford to be choosy.[4]

It took Kenneth less than a year to win Susan's hand. On July 12, 1842, the thirty-three-year-old congressman and the twenty-one-year-old debutante were married in Raleigh. At five o'clock that afternoon, three hours before the wedding, a friend of the groom paid a visit to the nervous Rayner. "Poor fellow he is as badly scared as tho' he were to be led to the gallows," Charles L. Hinton reported. The wedding must have been a rather intimidating affair. Sarah Polk threw a huge party, and as Hinton put it, "all the old Lady's children have *convened.*"[5]

If Hinton's depiction of the Polk clan "convening" sounds more like a corporate board meeting than a family wedding party, it is not surprising. In the antebellum South, one did not simply marry an individual—one wed the entire family. In effect, Kenneth became a Polk every bit as much as Susan became a Rayner. Sarah Polk now was "mother" to Kenneth, and the multitude of Susan's siblings were his "brothers" and "sisters." But marrying into the Polk family meant something more: on his wedding day Kenneth effectively gained control over Susan's share of the family fortune. The Polks never would have consented to one of their members marrying someone who might threaten that legacy. Although the family felt concern that the pampered, emotional Susan would have a difficult time adjusting to the reality of married life, three months after the wedding Susan's brother Lucius observed that the newlyweds seemed very happy. "He appears a most excellent man," Lucius wrote of Rayner, adding that Kenneth appeared to be a good "acquisition to the family." Lucius was "thankful that Susan has fallen in such good hands," provided that Kenneth did not "indulge her too much."[6]

The remaining years of Rayner's service in the House of Representatives were bittersweet ones for the couple. Many congressmen left their wives at home when Congress was in session, but Kenneth and Susan rented a suite of rooms in a Washington boardinghouse and set up housekeeping. Apart from official receptions, the capital social scene was dull in the 1840s, and the Rayners preferred quiet evenings in their apartment, where they were often joined by Kenneth's congressional friends James Pearce of Maryland, Richard Bayard of Delaware, and Leverett Saltonstall of Massachusetts. Bayard also brought his wife and daughters with him to Washington, and their companionship helped to relieve Susan's frequent bouts of home-

sickness. The new Mrs. Rayner, however, always looked forward to the ad-
journment of Congress, when she could return home to Raleigh. During the
recesses, she sometimes accompanied Kenneth to his plantation in Hertford
County, but she refused each year to venture into the swampy and unhealthful
tidewater country until the first two autumn frosts had rendered it less risky.[7]

Eleven months after the wedding, the couple's first child was born and
named after Susan's sister, Mary. Although Kenneth had hoped for a son, he
explained to James Pearce that "after a few days I became perfectly reconciled, and felt so thankful that it was a sound, healthy, and well-formed child,
that *now* I feel as though I would not have it otherwise." Like proud fathers in
all times and locales, Rayner thought his new daughter "the finest, best and
prettiest child in the world," although he admitted that his assessment was a
bit prejudiced.[8]

The Rayners' first two years of marriage, however, were also destined to
be marred by deaths on both sides of the family. Kenneth had done his best
to make his father, Amos, comfortable in the old man's declining years. Their
correspondence while Kenneth was in Washington shows the love and concern that the eighty-year-old Revolutionary veteran and his son felt for one
another, and Amos's death in 1843 came as a hard blow to Kenneth. Susan,
too, was saddened by the loss of her brother, Rufus, in late 1843, followed
by Sarah Polk's death in January 1844. Coming so soon after these losses,
Kenneth and Susan were truly stricken when, four days after their second
wedding anniversary, their one-year-old daughter died in Raleigh.[9]

Thus Kenneth's marriage to Susan, increasing financial responsibilities,
recurring ill health, and a series of family misfortunes—combined with his
dissatisfaction with the course of national politics—contributed to Rayner's
decision to leave the House of Representatives and settle down to the more
sedate and satisfying life of a gentleman planter. He and Susan would be
spared the uncomfortable Washington summers and equally disagreeable
winters, Susan could spend more time with family and friends in Raleigh,
and Kenneth could devote more time to his great love of agriculture. While in
Congress he had begun major improvements at Little Town, diversifying his
farming operation and constructing a fine house on the Hertford plantation.
With her mother's death, Susan had inherited the Polk mansion in Raleigh,
and the fortune now at his disposal made it possible for Kenneth to pursue
new planting ventures exceeding anything he could have imagined just a few
years earlier.

Only after the wedding did Rayner probably become fully aware of the
magnitude of his wife's fortune. Her inheritance consisted of approximately

twenty thousand acres in Carroll, Dyer, Gibson, Obion, Shelby, Tipton, and Weakley counties, Tennessee. The lands were worth about $50,000. In addition to the landholdings, Susan received stock in the Bank of North Carolina, the Raleigh & Gaston Railroad, and the Rockfish Manufacturing Company, valued at about $15,000. The Polk slaves were divided among the children, but unfortunately there is no way to determine how many were included in Susan's inheritance. There can be little doubt, however, that the Tennessee lands, stock, slaves, along with Susan's personal property and the valuable Polk mansion in Raleigh, constituted a wedding present in excess of $100,000. The master of Little Town was a rich man.[10]

After leaving Congress, Rayner wasted little time putting his planting dreams into motion. He had already broadened the scope of his agricultural operations by forming a partnership with his brother-in-law Andrew Jackson Polk, in which the two men jointly planted Polk's plantation in Fayette County, Tennessee. In November 1845, Rayner traveled to Tennessee to help oversee the cotton and corn harvest and the hog-slaughtering on Polk's property. Following a short stay in Memphis, he took a steamer down the Mississippi River to investigate the area, with the idea of purchasing a cotton plantation.[11]

Rayner made his temporary headquarters at the plantation of Isaac Hilliard, a transplanted North Carolinian related to the Polks by marriage. Hilliard's land lay on the banks of the Mississippi six miles north of the Louisiana border in Chicot County, Arkansas, and Rayner used it as a base for trips up and down the river to learn firsthand about agricultural prospects in the area. He liked what he saw. "It is certainly the most productive region I have ever seen," he wrote to his friend Duncan Cameron in North Carolina. "The inexhaustible fertility of the soil far exceeds any thing I have ever seen, or had ever conceived, and I have seen the best of the uplands of Alabama, Mississippi, Tennessee, &c. The cotton plant grows more luxuriantly than I had supposed possible." [12]

During the week Rayner spent as the Hilliards' houseguest, he ventured twenty or thirty miles in either direction along the river, talked with planters, inspected crops, and sought out land that might be bought. He discovered to his delight that one could reasonably expect to produce ten bales of cotton per hand (slave) and one to two bales per acre in the rich black soil. Purchasing a fine plantation, however, was difficult, for few owners wanted to sell. After years of depression, prosperity had returned to the nation, and no group was enjoying better times than Mississippi cotton planters. "There [are] a very few who have improved places, who are disposed to sell," Rayner reported.

"No place well improved, on the river, or the lakes contiguous, can be purchased for less than $25 per acre—and many ask $30 & $35." He could have
bought uncleared lands for half that price, but as he explained, "that will not
do for me, unless I was about to settle here permanently myself" and oversee
the clearing operations personally. There were some places "elegantly improved" for sale on the installment plan—for such was the usual practice in
the region—but Rayner was leery of credit. "I am too much afraid of debt to
incur the risk of a fatal revulsion in the cotton market," he told Cameron.[13]

Leaving Arkansas, Rayner traveled down the river to Louisiana, where
he looked at some more cotton plantations before investigating the sugar-
planting region. All things being equal, he would have preferred to buy in
Louisiana, probably because of the greater ease in conducting business in
New Orleans and closer proximity to the plantation of his brother-in-law
Leonidas. But in the end, he found nothing that appealed to him as much as
the area around Chicot County, and on December 20 Rayner consummated
the purchase of a 538-acre plantation on the Mississippi, immediately adjoining the Hilliard estate. The plantation contained three hundred cleared
acres, "with moderately comfortable houses, &c." He paid the owner, James
Dick of New Orleans, $8,640 cash. The scarcity of improved land for sale
had played a part in helping Rayner to decide upon this particular plantation,
but one other factor also influenced his decision. The area around Chicot
County, according to Rayner, was "remarkable for the humanity and attention to comfort, observed towards slaves." Slaves were "better housed than
in any country" he had ever seen. "They are well-fed, and are by no means
overworked," he noted. "I have been very minute in my inquiries on these
points."[14]

Rayner claimed slavery to be an "evil," but it was an evil that had been "entailed on [southerners] by their ancestors" and hence they could do little to
end it. In his mind this reality, rather than justifying harsh treatment, placed
heavy responsibilities upon the master. Traditional republican thought had
characterized human nature and thus society as imperfect and prone to corruption, and Rayner viewed slavery as one of those imperfections. Because
slavery could never (in the foreseeable future) be brought to a peaceful end
in the South, it was incumbent upon slaveholders to see that slaves were
decently fed, clothed, and housed. Slaves should not be sold, nor families
separated, except when such sale or separation was necessary to the peace
and order of the plantation. To Rayner, there was nothing sacred about the
South's social and economic arrangements; nothing about slavery made it an
ideal organizing principle for society, as the ultra-proslavery apologists often
suggested.[15]

When Democratic opponents, then, would later accuse Rayner of anti-slavery leanings, there was an abstract truth in the charge. Such favorite Whig measures as internal improvements and banks would help bind the various sections of the nation together and promote commerce and economic development. A South with a diversified economy, including manufacturing and mercantile establishments, would be less dependent upon plantation agriculture and perhaps ultimately less attached to slavery. Commenting on slavery in later years, Rayner would state, "I do not say it is the best condition they [blacks] are capable of. In the dispensation of Providence they may reach a higher standard of civilization in some other position." [16]

Thus, Rayner's attitudes toward slavery were in harmony with his Whiggish social and political outlook, an outlook that emphasized the role of environment in human improvement. As the sectional crisis deepened over the next few years, events would make it increasingly difficult for many men such as Rayner to maintain these mildly critical attitudes toward the South's peculiar institution. The ambivalence of some Whigs toward slavery contributed in two ways to their party's demise. First, the moderate views of men like Rayner helped to estrange them from the party when it began to take a more strident proslavery position in the South. Second, those Whigs who came to argue slavery as a positive good found their views better represented by the Democratic party. Although the issue has seldom been noticed, southern Whigs tended to be divided in attitudes toward slavery in much the same way as their northern counterparts.[17]

Rayner's concern as he purchased his new plantation on the Mississippi was not so much whether slavery constituted a just or unjust system, but rather that his slaves be treated humanely. When he described slavery as an evil, however, he was speaking primarily of its effects on the morals of the whites involved in the institution. On the effects of slavery upon enslaved blacks, Rayner said that he "regarded it as a blessing—I mean a blessing compared with any other condition I have ever seen them in, or heard or read of their being in." The widely held, ethnocentric American belief that blacks in Africa were barbaric rendered him unable to admit that Africans had ever occupied any status more desirable than that of the southern slave (and, surely, he believed that the poverty-stricken, discriminated-against free blacks in America were not materially better off than their enslaved brothers and sisters). But it is significant that Rayner qualified his description of slavery as a blessing to the slaves: it was only a blessing "compared with any other condition" he had ever known them to occupy. This was a clear admission that someday, somehow, blacks might rise above their current position. In a better future world, slavery would not be their ideal status. "We live in the age of improvement," Rayner had proclaimed from the floor of the House of Representatives four years earlier. His attitude suggests that he believed that at some point in the distant future whites might be relieved from the burdens imposed by the evil institution of slavery, and that blacks might be lifted to some higher and heretofore unobtainable station in life. This was neither a revolutionary blow for universal freedom nor a ringing denunciation of slavery, but it was an intellectual position that would become increasingly unpopular and politically untenable in the antebellum South.[18]

Where Rayner obtained the slaves to work his new plantation remains an unanswered question, because few of his antebellum financial records have survived. After the Civil War he maintained that he "never bought any [slaves], except to bring man and wife together," and that he "never sold any, except in three instances, where they had been guilty of such bad conduct as placed them in jeopardy, if I had kept them in the neighborhood." All of his slaves, he claimed, were the result of his and Susan's inheritances. This statement must be viewed with skepticism, because it is unlikely that Susan's inheritance included enough slaves to furnish labor sufficient for Kenneth's new Arkansas plantation. Most, if not all, of Susan's inherited lands in Tennessee were either unoccupied or leased out to tenants, meaning that she did not inherit slaves in proportion to her real estate. And on Kenneth's home plantation in Hertford County the slave population grew from eighteen in 1840 to fifty-two ten years later. On the Arkansas plantation he owned seventy-two taxable slaves in 1861 (a figure that includes only those between the ages of five and sixty). Furthermore, the Rayners were listed in 1860 as owning twenty-eight slaves in Wake County (Raleigh), where Kenneth had also bought a small farm. These were probably the slaves Susan inherited, along with their descendants. Of course, both Kenneth and Susan may have inherited more human property than is known about. For example, Kenneth's own relatives (such as his brother Henry, who died in 1842) may have willed some slaves to Kenneth, and Susan's legacy could have included far more black chattels than the slim evidence suggests, for daughters of elite North Carolina families were often given slaves by their parents in informal transfers. But there is still sufficient reason to doubt Rayner's claim that he never bought slaves. At any rate, on the eve of the Civil War, he owned at least two hundred slaves in Arkansas and North Carolina, and the figure may have been much higher.[19]

Rayner's statement that he never sold slaves appears much more credible than his denial of having ever bought any, but philanthropy need not be ascribed as the motive for keeping his slaveholdings intact. He constantly enlarged his planting operations throughout the antebellum period, buying new property and bringing increasing portions of existing lands into cultivation, thus insuring a constant need for the natural increase among his slaves. Until the war reduced his planting empire to ruins, Rayner never needed to sell slaves in order to meet financial exigencies. Thus his stated commitment to keeping black families intact was never seriously tested, as it was for many poorer slaveholders. Only when the war appeared lost did he consider selling his slaves. Then, according to his own self-serving account, he called a family consultation to discuss whether to sell the slaves or risk losing everything when the war was over. "I had a weakness on the subject," he recalled in the New York *Times* article of October 29, 1865. "Our slaves were family negroes. I feared if I sold them I should feel unhappy about it, and I concluded I had rather lose them than risk my happiness in selling them." According to Rayner, his neighbors remarked "that they had never witnessed so strong an attachment between owners and slaves as existed between my family and our slaves. I know the fact that it was the common boast of my slaves that 'they had the best master in the world.' "

The only real evidence that survives to indicate whether Rayner was indeed a humane master comes from his own testimony. Again, his postwar statements must be used. "I have all my life been regarded as a negro-spoiler by my neighbors," he wrote in 1865. He claimed that his North Carolina slaves "lived in better houses than a majority of the poor white people in the country—frame tenements, plastered and whitewashed, with every fixture and convenience necessary for comfort." Preparations to house his Arkansas slaves in the same manner were interrupted only by the war. "I have often thought I never saw a more joyous, happy and contented set of beings," Rayner added.[20]

Slavery, however, was an exploitative institution, no matter how ostensibly paternalistic the white master might be. Two separate occurrences from Rayner's experience illustrate this fact. First, he is known to have had a sexual relationship with at least one of his female slaves in the 1850s, a fact that will be dealt with in a later part of this book. At this point, it is sufficient to say that almost nothing is known about the woman in question or about the details of the liaison. Affection between master and slave was possible, and southern history is dotted with examples of such unions based on genuine love. Still, considering the age of the woman in question (she was fifteen at the time) Rayner's relationship must be considered exploitative, if not overtly coercive. Another episode also suggests the illusory nature of paternalism. It is the classic case of the master who thought himself loved by his slaves, only to have one run away at the first opportunity. Early in the Civil War, Union gunboats regularly began patrolling past Little Town on the Chowan River. The Yankees rarely went ashore due to Confederate cavalry, which followed their movements closely, but the presence of the boats provided a strong incentive for local slaves to run away and seek freedom. Rayner was genuinely hurt and puzzled when a trusted slave—a teenage boy who kept the plantation's keys "and was entrusted with everything"—defected to the Union troops and signed on as steward on one of the gunboats. "He was much better off than if free," reported a dismayed Rayner, "for he wanted for nothing; and I never struck him, since he was a child." It apparently never had occurred to Rayner that the "contented set of beings" whom he owned might consider freedom an improvement over bondage.[21]

The years following his retirement from Congress brought personal prosperity and happiness to the former representative from Hertford. As his planting and slaveholding fortune grew, so did his family. The great blow Kenneth and Susan had felt when their first daughter died was softened by the news in the same month that Susan was again pregnant. On March 30, 1845, Sallie Rayner was born in Raleigh. A steady succession of additions to the family arrived over the next fifteen years. In 1847, the son that Kenneth had so long desired was born and named Henry Albert, after Rayner's deceased brother. Henry was followed by Kenneth, Jr. (1849), Fanny (1851), Susan (1855), William (1857), and Hamilton (1860).[22]

Rayner naturally kept his finger on the pulse of political events, but throughout 1845 and most of 1846 he evinced little interest in personally seeking office. Private affairs consumed most of his time and attention, and his party seemed far more interested than Rayner himself in keeping him involved in politics. He was simply too valuable to the Whig cause to be allowed to drop from the scene, and the 1846 Whig state convention placed him on the party's central committee, even though Rayner was not present at the meeting. Throughout the antebellum period, the central committee largely dictated Whig policy in the state, and only the party's top echelon of leaders gained admittance.[23]

Whigs in his old congressional district particularly bemoaned Rayner's retirement from politics. As one eastern Whig expressed it, Rayner's refusal to seek a fourth term had "ruined we poor Whigs in this Dist[rict]." In 1845, Asa Biggs, a Democrat, had won Rayner's old seat in the House of Representatives, raising the total of North Carolina Democrats in Congress to six and further convincing Whig partisans of their former congressman's value. The following year, therefore, Rayner reluctantly permitted Hertford

County's Whigs to place his name in nomination for his old seat in the general assembly. Serving in the state legislature demanded far less time and energy than holding a congressional seat, and because Susan and the children made their home in Raleigh most of the time anyway, reentering the house of commons was far more palatable than returning to Washington. The state legislature met during the winter—after harvest but before planting—when Rayner could afford to be away from his plantations. The Whigs, furthermore, hoped to regain complete control of the general assembly in 1846. Thus state politics offered a far more promising arena for constructive legislation than the hopelessly Democratic national government.[24]

When the August election returns were counted, the Whigs had scored a sweeping victory in North Carolina. In Hertford County, Rayner defeated his Democratic opponent by a 235-vote majority. In comparison, the Whig candidates for state senator and governor carried the county only by margins of 135 and 160, respectively, indicating something of Rayner's continuing high personal popularity among his constituents. After the election, the Raleigh *Register* announced the first priority facing the new legislature: "We hold it to be the very first duty of the General Assembly, at the ensuing Session, to repeal the odious Gerrymander of 1842, and re-district the state."[25]

Rayner dominated the 1846–47 session of the state legislature. He wrote the Whig redistricting bill and on December 9 took the floor to defend the proposition. No one was more ideal for the task, for Rayner was a tremendously skillful floor captain and had little to fear politically. His position with Hertford County voters was impregnable, and he had repeatedly disclaimed all ambition for higher office. In his introductory speech on the bill, Rayner stated that he was "well aware of the vituperation and obloquy which awaited him" and that his course would provide "a theme of denunciation to a malignant party Press, and of unsparing abuse to every unscrupulous demagogue in the State." However, he had "counted the cost" of his actions and was prepared "to meet the peltings of many a pitiless storm of censure and denunciation."[26]

And a storm it was. One Democrat after another took the floor before packed galleries to denounce Rayner's redistricting scheme, and the Whigs answered with equal fervor. Both sides bandied about such terms as "Vandal Horde," "unscrupulous demagogues," "base fraud," and "corruption, treason, and tyranny." Rayner considered redistricting a "holy mission," while the Democrats characterized his efforts as being "stamped with the *cloven foot.*" A Whig partisan described Rayner's second speech on the bill as "a genteel rebuke, a severe flagellation, a most unmerciful excoriation." But no matter how fiercely the Democrats assailed the bill and its author, Whigs held clear majorities in both houses, and they succeeded in redrawing the districts.[27]

To a certain degree, redistricting is always an exercise in gerrymandering. A party in power would never purposefully injure its prospects by drawing districts in a politically disadvantageous manner. In the controversial session of 1846–47, Democrats charged the Whigs with "Raynermandering," and Whigs naturally replied that they were only undoing the gerrymander of 1842. By most standards of fairness, the Whig position was the more defensible of the two. Rayner's party had consistently polled sizable majorities in statewide elections, and they were understandably suspicious when the Democrats were able to elect six of nine congressmen while failing to elect their gubernatorial candidates. A look at maps of the districts before and after Rayner redrew them largely substantiates the Whig contention of redrawing the districts more fairly. Under the 1842 Democratic plan, several of the districts—especially the third and eighth—were narrow, twisted strings of counties. In comparison, the districts under the alleged "Raynermander" were composed of compact groups of contiguous counties and show no overt evidence of manipulation. Furthermore, Rayner left his old congressional district unchanged, even though the Democratic redistricting of 1842 had erased the traditionally large Whig majority there and had even allowed a Democrat to win in 1845. None of this, of course, is meant to imply that the Whig plan was impartial; Rayner's committee drew the new lines in order to give five of the nine districts to the Whigs, with one (his old district) capable of going either way. In the next election the Whigs succeeded in carrying these five districts and also in winning back the seat Rayner had once held.[28]

The result of this party warfare was strikingly similar to that of ten years earlier, when Rayner had led the movement to instruct the state's two Democratic senators: he emerged more popular than ever with North Carolina Whigs. This renewed popularity would have ironic consequences, for Rayner still had no discernible intention of seeking higher office. As the legislature prepared to adjourn, Charles L. Hinton stated that Rayner was "about the only member that has made much political capital during the session." Whig leader Richard Hines concurred, telling Willie P. Mangum that "Mr. Rayner is the only member that I think has gained much in popularity" and speculating that the legislator from Hertford would be "an acceptable Gubernatorial candidate at the next election to every section of the State." The redistricting episode underscores the influence that politicians at the state level in the antebellum period could wield indirectly in national politics. From his place in the general assembly, Rayner had twice been the key figure in determining who would hold seats in Congress. In 1838, his actions had helped to depose two U.S. senators, and in 1847 he played the leading role in giving his party three additional seats in the House of Representatives. In effect, he was exercising far greater influence in shaping national politics than he had been able to do with his single vote in Congress.[29]

Rayner's name had been mentioned in connection with the governorship since his first term in the House, although not with great seriousness until 1848. Whigs traditionally rotated the gubernatorial honors among the favorite sons of the state's three geographic sections—the east, west, and center. This system satisfied the party rank and file, who acquiesced in the selection of a man from a distant section knowing that their turn would come in due time. Geographic rotation also helped to deflect charges that a "Raleigh clique" dictated party affairs. Looking forward to the 1848 elections, most Whigs believed that the east's turn had come, and it was generally assumed that Rayner would be the nominee. In the fall of 1847, Whigs throughout the state held county conventions and stated their preferences for governor. Buncombe County, in the western mountains, inaugurated the movement for Rayner's candidacy, and counties in other sections soon began to follow suit. By the time of the March state convention, the nomination clearly would be his for the asking.[30]

Whigs, then, were dismayed when on November 27 the Raleigh *Register* published a letter from Rayner declining the nomination. The *Register*'s editor, Weston Gales, spoke for the Whigs of North Carolina when he expressed "real regret" at Rayner's withdrawal. "It is true," wrote Gales, "that public sentiment seemed to be concentrating all over the State, in favor of Mr. Rayner, as the Whig Candidate; and yet, we have been aware for months, that if he *did* accept the nomination, it would be done with very great reluctance." Gales understood that the governorship was something of a thankless job. As one leading student of North Carolina politics has pointed out, "at times, the parties nearly had to beg for a viable candidate." Candidates were required to engage in a long, difficult statewide speaking campaign; the office paid poorly and kept one away from one's regular occupation; and once in office, the governor had no veto power and limited patronage to dispense. The office was, of course, prestigious, and the governorship probably enhanced a politician's chances for higher honors (Graham, for example, was later secretary of the navy and Whig vice-presidential nominee). But party leaders knew that they could never automatically count on their first choice to agree to undertake the campaign.[31]

Rayner's stated reasons for declining the probable nomination were "of a personal character." Writing from Tennessee, he mentioned first his planting interests in the Southwest, explaining that until his Arkansas venture was more fully established, it would require frequent absences from the state. However, had his business interests been the only factor, he would have made the necessary sacrifices in order to answer the party's call. But Rayner also cited the "violent attacks of illness, caused by some derangement of my nervous system" that had plagued him throughout his congressional career. He believed these debilitating attacks were invariably brought on by "unusual excitement and fatigue" of the sort entailed by a political campaign. Thus he believed that to accept the nomination would risk his health and do a "great injustice" to his family and the Whig party.[32]

Rayner appears to have been sincere in this explanation of why he refused to seek the governor's office. His planting interests did necessitate frequent absences from Raleigh, and he had been plagued with the mysterious illness for years. The withdrawal certainly was not due to a fear of failure, for his election seemed almost certain. Whigs had not lost a gubernatorial race in more than a decade, and he was a far more able campaigner than some of the successful candidates of the past. Many observers viewed Rayner as the finest orator in North Carolina. His popularity extended to all sections; indeed, the far western part of the state had been among the first to advocate his candidacy. It is unlikely that at this point he had his eye on yet a higher office. The idea of a U.S. Senate seat could not help but tempt a man with as robust an ego as Rayner's, but it would have been difficult to choose a better stepping-stone to the Senate than the governorship. As Rayner himself argued in his letter of declination, to be governor was "an honor which should satisfy the ambition of any one." Therefore, beneath his genuine desire to have more time for private affairs and his nagging health problems remains the fact that Kenneth Rayner harbored little hope for the Whig party to save the Republic. He would do what he could to save the party—the Democrats were far worse—but with Whiggery rapidly becoming irrelevant, he had no intention of captaining the sinking ship.[33]

Rayner's refusal to run for governor placed the Whig party in a quandary. No single candidate emerged as a statewide favorite, and every county seemed to have a different preference. As Graham explained, since Rayner declined the honor there had been "no settled public opinion in favor of any Candidate." Rayner perhaps entertained second thoughts about his decision. After he and Susan visited Washington, Congressman David Outlaw suspected that Rayner regretted declining the nomination and would still accept the party's call. However, Rayner had ample opportunity to change his mind, for no frontrunner had emerged even on the eve of the state convention. For him to accept the nomination reluctantly, after having repeatedly stated his intention not to run, would have been interpreted as a selfless political act. To do so would be in keeping with the republican maxim that the "office should seek the man" and not vice-versa.[34]

When Rayner and his fellow Whigs assembled in Raleigh in March 1848 to choose a gubernatorial candidate, a number of names were mentioned for the honor. If Rayner persisted in declining the nomination, either Edward Stanly or Andrew Joyner—both easterners—were likely substitutes. However, nobody knew any longer whether or not an eastern man would get the nod; Rayner's withdrawal had rendered that assumption less certain. With Rayner engineering the proceedings, the nomination surprisingly went not to one of the eastern candidates, but rather to darkhorse Charles Manly of Raleigh. It was rumored that Rayner had colluded with the central clique and rigged the convention with the particular object of defeating Stanly. According to one Whig newspaper's account several years afterward, the convention had been "Raynerized"—it had voted by congressional districts—in order to prevent Stanly's nomination.[35]

The 1848 campaign marked the beginning of a long feud between Stanly and Rayner. The sources of the conflict are somewhat obscure. Stanly's biographer concluded that "Rayner opposed Stanly's nomination because he did not like him personally and feared his selection would prejudice his own political claims." The personal dislike appears to have resulted from the alliance between Stanly and Whig senator George E. Badger. Stanly and Badger were cousins, but Badger's first wife had been Susan Rayner's sister. When Mary Polk Badger died, her husband remarried more quickly than the Polks thought proper. David Outlaw elaborated upon this breach of etiquette in a letter to his wife, explaining that "scandal about Raleigh at the time further said that the present Mrs. Badger, was rather indecent in her haste in giving birth to twins after the marriage." Another Whig congressman, Thomas Clingman, reportedly told Rayner that Badger and Stanly were planning to use Stanly's governorship as a springboard for placing Stanly in the Senate. Presumably this would put him ahead of Rayner politically. According to this account, Rayner defeated Stanly's candidacy for governor owing to the Polk/Rayner-Badger/Stanly family feud and Rayner's own political jealousy. The validity of this theory can never be tested fully. Rayner still maintained a keen interest in political affairs, despite his growing disillusionment with the course of the national Whig party. That Stanly and Rayner had grown to dislike each other is beyond doubt. Rayner later provided the vague explanation that his and Stanly's differences "were of a private nature, growing out of our peculiar personal relations." But if Rayner were indeed as ambitious as this account suggests, it is difficult to see why he would have refused so steadfastly to run for governor himself.[36]

Charles Manly thus gained the Whig nomination. Accurately reflecting Whig sentiment in the state, Rayner's neighbor Valentine described the nominee as "a gentleman whom no body suspected they would nominate" and unenthusiastically supposed that "perhaps he will do as well as any." Manly won the election, but the margin of victory was razor-thin. Two years later the Democrats would defeat him in his quest for reelection. Many Whigs never fully forgave Rayner for refusing to answer his party's call in 1848, and when the party fell upon hard times they blamed him for selfishly contributing to the Whigs' downfall. Unable to see the extent of Rayner's disillusionment with the Whig party and with the course of American politics in general, most observers could do little besides question the integrity of his motives.[37]

With no viable political alternatives, and perhaps sensing the resentment that the state's Whigs were feeling for him, Rayner was not yet ready to abandon the party to which he had devoted most of his adult life. However, when the national Whig convention nominated war hero General Zachary Taylor for the presidency, Rayner received the news with coolness. Old Rough and Ready had been given the nomination on what Rayner believed to be unacceptable criteria: his military exploits in an immoral war and his total failure to commit himself to any clear set of programs or principles. Taylor had never voted in his life, and the national convention avoided even drafting a platform. Perhaps worse, much of Taylor's southern Whig support was due to the fact that he was a slaveholder. In Rayner's view, men like Henry Clay should be chosen for national leadership because they would patriotically set aside slavery-related considerations, not because they represented one side or the other of the sectional conflict.[38]

But if Rayner could find little to applaud in the selection of Taylor as the party's standard-bearer, he entertained no doubts whatever about which candidate would be the lesser of two evils. The Democratic party and its nominee, Lewis Cass, still represented spoilsmanship, executive usurpation, negative government, and reckless expansionism. The week after the national convention, Raleigh Whigs met to form a Rough and Ready Club. After former governor Morehead spoke to the assemblage, the audience called loudly for Rayner. Apparently doubts had already begun to circulate that he might not support Taylor's candidacy. Rayner meant to set the record straight. Some of his fellow citizens, he explained to the crowd, thought that he occupied a "peculiar" position with regard to the national party; he had "come forward to 'define it.'" Rayner then declared his preference for Clay but pledged his support for Taylor. Privately harboring great doubts, he was nonetheless ready to answer the party's call if his services were needed.[39]

The call soon came. The Ninth Congressional District Whig convention chose him as presidential elector, and soon he was dutifully waging the party's battle. Antebellum electors were expected to campaign actively for their candidates, and between the end of September and election day Rayner filled twenty-two speaking engagements throughout his old district on behalf of a candidate whom he did not truly trust. According to William Valentine, Rayner's misgivings apparently showed. In early October when Rayner debated his Democratic counterpart, John Bragg, Valentine pronounced the speech "a failure." The speech "did not answer my expectations and conceptions of him," wrote Rayner's neighbor, "but it is an uphill business to talk General Taylor into the Presidency."[40]

Uphill or not, Rayner and the Whigs did manage to talk and vote the hero of Buena Vista into the White House. But almost immediately Taylor had to deal with the mounting crisis over slavery in the new territories taken from Mexico in the war. Rayner, like countless other politicians throughout the nation, was forced to formulate a position on this critical problem. His analysis of the issue marked Rayner as a loyal southerner, but it also exhibited the political independence that was increasingly setting him apart from the mainstream of southern political thought.

Rayner took what appeared to be a thoroughly southern stance on the Wilmot Proviso, opposing it vehemently. Yet Rayner did not object on constitutional grounds as did many southerners. Admitting that Congress had the constitutional power to prohibit slavery in the territories, he argued that the Proviso was unfair to the South and antirepublican in nature. By passing the Proviso, Congress would be telling southerners that they did not possess the same rights and freedoms as northerners. The Proviso might be constitutional, but it was not consistent with the republican principle that all citizens deserved equal opportunities. With the reminder of slavery all around them, southern whites were especially sensitive to any act that might reduce them to a status beneath that of first-class citizens. "There is a great principle of freedom in it," Rayner wrote, "which is paramount to any literal provision in the constitution."[41]

This position placed Rayner in surprising agreement with the plan put forth by the new president, a plan most southerners strongly opposed. Taylor proposed dividing the Mexican cession into two states, California and New Mexico, allowing the inhabitants of each to draft constitutions and be admitted to statehood immediately. While this would eliminate the territorial stage altogether and thus render the Proviso moot, it would have the same practical effect as the Proviso, for the non-slaveholding Californians and New Mexicans would undoubtedly adopt free-soil constitutions. Rayner accepted the plan with equanimity, because although it would result in the addition of two new free states, the nation "was likely to be spared the enormity and injustice of the Wilmot Proviso, through the local action of New Mexico and California." It mattered little to him that the two states would draft free-soil constitutions; the important thing was that Congress would not use the Wilmot Proviso to render slaveholders second-class citizens. Indeed, Rayner thought the inhabitants of the territories possessed every right to "arrange this matter to suit themselves." Reflecting on Taylor's plan, an approving Rayner must have wondered if he had underestimated Old Rough and Ready.[42]

Whether or not he had underestimated Taylor's statesmanship, Rayner had clearly misjudged the tenor of his fellow Whigs. Unable to see the difference between the Proviso and Taylor's plan, the Whigs were rallying around the competing plan of Henry Clay, which would eventually be dubbed the Compromise of 1850.[43]

After championing the cause of Henry Clay for his entire adult life, it must have been difficult for Rayner to speak up against the Compromise. Therefore, while favoring Taylor's plan, he maintained an uncharacteristic silence during a cold, rainy spring spent at Little Town overseeing planting operations. Late in May the rumor began to spread that Rayner indeed was "opposed to the compromise." Congressman David Outlaw found it hard to believe that Rayner or "any sensible man" could favor Taylor's plan, which as far as the territories were concerned, was "no plan at all." It finally became apparent, however, that the president's plan was dead, and by August 1850 Rayner had relinquished his opposition to the Compromise. If the only choice were between the Compromise and the Wilmot Proviso, then Compromise it would have to be. Although he criticized both "Northern fanatics" and southern "Hotspurs" for their continuing intransigence, he reserved his sternest censure for the northerners who refused to settle for anything less than the Proviso. "It is the *duty* of Southern members," Rayner wrote, "to defeat by all *legal* means the passage of all Bills . . . that may have the 'Wilmot Proviso' tacked on to it."[44]

Just as it appeared that the Compromise would meet the same fate as

Taylor's plan, the president suddenly died and was succeeded by his vice president, Millard Fillmore. An old friend and congressional colleague of Rayner's, Fillmore helped push Clay's Compromise through Congress with the assistance of Daniel Webster and Stephen A. Douglas. In the subsequent session of the state legislature, a relieved Rayner introduced a set of resolutions declaring the Compromise of 1850 to be a final, binding solution to the vexing slavery issue. If the North violated that sacred agreement, the southern states should "resort to any mode of redress, not incompatible with the Constitution, before they should contemplate the alternative of disunion." Even then, secession would be available only as an oppressed people's inalienable right of revolution, a principle enshrined in the Declaration of Independence. Although Rayner reserved the right of secession as a desperate last resort, he made no mention of how, and under exactly what circumstances, it might occur. He clearly viewed it as little more than an abstraction.[45]

Kenneth Rayner, along with most Americans, breathed a tremendous sigh of relief with the passage of the Compromise of 1850. Now he could face the future with a degree of confidence that republican principles and the Whig program for economic and social improvement might once again get a fair trial. Millard Fillmore now occupied the White House. Unlike Harrison and Taylor, he was no war hero with untested political abilities; unlike Tyler, he was a proven Whig and could be trusted to promote the Whig agenda. Soon after taking office, the new president began purging the officeholding ranks of anti-Compromise Whigs and doing everything else in his power to rally the entire party behind the Compromise. This primarily meant proscribing northern antislavery Whigs, whose numbers had reached alarming proportions. Those southern Whigs who could not swallow the pro-northern aspects of the Compromise were already deserting the party. Rayner watched with satisfaction as his party again appeared ready to turn its attention to national rather than sectional politics. He celebrated by adding 960 acres to his Arkansas plantation.[46]

During these years in the general assembly, Rayner labored hard to legislate for what he perceived to be the welfare of the people of North Carolina. He had experienced unending frustration while in Congress over that body's inability to surmount purely partisan and sectional obstacles and engage in creative statecraft. Clearly, partisanship had been fierce at the state level as well, but despite the time spent campaigning for office, instructing senators, or gerrymandering districts, Rayner still actively pursued more socially beneficial causes.

His zeal in behalf of internal improvements rarely faltered. Indeed, no other issue occupied as much of the legislature's attention during the 1840s and early 1850s as the movement to improve navigation routes and construct railroads and turnpikes. Due to his prominence within the party, Rayner served perpetually on the Committee on Internal Improvements. He never abandoned his dream of a North Carolina commercially unified and thus economically strengthened by a state-aided transportation network. His personal experience as a planter in Hertford County, where virtually all imported necessities and exported produce traveled through Virginia, doubtless reinforced this attitude. Rayner's home county was a sort of microcosm of the state as a whole; as Hertford was cut off from the piedmont and mountains, so North Carolina was isolated from northern and overseas markets.[47]

But Rayner did not limit his positive-government philosophy to the realm of economic development. He was also one of the state's most consistent advocates of social reform and intellectual improvement. Drawing on Revolutionary-era ideology, Rayner believed that the survival of republican government depended upon a virtuous and intelligent citizenry. Ignorant or immoral voters could not be expected to choose wise leaders or support constructive measures. To the family and church fell the responsibility for instilling virtue, but the state could do something about intelligence. Only when citizens possessed intelligence could they resist the appeals of demagogues (who, of course, were usually Democrats). The solution lay in placing a basic education within the reach of average people. Therefore, Rayner had warmly supported the establishment in 1839 of the state's first public school system and was a friend to education throughout his legislative career. He always based his ardent advocacy of distribution of the public land proceeds on the argument that the proceeds would be used not only for internal improvements but also to establish a system of state-supported common schools.

Rayner was concerned about higher intellectual development as well. In 1849, a Frenchman named Alexander Vattemare visited Raleigh to promote a system of "international exchanges" that he had devised. Although a private citizen, Vattemare was laying the groundwork for a formal system of state-assisted, ongoing exchanges of literary, scientific, artistic, and governmental knowledge among all nations. An agency in Paris was to act as clearinghouse. Under the plan, for example, states such as North Carolina would contribute duplicate books from its state library and receive those of foreign countries. Vattemare was also petitioning legislatures for financial support for the system.[48]

Rayner chaired the committee appointed to study the Frenchman's plan and wrote an enthusiastic report recommending that the state participate in the venture. "This system of international literary exchanges may be considered as the commencement of a new era in the progress and dissemination of knowledge among men," he wrote. "It belongs emphatically to this age of rapid improvement and discovery, in which destiny has cast our lot. . . . Under this system, the Republic of Letters will soon become one and indivisible; knowing no national limits or sectional prejudices." Rayner based his recommendation on two grounds. First, he emphasized "the benefit it will confer upon every branch of science, art, and literature." Strongly influenced by the intellectual ferment of the Enlightenment, he believed in learning for learning's sake. Americans were "too utilitarian in our feelings and pursuits." They were ignoring the life of the mind in their "eager race of adventure, and efforts for physical comfort and worldly gain." Second, Rayner argued that Vattemare's plan had merit because of "the national and social blessings it will produce, and the national and social evils it will obviate." Rayner believed that wars were caused by a lack of understanding between nations, "growing mainly out of each others peculiar manner, character, habits of thought, condition, and surrounding influences." Here, as in so many of his actions and beliefs, environment played a key role. Nations, as well as individuals, could rise above their faults when placed under favorable environmental conditions. Knowledge and understanding were vital to this process, and the state could and should exercise its influence in promoting positive change. Confronted with these arguments, the legislature agreed to participate in the program.[49]

Rayner tried to practice what he preached. He cultivated a lifelong interest in science and literature and read widely in both. He also tried to instill his love for learning in his children; books were a favorite birthday gift in the Rayner household.[50] But his devotion to knowledge extended beyond either the purely ideological or exalted national and international benefits to be derived from education. Rayner saw great promise in the dissemination of practical knowledge to the masses. The best example of this—apart from his support of common schools—can be found in the role he played in establishing the North Carolina Agricultural Society.

Carolinians had founded an agricultural society in the early part of the century, but it had been defunct for decades. The widespread ignorance that led legislators to establish a public school system was reflected in the state's hopelessly inefficient and backward agricultural practices. In October 1852, Rayner and a group of concerned planters and political leaders met in Raleigh to draft a constitution and bylaws for a new state agricultural society and to request an appropriation from the general assembly to help promote the

venture. Perhaps most importantly, the founders created the North Carolina
State Fair, which rapidly grew to be an important social institution and a
major annual event. The society and its fair were huge successes.[51]

Rayner rapidly was earning a reputation as one of the state's leading proponents and practitioners of scientific agriculture. He turned his Hertford
and Raleigh plantations into showplaces for the latest in farming techniques
and crop varieties, experimenting with new strains of grains, fruits, vege-
tables, and an assortment of blooded livestock. Rayner's letters during the
next decade provide a glimpse at the diversity of his interests. He experi-
mented with exotic apples, cherries, cabbage, yams, and hay; five varieties
of pears, four of grapes, and two of wheat. He took great pride in breeding
fine Southdown sheep. At the annual state fairs in the 1850s, he served as
judge in such categories as Ayrshire, Holstein, and Durham cattle; small-
breed swine; and native wines and fruits. He became a zealous advocate of
scientific plowing techniques, crop rotation and diversification, and the use
of fertilizers.[52]

In a keynote address to the state agricultural society at the second annual
state fair in 1854, Rayner revealed the political and social ideology that would
shape his future political career.[53] Using the agricultural society and its state
fair as a point of reference, he explained how such voluntary associations
exemplified "the theory of the social contract" in action. Coming at a time
when the bonds that held the United States together were straining under
the weight of the sectional conflict, Rayner observed that "elements of political discord" had made it crucial for Americans to nurture institutions that
would "bring us together, make us acquainted with each others' advantages,
wants, pursuits and feelings." The fair helped to remind North Carolinians
that "sections and localities, though diversified in pursuits and resources,
are to a certain extent, dependent on each other, and identified in interest.
A common bond of union is thus secured—a bond of union, stronger than
one of statutes or parchments." In this manner Rayner affirmed the traditional republican commitment to unity and shared interests against which he
believed American individualism and sectional interests should be balanced.

Government, Rayner contended, must play a positive role in pursuit of
this unity. Because the American form of government "renders the direct
patronage and supervision of the objects of improvement in science, art, and
industrial enterprise a matter of questionable—or perhaps, I ought rather
to say, of *questioned*—policy," Rayner clearly believed that the government
should be taking an indirect part in fostering the kinds of associations and

institutions that would knit together the diverse sections and interests of the nation. However, until Americans were educated to the need for positive government, private citizens would have to promote collective enterprises like the agricultural society and its state fair. Something had to be done to counterbalance the unrestrained individualism of the modern liberal state and remind Americans that the blind pursuit of self-interest would ultimately endanger republican government.

The scope of Rayner's comments extended far beyond the relatively un-controversial matter of a state agricultural society. His speech shows just how out of step he was with the highly individualistic, laissez-faire, states'-rights philosophy held by so many southerners, especially by slaveholders. One of the most common criticisms northerners voiced in the 1850s was the way in which slavery tended to degrade manual labor in the South. Rayner ad-dressed this issue directly, arguing that a "social revolution" was needed, one that would elevate labor to a "high position" and thus grant it "that dignity to which it is justly entitled." He sternly criticized the fact "that for centuries, manual labor has been identified with degradation and vulgarity." Only now was humanity beginning to realize "that labor is the source of all wealth and prosperity."

In identifying labor as the source of all wealth, Rayner was expounding what has been called the labor theory of value—a notion seemingly at odds with a slaveholding economy. He seemed to realize that he was venturing onto precarious ground for an antebellum southerner. Without trying to sound judgmental, he noted that the government "in its organic structure, has done for labor all it could." Only "voluntary association" could presently "elevate labor in the social scale," an objective he clearly viewed as desirable. Seeking to clarify his position further, he claimed that he was "pandering to no spirit of political socialism when I say that I have long thought society needed a radical reformation in regard to the estimate placed on labor." Rayner con-tinued in a very Jeffersonian tone: "I wish not to be misunderstood. It is not to be expected, or desired that intellect shall fraternize with ignorance or virtue with vice. A natural incongruity forbids such association. Public opinion needs no reformation in this respect. But the reformation which is needed . . . is this—that the pursuits of honest labor shall no longer be a bar to the highest social position; and a stimulus thus [shall be] given to the laboring man for the cultivation of his intellect . . . and by holding out to him the rewards of virtue, the paths of vice and dissipation may be shunned."

Ironically, his belief in the labor theory of value and his affirmation of the dignity of labor placed Rayner (who, despite his status as a large slaveholder, always identified his occupation as "farmer") in a curious accord with some devotees of the nascent Republican party in the North. Just five years later, Abraham Lincoln would declare that "Labor is prior to, and independent of capital . . . in fact, capital is the fruit of labor." It comes as no surprise that slavery received no mention in Rayner's oration; it presented an insuperable intellectual problem for one holding such beliefs about the labor-capital relationship.[54]

If his conjectures about labor, capital, and wealth comported with those of Lincoln, it is less a sign of Rayner's liberalism than it is Lincoln's own devotion to republican ideals. Lincoln, of course, was also a former Whig congressman who had idolized Henry Clay. The Republican party of the 1850s gave little indication of the extent to which it would embrace modern liberal capitalism in the postwar decades. But Rayner was apparently far less committed to the values of individualism than even many antebellum Republicans. His experiences in public life had shown him that his notions of national progress could not be realized strictly through individual effort and laissez-faire government, and he deplored the mad race for wealth that he thought he detected in the urban North. Nevertheless, although taking an essentially Jeffersonian approach to social and governmental relationships, he knew that the market economy was a permanent and irreversible fact of American life. Therefore, his was a forward-looking vision of a nation peopled with virtuous, educated farmers, planters, laborers, craftsmen, and capitalists, bound together by a national government that used its rich resources to create strong economic and cultural bonds among the various sections, classes, and interests. In areas where the government either could not or should not exercise its influence, Americans ought to join together in private, voluntary associations to achieve the same goals. These bonds of common interest and mutual assistance were not intended to turn back the clock on capitalism, but to mitigate its excesses. Rayner's advocacy of a national bank, internal improvements, common schools, the cultural exchange program of Alexander Vattemare, and the North Carolina Agricultural Society all illustrate this vision. If it was a capitalistic vision, it was capitalism imbued with a humanistic sense of community and cooperation.

During these years Rayner advocated two other legislative causes that offer glimpses into his conception of the proper relationship between social welfare and the American polity. In December 1849 the distinguished reformer Dorothea Dix came to Raleigh as a part of her long-running crusade to help America's insane. Rayner and other Whig leaders had long recognized the need for an asylum, but most Democrats opposed it on the dual grounds of strict construction and fiscal conservatism. When Dix arrived in the state capital, she deftly lobbied leading Democrats, finally persuading one of them, John Ellis, to introduce an asylum bill in the legislature. In an impassioned speech in favor of the bill, Rayner reiterated many of the themes that had become his own personal orthodoxy. "The object of government," he stated, "is to take care of all." Painting an awful picture of the current status of North Carolina's insane, Rayner described the "hundreds within the borders of our State, who are immured in noxious cells, inhaling the 'vapors of dungeons,' confined with felons, and dragging out a miserable existence on beds of straw—and for no other crime, than that of being the victims of an afflicting dispensation from Heaven." He chided his fellow lawmakers, telling them that "if we fail to perform our duty, the shriek of every maniac in our borders will hereafter sound the note of reproach upon our names." The amount needed for the asylum was not great, he believed, compared with the benefits to be derived. In a footnote to the published version of the speech, Rayner told of Dix's effort to persuade Congress to appropriate five million acres of the public lands to support the asylum movement. "May her efforts be crowned with success," he wrote. Before Dix left Raleigh, the asylum bill became law.[55]

During the same session, Rayner supported another unusual reform effort. At about the same time as Dix's visit, a full-blooded Chippewa Indian chief named George Copway came to Raleigh to petition the legislature. A native of Canada, he had been educated by Wesleyan missionaries and later worked among his people as an agent both of the Methodists and the American Tract Society. Like Dix, Copway devoted his life to the uplift of unfortunate people and sought the government's aid in doing so. When he arrived in Raleigh, it was but one stop on an extended lecture and lobbying tour of the East Coast. The chief was promoting a scheme much more grandiose than that of Alexander Vattemare's or Dorothea Dix's. He wanted the federal government to set aside a territory in the West especially for the Indians.[56]

By the 1840s, the idea of reservations was not new, but Copway was not talking about a reservation. He wished to see the government create a territory that in due time would become an Indian *state*, to be admitted to the Union on terms just like those of other territories. It would be a place where the Indians, with secure property title and civil rights, could be civilized, Christianized, and "Americanized"—and take their place as regular citizens of the Republic. During a Saturday afternoon legislative session late in November 1848, Rayner requested that Copway be allowed use of the hall of the house of commons for a lecture. Permission was granted, and the following Monday night the polished and articulate Indian orator gave his speech before an overflow audience of legislators and leading citizens of Raleigh. The Raleigh *Star* explained that the Chippewa's object in seeking an Indian state was to secure for his people "a permanent home, a good government, education, agricultural knowledge, and all the arts and benefits of civilization."[57]

It might seem curious that a southern slaveholder would take an active interest in furthering the cause of a racial minority that in America rivaled blacks in the extent to which they were despised and oppressed. Yet Rayner expressed great enthusiasm over the chief's crusade, helping along the passage of a pro-Copway resolution in the general assembly. Rayner later wrote Copway, encouraging the "gigantic" undertaking and telling the Indian leader that if he succeeded, his name would "go down to posterity identified with one of the most glorious movements of the age in which we live."[58]

How could a man who owned two hundred slaves and believed in "the march of Anglo-Saxon improvement" rhapsodize over the prospect of having American Indians as fellow citizens of the Republic, with full rights and privileges? The answer lies in Rayner's unusual convictions about racial potentialities and his belief in the power of environmental influences. In an age when a majority of Americans—and even more southerners—had concluded that there existed inherent and irreversible moral and intellectual differences between the races, he had continued to suppose the opposite. No group in the South promoted "scientific" racism more enthusiastically than the ultra-proslavery apologists whose political views Rayner so detested, and no class of southerners was more eager than slaveholders to believe the new racist theories. But Rayner unquestionably accepted the premise that at least one racial minority—Indians—possessed the innate capability to exercise the heavy responsibilities of American citizenship. By virtue of the happy accident of American birth, these truly native Americans were free of the corrupting Old World influences that had made European immigrants such wretchedly misguided voters. But being born in America was not sufficient. If, however, the government would adopt Copway's scheme and place the Indians in an environment where they would receive the nurture of a Christian, republican education, they could be as good Americans as anyone. For proof, Rayner needed to look no farther than the example of George Copway himself.

By the early 1850s, as Rayner reflected on the past ten years, he had many reasons to feel satisfied. In the eyes of his constituents, he had served with distinction in the national House of Representatives. Before his fortieth birthday, his party had offered him the governorship of his home state, and his name was often mentioned for a U.S. Senate seat. He had married an attractive woman whose inheritance had made him a very wealthy man. He was recognized as one of his state's leading experts in his chosen vocation, agriculture. In his own state, his dearly held republican principles seemed alive and well in the hands of a still-healthy Whig party. Yet Rayner could not shake the feeling that he was somehow out of step with his time and section of the country.

He entertained no serious qualms about the necessity of preserving slavery. Human bondage, although an evil, was so much a part of the social and economic fabric of the South that there was no possible chance of it ending peaceably in the foreseeable future. And if by some miracle it could be abolished, what of the former slaves? Would white southerners accept them as free individuals and try to adapt to the new state of things? Certainly not. Would northerners welcome them as immigrants and neighbors? It was hardly possible. Even in the unlikely event that whites someday might accommodate black freedom, could the blacks themselves ever survive and prosper as free citizens? Perhaps—but Rayner seldom stopped to speculate this far, because he could see no way for the slaves ever to gain their freedom without a national bloodbath.

None of these views seemed—at least to him—controversial or debatable. Why, then, could not the deluded souls in both sections see that the only solution to the great American dilemma was the one the Founding Fathers had so wisely embraced in 1787: Slavery must be left alone, the agitation ceased. If the flawed Compromise of 1850 could somehow accomplish this, it was worthy of its great author, Henry Clay.

When Rayner turned his thoughts from slavery to more general political developments, the picture was equally clouded. Although Millard Fillmore, a fine Whig, occupied the White House, the party's national prospects were less than bright. As time had passed, it seemed that basic Whig ideology—a republic in which virtuous and intelligent freemen chose disinterested leaders who would legislate creatively for the national good—had been abandoned by all but a few true believers. Fillmore presumably held such principles, as did a fair number of faithful northern and southern Whigs. But far too many of those who had once supported the party had forgotten the wisdom of the Founders, just as the Democrats had done at the time of Jackson's rise to power. Whig disaffection was especially acute in the North, where thousands seemed to think that attacking the irremediable evil of slavery was worth jeopardizing the Union. This particularly distressed Rayner because it seemed so maddeningly misguided. Short of honor, nothing could be more valuable than the Union. Americans appeared to be forgetting that their country was still very much an experiment in freedom and self-government. America was humanity's best, and perhaps only, hope. Destroy the Republic, he suspected, and with it might be destroyed the only chance of freedom for all people, white, red, and black.

Unfortunately, things were rapidly growing worse. The Democratic party's grip on the nation's politics was tightening, helped immeasurably by the rapidly growing numbers of foreign immigrants in northern cities who could be controlled by corrupt Democratic bosses. Only a nationwide rejuvenation of the Whig party—or the creation of some new party that would embody the republican principles held by the original Whigs—would save the imperiled Union. For Kenneth Rayner, Henry Clay had always been the best hope of purifying the nation, but Clay's day had passed; he would be dead by mid-1852. But if the Whigs could rally behind Fillmore and carry the day in the upcoming elections, there was a chance, however slim, that the nation might be restored to republican rule, the "age of improvement" inaugurated, and the impending disaster averted.

CHAPTER 4

"A New Order of Things"

On the evening of April 28, 1852, Rayner's neighbor William Valentine took his pen in hand to make his customary diary entry. A failure in numerous professional pursuits as well as in his quest for a wife, Valentine found solace in the diary. Ranking high among his many personal disappointments was his inability to build a successful political career, for nothing more deeply interested him than politics. But Valentine long ago had found a way to experience, at least vicariously, the thrills and disappointments of public life. He did so by following the career of his famous and powerful Hertford County neighbor.

Valentine had closely studied Rayner's rapid rise to prominence in the Whig party. Up to the time he had declined the gubernatorial bid in 1848, Rayner's "course had been marked by sense and judgment," Valentine believed. But Rayner's role in the selection of Charles Manly, whose defeat after one term ended years of Whig supremacy in the state, had been "the falsest step in his political life." "Had Mr. R. accepted the nomination proposed to him it is not doubted he would have been easily elected; and the second term without opposition," wrote Valentine. "The State reeled and was thrown back from the whigs. Mr. R. was blamed for this. He declining to be governor and his course in the convention in making a nomination have, all believe, produced this effect[:] instead of his being now Governor as he might, a common party hack loco foco holds that huge office." [1]

No doubt many Whigs in North Carolina shared this opinion, and Rayner himself appears to have had second thoughts about his actions. Valentine observed that although Rayner continued to serve in the legislature, his influence and popularity waned. In "disgust and dissatisfaction" the former congressman had refused to run for another term in the legislature. Rayner's ambition had not been fulfilled when he resigned from the House in 1845, Valentine speculated; the United States Senate had been his goal. "To regard himself as a broken down political hack is no doubt excruciating to his sensitive nature. It is a torment to him. This is apparent to all who know him."[2]

Although Valentine's characterization rings true in a number of ways, there is something missing in this account of Rayner's supposed decline into "a broken down political hack." Valentine assumed that Rayner's actions had originated exclusively in poor judgment—refusing the gubernatorial nomination—and overweening ambition in his desire for a Senate seat. However, he failed to understand one thing: Rayner's adherence to the Whig party itself had been growing steadily weaker for years. It was difficult even for as astute an observer as Valentine to see this, for on the surface Rayner had remained a loyal Whig. After all, he had continued to fight the party's battles in the legislature and had campaigned hard as a Taylor elector. It never occurred to Valentine that, on the eve of the 1852 national elections, the one-time rising star of the North Carolina Whig party would soon cease to be a Whig at all.

Rayner's estrangement from his party became obvious when the Whigs nominated General Winfield Scott for the presidency. Observers were shocked when Rayner refused to support his party's ticket.[3] In a series of speeches in July and August, he strongly voiced his opposition to Scott's candidacy. Called upon to speak at a Hertford County militia muster, Rayner told his constituents that this was "perhaps the last time I shall ever address you." No longer able to support the national party, he declined renomination for the legislature and announced his retirement from politics. The national convention, he repeatedly reminded Whig gatherings, had "cheated us" by failing to nominate the rightful standard-bearer, Fillmore. Unfortunately, nothing like a full text of these speeches survives, so Rayner's arguments cannot be stated precisely. However, he clearly viewed the nomination of Scott as the final step in the betrayal of Whiggery by the party itself. Those who heard his speeches in the summer of 1852 doubtless assumed that his opposition arose from the same source as that of other southern Whigs—the belief that Scott would prove to be a free-soiler and thus threaten southern institutions. But Rayner would have been just as dissatisfied if Scott had run on an overtly proslavery platform and had promised to throw open the territories to slavery. The problem with Scott was not his stance on slavery pro or con; it was his apparent refusal to take an unequivocal position in favor of the Compromise as the final settlement of the issue. Moreover, the nominee's closeness to New York's antislavery senator William H. Seward suggested that a Scott administration would only exacerbate sectional tensions rather than set them to rest forever. Scott was also blatantly pandering to the immigrants in the northern cities, praising the "rich brogue" of the Irish in campaign speeches. All of this served as irrefutable proof that Scott's principles were no more sound than those of the Democrats. Rayner believed the Whig party as a voice for republican government was dead, and he had no intention of attending the funeral.[4]

North Carolina Whigs were alternately puzzled, distraught, and angry at this turn of events. After attending a Rayner speech in mid-July, William Valentine wrote that the address was "calculated to damp the ardor of the Whigs of the County; in a word to do harm." Another speech "abounded in false positions and his arguments in sophistry to a greater degree than I ever heard from him." According to Valentine, Rayner viewed the current political situation "with a jaundiced eye, every thing looks yellow and sickly." "To hear him talk, every thing is tumbling to pieces and destruction." Rayner refused to commit himself to voting for Scott, and "it was evident . . . if he could lead the people against Scott he would persist in doing so." Bewildered Whigs thought that Rayner was burning his political bridges. To persist on this course, thought Valentine, would soon "consign him to political oblivion."[5]

Rayner's actions threatened to disrupt Whiggery in northeastern North Carolina. "His influence is such," Valentine speculated, "that it is calculated to loosen the bonds of his party, in this Hertford County, at least." But as the campaign progressed, Rayner toned down his attacks on the national convention's decision. His friends implored him to erase all doubts by endorsing the ticket and taking the stump in its behalf. By August he had tendered a lukewarm public endorsement of Scott. He reportedly told a private acquaintance that "if he were at home at the election, he supposed he might vote for him [Scott], but that it would be a bitter pill." Of course, there was never the slightest possibility that Rayner would have voted for the Democratic candidate, Franklin Pierce. Unlike his fellow North Carolina Whig Thomas L. Clingman, Rayner's opposition to Scott was not sending him into the Democratic camp; for him, that would have been unthinkable. Adrift from the national Whig party but resolutely opposed to the Democrats, it appeared his political course was taking him nowhere.[6]

Appearances, in politics as elsewhere, can often be deceiving. Although Pierce carried North Carolina in November by a slim margin and the Democrats gained a two-seat majority in the state legislature, when the time came to elect a United States senator, Democratic legislators were unable to unite behind one candidate. Through ten ballots they tried unsuccessfully to close ranks, while the outnumbered Whigs lackadaisically cast their votes for a variety of candidates. During the early balloting Rayner had consistently received a sprinkling of Whig votes, but his party entertained no serious thoughts of electing a candidate. On the eleventh ballot, the Whigs sensed an opportunity. In the face of persistent disagreement among the Democrats, they believed it possible to garner a handful of dissident Democratic votes in favor of Rayner. Despite intense dissatisfaction with the role he had played in the fall campaign, Whig lawmakers dutifully fell into line and with only one exception voted solidly for Rayner. When the ballots were counted, he fell two votes short of winning. No Democrat had voted for Rayner. North Carolina passed the next two years with only one United States senator.[7]

As soon as the dust had settled on the failed senatorial election, Rayner became the focus of bitter recriminations among the state's prominent Whigs. Jealous or simply disappointed, some party leaders expressed displeasure that Rayner—a man who had offered only the most lukewarm support to the national ticket—had been chosen as the senatorial candidate. Legislators who voted for him complained that they had done so under coercion by dictatorial party managers. The bitterest denunciation came from Raleigh Whig Henry W. Miller, who, like Valentine, held Rayner personally responsible for all of the party's setbacks of the previous four years. "What, pray was Mr. Rayner—whose opinions had much weight with many—who had been regarded by all as a leading member of the Whig party, and who had ample time to devote to political matters—what was *he* doing during the three months between the August and November elections?" asked Miller. Rayner's actions, according to Miller, were "not only inexcusable, but highly censurable. . . . HE GAVE AID AND COMFORT TO THE ENEMY!"[8]

Rayner naturally defended himself, pointing out that he had campaigned actively for the Whig gubernatorial candidate and, despite his acknowledged dislike of Scott's candidacy, had voted for the general. Democratic editors gleefully fanned the fire in the Whig camp. The Fayetteville *North Carolinian* charged that while true Whigs were braving the elements campaigning for their party, Rayner was in Raleigh "protecting his fine personage from sun and weather; taking ease and pleasure in the enjoyment of his fine estate." William W. Holden, the acid-penned Democratic editor of the Raleigh *Standard*, joined in the fun: "The Whigs united almost to a man on Mr. Rayner— on a gentleman who is understood not to be acceptable to all of them. . . . By the way, who is Mr. Rayner? What is he for? What is he against? What did he think of Gen. Scott? Did he vote for him? Is he for Southern rights? If so, where is the proof?"[9]

Whigs usually tried to ignore Democratic editors—especially Holden.

But the war of words between Rayner and Miller and their respective Whig allies, punctuated by the snide remarks of Holden and other Democrats, continued for more than six months, growing increasingly bitter. The upshot of the conflict was that Miller believed Rayner's course during the presidential election had been specifically planned in order to position himself for the senatorship. According to Miller, Rayner had refused to take a firm stand in the presidential campaign "because he feared, as the two parties were tied in the Legislature, *such a course would injure his chance to get to the Senate of the United States!*" As the controversy deepened, the old feud between Rayner and Edward Stanly was dredged up and paraded through the state press as evidence that Rayner's senatorial ambition had been burning for four years. The anti-Rayner faction continued to believe that "all the troubles which the Whig party have been laboring under for four years were brought upon them by the extraordinary course of Mr. Rayner in the State convention of 1848," and that in his reckless pursuit of a Senate seat that year and in 1852, he had sacrificed the Whig party on the altar of his own ambition. Such criticisms were blind to the fact that Rayner had been growing steadily estranged from the Whig party for a number of years. They also failed to take into account the intensely personal nature of the family feud between Rayner and Stanly.[10]

It was mid-1853 before the controversy had died down, but Rayner's standing as a statewide Whig leader had been irreparably damaged. At odds with most of the Whig leadership in Hertford County, he had abruptly refused the 1852 nomination for his seat in the house of commons. However, in a vindictive mood at the conclusion of the senatorial contest, he had stated his intention to reenter the next legislature, which would be elected in 1854. Rayner declared that "he did not intend to allow a few personal enemies to obtain so great a triumph over him, as to make him swerve from the support of principles to which he had been so long devoted." He wished to repay those who had supported him in the senatorial election, "whilst those who had hunted him with a personal malignity unparalleled, should yet *feel* him, if life lasted."[11]

This respite from politics allowed Rayner to devote more time to personal affairs and his growing planting interests. In addition to the major expansion of his Arkansas estate in 1851, he had also purchased a valuable seventy-acre tract immediately adjoining the city of Raleigh in 1848. In 1853, he enlarged his property holdings in Hertford County and again in Arkansas. More than 150 slaves lived on the three plantations in 1850. By that same year he had brought 500 of the 1,200 acres comprising Little Town under cultivation, producing a variety of staple crops and livestock: 2,500 bushels of corn,

500 bushels of oats, 5 bales of cotton, 300 bushels of peas and beans, 400 bushels of Irish potatoes, 500 bushels of sweet potatoes, 35 head of cattle, 37 sheep, and 140 swine. The farm at Raleigh was similarly diversified, only on a much smaller scale. But the great cash crop in the South was cotton, and the Arkansas plantation possessed some of the finest soil anywhere on earth for growing the white staple. In 1849, on the 250 improved acres of the original purchase, Rayner's slaves grew two hundred bales of cotton. Ten years later, following the additions of adjacent acreage in 1851, 1853, and 1856, the plantation yielded 543 bales. Some years, it probably produced even more. The 1850s were a prosperous decade for Rayner.[12]

During his rest from active participation in politics, Rayner was able to distance himself from the immediate party battles of the state legislature and reap some of the rewards of a retired statesman. His fame as an orator well established, he found himself in high demand as a speaker at public occasions. One such opportunity came in June 1853, when, after being appointed by Fillmore to the Board of Visitors of the United States Military Academy, Rayner was invited to deliver the academy's commencement address. That same year he was a featured speaker at the grand opening of the Weldon and Gaston Railroad, where his oration reportedly outshown those of Governor David Reid and former President Tyler. In 1854 the opportunities for public appearances continued, with Rayner delivering formal addresses before the North Carolina State Agricultural Society and at several public events in Hertford County.[13]

This interlude also allowed Rayner to follow national political events more closely. As his estrangement from the Whig party had become more pronounced, he had watched the growing nativist movement in the northern states with great interest. By 1853 one nativist fraternal group, the Order of the Star Spangled Banner, was attracting national attention as it moved closer to third-party political action. With its odd rituals and vows of secrecy, members of the order were soon labeled "Know-Nothings." They swore to resist the antirepublican tendencies of the Roman Catholic church and foreign influence in general, to vote only for native-born Protestants, and to uphold the Union. Rayner's resentment of immigrants and their influence in politics had been on the rise for many years. Nothing had happened in the decade since his retirement from Congress to change his belief that naturalized citizens lacked "an abiding interest in the preservation of our free institutions." As he had stated in his retirement message to his congressional constituents, recent immigrants could not "appreciate the nature of our institutions, or estimate the theory of our glorious constitution." When the Order of the

Star Spangled Banner moved overtly into politics, it adopted the American party name and made a twenty-one-year waiting period for naturalization its main cause. Soon the Know-Nothings would be competing strongly with antislavery and anti-Kansas-Nebraska forces to see which would become the major opposition to the Democratic party in the North.[14]

Although the order's spread into North Carolina is poorly documented, Rayner claimed the distinction of being the first man to promulgate the order south of Maryland, and he is generally credited with the introduction of Know-Nothingism into his home state sometime in late 1854. Circumstantial evidence suggests the accuracy of this claim, for Hertford County was one of the earliest strongholds of the organization. In September the Democratic *North Carolina Standard* reported that "it is now certain that we have in Raleigh a regularly organized band of Know Nothings." The editor, Holden, claimed that the order numbered two or three hundred members and gave the location of the lodge. Certainly by October Rayner had become deeply involved in Know-Nothingism. In his keynote speech before the state agricultural society, he went out of his way to enunciate anti-Catholic doctrine. Drawing on his Enlightenment intellectual heritage, he spoke broadly of how "the theory of the social contract" sanctioned voluntary associations. "The early founders of the Christian Church," he said, "availed themselves of the social tendency of man, in organizing a pure worship, and in disseminating a pure faith." Early Christianity was pure because its members recognized the "correlative duties, benefits and burdens" of social life. On the other hand, Rayner pointed out, "the cloister of the monk and the cell of the anchorite, is as much a perversion of man's religious, as the cave of the hermit, is of his social nature." Here was a subtle defense of the Know-Nothing organizational principles, combined with an attack on the alleged antisocial and thus antirepublican nature of Catholicism. Sending a copy of the speech to a Know-Nothing colleague a few weeks later, Rayner noted that the careful reader would "find some *Americanism* in it."[15]

In North Carolina the organization of the order had apparently progressed far enough by November 1854 to elect a state council, which in turn sent representatives, including Rayner, to the national council scheduled to meet in Cincinnati on the fifteenth. The national council was made up of seven delegates from each state, and it determined the order's national political direction and served as the supreme governing body for the fraternal aspects of the organization. The Cincinnati meeting marked the first truly national Know-Nothing convention. Secrecy was strictly enforced, so only the vaguest sketches of the proceedings have survived. It appears, however, that the meeting's primary purposes were to revise the order's ritual and help perfect the organizational structure, thus laying the groundwork for future political action. Discussions about actual candidates were to take place only on an informal basis.

Rayner traveled by train to Cincinnati, whiling away the long hours discussing political strategy with fellow delegate Joseph Segar of Richmond. Although his primary attraction to the new movement was its political nativism, Rayner feared that the order, as then constituted, was too vulnerable to the forces of sectionalism. To remedy this Rayner had formulated an oath called the Third, or Union, Degree. The Know-Nothings, like other fraternal groups, took a series of oaths, or "degrees," and as delegates to the national council, Rayner and Segar were both second-degree members of the organization. In Know-Nothing ritual the first two degrees bound initiates to keep the order's secrets, to support native-born Protestants for public office, and to acquiesce in the political will of the order's majority as far as these things were constitutionally possible. The Union Degree, as Rayner explained it, obligated its takers "to protect, maintain, and defend the Union, at all time, under all circumstances, and at all hazards, and to vote for no one, who entertained sentiments unfriendly to the Union, or who were plotting and intriguing for its overthrow or injury." After hearing Rayner's proposal, Segar thought it a good idea and promised to sustain him in his efforts to secure its adoption by the national body.[16]

The convention that assembled in Cincinnati was led mostly by former Whigs like Rayner, men who were nationally known but who were not generally considered among the most prominent national leaders of the old party. Garrett Davis of Kentucky, Robert T. Conrad of Pennsylvania, Daniel Ullman of New York, John M. Clayton of Delaware, Segar of Virginia, and Rayner headed the list. Most of the delegates, however, were not known as public men at all. When Rayner arrived in Cincinnati, he began seeking advice and approval for his plan. Immediately, opposition arose from northern delegates who wanted the order to assume a more aggressive stance against slavery expansion and from southerners who thought its unionism too unconditional. When the council formally met, he moved that a committee composed of one delegate from each state be appointed to consider his proposition. Rayner chaired the committee, which favorably reported the Union Degree to the convention. He spoke before the delegates in its behalf and secured the passage of the degree, although antislavery Know-Nothings would later express great displeasure with it. The American party was now officially the party of Unionism as well as that of nativism. In Rayner's mind, the two were inseparable.[17]

After the adoption of the degree, Rayner presided over the ceremony that conferred it on all of the Cincinnati delegates. The ceremony, melodramatic by modern standards, was undertaken with tremendous seriousness. In a solemn ritual that would soon be repeated throughout the nation, Rayner directed the party's leaders to form a circle. With their arms crossed over their chests, they joined hands to form an unbroken human chain symbolic of the eternal Union. An American flag was raised in the center of the circle, and Rayner administered the oath:

> You, and each of you . . . do hereby solemnly declare your devotion to the Union of these States; . . . that you will discourage and discountenance any and every attempt . . . to weaken its bonds; and that you will use your influence, as far as in your power, in endeavoring to procure an amicable and equitable adjustment of all political discontents and differences, which may threaten its injury or overthrow. You do further promise . . . that you will not vote for any one . . . in favor of a dissolution of the Union of these States, or who is endeavoring to produce that result; that you will vote for . . . Union Degree members of this Order, in preference to all others; that if it may be done consistently with the Constitution and laws of the land, you will, when elected or appointed to official station . . . remove from office or place all persons whom you know or believe to be in favor of a dissolution of the Union, or are endeavoring to produce that result; and that you will in no case appoint any such persons to any political office or place whatever. All this you promise and swear (or affirm) upon your honor as American citizens and friends of the American Union. . . . To all this you pledge your lives, your fortunes, and your sacred honors. So help you God and keep you steadfast!

After taking the oath, the members of the national council were to return to their home states and repeat the process. By this method the new ritual would rapidly filter down to the local lodges, binding hundreds of thousands of Americans to uphold the Union under all circumstances.[18]

Rayner left Cincinnati with a tremendous feeling of satisfaction over his role in committing the Know-Nothings to militant Unionism. Thousands took the oath over the next few months, and Rayner believed that more than a million Americans were eventually initiated into the Third Degree. He returned to North Carolina and commenced the work of conferring it on his fellow Know-Nothings. "It is always received with delight and enthusiasm," he reported to Daniel Ullman. "It seems to me that when 2 millions of men in this country have taken that third degree, that this union *must* be safe."[19]

The fall 1854 elections also gave Rayner and the Know-Nothings cause for optimism. In Massachusetts, the governor, all state officers, the entire state senate, and all but two members of the state house of representatives were members of the order. Know-Nothings also carried Delaware and, in a fusion with the Whigs, Pennsylvania. In North Carolina, the order spread rapidly, but the old party lines were very resilient. The Whig party had survived intact to a much greater degree than in most states, and politicians were reluctant to sever the old ties. However, before many North Carolinians were even fully aware of the Know-Nothings' existence, the organization succeeded in electing a significant number of local candidates—mostly to municipal offices. Political leaders were forced to take a hard second look at the power of the order.[20]

Rayner's work on behalf of the Know-Nothings back home in Hertford County can readily be seen in the diary of William Valentine. In language that undoubtedly echoed Rayner's own rhetoric, Rayner's neighbor in late 1854 approvingly noted that the new organization had "turned up more disappointments to politicians than any thing for twenty years. They are successful. They are quiet and irresistible." While Valentine applauded the fact that the Know-Nothings had "paralised" both of the old parties in the North, he emphasized that "their views and objects are truly American and conservative. . . . Their leading object is to prevent immigrants and foreign influence from disturbing and influencing our pure republican government." The American party represented "a new order of things" that would redeem republican government "from the deadly clutches of Roman Catholicism which is an enemy to free judgment & temporal government and free conscience in spiritual Christian religion."[21]

For Rayner, the American party clearly meant more than simply politics as usual; it signified a purification of American politics, a return to pristine republicanism. Know-Nothingism promised to erase the old party lines, purging the nation of corruption and recasting the country's politics in the mold designed by the Founding Fathers. It comes as no surprise that old Whigs like Rayner and Valentine were drawn to the order, because the movement was fueled by much of the same reformist conservatism that twenty years earlier had helped to create an opposition party to Andrew Jackson. The leading issue was now different; fear of Catholics and immigrants replaced excessive executive power as the great threat to republican institutions. But at the heart of Know-Nothing ideology lay the same anxiety: corruption—or more precisely, the undermining of the political process as designed by the Founders—threatened American liberty and self-government.

Know-Nothing ideologues such as Rayner were not simply paranoically hunting for new scapegoats on which to blame the ongoing deterioration of American politics. There was, in fact, a surprising consistency in Rayner's newfound identification of immigrants as a serious threat to republican institutions. By the 1850s politicians who in the past had identified a corrupt Democratic executive as the great menace to republicanism increasingly identified corrupt Democratic-voting immigrants as the source of that threat. The transformation was easily made, because the immigrant vote kept Democratic administrations in power, perpetuating the arbitrary and corrupt exercise of executive power that had been the opposition's complaint for so long.

The fact that large numbers of the recent immigrants were Roman Catholics greatly expedited this identification of immigrants as a threat to republican institutions. Anti-Catholicism had always been strong in America. But in the early 1850s it was heightened as some Catholic leaders, led by Archbishop John Hughes of New York, began an aggressive assertion of church authority. Encouraged by the rapid growth of the church in America, Hughes publicly suggested that Catholicism was on its way to becoming the predominant faith of the United States. In many areas Catholics began demanding that public school funds be shared with church schools, or if this failed, that the reading of Protestant Bibles be prohibited in public schools. The Catholic hierarchy also mounted a campaign to have ownership of church property taken away from lay trustees and be vested in the clergy, a policy that seemed decidedly antirepublican to most Protestants. Finally, the 1853 visit of papal nuncio Gaetano Bedini, who was empowered by Rome to settle the trusteeship controversy and to bestow the pope's blessing on American Catholics, provided a ready symbol of the aggressive intentions of the Vatican. To native-born Protestants, the Catholic church's alleged monarchical, hierarchical, ostentatious, arrogant, and corrupt nature conflicted sharply with republican equality, simplicity, and virtue. The church's real or imagined influence in American politics, via its immigrant devotees, convinced nativists such as Rayner that it now posed the greatest single threat to the Republic. If the United States was to overcome corruption—which most nativists associated with the Democratic party but which some believed had ruined both the old parties—some way would have to be found to counter Catholic aggression and to neutralize foreign influence in politics.[22]

These themes emerge clearly in Rayner's nativist rhetoric. Beginning in December 1854, he wrote a series of replies to an anti-Know-Nothing manifesto written by his old congressional colleague Henry A. Wise, now running as a Democrat for the Virginia governorship. Wise had castigated the Know-

Nothings for their secrecy, bigotry, and antidemocratic tendencies. Rayner defended the order with an argument taken straight from Revolutionary-era Whig ideology. Recounting the blessings of liberty and republican government, he reminded Wise that "the tendencies of human nature, and the bias of human government" made it crucial for Americans to be alert to the "insidious approaches of despotic power." Employing orthodox republican rhetoric that would have sounded very familiar in the 1770s, Rayner pointed out that "the liberties of every free people have been undermined by slow and gradual approaches, by a failure on their part to guard against the first incipient assaults upon their rights." The American party had been created specifically to protect the nation against these kinds of assaults, he believed.[23]

In defending the order against Wise's charge that the Know-Nothings' secrecy was subversive, Rayner naturally relied on constitutional arguments. The Constitution guarantees "the right peaceably to assemble together to consult upon grievances," he noted, claiming that this was exactly what the Know-Nothings were doing in their lodges. Wise admitted the right of a party caucus to meet behind closed doors; how was that different from a secret Know-Nothing meeting? Even party caucuses were "reprehensible, if carried too far," Wise said. "And so I say 'Know-Nothingism' is 'reprehensible, when carried too far,'" countered Rayner.

Wise criticized the Know-Nothings for the same reasons that many historians have; he accused the order of bigotry and charged that its members proscribed Catholics and immigrants simply because of their religious beliefs and place of birth. Rayner admitted "that opposition to foreign and Roman Catholic influence in the administration of the government is one of the principal objects of this movement," but he denied that the order sought to proscribe anyone. The American party, he maintained, had no intention of depriving Catholics or immigrants of the privileges of citizenship, equality under the law, trial by jury, or "eligibility to official station by the people, if the people see fit to elect them." The party did not seek to impose additional taxes on immigrants or Catholics, to interfere with the freedom of religion, to exclude them from any professions, to deprive their children of public education, or to proscribe them socially. The only legal or constitutional remedy that Know-Nothings suggested for curing the ills caused by immigrants was a lengthening of the period required for naturalization. "Of what, then, can Mr. Wise complain?" Rayner asked. "Does he allude merely to the disposition to extend the time of their residence in the country before naturalization?" If he did, Rayner noted, then he might as well say that the present five-year law was antirepublican. "For whether it shall be five years, or twenty-one years, is a question of mere policy—the principle is the same."

Rayner's defense of the order against charges of prejudice was standard Know-Nothing fare. It was not so much for whom the foreigners voted as the fact that they voted "as a unit" in alleged obedience to the dictates of priests; consequently, both of the old parties had been forced to compromise their principles. It was, according to Rayner, "a spectacle calculated to humiliate every patriotic heart, of both the great parties, bowing down before this foreign horde, truckling to them for votes—and of a Protestant people huckstering for votes with the Romish priesthood." Having read the rhetoric of militant Catholic spokesmen such as Archbishop Hughes, Rayner charged that Catholics, "in a tone of increasing arrogance . . . are now asserting . . . that the Pope is not only the spiritual head of the church, but that, even in temporal matters, he is paramount to all other kings, princes, powers, or authorities on earth." Although it is tempting to dismiss Rayner's anxieties as either paranoia or plain bigotry, to do so is to disregard his lifelong concern for the fragility of republican institutions, the very real influence that the immigrant bloc exercised in elections, and the genuine stridency of some Catholics' rhetoric.

The key to understanding Rayner's nativist ideology lies in his conception of American nationality. "When we speak of foreigners, we mean foreign to the government, not foreign to the soil," he wrote in a crucial passage of the reply to Wise. He went on to explain that the children of Americans who were born while their parents were temporarily on foreign soil were rightfully recognized by the Constitution as full-fledged citizens. According to Rayner, if Wise "knew the principles of the association he is assailing, he would understand that it is not against foreigners on account of their birthplace, it is not against Roman Catholics on account or their faith, that the 'Know-Nothings' are organized." Rather, it was the fact that Catholic immigrants came to America "without any knowledge, or the ability to appreciate the value of our institutions; with preconceived notions that a 'land of liberty' means a land of unrestrained licentiousness—many of them refugees from justice or lately released from the prison-houses and chain-gangs of Europe, . . . ready to sell their political influence to whichever party or local faction that will pander most abjectly to their passions, flatter their prejudices, and barter away the country's honor for selfish ends."

Perhaps sensing his personal vulnerability on the issue in light of his passionate defense of Catholic rights in the 1835 constitutional convention, Rayner explained why Catholics and immigrants posed so much greater a threat than they had in the past. Until the last thirty years, he argued, immigrants had been "an industrious, enterprising, and orderly population" who had come to America to seek freedom and economic opportunity. In

the early days of the Republic there had been "no distinctive class organization among them for political purposes; no concerted action among them as
a foreign, contra-distinguished from an American party; no disgracing the
streets of our cities with scenes of riot and bloodshed; no driving and beating
away peaceable and orderly American citizens from the polls; no emptying
the prisons and almshouses of Europe upon our shores; no huckstering with
parties, corrupting the ballot-box for reward or the promise of reward." And
so it was with Catholics, he added. "In the early history of the country, when
they were weak in numbers, they were modest and unpretending." In short,
Rayner believed that Catholics in the early republic had acted like other citizens, dividing along the same political lines as Protestants and contributing
positively to the American experiment in self-government. His critique of
both immigrants and Catholics had nothing to do with their foreign birth or
spiritual beliefs per se; it was with the manner in which these groups were
exercising the privileges of American citizenship.

Rayner's enthusiasm a few years earlier for the Chippewa chief George
Copway and his scheme for making the Indians American citizens through
the creation of an Indian state in the West sheds light on Rayner's brand of
nativism. It will be recalled that Rayner warmly supported Copway's plan (as
the American party itself later did), believing that Indians—although they
were not Anglo-Saxons—could be trained in the ways of Americanism by
placing them under the proper environmental influences. It was precisely
this environmentalist outlook that led Rayner to feel so concerned about the
abilities of Catholic immigrants to exercise wisely the rights and duties of
citizenship. Foreigners arrived in America laden with the cultural baggage of
the European monarchies from which they came—a heritage not bred into
them in a genetic sense, but rather a product of the environment in which they
had grown up. Rayner suggested that Catholics, or at least the bulk of those
who had arrived in the last several years, carried with them a similar cultural heritage of superstition and blind obedience to Rome. These liabilities
were not easily surmountable, but even Catholic immigrants could eventually
overcome their antirepublican backgrounds to become real "Americans." It
would simply take a longer period of time for them to become inculcated with
American values. The Know-Nothings suggested twenty-one years, the same
period that it took a native-born child to reach majority and be granted the
privilege of voting. For Know-Nothings like Rayner, steeped in the ideology
of Revolutionary-era America, nothing could have seemed more consistent
with logic and justice.[24]

Rayner himself clearly understood that Know-Nothingism was attempting to reform American political life not by introducing new, innovative programs, but rather by bringing the nation back to its original principles. As he saw it, the movement drew its great strength from the fact that it began with neither the clergy, the politicians, the intellectuals, nor the wealthy. He argued that "it originated with the great middle class—the laboring mechanics and artisans of the country—men who had no ambitious purposes to serve—men who could have had no object but the good of their country, and the vindication of their rights and liberties." This, Rayner suggested, was "the most beautiful feature" of the order. "It proves," he wrote, "that there is a great conservative element, a great moral power, underlying the framework of our social organization potent for the preservation of our liberties, even when the functionaries of authority have become utterly corrupt." With considerable accuracy he noted that "the politicians cautiously avoided this organization until they saw it was becoming popular." Echoing the sentiments of the Founding Fathers, he praised the party for adhering to the principle that the "office must seek the man, and not man the office."[25]

By appearances, at least, Rayner was adhering to this principle. Although in the wake of the unsuccessful 1852 senatorial election he had vowed to return to the state legislature two years later, when the Hertford County Whigs met in mid-summer of 1854 he "positively declined" the nomination for office. The party dutifully nominated alternate candidates. Perhaps Rayner was reluctant to unseat the man who had replaced him in the house of commons when he had refused to run in 1852. However, a month after the county nominations, the name of Hertford's candidate for the state senate, R. G. Cowper, was withdrawn from the race and Rayner took his place. Whether he withdrew in order to make way for Rayner, was pressured to withdraw, or for some reason was unable to make the race remains unclear. Whatever the circumstances, Rayner won election without serious opposition and took his place in the upper house of the legislature for the first time. The *Standard* took a jab at the new senator for living much of the year in Raleigh, saying that Whigs obviously supported "the British practice . . . of electing members for localities in which they do not reside," but the race proved once again that among his own constituents, Rayner was virtually invulnerable. He did not have to seek office, for in Hertford County the office still sought him.[26]

Returning to the state legislature, however, was important to Rayner, because it provided the ideal staging ground for spreading the emerging Know-Nothing gospel. He naturally continued to support internal improvements and education, but there was a greater work to be done in furthering the cause of the new party. As soon as the national meeting in Cincinnati had adjourned, Rayner traveled 1,300 miles in fifty-three hours in order to return to Raleigh quickly. As soon as he arrived, the Know-Nothings in the state capital held a large meeting so that Rayner could report on the national council's proceedings. Many members of the state legislature were initiated into the order then, and Rayner predicted that "we will have the greater portion of them, in a few weeks." In mid-January 1855, the state council met in "a harmonious and enthusiastic" session, and soon Rayner had conferred the Union Degree on "a goodly number" of men in Raleigh. By the spring of 1855 Know-Nothingism had spread throughout North Carolina, and most of the state's Whig newspapers had formally allied themselves with the new party or had endorsed its principles.[27]

Because of his leading role in the Cincinnati convention, his widely circulated "Reply" to Wise, and his activism on behalf of Know-Nothingism in North Carolina, newspapers throughout the nation were now mentioning Rayner for national office. As soon as the Cincinnati meeting had adjourned, the ever-critical *North Carolina Standard* asked point-blank, "Is Mr. Rayner a candidate for the Vice Presidency at the next election?" The Baltimore *Sun* speculated that Rayner would be the party's candidate for president in 1856. A correspondent for the Cincinnati *Daily Times* wrote, "In the ranks of the American party he stands pre-eminent, and he is the favorite candidate of thousands of his fellow citizens for the next Presidency." The New York *Herald* and Wheeling (Virginia) *Intelligencer* listed him among the party's probable presidential choices. A traveling correspondent of the New York *Express* visited the state, concluded that Rayner's "star is more in the ascendant than any I have seen in North Carolina," and noted "that recent events, purely American, have placed him more conspicuously, not only before the people of this State, but the people of the United States."[28]

Rayner felt flattered by such publicity, and he doubtless would have liked to be president or vice president. But he honestly believed that all talk of specific candidates so far in advance of the elections would work to the detriment of the party. "This struggling and scrambling for office and promotion," he told his friend Ullman, "was one of the very great evils it was the object of our organization to remedy—and yet our success is likely to be jeopardized by the very same evil." He did not question the soundness of the masses, but warned that "the old party leaders and political hacks" who had joined the order "from selfish purposes" could ruin the party. As for the movement in his own favor, Rayner claimed that he had "seen it with regret." It was not only too early to be talking about candidates, he explained, but also he feared that it would impair his own usefulness to the cause. "Intending as I do, to devote myself, for the next year or two of my life (if it should be spared so long) to the promotion of the order, my motives are liable to be suspected, and my energies paralyzed, if the idea should be entertained that there is any taint of selfishness in my course," he wrote.[29]

Rayner probably realized that the odds worked against his own chances for high office. His popularity with the masses was nothing like that of Millard Fillmore's or Sam Houston's, two men frequently mentioned in Know-Nothing circles for the presidency. Still, no one could predict what the national council might do when the time came to nominate candidates. In early 1855 little unanimity existed in the American ranks, and some strange movements were afoot in the party. The strangest was the sentiment among a large segment of the northern Know-Nothings in favor of New York's George Law, a wealthy businessman and shipowner who had earned notoriety when he sent one of his vessels to the Caribbean to capture a Democratic gang leader who had fled the country after murdering a member of a nativist gang. Rayner was understandably suspicious of the Law movement. "Upon what grounds will his name be pressed?" he asked Ullman, who, as a New Yorker, was in a position to know. "Is he remarkable for talent, for any peculiar moral traits of character, that endear him to those who know him? Has he made any special sacrifices for the order—was he one of its early founders—has he done a great deal to sustain and promote it?" Rayner clearly thought that whomever the party chose as its standard-bearer in 1856, the man should have such qualities. It should be a man like Kenneth Rayner.[30]

As usual, Rayner spent the spring of 1855 attending to planting affairs in Hertford County. However, he kept a close watch on national affairs and maintained correspondence with Know-Nothing leaders in other states. Two things worried him about the party's future. First, he was alarmed by the desire of Know-Nothings in certain states, especially Louisiana, to admit native-born Catholics to the order. The national council was slated to meet in Philadelphia in June, and Rayner had learned that "another strong attempt [would] be made, to induce us to relax our stringent position in regard to Roman Catholics." If such an effort proved successful, Rayner predicted, the American party would be "done for." He warned Ullman that outside of the large cities "the Protestant feeling is our great element of strength" and stated his conviction that the pope and the Jesuits were at work planning "to induce us to yield the point as to native Roman Catholics." Rayner vowed to "resist this movement to the bitter end." History, he believed, had shown conclusively "that whenever Protestantism makes a concession to Romanism, disaster and ruin, to the former inevitably follow."[31]

The second troubling aspect of the party's future was the ever-present issue of slavery. Rayner had seen a preview of the problem in Cincinnati, where some of the delegates from both sections had balked at the Union Degree. Their forces would be better organized in Philadelphia. The great issue confronting the nation in 1855 was the Kansas-Nebraska Act, which repealed the time-honored Missouri Compromise and allowed the settlers of the Kansas and Nebraska territories to decide for themselves whether slavery was to be permitted within their boundaries. As proslavery and antislavery settlers clashed violently in Kansas, the whole issue of slavery's extension threatened to divide the American party irreparably. Even the Union Degree might not be enough to prevent it.

Rayner's actions in Cincinnati set the tone for his position on slavery during the next two years. He understood with great clarity that slavery had to be excluded entirely from the party's debates if Know-Nothingism was to survive as a national organization. The failure of the national American party would surely lead to the triumph of the purely sectional Republicans. Even more troubling was the growing willingness of some northern Know-Nothings to support Republican candidates in fusion arrangements. For instance, when New York's William H. Seward sought Know-Nothing votes in his bid for reelection to the Senate in 1855, Rayner wrote to Ullman, urging him to work hard for Seward's defeat. "It will hurt us greatly in our part of the Country, if he should be elected by 'Know-Nothing' votes," warned Rayner. His personal objections to Seward are instructive: "I hope in God, he may be defeated—not because he is an anti-slavery man, but because he is an *anti-union* man." Seward won the race, and to Rayner it was yet another sign that sectionalism was triumphing over nationalism.[32]

The only thing worse than Know-Nothings supporting a Republican candidate was the prospect of northern candidates of the American party themselves openly championing the antislavery cause. Rayner was mortified when the Massachusetts legislature elected an avowed antislavery Know-Nothing, Henry Wilson, to the U.S. Senate. "That Wilson is an extreme man of the Seward, higher law stripe, there is no doubt," he complained. Rayner noted Wilson's participation in a recent abolitionist lecture in Boston, in which Wilson reportedly endorsed the concept of a law higher than the Constitution. "How is this?" Rayner asked. To him, Americanism meant the rule of law over anarchy, pursuit of national rather than sectional interests, and the supremacy of reason over emotion. Americanism, by definition, could never be sectional or place any set of rules ahead of the Constitution. That Massachusetts Americans would support Wilson seemed to Rayner a perversion of everything the party represented. His response to Wilson's election was both candid and revealing. "I can't understand it," wrote a frustrated Rayner.[33]

Rayner increasingly stood alone as a major American party leader who wished to seek a true middle ground between the southern and northern positions on slavery. For example, he criticized the course of the order's national newspaper, the Washington-based *American Organ,* as "too violent in its *proslavery* views, for a national organ." Rayner agreed that its editor, Vespasian Ellis, was correct "in the abstract" in championing the constitutional rights of slaveholders, but in the world of practical politics, Rayner believed that "respect should be had for the feelings, and even the prejudices of peculiar sections." Thus he argued that Ellis should tone down his defense of slaveholders' rights in order not to offend northern members. "If I understand the spirit of this order," Rayner told Ullman, "it is, to leave the question of slavery exactly where the institutions of our country have left it, and not to hazard the integrity of the Union, by discussing or agitating the question, either at the North or South." [34]

But leaving the question entirely out of political discussions was fast proving impossible in both sections. In May 1855, the nation's attention focused on Virginia, where the Know-Nothings were expected to make a strong effort to win the governorship. The contest pitted the American candidate, Thomas S. Flournoy, against Rayner's old congressional colleague and nemesis, the Whig-turned-Tylerite-turned-Democrat Henry A. Wise. Throughout the country it was believed that the Virginia election would either establish the American party as a viable force in southern politics or else deal it a crippling blow. Wise campaigned hard and brilliantly, condemning the Know-Nothings for their secrecy and bigotry and ridiculing their ritual. His most effective weapon, however, was the charge that the American party sympathized with abolitionism. The actions of the Massachusetts and New Hampshire Know-Nothing councils in repudiating the Union Degree and in elevating men like Wilson gave Rayner cause for deep concern about the effects on the Virginia election. With avowed abolitionists occupying high places in the order, Know-Nothings found it almost impossible to defend against Wise's charges.[35]

In the final two weeks before the critical election, Virginia Know-Nothings asked Rayner to deliver speeches in Petersburg, Portsmouth, and Richmond. Wise's charges of abolitionism had gone largely unanswered by the lackluster campaigning of Flournoy, and the Virginians desperately needed someone who could take the offensive against Wise. In Petersburg Rayner began with his standard nativist appeals, hoping to keep political attention focused on the threat that Catholics and immigrants posed to republican institutions. Only after the party's principles had been outlined did Rayner attempt to answer the charges of abolitionism. He did so by turning the tables on the Democrats, accusing them "of being the real aiders and abettors of the Northern fanatics, by their constant practice of holding up to public view the truest men in the Commonwealth as branded Abolitionists." With more than a little accuracy, Rayner told his audience that each blow against the American party strengthened the Republican party in the North. If the Sewards of the North and the Wises of the South succeeded, he predicted, "the slavery agitation shall rend this Union into fragments."[36]

Virginians received his speeches with great enthusiasm. At Portsmouth, the address reportedly attracted the largest audience of any political gathering in years, with more than two thousand in attendance. Rayner spoke until midnight and was escorted back to his lodgings by a torch-light procession and a band. But as he had feared, the Know-Nothings were unable to convince enough Virginians of the party's righteousness and its safety on the slavery question. On election day Wise won by a margin of ten thousand votes out of 155,000 cast. Rayner's concern that the American party was being "converted into a stalking-horse for fanatical agitators" seemed to be coming true.[37]

The stage, then, was set for the June 1855 meeting of the national council at Philadelphia, where the party's platform was to be drafted. A month before the convention Rayner was already anticipating the battle that would be waged over the slavery issue and was trying to impress his views on northern leaders. "We do not ask you to say one word in favor of slavery," he told Ullman. "We do not ask you to say that your people shall, or ought to, give up their anti-slavery opinions, *as individuals*—not at all." Rayner desperately sought to persuade the northerners "that if this order is to be *National*, it must, *as an order*, ignore questions that are sectional."[38]

The meeting came at a bad time. The week before Rayner left for Philadelphia, his three-year-old daughter, Fanny, fell ill and died. But duty called, and Kenneth left Susan to grieve in Raleigh with ten-year-old Sallie, eight-year-old Henry, six-year-old Kenneth, Jr., and two-month-old Susan. As the delegates gathered on June 5, the crucial issue of credentials had to be settled. Many southerners wished to see Henry Wilson and the Massachusetts antislavery delegates expelled on the basis of having failed to take the Union Degree or having ignored its tenets. The Virginians, who blamed Wilson for their party's defeat in the recent elections, especially hoped that the New Englanders would be excluded. The other major dispute, as Rayner had predicted, involved the Louisiana delegation, which included several Catholic members. After two days of heated debate between northern and southern members, the council admitted the Massachusetts delegation and, to Rayner's relief, excluded the Louisiana Catholics. A majority of the delegates apparently realized that without the Massachusetts men seated in the council, it could hardly be considered a national convention. At the same time, they concluded that admitting Catholics would seriously undermine the entire reason for the party's existence. At one point it appeared that the Louisiana Catholics would win their fight to be seated, but "a strong speech" by Rayner "carried the issue" against them. It was not the last time that he would occupy center stage in Philadelphia.[39]

On the third evening of the convention, with no platform yet reported out of committee, local Know-Nothings held a grand banquet at the Samson Street Hall. About 450 dignitaries attended the function, which featured a sumptuous meal and elaborate patriotic decorations in the banquet room. The master of ceremonies, Philadelphia's Mayor Robert Conrad, offered the first toast to "the Union." Rayner responded with what the New York *Times* called "an old-time, patriotic, glorification, Star-Spangled Banner speech." The applause when he rose to speak was overpowering, and it took several minutes for the chairman to restore order. The address was one of the super-patriotic efforts that so frequently characterized Know-Nothing rhetoric. Rayner had long since concluded that the party's—and the Union's—only hope lay in rekindling the emotional patriotism that had characterized the early Republic.[40]

His speech hammered away at "the idea of the Union." He opened with a history lesson, detailing the hardships endured by the early colonists, the sacrifices demanded by the Revolution, and the human costs of the country's wars. But what was remarkable about this particular oration was not so much its content but the response of the audience. Early in the speech Rayner commented that being so close to Independence Hall made him feel like Moses beholding the burning bush. Before he could finish the sentence, his remarks were drowned out by "vehement and prolonged cheering," according to the New York *Times* report. A few minutes later the mention of George Washington's name elicited "vociferous cheers." When he spoke of the Founding Fathers as "immortal names 'that were not born to die,'" the crowd broke into "tremendous applause and cheering." "What is it that has peopled the wilderness?" Rayner passionately asked. "What is it that has substituted for the shrubbery of the wilderness fields of waving grain? What is it that has whitened with sails of commerce those lakes and rivers upon whose shores solitude had brooded for ages? What is it that has carried our literature, our science, our arts, our manufactures, our arms, from the shelving beach of the Atlantic to the beetling crags of the Pacific? It is the Union of these States." The audience responded with "loud and prolonged cheering." By this time Rayner was interrupted by hysterical displays of approval after nearly every sentence.[41]

Halfway through the address Rayner's tone suddenly changed. "But, my friends," he asked gravely, "who is so irrational—who dare lift that veil which shrouds the future in darkness, and beyond which shadows, cloud, and darkness rest upon the prospect?" The Union, he claimed, was "identical with liberty itself. Destroy this Union and the very idea of Liberty becomes a mere wild and senseless abstraction." After reminding his listeners of the blood spilled in the Revolution, he appealed to them "by the blood of your fathers" and asked, "will you lay your unhallowed hands upon this Union which was so cemented by their blood?" His appeal was met with "frantic cheering, howling, clapping of hands, and the most intense and half ludicrous exhibitions of patriotic excitement" that prevented him from resuming for some time.[42]

Rayner approached his finale with devastating effectiveness: "Then, my brethren, I appeal to you in conclusion—I appeal to you by these glorious associations of the past, by these glories of the present, by the bright prospect of the future—I appeal to the North by her glorious associations; to the South by her glorious associations—and by the common prosperity of both, that before we leave this city of Philadelphia, we shall have laid the foundations broad and deep, and everlasting, of the preservation of the Union of these States." Words finally failed the *Times*'s reporter. "The rapturous enthusiasm and uncontrollable confusion with which this sentiment was received is indescribable," he wrote, noting that "some minutes elapsed before the speaker could proceed." With continuing cheers that made it difficult for him to be heard, Rayner finished by admonishing his fellow delegates: "Let us do our duty. Let us make these small sectional sacrifices which may be necessary, under the exigencies of this case, to preserve this Union. We then shall have secured our nationality, thank God. We shall have secured the great principle of religious freedom, and, after having secured these, we shall die with the proud consciousness that owing to our efforts in a great part, 'The Star Spangled Banner for ever shall wave / O'er the land of the free, and the home of the brave.'" He took his seat amid the thunderous applause and cheering of the crowd. Someone wanted to know if Massachusetts—meaning Wilson and the antislavery delegates—had anything to say. They did not.[43]

Although Rayner had seemingly reached the pinnacle of his popularity in the Know-Nothing movement, he knew that the principles he had striven to instill in the party hung precariously in the balance. The next few days would do much to determine whether he and the other Know-Nothing leaders who thought as he did would succeed in making the party the voice of conservative republicanism in America. If they failed, he believed it would be because selfish politicians had gained control of the national organization, surrendering the party's principles in favor of antirepublican sectionalism. In short, the American party would suffer the same fate as the Whigs, and the days of the Union would be numbered.

CHAPTER 5

"Engulphed in the Vortex"

◆◇◆

As the platform committee of the American party deliberated in Philadelphia in June 1855, the controversy born of the Kansas-Nebraska Act raged fiercely in the United States. Kenneth Rayner soon found himself at the eye of the storm. The committee completed its work and submitted a majority report endorsing existing laws—meaning the Kansas-Nebraska Act as well as the Fugitive Slave Law—as final settlements of the slavery question. In the ensuing two-day debate over the platform, Rayner strove heroically to play the part of peacemaker in a convention badly split along sectional lines. During one of the most heated exchanges, Thomas A. Ford of Ohio, an eloquent antislavery spokesman, delivered a strong speech condemning Kansas-Nebraska. After several southern delegates responded, Rayner gained the floor and dropped a bombshell. "Well, then," he thundered, "I have to say that the repeal of the Missouri Compromise was an uncalled for and unnecessary act, an outrage even, a violation of plighted faith; and I would have seen my right arm wither and my tongue palsied before I would have voted for it." This declaration brought forth "great indignation, hissing and exclamations" from the southern delegates. An Alabamian asked if these remarks were intended as a personal attack on him. Rayner replied that they were not; he allowed every man freedom of opinion on the matter. A handful of other southern moderates agreed in principle with Rayner, but most southerners denounced him for his bold stance against the Kansas bill and the repeal of the Missouri Compromise. One warned that he would "suffer for this at home; that he would be put down there." Rayner defiantly answered that he would "trust in the generosity and justice of the old North State," and that if his enemies chose to make an issue of his opinions, he would stump the entire state in his own defense.[1]

The speech, according to the New York *Tribune*'s undercover reporter, "created a great storm among the Southern members." Before taking his seat, Rayner proposed a set of substitute resolutions. After reiterating the American party's commitment to nativism and Unionism, Rayner's substitute declared "that the attempts of our enemies to identify the American Party with the agitation of the question of negro-slavery, either *pro* or *con*, are based on misrepresentation and deception—that the question of slavery does not come within the purview of the objects of this organization." The party should simply leave slavery "where it is placed by the Constitution and the laws made in pursuance thereof, regarding it as a sectional question subject to the regulation of local law."[2]

Although he had branded the repeal of the Missouri Compromise "an outrage," Rayner's proposed resolutions were in keeping with his long-standing belief that slavery should be kept out of the political dialogue altogether. They did not endorse the Kansas-Nebraska Act, but neither did they reflect their author's professed repugnance toward it. But to leave the slavery issue where it currently stood under the Constitution and the current laws was, in effect, to sanction Kansas-Nebraska, popular sovereignty, and the Fugitive Slave Law. Rayner hated these measures, but he was convinced that the Know-Nothings would never survive as a national party unless they simply left slavery legislation—good or bad—alone.

As the convention moved into its eighth day, the *Tribune*'s correspondent reported that "the excitement in reference to Rayner is intense." His object, the reporter accurately deduced, was to create a platform upon which the upper South and the North could unite. Nobody believed that the deep South would rest contented with any platform that did not expressly endorse Kansas-Nebraska and the Fugitive Slave Law. But the *Tribune*'s perceptive correspondent realized that the effort would fail, even if the upper South went along with Rayner's substitute. "He labors in a hopeless cause," wrote the reporter. "The very moment the Convention refuses to recognize the unconditional restoration of the Missouri Compromise, the vitality of the Organization is gone."[3]

This analysis soon proved entirely accurate. Rayner's proposal was defeated by a 97 to 46 margin and the proslavery majority report adopted. Only seven slave-state representatives scattered among the Delaware, Maryland, and the District of Columbia delegations supported Rayner in his attempt to have the slavery controversy laid to rest, while thirty-six of the free-state members voted for it. The South—including upper-South states of Virginia, Kentucky, Tennessee, Maryland, Arkansas, and Rayner's home state of North Carolina—formed a nearly unbroken phalanx in uncompromising support of the proslavery resolutions. After seeing his measure defeated, Rayner himself reluctantly voted with the pro-southern majority, perhaps realizing that to go on record as having voted with the North would endanger his political standing, if not his life, in the South. Later he claimed that he had consulted privately with almost all of the delegates, and "a very decided majority" had pledged to support his measure. "But when the vote came to be taken," he explained, "whilst 'the spirit was willing the flesh was weak.'"[4]

Rayner thus saw his hopes of keeping slavery out of the party's official dialogue dashed upon the rock of the Kansas-Nebraska Act. At eight o'clock the next morning, to the surprise of no one, Henry Wilson led the bulk of the northern delegates in a bolt from the convention. They convened in a nearby hotel and endorsed the minority platform. It signaled the first time that northern delegates to a national political convention had refused to allow the slavery issue to be ignored or couched in innocuous terms. The New York *Tribune* correspondent who had clandestinely followed the entire convention also covered the bolters' meeting, and after it had adjourned he echoed a sentiment that to Rayner must have seemed a frightful portent: "There is reason to believe now that there is a North!"[5]

Following the convention, Rayner and a number of the more prominent delegates traveled to New York City to participate in a mass meeting celebrating the completion of the party's work at Philadelphia. Ten or twelve thousand Know-Nothings assembled in Central Park to hear speeches before forming a huge procession that conveyed Rayner and other dignitaries around the city to the cheers of the party faithful. Leaving New York on his way home, Rayner participated in another massive rally in Baltimore and then stopped in Washington, D.C., where a similar gathering attracted six thousand participants. Addressing the large crowd, he remarked that when he resigned his House seat a decade earlier in disgust over the corruption of both political parties, he never thought that he might be called back to Washington to advocate even higher principles than those he had championed during his congressional career.[6]

Rayner knew he faced a tremendous challenge in the months to come. The Philadelphia convention had been disastrous to party unity. He now tried to put the best face on things by saying that the northern delegates had merely protested against Section Twelve of the platform (as the pro-Kansas-Nebraska plank was now universally known) and that there had not been a true bolt. The cardinal principles of the order—opposition to the political influence of Catholics and immigrants—were still in place, he pointed out.

He played to the emotions of his Washington audience by expressing sympathy for government employees who, because they were Know-Nothings, had been turned out of office by the Pierce administration. "The minions of power are watching you, to be turned out by the pimp of the White House, if you refuse to sustain him," he told the crowd. Rayner usually scrupulously avoided personal name-calling in his speeches, but the cheers of the rabidly anti-Democratic throng goaded him to even more intemperate language. He described the president as "a man sunk so low we can hardly hate. We have nothing but disgust, pity, and contempt." Referring to Pierce's cabinet, he characterized them as "seven waiters [who] look and act like whipt curs" and "seven slaves who wait upon his bidding." Rayner concluded with the explosive charge that a papal nuncio in Madrid had known of the selection of Catholic James Campbell to Pierce's cabinet before the news had reached Spain, suggesting that a corrupt bargain had been struck between American Catholics and Pierce. This information had come from former North Carolina Whig Congressman Daniel Barringer, who as minister to Spain had conversed with the nuncio in Madrid. Later that evening a group of Know-Nothings, allegedly incited by Rayner's inflammatory speech, carried transparencies and banners to the White House, where they cursed and harangued the president outside the windows of his private quarters.[7]

The threats voiced by the southern delegates at Philadelphia that Rayner would suffer at home for his denunciation of Kansas-Nebraska quickly came true. Arriving in Raleigh, he was greeted with a fierce storm of denunciation and ridicule. The editor of the Democratic Raleigh *North Carolina Standard*, Holden, had been conducting a war of words against Rayner for six months. Now he stepped up his attack, relentlessly castigating Rayner for the harsh language he had used in Washington, lambasting him for his alleged political ambition, laboring to disprove the papal nuncio story, and charging him with making "common cause with the traitors, the abolitionists, and the disunionists of Massachusetts and New Hampshire." Of all possible accusations that could be leveled at a politician in the antebellum South, the charge of anti-slavery sympathies was probably the most damaging. Holden was not satisfied to make the charge once or twice. Instead, he harped upon it issue after issue, week after week, for the rest of 1855 and most of 1856. He became almost obsessed with Rayner and his "northern allies," devoting not just individual articles but entire pages to the cause of discrediting him.[8]

Rayner spent the rest of the summer defending himself in speeches throughout eastern and central North Carolina. The effort began immediately upon his return to the state capital, when one of the largest public assemblages in Raleigh's history met to ratify the Philadelphia convention's work. That Rayner was on the defensive is evidenced by the fact that he answered the charges of abolitionism and bigotry before advocating the positive principles of the party; usually he addressed such charges at the end of his speeches. No doubt referring to Holden, he argued that his course in the national convention had been the subject of "vile and malicious misrepresentations of the locofoco press and of small-potato politicians and street-brawlers." In order to demonstrate Rayner's about-face on the issue of religious freedom, Holden and the Wake County Democratic Club had issued his 1835 constitutional convention speech, which advocated repeal of the religious test, in pamphlet form. Rayner replied that, if need be, he would make the same speech and vote against a religious test again. He accurately pointed out that neither he nor the Know-Nothing party had ever advocated any law or constitutional amendment banning Catholics from holding public office; theirs was simply an effort to persuade people to vote against Catholics because of their corrupting influence on politics. Only toward the end of the speech did he remind the crowd of the three great objectives of the American party, as he defined them: "1. The cultivation of a spirit of intense American nationality. 2. Opposition to any church that would attempt to wield its influence as an organization in favor of any particular party. 3. A devoted and unalterable attachment to the Union of the States." As he conceived it, the party clearly stood for more than mere proscription.[9]

Holden and the Democrats followed Rayner's every utterance, missing no opportunity to turn his words against him. "KENNETH RAYNER DESPERATE" read one headline in the July 4 Standard. Seizing on Rayner's unseemly attack on Pierce and the cabinet in the Washington speech, Holden, unparalleled in the art of exaggerated and inflammatory rhetoric, hypocritically asked, "Can it be possible that Kenneth Rayner used that language?" Rayner, according to Holden, was exhibiting "rage, malice, and envy characteristic only of the desperate but baffled and disappointed place-hunter." Noting that the Know-Nothing leader had referred to his opponents as "small-potato" politicians, Holden jeered that "if others are small, surely Mr. Rayner is himself a *big* potato." Rayner henceforth became known in the Democratic press as "Mr. Big Potato Rayner," soon shortened to "Mr. (B. P.) Rayner."[10]

These attacks, if anything, motivated Rayner to work harder for his party in North Carolina. Congressional elections were to be held in August, and after an extensive speaking and debating tour through the central counties, he returned to his old district to try to redeem it for the American party. Rayner's strength in the northeastern part of the state remained undiminished. He knew his former constituents better than any man alive. Sensing, for example, that some North Carolinians were associating Know-Nothingism with temperance, he would down a "stiff toddy" from the speaker's stand to demonstrate the party's correctness on the liquor question. Rayner's efforts in his old district paid off handsomely, with the American candidate defeating the incumbent Democrat. Statewide, however, the party won only three of the eight house seats. Reflecting on the victory in his own district, Rayner was convinced that "our principles are strong, when fairly and boldly maintained." But there simply were not enough Rayners in the rest of North Carolina or the South.[11]

Despite his public professions of confidence in the party's future and his strenuous efforts on the stump, Rayner realized that the American party, as a national organization, was in serious danger. There was a growing movement on the part of southern councils to allow native-born Catholics into the order and of northern councils to admit foreign-born Protestants. "In the main," he wrote, "the native papists are as intolerant as the foreign." At the same time, he thought it wrong "to put the staid and peac[e]able and industrious Germans & Swedes & Swiss Protestants upon a level with the Irish Romanists." But while readily admitting that individual exceptions existed among both groups, Rayner was convinced that to alter the party's stance toward either Catholics or immigrants would be a fatal political mistake. Such actions aided Know-Nothings in winning state and local elections, but they seriously compromised the party's principles on the national level.[12]

Rayner's anxieties were compounded by the near-fatal intrusion of the slavery question into the party dialogue. In the wake of the Philadelphia convention, one northern state council after another had formally repudiated the infamous Section Twelve of the platform. "With the lessons of the past before us, why could we not avoid that dangerous rock of slavery," he asked Ullman? "It *was* extraneous to the objects of our organization—the taunts of our enemies drove us to the attempt to harmonise the conflicting views of the two sections of the Union on this distracting subject—and these same enemies are now laughing and cajoling over our troubles." More than ever, Rayner was convinced that he had pursued the proper course in Philadelphia. Now he could say with justification, "Well, has it not turned out as I predicted? Did the platform strengthen us *in the Union*—did it strengthen us *in the South*—or did it weaken us?" It mattered not whether the pro-Kansas-Nebraska platform was right in the abstract; it was not "politic as a party movement." Rayner had learned from bitter personal experience on the campaign trail that the platform had not aided the cause in the South at all. When

Know-Nothings in the South emphasized the pro-southern nature of Section Twelve, their opponents simply pointed to the actions of the northern delegates and state councils in repudiating it in favor of a free-soil platform. "I confess to you, in all candor, that I feel depressed, when I look forward to the future," he confided to Ullman. "I do not see how we are to succeed, without harmony."[13]

Political excitement abated somewhat by late 1855. Early in 1856 the Rayners made their annual spring migration to Hertford, where they would remain until June. The American party's national nominating convention was scheduled to convene in Philadelphia in February. Immediately before the convention, the order's national council (technically different than the nominating convention but consisting mostly of the same membership) would meet in hopes of restoring sectional harmony to the party. Rayner wisely believed that February was too early; another sectional clash was almost inevitable, and it would give opponents eight long months in which to bash the Know-Nothing candidate, whomever it might be. He nevertheless planned to attend the gathering, but on the eve of his departure chose not to go. Later he cited "a press of business" and the serious illness of one of his children as his reasons for remaining at home. Perhaps Rayner felt forced to stay at his child's bedside after having deserted Susan to go to the last national council meeting scarcely a week after Fanny's death. But had his excitement over the upcoming convention been equal to that he had felt before the 1854 and 1855 gatherings, he almost certainly would have been there. Since the June meeting, Rayner had seen the crucial national principles of the party—doctrinaire political nativism and exclusion of slavery from the party platform—crippled by political trimming and sectional animosities. The February nominating convention would be a showdown, with disaster as its only result, no matter which faction or section prevailed. It came as no great disappointment to him to stay home.[14]

Carefully following the Philadelphia proceedings in the newspapers, Rayner found little to brighten his pessimistic outlook. The national council meeting and the ensuing nominating convention both were marked by extreme confusion and disorder, bordering at times on anarchy. Rayner confessed feeling "deep mortification" when, on the second day of the council meeting, the Catholic delegates from Louisiana were seated. With that move he believed the order had "surrendered to the enemy the citadel of our strength." The admittance of Catholics was only a prelude to the central battle of the four-day council meeting: the fight over the platform. After a long debate the delegates voted to eliminate the divisive Section Twelve, which had essentially endorsed Kansas-Nebraska, popular sovereignty, and the Fugitive Slave Law, and replace it with a vague resolution resembling Rayner's earlier proposal. But the political damage had already been done; simply leaving existing slavery laws where they stood would please neither section. The Kansas-Nebraska Act and the Fugitive Slave Law *were* the existing laws in 1855, measures that hundreds of thousands of Americans in the two sections were grimly determined either to preserve or repeal. With these statutes on the books there was no middle ground in the politics of slavery.[15]

Although Rayner had remained in North Carolina, he was not entirely forgotten when the delegates at last proceeded to the nomination of a presidential ticket. Fillmore and Law were the principal contenders, with Houston, Rayner, and others as possible compromise choices in case of a deadlock. The balloting, like the convention as a whole, was highly irregular. But with strong southern support, Fillmore easily won the nomination for president. Garnering fourteen votes from among the Pennsylvania, Illinois, and Wisconsin delegations, Rayner finished third in the balloting behind George Law. His name was also placed in nomination for the vice-presidency, but Tennessee's Andrew Jackson Donelson—the nephew of Old Hickory—received almost unanimous support.[16]

The antislavery delegates, already unhappy with a platform that had stopped short of repudiating Kansas-Nebraska, refused to accept the selection of Fillmore and Donelson. As soon as the results were known, some seventy northern members seceded from the convention. Labelled "North Americans," they retired to another hall, drafted resolutions of protest, and scheduled their own presidential nominating convention to be held in New York in June, immediately before the Republican convention. A number of disgruntled Law and Houston supporters later joined them. For Know-Nothings like Rayner who were ideologically committed to both nativism and Unionism, the handwriting was plain to read: the day of the American party as a national movement was rapidly passing.[17]

Kenneth Rayner and Millard Fillmore were, of course, old friends. Yet Rayner certainly would have preferred to see the national convention nominate a man with stronger Know-Nothing credentials and a greater base of support in the North. Fillmore had never participated actively in the nativist movement and only recently had been hurriedly initiated into the order as a means of qualifying him for the nomination. In the former president, most northerners could only see an old Whig who by supporting the Compromise of 1850 had destroyed the Wilmot Proviso and foisted the Fugitive Slave Law onto an unwilling North.

Rayner soon endorsed Fillmore's nomination and began making speeches in his behalf in North Carolina, but he felt "mortified and discouraged by the 'signs of the times' in the North." The practical politician in Rayner realized that Fillmore's chances of carrying enough northern states in November were very slim. The last chance of any sort to reunite the divided party would come when the North Americans met. Rayner's correspondence with other party leaders in the spring of 1856 shows his understanding of the importance of the North Americans' actions. "Much, very much, yes every thing depends on the convention of the seceding Americans of the 12th June," he wrote to Ullman. "Can't they be induced to compromise on Fillmore, as the best thing they can do under the circumstances? If they persist, and thoroughly repudiate Fillmore, & nominate a separate ticket—what chance is there of contending successfully with the hosts of Loco-focoism? . . . Will they—*can* they—fuse with the "Republicans," as they call themselves—or will they nominate another independent ticket? If the latter, whom will they select as standard-bearers?" [18]

These indeed were among the crucial questions on all political minds in the United States in June 1856. Rayner, having spent the spring "rusticating" on his remote plantation in Hertford County, possessed no means of knowing exactly how far the plans to unite the North Americans with the Republicans had progressed. But he knew enough to suspect the worst. Those plans, in fact, were well developed by the time of the North American convention. An influential group of North American leaders, working in close concert with Thurlow Weed and other Republican strategists, were actively scheming to merge the North Americans into the Republican party. With these plans afoot there was never the slightest possibility that the North Americans would reunite with the rest of their party and rally around Fillmore. "We feel as if we were '*leading a forlorn hope*,' unsustained by our American Brethren North," Rayner glumly remarked ten days before the New York convention.[19]

Rayner's fears were substantiated when the North American convention met. Although very little was said about nativism or Unionism, Republican managers were to be seen everywhere. However, not all of the North American delegates were headed for the Republican camp; some had bolted the Philadelphia convention not so much because the platform and the presidential nominee were soft on slavery but because Fillmore was not really a Know-Nothing. They had no desire to see the American party absorbed bodily into the Republican organization; they in fact wanted to see it purified.

On the fourth day of the gathering the New Jersey delegation withdrew from the convention, followed by a handful of members from the Pennsylvania, New York, Massachusetts, Illinois, Iowa, Delaware, Indiana, and Tennessee delegations. The bolters had realized that the ultra free-soilers were "violating the integrity of the American Party, and merging it into an organization which may prove to be nothing else but that of the Abolition Party." While the remaining North Americans proceeded with their plans to merge with the Republicans, the bolters held their own convention. They nominated a genuine nativist and original Know-Nothing, New Jersey's Commodore Robert F. Stockton, for the presidency. To balance the ticket they unanimously chose Kenneth Rayner as their vice-presidential nominee. Meeting the following day to draft a platform, the rump convention passed several strongly nativist resolutions, endorsed a protective tariff, called for government aid for internal improvements (including a transcontinental railroad), and condemned the Kansas-Nebraska Act. With the noncommittal Fillmore as the regular Know-Nothing nominee and the rest of the North Americans headed for the Republican party, this was the only truly nativist American ticket remaining in the field.[20]

Rayner received word of these developments in Raleigh, where he and his family had just returned to spend the summer. Composing a long public letter on June 30, he expressed his appreciation for the vice-presidential nomination, even though the convention had been a fragment of a fragment of the American party. Although the delegates had been "few in numbers," Rayner thought it made their actions all the more sincere. "Those who volunteer as 'a forlorn hope,'" he wrote, "are not likely to be moved by selfish considerations." Although honored, Rayner could see no choice but to support the Fillmore-Donelson ticket. "Americans must bide their time," he forlornly wrote as he graciously declined the nomination. Fillmore, at least, was a man with "a sound head, an honest heart, and national conservative, and statesmanlike views. If he erred during his Presidential service, I believe he erred from honest and conscientious convictions of duty." This was hardly a ringing endorsement, but Rayner was "unwilling to be instrumental in adding to the discord which already exists." Defeat, he hoped, would at least teach the party the wisdom of unity.[21]

If Rayner anticipated defeat, it did nothing to diminish his exertions in favor of the American cause. He stumped North Carolina in August on behalf of the Know-Nothings, ardently promoting the candidacy of gubernatorial nominee John Gilmer and the Fillmore-Donelson ticket. Gilmer lost, but in the fall Rayner again toured widely in support of Fillmore. In late October, with the national election just two weeks away, he received a letter from an unidentified friend in Pennsylvania. The writer asked for Rayner's opinion on the political situation. In his reply, which was published in the New York *Times* and widely circulated, Rayner again laid the blame for the current national political crisis at the doorstep of the Democratic party. He repeated his frequent charge that the Kansas-Nebraska Act had been gotten up by the Democrats following the success of the Compromise of 1850 because it represented "a hook on which they could hang a 'slavery' issue" and thereby revive their political fortunes.[22]

The writer also asked about the South's attitude toward John C. Frémont, the Republican presidential nominee. Rayner answered that if he were fairly elected, southern people would wait to see what his policy would be. If Frémont should attempt any violation of the South's constitutional rights, southerners would resist "without reckoning the cost." But whatever the intentions of Republicans or southern disunionists, Rayner believed defeating the Democrats to be of the utmost importance. In this matter, he told his friend, "almost everything" depended upon Pennsylvania. No one doubted that the Democratic candidate, James Buchanan, would carry most of the South. Likewise, Frémont would be unbeatable in the majority of northern states. Pennsylvania was the most populous state in which the Americans and Republicans each had large followings. It was also Buchanan's home state, and against divided opposition he would certainly triumph. Those who closely followed national politics knew that Republicans and Know-Nothings had recently attempted to arrange a type of fusion agreement in Pennsylvania. At stake in the state were twenty-seven electors. This fusion, or "Union," ticket, was to work as follows: Two sets of electoral ballots were to be printed, with twenty-six of the electors being the same on both sets. On the version of this ballot to be cast by Republicans, the twenty-seventh elector would be Frémont. On the Americans' version it would be Fillmore. In the event of victory, the twenty-six joint electors pledged to cast their votes for Fillmore and Frémont according to the proportion of the popular vote each version of the ticket received.[23] Pennsylvania Know-Nothings were seriously divided over the scheme. The majority of the state executive committee decided against fusion and kept a straight Fillmore ticket in the field. A minority of the committee liked the idea and went along with the fusion ticket as planned. Thus the American party in the state had two competing tickets when Rayner received the inquiry from his friend in Pennsylvania.[24]

The casual observer in the fall of 1856 never would have guessed that Millard Fillmore was running for president of the United States. He held himself aloof from the turmoil of the campaign, content to let his supporters do as they saw fit. Beginning in mid-summer, Pennsylvania Know-Nothings swamped him with letters asking advice on the propriety of fusion or arguing the case for or against. No definitive answer was forthcoming. Meanwhile, Philadelphia Republicans worked diligently to convince the Americans to drop their straight Fillmore ticket and support fusion. On Tuesday, October 27, Republican managers telegraphed Rayner in Raleigh, asking him to come to the city "to exercise his influence with his American friends in favor of a Union ticket." He arrived in Philadelphia the following Friday and took control of the movement from the American side. It would be the boldest and most costly decision of his political career.[25]

Rayner hurried to American party headquarters as soon as he reached Philadelphia. After meeting all afternoon with Know-Nothing leaders, he delivered the first of six speeches that he would make while in the city. The Republicans wisely kept their distance. "If the Fil[l]more men here knew that he was here at my suggestion," wrote Republican manager Alexander Cummings to New York boss Thurlow Weed, "there would be a row of the tallest kind—but when they find it out, (if ever) it will be too late." On the second night of his visit, Rayner spoke before an overflow Know-Nothing crowd at the Musical Fund Hall. After a lengthy disquisition on American principles and exposure of Democratic corruption, he asked the crowd, "Does any body doubt me as an American?" His listeners replied with cries of "No, no." "But gentlemen," he counseled a moment later, "we are *practical* men, as well as patriots. . . . we cannot always control events. We must sometimes bow to the storm which we cannot breast." "Never," came a voice from the audience, sensing what was to come.

Rayner was forced to explain that he was not "the representative of any clique or faction." "I know nothing of your straight-out ticket," he told them. "I know nothing of your Union ticket; I know nothing of Frémont." Finally he came to the moment of truth: "Then I say, can't you combine the vote of this State and beat Buchanan?" The question elicited a hail of competing cheers and hisses that continued for several minutes before Rayner could resume. When the excitement abated, he pleaded with the Know-Nothings to put aside their differences of opinion. He told them to go ahead and vote the straight ticket if they thought it would carry the state for Fillmore. Few believed it could. "I would not vote a ticket that had on it the name of Frémont," he stated, "but I would vote a ticket with Fillmore's name upon it, and which would give him, (if not twenty-seven electoral votes) seven, or ten, or twenty, just as the numerical proportion of the votes might decide." Rayner stopped short of actually telling his fellow Know-Nothings to vote the Union ticket, but the implication was unmistakable. Depriving Buchanan of twenty-six Pennsylvania electoral votes—even though some of them would go to Frémont—might keep any of the three candidates from receiving a national majority. This would throw the election into the House of Representatives, where Fillmore would be the probable compromise choice. Rayner communicated this arithmetic to the audience and then closed "amid a storm of applause, which continued for some time." [26]

After hearing one of Rayner's addresses, Alexander Cummings, the Republican leader who had been instrumental in summoning him to Philadelphia expressed the opinion that Rayner would "be the means of saving us if we are saved at all." But time was running out for eliminating the straight ticket and combining all American votes on the Union slate. If only Fillmore himself would endorse the fusion effort, it might still be accomplished. On October 30—five days before the election—a worried Know-Nothing manager had written Fillmore to ask for approval of the plan. Fillmore replied weakly, "Do as our friends there think best." This provided little ammunition for Rayner and the advocates of the Union ticket to use in their efforts to have the straight ticket abandoned. The day before the election Rayner himself desperately telegraphed Fillmore: "I am convinced the defeat of Buchanan depends on depriving him of Pennsylvania. Can't you give me an intimation to be used here that you would be pleased to see your friends in this state united on the same ticket. This city will probably decide the vote of the state." Fillmore's enigmatic answer came quickly: "Success alone can justify any union; but that may my friends there determine." The wording of the first part of this message was crucial. Interpreting it as approval for his course, Rayner read the telegram to his final Philadelphia audience on the eve of the election, hoping against hope that it would sway the straight Fillmore men to support the Union ticket. The vote in Philadelphia might well determine how the state went, and upon Pennsylvania hinged James Buchanan's chances for the presidency.[27]

It was not to be. Buchanan swept the South and captured New Jersey, Indiana, Illinois, California, and Pennsylvania. Frémont carried the rest of the free states, leaving only Maryland to Fillmore. The election returns of 1856 proved, if nothing else, that Rayner was a political prognosticator of the first degree. In the electoral college, 149 votes constituted the minimum needed to elect a candidate. Buchanan received 174. With all of her twenty-seven votes going to the Democratic candidate, Pennsylvania indeed proved to be the difference in the election. Had the Union ticket succeeded, twenty-six of those votes would have been divided between Fillmore and Frémont, leaving Buchanan with 148—one electoral vote short of a majority. The contest would have gone to the House of Representatives, with Fillmore's election the likely result.

Rayner's frenzied campaigning in the City of Brotherly Love demonstrates how far he was willing to go to secure the defeat of Buchanan. Denying that he was pursuing fusion with the Republicans, Rayner later argued that "the purpose was to avoid fusion, and thus enable each party to ascertain its numerical strength at the ballot-box." Despite this distinction, Rayner's strategy was intended primarily to defeat Buchanan; it might have resulted in the election of Fillmore in the House, but it just as likely could have made Frémont the first Republican president. In the end, Rayner considered either of those options preferable to four more years of Democratic misrule.[28]

Three days after the election, Know-Nothing leaders in Philadelphia tendered Rayner a public dinner to express their gratitude for his work in the campaign. He was forced, however, to decline the honor, for events had taken an alarming turn in North Carolina. Word had spread of his advocacy of the Union ticket. Before Rayner left Philadelphia, Susan apparently had written or telegraphed, urging him to hurry home. The streets of Raleigh were abuzz with talk of personal violence against the man who had gone to Pennsylvania "to advise the American party *to a cohabitation with black Republicanism and Northern Sectionalism,* whose crusade aims the ASSASSIN'S KNIFE AT THE HEART OF NORTH-CAROLINA, as of every other State south of Mason and Dixon's line." Acts ranging from effigy-burnings, mob violence, death threats, and expulsion from the state were spoken of. One could not simply dismiss such talk as empty bluster, for just a month earlier a bright young professor at the University of North Carolina, Benjamin Sherwood Hedrick, had been forced to flee the state after admitting his preference for Frémont in the election. Rayner's old nemesis William Holden had orchestrated the persecution. Hedrick, however, was small game compared to the Big Potato.[29]

As soon as reports of Rayner's activities in Philadelphia had reached Raleigh, Holden had renewed his campaign of abuse and vilification. Under the Democratic editor's expert guidance, it soon escalated into the most vicious personal attack of Rayner's career and perhaps in the history of North Carolina. Holden not only reiterated all the old charges of Rayner being in league with traitors and abolitionists, but he also scoured the national press and reprinted their condemnatory editorials. The Democratic press repeated accusations that Rayner had gone to Philadelphia explicitly "to secure the election of John C. Frémont, and earn a seat in his cabinet." He was charged with neglecting his own state in order to attend black Republican caucuses and betray Fillmore. By the time he arrived back in Raleigh, the recriminations had grown so shrill that he felt compelled to take extreme measures. "I saw plainly," he later recalled, "that I must breast this storm, or succumb to it."[30]

On November 10 Rayner threw down the gauntlet before a large bipartisan outdoor crowd in Raleigh, pronouncing "that those who were uttering, sanctioning and endorsing the charges against me . . . were a pack of cowards, liars, and scoundrels." He stated that his purpose was "not to *provoke* a difficulty" with anyone. No doubt with Holden in mind, he claimed to "prefer peace" and wished only to define his position: "Whilst I shall studiously avoid giving personal offence to the unoffending—I shall be prepared to resist all assaults that may be made on my person or character." He began quietly wearing a pistol when venturing away from his home.[31]

More than a year earlier, at the time of bitter controversy that followed Rayner's Washington, D.C., speech, he had privately sent a message to Holden professing his desire for peace. Warning Holden that the *Standard*'s course was one "of violence and outrage not warranted by the rules of political opposition," Rayner proposed " 'a child's bargain' to Mr. Holden—that he will continue to let Mr. Holden alone, if he (Mr. H.) will let him alone— that the world is large enough for both of them, and there is no necessity for their coming in conflict." Holden responded by denying that he had been excessively harsh in his attacks. So things stood fourteen months later, when the Democratic campaign of denunciation entered its final and most scurrilous stage. Several days after issuing his public ultimatum, Rayner encountered Holden in a downtown store, where the accumulated tensions of eighteen months finally reached the breaking point. "Many bitter expressions were used on both sides," and the two men quickly came to blows. According to Holden, Rayner "endeavored to wield, with some effect, a heavy stick." Fortunately the pistol was not drawn. Neither of the combatants suffered physical injury, but the altercation only heightened the strained political atmosphere surrounding Rayner and his Democratic antagonists. Soon after the caning, Raleigh Democrats met in the capitol and drew up resolutions censuring Rayner's course during the election, saying that he had "forfeited the confidence and respect of all true Southern men." They also condemned the assault on Holden as "an unjustifiable and cowardly attempt to restrain the freedom of the press."[32]

The final phase of the drama was acted out on December 8, more than a month after the presidential election. On that evening a large audience from both parties gathered in the Hall of Commons to hear Rayner formally defend himself from accusations of treason to the South. He sat quietly while former Whig congressman Alfred Dockery explained the purpose of the meeting and introduced the featured speaker. Middle age and fine food and wine had added to Rayner's already stout frame, and his face bore the lines of a man who had fought too many battles against overwhelming odds. Dark, intense eyes glowered irritably from their sunken sockets. The broad forehead and resolute jaw were framed by thick, unruly hair and a closely trimmed beard. The audience of politicians and civic leaders grew quiet, and ladies watched with interest from the galleries as the embattled Rayner solemnly made his way to the podium. It was a remarkable change from the cheering, hysterical crowds that he had become accustomed to addressing over the past two years.[33]

After an introduction in which he compared his situation with that of the apostle Paul when arraigned before Festus and Agrippa, Rayner spoke of his accusers. "For them, and for the bitter hostility they have exhibited towards me, I have nothing but *defiance, contempt and scorn.* . . . When was it ever before known, that the entire party of a great State made war upon one man?" He presented a long history of the Democratic offensive against him, tracing its origin to the period immediately following the Know-Nothings' 1855 national convention. Yet the Democrats did not suffer alone in his analysis. The "conservative parties" of the United States, which he identified as the Whigs and Americans, had themselves possessed one "great defect"—"a want of *nerve.*" Their leaders too often had not measured up to the principles they professed to support. Rayner, however, suffered from no want of nerve on this occasion. He spoke out boldly in criticism of the lack of free speech in the South: "If it be treason in the South to say, that the mere election of Frémont would not have been valid cause for dissolving the Union—if that be treason, then my enemies may make the most of it. . . . Suppose Frémont had been elected—and the South had dissolved the Union in consequence— how should we have appeared in the eyes of posterity, on the page of history—if in appealing to the moral sense of the christian world, we should state our grievance to have been, that *we were beaten in an election?*"[34]

Rayner explained his course during election week in Philadelphia, again laboring to show that the Union ticket did not constitute fusion because it required no American to vote for a Republican. The politics of slavery occupied the final passages of his address: "I am proud to number among my friends—men who supported Frémont, not on account of any abolition proclivities, but because they considered him the most available candidate to beat Buchanan." Rayner followed this unpopular sentiment by reiterating a theme that had been a constant with him since the congressional days. The real enemies of the South and slavery, he contended, were the Democrats:

> I say here, boldly, what I have often said before: that the Democratic party, if not overthrown, will destroy slavery in the South, in less than a quarter of a century. I do not mean that such is their design, for I do not think so.
>
> But that party seems determined for political purposes, to keep up an endless agitation, on the subject of slavery. Just as soon as one slavery difficulty is settled, they reopen the agitation in some other shape. . . . And every Southern man who may then dare to oppose such policy, will be *tabooed* as an abolitionist. . . . The true interest of a slave-holding community is a defensive one. The moral sense of the christian world and of a large portion of our own country, is against us, in regard to slavery. We can't afford to be aggressive. We are in a minority. . . . This moral influence, of itself, would ultimately destroy the institution, if not counteracted by some other moral influence. Fortunately for us, we have the counteracting moral influence, in the respect and reverence of the world for the guaranties of constitutional compact and compromises, and in that sense of justice, which blames no people for evils entailed on them by their ancestors. The position of the slave-holding States is strong enough. It rests upon the Constitution.[35]

Rayner closed the address with some words about the fate of prophets: "It seems to be the development of one of the great laws of the Governor of all things that those who are in advance of the public opinion of their age, those who boldly assail evil in evil times, are always subjected to contumely, insult, and martyrdom." It had become clear to him that Americans of all parties and sections would continue to ignore the warnings he had been issuing for fifteen years about the inevitable consequences of sectional politics and reckless slavery agitation. Amid lukewarm applause, and looking "ill at ease and dissatisfied," he stepped from the podium into political retirement.[36]

Rayner's political career lay in ruins. He had gambled everything on the American party, which he viewed as the nation's last chance to reclaim the republican principles of the Revolutionary generation. As a leading Know-Nothing ideologue, he had tried to make the party a "conservative" party in the most literal sense of the word, that is, a party that would conserve a hallowed set of beliefs in the face of rapid change. But he believed that corruption on the part of demagogic politicians and their immigrant pawns, and the rising tide of unpatriotic sectional extremism both North and South, had seduced even the American party from its mission.

With the defeat of Know-Nothingism, Rayner could see little chance of avoiding the sectional bloodbath that he had long predicted. Whether they were northerners concerned with extending the theory of natural rights to blacks or southerners dedicated to the protection of slaveholders' property rights, very few Americans apprehended the cost in human lives that would be required to settle the conflict. But because he understood clearly that continuing the sectional agitation would bring war, Rayner refused to abandon the American party, even after it became apparent that its day as a political force was over. He knew, however, that in championing a cause that had failed to pass the South's test of racial fidelity, he had overstepped the limits of southern dissent. In his letter to the New York convention that nominated him for the vice-presidency, he had darkly alluded to what the future held for him personally. "For one, my destiny is linked to the cause of pure and unadulterated Americanism," he wrote. "In this bark I have shipped with my fortunes. . . . If, in the Providence of God, it is doomed to destruction, I will cling to the wreck, as long as there is a spar or a timber afloat, and when it goes down in the deep, I will be engulphed in the vortex." [37]

CHAPTER 6

"The Most Extraordinary Summerset in History"

As the nation careened toward disunion and civil war in the late 1850s, Kenneth Rayner's political course was marked by inconsistency, confusion, and, at times, irrationality. Following the defeat of Know-Nothingism, he became a politician without a party. Despised by the North Carolina Democrats, against whom he had waged relentless war for two decades, and resented by many Whigs, who blamed him for their party's decline and fall, he had become a political orphan, welcome in neither party. Although the American party had briefly captivated the Whig masses of North Carolina, it had failed to attract enough of the state's Democrats or new voters. After the national organization split asunder over the slavery issue, those who in the past had supported the American ticket found themselves disorganized and demoralized. And, in a replay of the events of 1852, Rayner's outspoken independence had cast him as scapegoat. Such deviation from the South's racial orthodoxy and its standards of partisan conduct could leave a man a political outcast. Rayner, who had cooperated with Republicans in Philadelphia in 1856, had overstepped the limits of southern dissent.

Nobody delighted more in this state of affairs than his Democratic opponents. When the time came in late 1858 for the "Whig-Americans" to nominate candidates for the U.S. Senate, Rayner was passed over in favor of the Whig patriarchs George Badger and William Graham. "This is indeed a strange world," commented one Democrat in Holden's *Standard*. Identifying himself only as "Nestor," the editorialist wrote facetiously of the injustice done to Rayner, noting that Rayner was "covered *all over* with wounds received" in the past few years' battles against the Democrats but now was shunned by his own party. "While *he* was fighting and leading on the forlorn hope of that party, where were they who are now thought the only men worthy of honor, emolument, rank, position?" Nestor asked. "What were *they* doing to insure victory or save their friends, when defeated, from being cut to pieces by the victorious enemy?" It was a fair question. "I really pity Rayner," concluded the editorialist. "He deserves sympathy for the injustice done him."[1]

Rayner himself was tempted to give up altogether on politics. Corresponding with the Know-Nothing propagandist Anna Ella Carroll in mid-1857, he confessed that "since the result of the late Presidential election was known, I have felt so depressed in regard to the prospects of the future, that I have mingled but little in the political world—but have been attending to my own domestic affairs." His spirit, he claimed, remained "unconquered as ever," and he was still "ready to do battle for the great cause" of Americanism whenever he could "see an efficient blow can be struck." But the opportunities to strike such blows did not come very often.[2]

Rayner's political views in the late 1850s seemed oddly irrelevant in a national political environment in which the chief issue had become either the defense or the criticism of slavery. His political writings of this period harped upon the theme of corruption, which assumed many forms: government patronage "prostituted for political purposes," influence-peddling in Congress by "mammoth corporations" and "millionaire speculators," and rampant voter fraud. But the worst kind of corruption, as Rayner had long believed, was sectionalism itself. The Democratic party's "continued and systematic agitation of the question of slavery, merely to subserve party purposes," had brought the nation to the brink of disunion.

Rayner harbored an intense bitterness over the treatment dissenters received in the South. Drawing upon his own experience, he wrote in 1858 of how "the reign of terror which party proscription has installed over public opinion in the south" had caused dissenters like himself to be "reviled and stigmatized as false to its interests and traitors to its cause." He placed the blame for this squarely on the Democrats. It was the national Democratic party—not just southern Democrats—who had supported such measures as the Kansas-Nebraska Act; Stephen Douglas, Franklin Pierce, and James Buchanan were northerners. He also felt that public opinion in the North unjustly held the South, "*as a section,*" responsible for all the slavery agitation. "The cant phrase of 'the slave power' is frequently applied to us without discrimination," he complained. The great error under which the North labored was its belief that the South was monolithic in its opinions. "*It is not the south,* but the self-styled democratic party, that has committed these wrongs," Rayner emphasized. "It is *not* the 'slave power,' but the self-styled

Democratic power, that keeps the two sections of the Union embroiled on this question of slavery. It is *not* the people of the south but the self-styled Democratic party of the south, that keeps up the slavery agitation by party concert, and for party ends." [3]

Such are the beliefs and attitudes Rayner took with him into the final phase of the sectional crisis. Never had he portrayed himself as an unconditional Unionist, a man who would stand by the Union under any circumstance. Virtually all of his efforts over his thirty-year public career had been directed toward reforming the political system to prevent the sections from becoming irreparably divided—efforts aimed at insuring that the North would never have to wage war on the South, and the South would not have to defend itself. Rather than deny the necessity of revolt against northern aggression, he had instead battled to keep that aggression from occurring. At the heart of his efforts lay attitudes that can be summarized plainly: The hundreds of thousands of black slaves in the South were grossly unprepared for—although theoretically capable of—exercising the responsibilities of freemen. Therefore, slavery, although an evil, must for the foreseeable future be preserved at all costs, lest the freed slaves drag down American civilization with them. The final national triumph of a purely sectional party would almost certainly mean civil war, a war that would be a protracted and bloody affair that would probably result in the ruin of the South and the abolition of slavery. Holding these views as the critical year 1860 approached, the reality was that sectionalism, despite Rayner's best efforts, was in the final stage of consolidating its victory. [4]

Soon that reality struck nearer to home than Rayner could ever have imagined, and he was ill-prepared to meet it. Following the disastrous 1858 elections that saw the Democrats virtually sweep the field in North Carolina, the state's Whigs and Americans regrouped and reestablished their organization, calling it the Opposition party. Rayner took no part in the reorganization, and as of late 1859 he confessed that he had paid "little attention to what has been going on in the world . . . in regard to political affairs." In its attempts to reorganize the party on the broadest base possible, however, the Whig hierarchy reluctantly named him to the party's state executive committee. After all the tribulations of the past several years, Opposition leaders were nonetheless forced to recognize Rayner's personal popularity among the Whig-American rank and file, at least in his old congressional district. They needed him—if he would behave. In February 1860 the Hertford County anti-Democratic forces appointed their former representative as a delegate to the Opposition state convention. Although skeptical of its purposes, Rayner agreed to attend the Raleigh meeting. [5]

The convention, heralded by Whigs and Americans as the rebirth of a viable anti-Democratic party in the state, introduced a revolutionary new issue into North Carolina politics. Over Rayner's objections the delegates drafted a platform calling for the ad valorem taxation of slaves. Throughout the state's history, slave property had been subject to a flat-rate poll tax in the same amount as that placed upon whites. At the beginning of the 1850s that rate stood at twenty cents, with freed slaves paying it for themselves and masters for each slave they owned. By the end of the decade the tax had increased fourfold to eighty cents. Only land was taxed on an ad valorem basis. Still, many people who did not hold slaves believed with some justification that they shouldered a disproportionate share of the state's tax burden. Whigs astutely realized that ad valorem could serve as the perfect "hobby" on which they might ride to victory at the polls.[6]

Rayner was horrified by the convention's action. Again he was about to run afoul of Badger, Graham, and the Whig patriarchs. Changing the method of taxation would require a change in the state constitution, something that Rayner had consistently opposed. As in 1835, when he voted against adoption of the new constitution, and again in the early 1850s, when he objected to the Democratic move to erase the traditional property requirements for voting in state senatorial elections, he felt that any tampering with the time-honored charter of the founders was unwise and unnecessary. "Having been a member of the Convention of 1835 . . . I feel that I am particularly called on to resist this movement," he wrote in March 1860. But his objections to ad valorem went beyond theoretical questions of original intent or his moral obligation as one of the framers of the 1835 constitution. Rayner primarily opposed it because he believed it represented, for the first time in any concrete sense, an attempt to reorganize state politics on the basis of a slavery-related consideration. Ad valorem threatened to array slaveholder against yeoman, rich against poor, neighbor against neighbor. Worst of all, by thrusting an emotional issue connected with slavery to the forefront of state politics, it would legitimize slavery as an appropriate topic for political debate among North Carolinians. This was exactly the sort of movement that Rayner had spent so many years trying to discourage in national politics.[7]

Despite Rayner's vehement opposition, the convention adopted the measure by a large margin. Soon after the meeting adjourned, he traveled to Hertford County on plantation business. The week he spent in the eastern part of the state gave him time to reflect on the convention's decision and to sound out public opinion. His travels only strengthened his concern about the "mischievous consequences" that ad valorem threatened. On his return trip he took time to write to his old law mentor, Democratic chief justice Thomas

Ruffin. Their close friendship had never been affected by their political differences, and now they found themselves on the same side. "I have publicly given notice to our people in Hertford that I will resist the thing; and I mean to do it with all the character, influence, and ability I possess," Rayner wrote, adding matter-of-factly, "of course I may expect nothing but denunciation in return." Imploring Ruffin to come to Raleigh to confer with him, he shrewdly evaluated what the upcoming campaign would bring. "There will be a desperate effort made to revolutionize the State, upon the *ad-valorem* principle of taxation. The attempt will be made to carry it in the West, by getting up a furor against the *negroes* in the East. In the East, it is to be urged on the ground of its being a poor man's law. Much as I dislike the word, you may rely on it we are in a *crisis.*" Rayner urged that "the conservative men without reference to *past* party issues confer together" to save the state from its own version of slavery agitation. "This movement, as I honestly believe, contains the mischievous elements of Seward's 'irrepressible conflict,' brought home to us."[8]

The Opposition's embrace of ad valorem placed Rayner in the nearly unbearable position (for him) of agreeing with North Carolina Democrats on the leading issue of the day. Holden editorialized in the *Standard* that "the Hon. K. Rayner, who has fought so many battles for Whiggery and Know Nothingism—who has given the Democracy more hard knocks, and received them more in return than any man in the State—refuses to sustain *ad valorem,* and openly avows his opposition to it." But according to Holden, Rayner had been "whipped into the traces before, and if the interests of Messrs. Graham and Badger require it he may have to pull in harness again." Holden facetiously warned Rayner to "take care," because Badger's and Graham's "drill sergeants" were following his every move, preparing to read him out of the party if he complained too vigorously.[9]

Opposition leaders, in fact, apparently had foreseen the possibility of Rayner's revolt, and as insurance the convention had appointed him as one of the state's delegates to the upcoming Baltimore convention of the party's national counterpart, the Constitutional Union party. He thus either had to buckle to the pressure and adhere to his party's state platform, including ad valorem, or to decline the nomination as national delegate. The Raleigh *Register* acknowledged Holden's comments on the rift in the Opposition ranks and definitively stated that one's stance on ad valorem constituted the test of fidelity not only to the state Opposition party but also to the national anti-Democratic organization as represented by the Constitutional Union party. "In regard to the 'hard *knocks*' which Mr. Rayner has given to the Democrats, we humbly defer to the editor of the Standard's more enlarged and practical experience on *that* subject," the *Register*'s John Syme snidely added.[10]

Whigs might try to joke about the Rayner-Holden caning incident of 1856 in an effort to deflect attention from Rayner's displeasure over ad valorem, but they knew he could cause serious problems if that disaffection turned into open revolt. In April, matters took a turn for the worse as Rayner was indeed forced to decline the appointment as delegate to the Baltimore convention because he could not support the party in its upcoming state campaign. Soon it was being rumored in North Carolina that Rayner would not sustain the Constitutional Union party's national ticket and that he actually intended to support the southern Democratic presidential ticket. "If this be true," exclaimed Kemp Battle, an Opposition leader, "it is the most extraordinary summerset in history."[11]

The rumors persisted well into the summer as the rift between Rayner and the Opposition party widened. The gubernatorial election had become a bitterly contested referendum on ad valorem, with Rayner's old Whig friend from neighboring Pasquotank County, John Pool, running on the Opposition's pro-ad valorem platform and incumbent governor John Ellis seeking reelection and leading the Democrats' fight against ad valorem. As Rayner had predicted, the Opposition's determination to link the state race inextricably to national politics resulted in a significant recasting of party lines, especially among slaveholding Whigs. Capitalizing on Rayner's dilemma, Democrats made overtures to him to announce publicly his conversion to the Democratic party at an upcoming mass meeting. "Great God!" wrote one Opposition editor in Hertford County, "has it come to this? that the Democratic party has got so low that it is compelled to implore and beg the aid of Kenneth Rayner . . . to save them from inevitable defeat?" The editor plainly expressed Opposition disbelief in the rumors, saying that "the Sun will turn to green cheese . . . [before] Kenneth Rayner, the idol of our hearts," would support a Democrat. "Kenneth Rayner address a Democratic Mass Meeting!! Great God, what a preposterousness!!!"[12]

For the first time in his life, Rayner did in fact support the Democratic gubernatorial candidate in the August elections, and Ellis managed to win a surprisingly close contest against the pro-ad valorem Pool. In Hertford County, Pool eked out only a narrow forty-six-vote majority, indicating that the county's traditional Whig loyalties had been seriously undermined by ad valorem and Rayner's opposition to it. But the presidential election was still three months away, and the furor over ad valorem, combined with the breakup of the national Democratic party into northern and southern factions, resulted in a complex scrambling of party lines and traditional political ties. No one, including Rayner, knew what to expect from the future.[13]

For perhaps the first time in his career, Rayner was at a loss about what course he should pursue. His confusion and frustration can be clearly traced in his public and private correspondence in the weeks and months before the November election. As late as November 1859 Rayner had still clung to hopes that conservative men from both sections, including moderate Republicans in the North, would find some way to cooperate honorably in the resolution of the sectional crisis. For example, Rayner privately advocated the election of Thomas Corwin as speaker of the House, calling the Ohio Republican leader "a national conservative patriot." He even corresponded with Corwin himself in the spring of 1860, discussing some sort of fusion between old Whigs, Know-Nothings, and moderate Republicans—perhaps the same kind of arrangement that Rayner had worked for in Philadelphia in 1856. Corwin replied in April that he had labored hard "to bring about the results" Rayner desired and pleaded with him to attend the Constitutional Union convention to work for such a fusion. "The great end we all have at heart is, if possible, to unite the vote of the Union party with that of the Republicans," Corwin told his southern friend.[14]

At the time of the state Opposition convention, Rayner likewise had made public—or as public as he dared—this conviction that moderate Republicans posed no greater threat to the nation than did Democrats. The convention had framed a resolution commending the state's congressional delegation for supporting a Democrat over a Republican in the recent speaker's contest. Rayner took the floor to say that he placed "no more confidence in the Democratic party, in regard to the question of slavery, than he had in the Black Republican party. The Opposition," he stated, "should not have voted for a Democrat for the purpose of defeating a Republican." Because at this point he was still slated to attend the Constitutional Union party's national convention, he made it clear that under no circumstances would he vote for a Democrat at that gathering. This refusal, in addition to his opposition to ad valorem, probably influenced his decision to ignore Corwin's pleadings and not attend the Baltimore convention.[15]

Clearly, Rayner's position by the fall of 1860 was a grim one. Unable to attend the Constitutional Union convention because of his disagreements with his fellow Whig-Americans at home, he could only stand by helplessly and see any hope disappear of achieving a viable national conservative coalition of the sort he and Corwin envisioned. The northern Democrats had nominated Stephen A. Douglas, and the southern Democrats had named their own candidate, Vice-President John C. Breckinridge. It would have been difficult to say which man Rayner despised the most. In contrast, he had great respect for the Constitutional Union candidates, his old Whigs friends John Bell of Tennessee and Edward Everett of Massachusetts, but the Bell-Everett ticket's chances of winning were nonexistent. The North, as Rayner well knew, would vote for the Republican nominee, Abraham Lincoln, in a solid phalanx. His victory, if it happened, would mean civil war.[16]

Following the August state elections, the Democratic press in Hertford County reported that Rayner was committed to Breckinridge in the fall. Finally feeling the need to explain his position, Rayner composed a public letter in which he denied supporting the South's Democratic standard-bearer. But his denial was strangely qualified. "So far as any committal may be involved in the expression of my opinions and purposes in conversation, that committal has been in favor of Bell and Everett," Rayner noted. "But I am in fact, committed to no one, any farther than my convictions of duty to my country, dependent upon the developments of the next month or six weeks, may regulate and govern my course."

The explanation that followed was that of a man whose political options had reached the vanishing point. At the outset he made it clear that "every patriot, North as well as South, should try to prevent" Lincoln's election. "I speak not of his anti-slavery sentiments, which alone are odious enough to repel every national man in every section of the country," Rayner noted. "I speak more particularly of consequences which *must* in all probability follow his election." If Lincoln were elected president, "a dissolution of the Union can hardly be avoided." Rayner did not want to discuss the question of whether disunion was right or wrong, or even what means Lincoln might use to force the seceding states back into the Union. The only question facing patriotic Americans at this point was how to prevent the impending civil war that Lincoln's election was certain to inaugurate. There could be but one answer, repugnant though it might be: defeat Lincoln, even if it meant supporting a Democrat.

Rayner held out one slender chance for Lincoln's defeat, and thus for postponement of the war. He made it known that he favored a plan whereby all the southern states would agree to run one slate of electors, leaving those electors uncommitted to any one candidate. Therefore, when the electoral votes were cast, the southern electors could join forces with anti-Lincoln states in the North—perhaps New York—on a common candidate. This was the only conceivable way Lincoln could be beaten. Perhaps North Carolina could set this plan in motion. Rayner realized how far-fetched the plan was, but desperate times made desperate men. However, he also explained how he would vote if the fusion plan could not be worked out. If any of the announced candidates would "afford reasonable grounds of hope that he may compete formidably with Lincoln," Rayner would feel compelled to vote for that candidate. But if Lincoln's election was as inevitable as it appeared to be, Rayner would vote for John Bell out of "personal regard" for the Tennessean. Rayner thus frankly summarized his position as of August 1860: "I commit myself absolutely to no man, and to no party. As I have before said, I don't know, I can't possibly foresee what a sense of duty may require of me."

Before closing his letter, Rayner provided what would serve as a poignant postscript to a thirty-year career spent in defense of republican principles as he interpreted them:

> As to mere party trammels, they have no hold on me—nor do I mean they shall have, whilst the very existence of the government and its institutions are in peril. As to the old Whig party, I spent the morning of my days in fighting its battles. It had no more loyal subject, no more faithful servant, no more affectionate son, than me. I honored and loved it while it lived, I grieved with an unaffected sorrow when it died. . . . I intend to stand at guard over its grave. . . .
>
> As to the American party, I am guilty of no vain pretension when I say that I performed more labor in its service, incurred more pecuniary loss, made greater sacrifices of time, of personal comfort, and encountered more contumely and vilification in its cause, than any man in North Carolina. What I said and did in its support were from the honest impulses of my head and heart. I declared in a published letter four years ago that I would abide by its fortunes—that if it was doomed to shipwreck, I would either cling to the last plank that floated, or that I would be engulphed in its vortex. I was as good as my word. It did encounter shipwreck; I was among the last on deck; and since then I have been buffeted by the winds and the waves, without sympathy or compassion on the part of those in whose cause I had labored so hard and endured so much. Times have changed, and issues have changed. The old issues, which divided public opinion in the days of the Whig party, and those which were represented by the "American" party, are no longer living issues. They belong to the past. . . .
>
> As to the "Constitutional Union" party, no matter how pure and patriotic may have been the motives and aims of those who organized it, yet it [is] a mere negation. The fact that it laid down no code of prin-

ciples, no political creed, shows that its founders regarded its mission as one of prevention of evil rather than of positive action for good. . . . At the present time, something higher than this calls for the most serious and anxious consideration of the people of this great Republic. This issue is not what system of governmental policy shall prevail in the administration of our affairs, but whether the government itself shall stand on those foundations whereon our fathers placed it. If this storm shall, in the mercy of God, happily pass over—and our government be left to us unchanged and unharmed; then, in regard to the system of policy hereafter to be pursued by its administration, with the independence of a freeman, who acts and thinks for himself, I shall identify with whatever organization I may regard as most conservative in its character, most loyal to the constitution, and as most fully representing the genius and spirit of our free institutions.

A few weeks later Abraham Lincoln was elected sixteenth president of the United States, and Kenneth Rayner relinquished hope that the Union could be saved. Nevertheless, he did not advocate immediate secession. South Carolina was the first state to sever its ties with the Union, doing so on December 20. The same week Rayner made a hasty trip to Hertford County to oversee winter hog-slaughtering at Little Town. While there, he "tried to sound public opinion, as it exists among the plain country people." Returning to Raleigh, he reported to Ruffin on Christmas Day that he was "mortified" to find that the feeling in Hertford and surrounding counties "was in great measure in favour of 'the Union at any and all hazards'—in other words, unqualified submission." People who did not hold slaves, he discovered, "were swearing that they 'would not lift a finger to protect rich men's negroes.'" Rayner attributed the hostility of his neighbors to the "mischief done last summer, by the advocates of 'ad-valorem.'" He believed that the Whigs, in their zeal to regain office, had "infused among the ignorant poor, the idea that there is an antagonism between poor people and slave-owners—in other words Seward's 'irrepressible conflict,' was insidiously preached." And in those places where ad valorem sentiment had been the strongest, the "feeling of absolute submission to abolition outrage" was the most pronounced.[17]

Publicly Rayner had kept rather quiet since the elections. As late as the year's end few people outside his private circle of friends knew where he stood on the secession question.[18] If North Carolinians were uncertain about his position, it is not surprising that politicians in the North believed him still to be unconditionally for the Union. John W. Forney of the influential Philadelphia *Press* had speculated two months earlier that Rayner would be willing to accept a position in Lincoln's cabinet. Evidently Seward believed the same, for on Christmas Day—ironically, the same day that Rayner had complained so bitterly to Ruffin about "Seward's 'irrepressible conflict'" having been "insidiously preached" in Hertford County—Seward himself wrote to President-elect Lincoln suggesting that he name Rayner to a cabinet post. Upon receipt of Seward's letter, Lincoln vaguely replied that he had considered Rayner along with three others, "but not very definitely." In subsequent discussions with Vice-President-elect Hannibal Hamlin, Lincoln again "in a general way mentioned" Rayner's name, but he pursued the possibility no further.[19]

It was just as well, for Rayner almost certainly would not have accepted a post in the Lincoln administration. By February 1, 1861, the seven states of the lower South had seceded, and North Carolina was debating whether to follow them. In his Christmas Day letter to Ruffin, Rayner had expressed his original intention to be a candidate for the state secession convention if one were to be called, but after gauging the strength of unconditional Unionism in Hertford, he had come to doubt whether he could be elected. He believed that Hertford's voters, who had not dealt him a defeat in more than twenty-five years, would sustain no man unless he pledged himself "to the maintenance of the Union at all hazards, and under all circumstances." Rayner would not do that. "Although a decided Union-man in sentiment," he wrote, "—although ready to make any reasonable sacrifices and delays, in order to save it; yet, I have no hesitation in saying, that I will surrender the Union rather than surrender the equality of my State with the other states, or our rights and property under the Constitution." He was willing to wait until Lincoln "developed his policy" to proceed with secession. He entertained little doubt, however, about what that policy would be. If civil war indeed were coming, it would not do for North Carolina to remain indecisive too long. Rayner dreaded the war, but if it came, he intended for the South to do everything in its power to win.[20]

The state legislature did finally call an election submitting the question of a convention to the voters and providing for the election of delegates in case the question was decided in the affirmative. On February 28, North Carolinians narrowly rejected the call for a convention. Thinking he could not be elected, Rayner had chosen not to enter the contest for a delegate's seat. And so it would have turned out, for Hertford voters returned a fifty-three-vote majority against holding the convention and elected an unconditional Unionist as their delegate. The victorious opponents of secession considered the question of disunion settled, at least until Lincoln made some overt move against southern rights. With the question of secession temporarily settled, and perhaps wishing to divert his attention from the spectacle of the Union disintegrating around him, Rayner departed for his plantation in Arkansas.[21]

Events proceeded at a dizzying pace during his absence. A hastily called peace conference in Washington had failed to result in a workable adjustment of the secession crisis, and on April 12, South Carolina troops opened fire on the Union garrison at Fort Sumter in Charleston Harbor. The Civil War had begun. Rayner later related the story of how he heard the news. "I was standing on the bank of the Mississippi, waiting for a boat, on my return home," he recalled. "As the boat approached the shore, the captain cried out from the upper deck, that 'Fort Sumpter has fallen.' 'Yes,' " remarked Rayner to a man standing next to him, " 'and I fear the South has fallen with it.' " [22]

CHAPTER 7

"Some Strange and Unaccountable Influence"

Rayner returned home to Raleigh to find that "a tremendous revolution in public opinion had taken place" on the question of secession. Within two weeks of Sumter's fall and Lincoln's subsequent call for seventy-five thousand volunteers to suppress the rebellion, the state legislature passed a bill calling for a secession convention. Rayner was not present on May 9 when the citizens of Hertford County nominated him as their delegate to the convention, the unconditional Unionist candidate having withdrawn his name from consideration. Rayner's election was nearly unanimous. Voters who for twenty-five years had called on him to represent their strong Unionist sympathies in Raleigh and Washington now summoned him—for the last time—to help take their state out of the Union.[1]

Although he had been convinced of the war's inevitability since Lincoln's election, Rayner made the transformation from Union man to outspoken secessionist only after the northern call for troops. When the convention assembled in Raleigh on May 20, the delegates required just one day of debate to pass an ordinance of secession by a unanimous vote, making North Carolina the last southern state to decide to leave the Union and join the Confederacy. In a very real and tragic sense, the secession crisis of 1860–61 had turned Rayner's world upside down. Although his own accounts of the events of 1861 date primarily from the postwar period when he had a vested interest in putting his actions in the best possible light, it is necessary to view his torturous course during the 1860 elections and his eventual advocacy of secession in 1861 in the context of twenty-five years as an uncompromising foe of sectionalism and disunion. Rayner had devoted the best years of his life to preserving the Union on the basis established by the Founding Fathers and the Constitution. When the vast majority of his countrymen repudiated the republican ideology that had informed his actions and beliefs for a lifetime and, as a result, the Union crumbled, he was unable to envision how any new order of things might ever rise from the ruins.

Rayner's story offers unique insight into the psychology of Unionism and secessionism. After the war he sometimes conveniently failed to mention his support of disunion when it was politically expedient to do so. But in his twenty-page application for amnesty in 1865, there was no hiding his vote for secession. Rayner set the scene; it was May 1861, Lincoln had called for troops, "and the cry for resistance was wide-spread and universal": "This fever, this moral epidemic, swept over the country like a tempest before which the entire populace seemed to succumb. And thus . . . some way or somehow, by some strange and unaccountable influence, which I can not comprehend, I soon found myself being swept along by this irresistible current. I found that I had imbibed this moral poison, without being able to understand the why or the wherefore." [2]

In short, he was suggesting that his actions had been irrational—a kind of madness. Had such an explanation come from one whose antebellum Unionism was questionable, who had warmly supported Breckinridge in the 1860 elections, or who hated all Republicans, it would sound hypocritical at best. But as the preceding account has shown, Rayner steadfastly had resisted secession and the sectionalization of national politics at least until Lincoln's election and even thereafter had been "ready to make any reasonable sacrifices and delays, in order to save" the Union. In both 1856 and 1860 he had been anxious to see some sort of alliance effected between moderate Republicans and southern conservatives. However, his own actions in the final stages of the secession crisis and throughout the war itself provide the most convincing proof that his self-analysis contained a large measure of truth. Whether through personal weakness or the overwhelming pressure to conform—or some combination of both—events had come to control Rayner instead of his controlling them. Testing the limits of southern dissent could take a heavy psychological toll.

His utterances in the spring of 1861 concerning the South's need to resist any overt act of northern aggression were not truly inconsistent with his long-standing opinion that secession was a viable option in the last extremity. But he had long held the conviction that secession was not a constitutional remedy; it was, in Rayner's words, "nothing but the right to fight—the right of revolution." And throughout the antebellum period most Unionist Whigs in the state had agreed with him. When the secession convention met, the delegates immediately confronted this very question. Would they frame an ordinance declaring it their constitutional right to repeal the state's ratification of the 1787 federal Constitution, or would they simply declare independence from the United States based on the right of revolution? Both points of view were clearly represented at the convention. The first test came when the revolutionists nominated William A. Graham as convention president. The constitutionalists nominated Weldon N. Edwards. Inexplicably, Rayner voted for Edwards, who was elected. The convention next voted on opposing ordinances designed to sever the state's ties with the Union. Again Rayner supported the constitutionalist measure over its revolutionist counterpart, negating a stance that he had held for twenty years. Bells were soon ringing and guns booming to announce secession to the people of Raleigh, and Rayner had given the first indication of that "strange and unaccountable influence" that would carry him in an often-irrational course along with his section down the path to defeat and ruin.[3]

Reading Rayner's correspondence from the early years of the war, one finds nothing to suggest that he had ever been anything but a fire-eating secessionist. In the convention—which essentially ran the state government until May 1862—and as a private citizen, he consistently championed measures intended to bolster the war effort and Confederate unity. "I am still of [the] opinion that we ought to *fight them—fight them* and continue to fight them," he wrote after the first skirmishes of 1861. Although he doubted the propriety of mass conscription, he did not hesitate to advocate it in the event of an actual invasion by the North. "Necessity will then override every other consideration."[4]

Like other southerners, Rayner followed the news of military victories and setbacks with alternating enthusiasm and discouragement. But unlike many other North Carolinians (especially the state's Unionists) who criticized the Confederate government for exercising its power in a high-handed manner, he faulted it for not pursuing the fight with the Yankees more vigorously. Jefferson Davis was too much a southern gentleman in a war against a ruthless foe, Rayner believed. In early 1862 the invasion he had feared finally materialized. Union troops under the command of General Ambrose E. Burnside mounted a successful amphibious invasion of the northeastern coast and gained control of Pamlico and Albemarle sounds. The Yankees seized Roanoke Island and New Berne and established a solid military presence across much of Rayner's old congressional district. In February an expedition touched as far north as Hertford's county seat, Winton, just a few miles up river from Rayner's landing on the Chowan River. Union troops never went ashore at his plantation, but the gunboats constantly patrolled up and down the river, keeping local planters nervous and inciting many slaves to run away.[5]

Distressed by these developments, in early December 1862 Rayner wrote a long letter to Jefferson Davis, whom he had known personally for many years as a Democratic opponent to Whiggery and Know-Nothingism. Cataloging the many "outrages" and "barbarities" perpetrated by the Yankees in his home region, Rayner implored Davis to adopt an ironhanded policy of retaliation. Union troops caught on southern soil, trying to carry out Lincoln's Emancipation Proclamation, he insisted, "should be regarded as savages and outlaws, and if taken with arms in their hands should suffer death." Rayner admitted that it was "a *very, very* difficult question. It is a dreadful, a horrid alternative. But so is all war, no matter how humanely conducted."[6]

Two weeks later Rayner was delighted by Davis's proclamation branding Union general Benjamin F. Butler an outlaw and forbidding the parole of any Yankee officer until the general had been caught and hanged. Butler had executed a southern citizen in New Orleans for tearing down the Union flag, and Rayner shared in the outrage felt by almost all southerners in connection with the act. Reading Davis's proclamation, Rayner exclaimed, "It is just the very thing! The more I study Davis' character, the better I think of him." Rayner, who before the war had hated Jefferson Davis's party "with a perfect hatred," suddenly became profuse in his praise for the "philosophic statesman" in the Confederate White House. Davis had "at last taken his position. He will not be moved from it! If Butler is ever taken, he will die, 'by hanging'!!"[7]

Jefferson Davis a philosophic statesman! It was indeed a strange world in which Rayner found himself. But by mid-1863 his enthusiasm was beginning to wane. In March of that year he admitted feeling "gloomy" about the progress of the southern struggle. The northern congress had given Lincoln the financial as well as military power to continue the war on a massive scale, and Rayner concluded that the war was certain to last at least another year, barring a revolution in the North. Davis had rescinded a recent order calling for retaliation for Yankee atrocities in Missouri. "Between you and me," Rayner now told Thomas Ruffin, "I fear Davis has not enough of old Genl. Jackson in him, to suit this crisis." He also was becoming increasingly alarmed about the state of the southern economy. Southern securities were depreciating rapidly, and Rayner feared that even if the Confederacy could survive another year of war, the mountain of debt would drag the nation down: "To me, the future looks dark and forbidding."[8]

Anxiety over the war and the press of personal and family business were beginning to tell on Rayner by the late spring of 1863. His family life in the preceding several years had not been easy. True, he and Susan had two more sons, William and Hamilton, born in 1857 and 1860, respectively. But the family had also been stricken by tragedy in 1859 with the death of yet another child, their eldest son, Henry Albert, the third Rayner child to die before reaching adolescence. Kenneth and Susan were again grief-stricken in June 1863, when a close family friend, Robin Jones, was killed in battle.[9]

In addition to these blows, the war brought great personal financial worries. Virtually all of the family fortune was invested in land and slaves. The repeated Yankee incursions into the Albemarle country seriously jeopardized Rayner's plantation in Hertford County, and Union armies threatened to disrupt planting operations in Arkansas. In July 1862 he was forced to have between $25,000 and $30,000 worth of cotton burned at the Arkansas plantation to prevent its falling into enemy hands. When Union gunboats made their appearance on the Mississippi near his property later that year, he narrowly managed to have his slaves evacuated to a safe location twenty-eight miles from the river. To make things worse, a violent hailstorm completely destroyed his 1862 crop in Hertford County. At the end of May 1863, Rayner's health broke under the strain. As he waited anxiously for news from the siege at Vicksburg, he was bedridden with what he described as *"nervous irritability & excitement."* By the year's end his malady, a "terrible *neuralgia,"* was causing him serious problems. "I very much fear, that all my capacity for usefulness, is about at an end," he confided to Ruffin, "I can[']t stand the least exposure."[10]

Political developments in North Carolina did little to ease his affliction. Because he had strongly supported secession and the war effort once Lincoln called for troops, Rayner had become identified with the southern rights faction in Raleigh. After the initial euphoria surrounding secession subsided, the state's politics again settled into a rough two-party system. Ironically, the Unionist faction was now led by Holden, who for a decade before the war had been the shrillest southern-rights voice in North Carolina. Holden's party adopted the label "Conservative," and according to Rayner the *Standard* became "perfectly rabid" in its criticism of the secessionists. "What a shame it is to see an attempt," he wrote in July 1862, "to get up a bitter party contest in the midst of a war!" He observed that the Conservative movement would likely succeed in capturing the state, for its supporters were "working like beavers" to have their candidate, former Whig Zebulon Vance, elected governor. The southern rights men, in contrast, were disorganized and apathetic.[11]

His prediction was born out when the Conservatives captured all the state offices, elected Graham to the Confederate senate, and began turning out all appointees who did not agree with Holden and Vance. The Conservatives did not advocate an end to the war or a return to the Union, but they did seek to strengthen the power of the state at the expense of the central Confederate government. For the remainder of the war they would oppose stringent war measures such as conscription and the suspension of habeas corpus. "The heart sickens at the sight of such doings," Rayner complained soon after the elections. "Never, never, in the worst days of party bitterness, did I witness any intolerance to be compared with it."[12]

By mid-1863 many North Carolina Conservatives had become so emboldened by their success that they began to talk, first in whispers and soon openly, about peace. Holden led and encouraged such talk. He stopped short of explicitly advocating a Confederate surrender or the state's immediate return to the Union, but his outspoken editorials soon had Unionists throughout the state holding peace meetings and discussing the best means of ending the bloodshed. Rayner's opposition to the peace movement and his continued support of the war effort undoubtedly sprang in part from his own pecuniary interests that were so tied to Confederate success, but they were also influenced by his closeness to his brother-in-law Leonidas Polk, who by then was a lieutenant general in the Confederate army. Rayner and Polk corresponded during the war, apprising one another of political and military developments from their respective vantage points. The "Fighting Bishop" communicated to Rayner his deep concerns about the conduct of the war—especially the incompetence of President Davis and General Braxton Bragg—and his alarm over the peace movement in his native state. "An eye should be placed on these men," Polk told Rayner in an August 1863 reference to the peace agitators, "and the strongest measures adopted to put it down." Polk was horrified to learn from General Bragg (who in turn had heard it from his brother, former North Carolina governor and Confederate attorney general Thomas Bragg) that Holden wished a return to the Union and that Graham supported him. "Can this be so?" Polk asked Rayner in disbelief.[13]

By the end of 1863 the peace movement had assumed such proportions that even Conservative Governor Vance concluded that Holden had gone too far. In January 1864 Holden introduced resolutions at a peace meeting suggesting that North Carolina might have to withdraw from the Confederacy if the "despotism" of the central government continued. This meeting sparked a series of similar gatherings across the state, and Vance promptly broke with Holden. Holden responded by announcing that he would oppose Vance in the 1864 state gubernatorial election.[14]

Holden hoped to force the legislature into calling a state convention to consider his peace proposals. The Confederacy's worsening military prospects and the terrible conflict brewing in North Carolina politics virtually paralyzed Rayner, both mentally and physically. He wrote to Thomas Ruffin that "something must be done and that speedily, if anything is to be done" about the movement to call a convention. "Talking about it and ridiculing the movement, are about as vain and insufficient a method of dealing with this difficulty, as is reading the riot act to an infuriated mob." [15]

His mysterious illness continued almost unabated into 1864, keeping him confined mostly to his house. In February he shook off his lassitude sufficiently to write three editorials that were published in the newly established southern-rights paper, the Raleigh *Confederate*. In them he argued against the peace movement and the convention-calling scheme from a constitutional standpoint, insisting in a manner reminiscent of his nationalistic congressional speeches that the central government possessed the needed power to enforce conscription laws and suspend habeas corpus in extraordinary cases. The peace planners, he wrote, were mistaken if they believed that negotiating a separate peace would preserve slavery. The only way to save the peculiar institution was to continue the war to its successful conclusion. But by this point it is clear from Rayner's private correspondence that he himself had grown to doubt that the South would ever secure its independence. Significantly, he published the three editorials under a pseudonym.[16]

The summer of 1864 signaled the first outward signs of a dramatic shift in Rayner's feelings and approach toward the war. On June 14 the news reached Raleigh that Leonidas Polk had been killed in action. The family was crushed. Rayner could only mourn over the "inscrutable . . . ways of Providence" and the "moral desolation" brought by Polk's death. He tried to keep "from brooding over the horrors produced by this war" by writing to Ruffin about crops, livestock, and other mundane matters, but he confessed that his "heart was aching." The war had changed his "whole character," Rayner confessed. He seldom ventured from the house unless business absolutely required it. "Every day,—year, almost every hour, I ask myself the question—what is to be the end of all this?" As the summer of 1864 progressed, he continued to mouth token expressions of hope in a southern victory, but he only grew more "gloomy at the complexion of our affairs." His letters reflected his anguish. "Oh, that God, in his mercy, would bring us peace!" he prayed. After North Carolina voters went to the polls and repudiated Holden's peace movement by overwhelmingly reelecting Governor Vance, Rayner's physical health improved somewhat, although he was still unwell. But it was his mental and emotional condition that worried him the most. "I am so *sick at heart*, in regard to our military prospects," he told Ruffin, "that I hardly know what to say on that score, or what to think. . . . these things are prostrating and crushing me, day by day."[17]

Exactly what transpired in the ensuing weeks and months is mysterious at best. In late September his correspondence with Ruffin, who had been his confidant and fellow-traveler in the cause for southern independence since the beginning of the war, came to an abrupt halt. The reason is understandable, for Rayner had finally abandoned all hope of the South winning the war and entered into discussions with Holden and other peace leaders concerning possible means of ending the fighting. Although evidence regarding the nature of these discussions is sketchy and contradictory, in his application to Andrew Johnson for amnesty in June 1865 Rayner told an astonishing story. He claimed that "for the past two years" (i.e., beginning sometime in 1863) he had been "most anxious for peace, on any the best terms we could get," knowing "that the longer the South persisted in the war, the harder would be the terms to which it would ultimately have to submit." Rayner explained that he had desired peace so badly "that it was agreed upon with certain union men here last fall, that I was to make a public speech, declare for peace on the basis of reconstruction, and then make the effort to inaugurate a counter-revolution." This incredible scheme, he suggested, would have been put in motion had he not been stricken by serious illness a few days afterward and confined to his house for two months.[18]

If Rayner's own telling of these events were the only existing account, the story would have to be dismissed as an outright lie or at least the self-serving fantasy of a defeated and perhaps unbalanced man trying to salvage his political standing. But there are enough surviving pieces of corroborative evidence to make it impossible to dismiss the tale out of hand. First, in the amnesty application he said that the events were "well known to Gov. Holden, with whom I had a consultation on the subject, and to whom I have freely communicated my views, for the last two years." By then, Johnson had appointed Holden provisional governor of the state, and it was Holden's job to recommend or reject applications such as Rayner's. Rayner submitted the application to Holden personally and the governor endorsed it, enclosing a note to Johnson saying, "I believe Mr. Rayner is sincere. I respectfully advise that he be pardoned. I believe he will prove himself a peaceable, loyal, and useful citizen." Yet Holden had refused to support the applications of Vance, Gilmer, and Graham—all prominent Conservatives who had supported Holden until he came out overtly for peace. Furthermore, at the time Rayner wrote the application, Johnson's personal envoy, Harvey M. Watterson, was in Raleigh on a fact-finding mission for the president. Watterson, Johnson, and Rayner had all served in Congress together. When Rayner finished writing the application, he visited Watterson and read it to him. In a report back to Johnson, Watterson mentioned the letter. "Notwithstanding its length [twenty pages] I trust that you will find time to read it," he told the president. "It is so true, so sincere, and so manly, that I regard it as a model paper." In short, both Holden and Watterson had seen Rayner's account of his role in the abortive counterrevolutionary conspiracy and found nothing in it to dispute.[19]

Another, even more curious, piece of evidence survives to add credence to Rayner's story of a contemplated counterrevolution. In May 1866 Graham received a letter from one George B. Simpson, a Union army officer who had been stationed in occupied Washington, North Carolina, during the war. Simpson asked for confirmation or denial of a story he had heard in December 1863. It seems that "a gentleman by the name of Rich" had told Simpson that he held a permit from Lincoln that allowed him to cross Union military lines "at pleasure" and a similar pass from North Carolina officials permitting him to cross Confederate lines. Rich had told Simpson that he personally knew Vance, Rayner, Graham, and other political leaders in the state and that one of the aforementioned leaders had told him of a conspiracy similar to the one Rayner later related to Johnson. According to Rich, after the rupture between Vance and Holden, Rayner and other conspirators had proceeded with the plot. Simpson related Rich's account of the conspiracy in considerable detail.

> It was as follows, to wit: That the Federal Army in North Carolina should be sufficiently strengthened to enable it to move from the seaboard to the interior of the State; that it should take and hold the Railroads communicating with Richmond, and Charleston; that this would effectually cut the Rebellion in two and would unite the Federal Army in the valley of the Mississippi with the same Army on the Atlantic, through the States of Tennessee and North Carolina; this being accomplished, the distinguished gentlemen submitting the proposition to the Government at Washington and other prominent gentlemen of

the State would take the stump, go before the people on the proposition, and within sixty days would put *seventy thousand* North Carolina soldiers into the Federal ranks, and thus turn the State over to the Federal Government, and the Union. It was argued that this course would cut off Richmond from its supplies of provisions and men from the South, and would cut off Charleston from its supplies of men from Lee's Army, and thus effectually *crush* the Rebellion, as neither could hold out ninety days thereafter, when the Union Army could retire and rest upon its laurels.

Rich had insisted to Simpson that Rayner and the others had submitted this proposition to the Lincoln administration via Union officers in occupied North Carolina and General Benjamin Butler.[20]

Graham read Simpson's letter and denied having ever participated in any such conspiracy. He had never heard of anyone named Rich and presumed that he was "an adventurer engaged in illicit trade." Max R. Williams, the editor of the Graham Papers, agrees that the episode was "not creditable" and speculates that the Rich mentioned in the letter was one David J. Rich, "a carpetbagger of unsavory reputation." Graham's denial, however, does not necessarily discount the veracity of the Simpson-Rich story. For when Vance broke with Holden, Graham sided with Vance. Neither would have been parties to the subsequent conspiracy—if it occurred—and Simpson's letter did not specifically name which of the North Carolinians hatched the plan to go public with counterrevolutionary scheme following the Vance-Holden split. Rayner, on the other hand, was not a Vance partisan and along with Holden could have proceeded with the plan after Holden parted ways with Vance and Graham. In other words, Graham might have been involved in the early peace discussions (as Leonidas Polk had heard it told through the Bragg brothers) but did not participate in the radical scheme Simpson described. Curiously, Rayner himself wrote to Graham in September 1865, expressing the opinion that "you owe it to yourself to make some public statement in regard to your connection with passing events, for the last 12 or 18 months." Rayner refused to elaborate in the letter, saying that they needed to discuss the matter in person. Perhaps he was gently pressing Graham to own up to his part in the peace movement, whatever that part may have been.[21]

The incidents related in the Simpson letter must be taken with a very large dose of skepticism. Even Rich (whoever he was) admitted that he actually had not been present at the conspirators' meetings; it merely had been "stated to him by one or more" of the men mentioned in the letter that the meetings took place. Records of negotiations with Union officials such as he described surely would have come to the attention of historians. But at the same time, it appears undeniable that Rayner was telling the truth about his involvement in some sort of serious peace discussions, even while he was complaining to Ruffin about Confederate military reverses. The events related in the Simpson letter bear an uncanny resemblance to those in Rayner's amnesty application, and Simpson himself placed enough stock in the story to want to verify it. Could two men as diverse as an alleged Union messenger and a known southern secessionist have told such similar stories and it be nothing but a coincidence? Is it conceivable that Holden, who had suffered twenty years of abuse and a humiliating caning at the hands of Rayner, would have sanctioned Rayner's account of the conspiracy and urged his pardon if it had contained no significant measure of truth? We will never know for certain what went on in the meetings that Rayner and Rich described. But Rayner repeated the essentials of his story for the rest of his life and was never questioned or corrected, even by the several North Carolina politicians who eventually heard him tell it. And Holden and Rayner remained close friends for the remainder of their days.[22]

Rayner's desire for a negotiated peace while nominally professing allegiance to the southern cause quite likely contributed to his debilitating illness during the latter part of the war. As early as his congressional days he had exhibited a tendency to fall ill when he perceived political matters slipping beyond his control. His "neuralgia" in 1863 and 1864 came when he found himself torn between two conflicting sets of loyalties, with little power to influence the course of events in one direction or the other. On one hand, his personal financial stake in slavery, his initial record as a war supporter, and his close family ties to Confederate military leadership kept him wishing for a southern victory. On the other hand, his life-long devotion to the Union, his conviction that the war was lost and slavery dead, and his wish to see an end to the killing made him realize that steps must be taken to terminate the conflict. It is not surprising that when he fully determined to take the stump to advocate an end to the war, he was again stricken with the incapacitating malady. Confined to the safety of his bed, he could earnestly say that he had determined to strike for peace, while in reality he could keep from relinquishing the futile hope that his fortune, his political future, and his very way of life might yet be salvaged by a miraculous southern victory. The sudden end of his correspondence with Ruffin, however, suggests that he no longer could maintain the pretense of sympathy for the Confederate cause when he actually wished to hurry the surrender. Rather than keep up the charade with his oldest friend, he simply quit writing.

On April 9, 1865, Lee surrendered to Grant at Appomattox. Meanwhile, Sherman's juggernaut, having ravaged Georgia and South Carolina, rapidly approached Raleigh from the south. On Tuesday morning, April 11, a still-ailing Rayner attended the funeral of his neighbor, Samuel Mordecai. When the funeral procession left the Mordecai home and began its march to the burying ground, Rayner and Raleigh lawyer B. F. Moore lagged behind the mourners and conversed quietly about the need to surrender the city. Everyone feared that Raleigh would meet with the same fate as Columbia, South Carolina, and be put to the torch. The only way to prevent such a disaster would be to surrender the city formally and secure promises from Sherman that lives and property would be protected. Rayner, in fact, had called on Governor Vance a few days earlier to implore him to take such steps, but the governor had balked at the idea, fearing the public reaction in the rest of the Confederacy. Dropping farther behind the procession, Rayner and Moore decided that one final effort must be made to persuade Vance. When they had fallen out of sight of the funeral procession, Rayner hurried to the executive mansion.[23]

As he neared the governor's residence, he met former governor David Swain, who was leaving the city to escape the occupation. Rayner convinced Swain to accompany him to see Vance, for the governor valued Swain's opinion. They reached the mansion at the same time that news of Lee's surrender arrived, and they found Vance and beseeched him to send commissioners to meet with Sherman. At one point during the conversation Confederate General Joseph Johnston came into the room, and Rayner and the others kept quiet about the purpose of their mission until he had left. Vance postponed his decision until the next day, when Graham arrived in the city and he, Swain, Vance, and Rayner again conferred. The governor finally agreed to send a commission, headed by Graham and Swain, to meet with Sherman and negotiate the surrender. The party left immediately for the Union lines. In the meantime, Rayner, with Vance's approval, put contingency plans into motion in case the Graham-Swain expedition did not meet with success. He sought out Raleigh's mayor, William H. Harrison, and urged that he appoint a city commission to meet the Union army and surrender the city. Harrison agreed and appointed Rayner to the commission.

It was fortunate that Rayner initiated the city commission, for Graham and Swain had met with problems. After some difficulty in passing through the lines, they had gotten through to Sherman, who received them cordially and seemed anxious to effect an agreement with Vance. Unfortunately, the delays they had experienced in crossing the lines rendered it impossible for them to return on the twelfth to Raleigh with Sherman's offer to the governor. Vance waited until midnight for them and, fearing what might happen if he remained any longer, he fled, leaving an unprotected and frightened citizenry to await Sherman's advance the next day.

Although still ill, Rayner slept in his clothes that night and rose at daybreak on the morning of April 13. The skies were gray and threatening. He hurried to Mayor Harrison's house, and the two men then went to the place where they were to meet the rest of their surrender party. In the confusion that prevailed in Raleigh that morning, only two others made their appearance. Several people tried to dissuade them from carrying out their mission, arguing that four men was too small a party to accomplish their purpose, but Rayner insisted that they proceed. "I felt sure," he later recalled, "that if some guaranty of protection to private persons and private property was not obtained, by a formal surrender of the town, we should all be at the mercy of an unbridled soldiery." Preparing a flag of truce, the four men solemnly rode to a place a mile outside of town. Rain soon began to fall in torrents, and the small party waited for Sherman's troops to appear. After an hour's wait in the rain, the advance guard commanded by General Judson Kilpatrick arrived. Rayner made a short but formal speech surrendering Raleigh, "pledging a quiet submission on the part of the inhabitants—and bespeaking his clemency and protection for a powerless and unresisting people." Kilpatrick gave his word that the city would be spared and private property protected, and within a few hours the Union army peacefully occupied the state capital.[24]

Thus the Civil War came to an end for Kenneth Rayner that day in the rain and mud outside Raleigh. Within forty-eight hours of the surrender, news arrived of Lincoln's assassination. Rayner was convinced that had he not secured formal assurances of protection, vengeance-seeking Union soldiers would have taken out their grief and anger on the citizens of Raleigh and their property. After turning the city over to the Yankees he forlornly made his way back home. His fortune in shambles, his health shattered, and his spirit broken, he might have reflected on the words he had spoken more than twenty years before in the House of Representatives. "We never shall know how to estimate [the Union's] value, until it shall be severed by discord," he had told the House. But "when brothers' hands shall reek with brothers' slaughter, and the sun of our liberty shall go down in blood; then, and not till then, shall we appreciate the blessings of this Union." Now everything he had once predicted had come true. The Union lay in ruins, facing an uncertain future. The curse of slavery had been lifted, but how would the nation deal with the four million destitute and uneducated former slaves? Those southern dissenters who had been branded as abolitionists because they opposed sectionalism were now in a sense vindicated, but it was a bitter vindication purchased at the cost of six hundred thousand American lives. And what of those like Rayner who in the final hour had chosen to go with their section instead of the Union—what would the future hold for them? The questions were many and the answers few in April 1865, as southerners waited to see what would be the price of their tragic folly.[25]

CHAPTER 8

"Crushed and Overwhelmed"

Two colors seemed to dominate the streets of Raleigh in the weeks following the surrender. Everywhere one turned, the blue of Union army uniforms and the black faces of the newly freed slaves were to be seen. Civil government at all levels had collapsed, and until it could be restored military officials had all they could do to maintain order and provide the necessities of life for the thousands of destitute North Carolinians, black and white, who flocked to the capital with no other place to turn. As one of Raleigh's wealthiest families, the Rayners emerged from the war in far better financial shape than other southern families. But when compared to its position before the war, the Rayner fortune truly had been devastated.

Like other great planters of the Old South, Kenneth Rayner had more capital invested in his human labor force than in any other single asset. In 1860 he owned about 250 slaves, which even by a conservative estimate would place his loss by emancipation at $200,000. The location of his two principal plantations in or near the theaters of war meant that he realized very little income from them during the conflict. He claimed to have spent $70,000 (Confederate money) to buy provisions for his slaves during the war without realizing any profit in return. His Arkansas slaves spent most of the war in the safety of Texas, transported and supported there at their master's expense. Also during the course of the war Confederate authorities burned some six hundred bales of his cotton to prevent its falling into federal hands. Perhaps most painful of all, Rayner was forced in 1863 to sell his home plantation in Hertford County. He received $17,000 for the property, which over the years he had enlarged to 1,900 acres. Unfortunately, the $17,000 was paid in Confederate money and suffered the same fate as the $60,000 in various securities that he owned: it depreciated rapidly in the last two years of the war and was rendered worthless when Lee surrendered to Grant.[1]

What remained of his fortune was his property in and around Raleigh, a wooded two-thousand-acre tract north of Memphis, and the Arkansas cotton plantation. Although during the final days of the Confederacy land was a far better asset than money, simply looking at Rayner's acreage is a deceptive measure of his financial condition in 1865. With the abolition of slavery, who would work the land? Rayner feared that "the labor of the black race cannot be made available here in the South. As far as it has been tried it does not work favorably at all." Furthermore, there were virtually no solvent banks or other sources of credit to enable planters to resume operations.[2]

Thus Rayner found himself in the classic predicament facing other southern planters at the war's conclusion. While he still owned some of the finest cotton-growing soil in the world, he had no way to profit from it. The outlook for selling it was poor, and taxes were mounting. He estimated his prewar net worth as high as $400,000; by 1865 it was perhaps a tenth of that. Politics had never been a source of income, and even if it had been, he was now disfranchised because of his participation in the secession convention and the fact that his remaining assets placed him outside the terms of President Johnson's amnesty proclamation. The only other occupation he had ever known was planting, and its prospects were discouraging at best. "The hardest part of it," he later explained, "was, my reverses were caused by a war, which I had done every thing in my power to prevent."[3]

Andrew Johnson, like Abraham Lincoln, wished to see the South quickly reconstructed and the Union reconstituted. But which southerners would be entrusted with power was a complicated and divisive issue. Even in North Carolina few prominent leaders could pass a test of consistent loyalty to the Union. William W. Holden, who had led the peace forces through most of the war, had advocated disunion for a decade before the conflict and voted for secession along with everyone else in the state convention. Antebellum Whig Unionists such as Zebulon Vance and William A. Graham had likewise served the Confederacy. In Rayner's case, his claim that for twenty years before the war he was as uncompromising a Unionist as any man in the South was no idle boast. But his eleventh-hour conversion to secessionism and his strong support for the war during its early stages disqualified him from any claim to preferment in the postwar political order.

A month after the surrender Johnson made his decision. He appointed Holden provisional governor, placing the editor of the *Standard* in charge of reestablishing civil government and relying upon him to recommend men for pardon. Rayner had continued to cooperate with his old nemesis in the immediate postwar weeks, publishing in Holden's paper a number of leading editorials calling for the southern people to acquiesce quietly in whatever

Reconstruction measures the government might impose. On July 6, Holden endorsed Rayner's laborious twenty-page application for amnesty, and Johnson granted the pardon. It was a strange alliance—the former secessionist editor, the president who before the war had been a staunch Jacksonian Democrat, and the old Whig congressman who had fiercely opposed them both for most of his career. For the remainder of Johnson's stormy term in office Rayner would be a vocal supporter of the administration's Reconstruction policies. He realized, more clearly than most southerners, that the only alternative to Johnson was Radical Republicanism, with its harsh medicine for the conquered South.[4]

The sincerity of Rayner's commitment to Johnsonian Reconstruction cannot be doubted. The conclusion of the war had marked the beginning of his recovery from the mysterious malady that had so incapacitated him for most of the previous two years, and in October he announced his candidacy for the first postwar state legislature. Running successfully with the backing of the pro-Johnson "Holden men" to represent Raleigh in the house of commons, Rayner took his seat for the brief fall session. The house did little in the session besides electing officers and endorsing the Thirteenth Amendment abolishing slavery. The more serious work—specific legislation touching on the status of former slaves—would not be entered into until the January session.[5]

In the meantime Rayner turned his attention to a new project. Sometime in September or October 1865 he concluded that the best service he could render to the cause of reconstructing the Union was to aid in publicizing Johnson's program. With this in mind, he commenced an ambitious undertaking: writing a campaign biography of the president. The work took more than six months to complete, ultimately reaching a length of 363 pages. In November he traveled to Washington and met with Johnson, who apparently approved of the project. One Raleigh skeptic speculated that Rayner hoped "to get a mission or some other federal office," but if the speculation was accurate, Rayner never pursued such an appointment with any additional vigor. In fact, he continued to work on private business plans that would have made it impossible for him to accept a federal appointment even if one had been offered. Beyond serving in the legislature he appeared to have no further interest in politics.[6]

The Life and Times of Andrew Johnson was in many ways a remarkable work, not because of its dubious literary merit, but because of the insight it provides into its author's political views immediately following the Civil War. Published anonymously, the title page credits the work as being "Written

From a National Stand-point. By A National Man." As he explained in the book itself, the biography was clothed in "the garb of 'hero-worship' . . . The author frankly admits that he regards Andrew Johnson as *a man of destiny*, that he has a mission to accomplish, that he is the chosen instrument in the hands of a Higher Power, to carry out its inscrutable plans." In publishing the book anonymously, Rayner explained that he would thus avoid securing personal political advantage and at the same time protect himself personally "against the shafts of unfriendly criticism."[7]

Immediately apparent in *The Life and Times* is Rayner's continuing devotion to classical republican theory. The majority of the book consists of an effort to portray Johnson as the guardian of the Founding Fathers' principles, a man who would "rear up again the old landmarks of principle erected by the fathers, and will bring back the administration of the Government to the intent and purpose of its immortal founders." Although Johnson was a Democrat, Rayner argues that he was "not merely a Democrat in the ordinary *party* sense of the term," but rather a democrat devoted "to the philosophy of democratic principles, as constituting the groundwork of republican institutions."[8]

As a former Whig and Know-Nothing, Rayner had to find some way to defend Johnson's record without renouncing his own old allegiances. Thus Rayner excused Johnson's past opposition to Whiggery and Know-Nothingism simply by saying that he was "honest and conscientious in his course." But Rayner could not resist noting that Johnson's opposition to Know-Nothingism would have been "moderated . . . if he had been more thoroughly informed as to its principles and objects." The anonymous author explained the Union Degree and the Honorable Kenneth Rayner's part in its adoption: "he is, no doubt, the first man in this country who ever administered an oath to any one binding the recipient to maintain and defend the Union against all assaults from any and every quarter under the same pledge given by our fathers in support of the Declaration of Independence—that of 'life, fortune, and sacred honor.' " Rayner's defense of himself and Know-Nothingism occupies more than three pages, a curious feature for a biography of Andrew Johnson.[9]

Large portions of *The Life and Times* scarcely refer to Johnson at all, but rather are devoted to Rayner's own interpretation of the history of the sectional crisis. So sophisticated is this formal historical study that it must place Rayner among the earliest serious historians of the Civil War. Not surprisingly, he paid particular attention to the formation, growth, and destruction of the Second Party System. Rayner's account of American political history suggests that, with the possible exception of the original Federalist party, the Democratic party had been the only *"positive representative"* party in the nation's history. Other parties such as the Whigs had been "parties of *negation,* of opposition to what they regarded as the corruptions and excesses" of the Democratic party. These parties had not lasted because each time they triumphed over the Democrats, their mission was fulfilled, and they disintegrated. Rayner explored at great lengths the relationship between the two great antebellum parties and "democratic principles" (small *d*). In the Jacksonian period, the Democratic party "was sometimes found contending for measures in direct contravention of pure democratic principles, and in support of official prerogative and power, whilst the Whig party was found maintaining the former and resisting the latter. Still, it was in the name of democracy and of democratic principles, that the Democratic party was so long able to sustain themselves in power." [10]

Rayner displayed a sophisticated understanding not only of the origins of the second party system, but also why it worked so well in preserving sectional harmony. Despite his staunch Whig and Know-Nothing partisanship, he had long recognized the importance of the parties as national institutions. A united South was not a thing that southerners should have sought before the war, he contended. As some modern historians have done, he used South Carolina as a case in point: "It was the only State in the Union where no party divisions existed. All party organizations were merged in the paramount organization against the Union." Moving to 1860 and the final split in the national Democratic party, he noted the effect of its destruction on old-line Whigs: "strange to say, those . . . belonging to the old Whig party were pained and distressed at the disruption of the Democratic party. Much as they had differed with that party on questions of governmental policy, they yet believed as long as the integrity of that party was preserved that the Union was safe." In short, Rayner comprehended a fact that has taken historians more than a century to rediscover: The final crisis of the Union took place not because Americans had suddenly grown estranged from each other in the late 1850s, but because the differences that had allowed them to take sides in national parties had ceased to operate, thus permitting long-standing disagreements about slavery to become the organizing principle of American politics.[11]

Moving from the general cause of the war—the disintegration of national parties—to the specific, Rayner offered his own interpretation of the secession movement. Secession, he contended, was no accident but rather "the consummation of a fixed purpose and of a deep-laid conspiracy to destroy the Union, that had been organized for thirty years." The South Carolina fire-eaters had organized the nullification movement of 1832 knowing that

Jackson would put it down. The nullifiers supposed that "the other Southern States would, from the sympathy of a common interest and a common locality, take part with her in case of a conflict," thus inaugurating secession. "After the abortive attempt at nullification in 1832, the leaders and agitators, who had been foiled in that movement, started the idea of 'uniting the South,' as they termed it," Rayner wrote. Their strategy clearly went against the "doctrine of the early fathers of the Republic . . . that slavery, as a mere institution considered in the abstract, had been an evil to the white race, wherever it existed." [12]

His depiction of the fire-eaters as treasonous conspirators consciously seeking to destroy all Unionist opposition brought Rayner to a discussion of the central tragedy in his own political life: the treatment of dissenters in the South. He rejected the common northern contention that slaveholders as a class were the main power behind secession. It was "in the very nature of property, of invested capital, to shrink from agitation," Rayner claimed. In fact, he believed that if the entire question had been left to the slaveholders, secession would never have taken place, even in 1861. Who, then, kept up the agitation that finally prepared the southern mind for disunion? "It was the *politicians* who did it," Rayner bitterly noted. Drawing upon his own personal experience he explained how:

> For many years past, in almost every election of any importance, the main issue between the opposing candidates was, who was the best Southern man. . . . It might perhaps be asked, what interest had the great mass of the non-slave-owners in an issue of that sort? . . . The non-slave-owners had no sort of sympathy with the slave-owners, and the protection of their property *as such*. . . . The *rationale* of the matter is this: The masses of the non-slaveholding population of the South were more violent in their opposition to *"abolition"* and *"abolitionists"* than were the slave-owners themselves. They had in their minds a fixed and definite meaning attached to the word "abolitionist." They regarded it as meaning one who was "in favor of setting free all the negroes in the country, to remain there among themselves, and to have all the rights and privileges of, and be on an equality with, the poor white men." Thus it was a question of caste, of social position, of personal pride, in regard to which, above all other things in the world, human nature is most sensitive. [13]

It all boiled down to that old enemy of republican government, demagoguery. Corrupt, self-serving politicians with no regard for the best interests of the people had deceived the nonslaveholding masses into believing that the free-soil program would inevitably raise the dreaded specter of "social equality." The resulting hysteria led southern people rashly to follow South Carolina out of the Union.

When the manuscript was finished, there remained the problem of getting it published. Rayner had no connections or experience with publishers, so he asked the help of his old friend and congressional colleague, former New York governor Hamilton Fish. Through Fish he made contact with the prestigious New York publishing house of D. Appleton and Company, who agreed to publish the work. Rayner hoped to reap considerable profit from the biography, but by the time the book was released in June 1866 Johnson was already under fierce attack by Radical Republicans and rapidly losing face with the northern public. It was too late for any printed defense of the president to gain a large readership or to change the course of national affairs.[14]

Rayner's defense of the embattled Democrat in the White House may have been inconsistent with his prewar anti-Democratic partisanship, but at a more fundamental level the two men now had much in common. Both Rayner and Johnson clung to a vision of a nation returning to republican values; with slavery destroyed, the country could reestablish the rule of intelligence and virtue, curb official corruption, and judiciously balance the powers of state and federal government in order to strike a compromise between individual self-interest and the common good of the nation. Prolonged military rule in the South would violate the republican injunction against large standing armies. A harshly punitive Reconstruction policy would continue the antirepublican politics of sectionalism when the main reason for the rise of sectionalism in the first place—slavery—had already been destroyed. Enfranchisement of blacks would thrust millions of ignorant and corruptible voters into the electorate. The Radical Republicans, on the other hand, were far more concerned with insuring individual liberties and creating a social, political, and economic climate conducive to the pursuit of private interests. These values of liberal capitalism—and the policies necessary for their implementation—clashed with the republican values that Rayner held so dear. The president's conservative program came much closer to embodying the theories of classical republicanism.

Rayner understood that the status of blacks would be the central issue of Reconstruction. His postemancipation outlook toward blacks bears careful examination because it would play a major role in determining his political affiliations during Reconstruction and beyond. As indicated in chapter 1, one of his first acts in public life had been to speak out in support of preserving a limited suffrage for free blacks during the 1835 North Carolina constitutional convention. His opinions had changed little in thirty years, but he always believed that granting unlimited suffrage to the ignorant violated republican principles. Nobody could deny that the majority of the freed slaves were uneducated and unversed in politics. In the Johnson biography, therefore, Rayner took his usual cautious and moderate approach. Caution and moderation on the subject of black rights marked one as a dissenter in the Civil War-era South.

Suffrage for the masses of illiterate former slaves, Rayner wrote, was a subject "unwisely and prematurely thrust forward as an element of mischief." Introducing the question of black voting immediately could "do no good, and it may do much harm." Give Americans in both sections some time to recover from the war and "take a calm and fair view of the subject," Rayner urged his readers. Let southern whites "have time to acquiesce gracefully in the loss of such an immense amount of property." Give blacks a chance "to adjust themselves to the great change already taken place in their condition." Rayner chose his next words carefully: "As to whether it may be advisable for the Southern States hereafter to extend the privilege of voting to the colored race, when they shall have become sufficiently enlightened and improved to appreciate the importance of civil and political rights, that is another question. It is a question on which it is not deemed proper now to express any opinion." [15]

If Rayner was prepared to entertain the possibility of eventual black suffrage, he was nonetheless extremely worried about the status of several million freed slaves in the South. He considered it unavoidable that the mass of former slaves would continue as agricultural laborers for the foreseeable future. The early indications of the postwar months suggested to him that blacks would not work steadily and efficiently except by compulsion. Still, he was reluctant to recommend any sort of peonage or quasi-slavery for former slaves. Such a status was antirepublican. Yet as his interpretation of the causes of secession had shown, Rayner understood clearly the temper of the white southern masses. They would not live in peace with blacks on a basis of equality. Four months after the war's end he elaborated on his fears in a long public letter published in the New York *Times* and other major newspapers. "You may rely on it, the two races cannot co-exist in the same country where there is anything like the same approximation to equality in numbers as there is in the South." He could offer only one possible solution: "The good of both races requires their separation." Rayner was not talking about segregation or some sort of apartheid; he urged the federal government to begin immediately formulating a massive plan for colonizing freed slaves in some foreign land: "if this separation does not take place, in less than ten years the Southern States will retrograde into a state of semi-barbarism." [16]

This drastic and impractical suggestion was entirely consistent with Rayner's conception of the requirements of a republican form of government. Blacks comprised about 40 percent of the South's population, and virtually all were uneducated and presumably unschooled in the ways of republicanism. Whether or not they were given the right to vote, to turn them loose among the free citizens of the South would spell disaster. Not surprisingly, colonization was the same remedy that slaveholders of Jefferson's generation embraced when they contemplated an alternative to black slavery.

Rayner soon abandoned the idea of colonization, but not before the Republican press in the North and a newly established black newspaper in Raleigh ridiculed the impracticality of his suggestion. The Washington *National Republican* asked Rayner whether blacks could have done any worse a job of governing the South than he and other white legislators did before the war. The Raleigh *Journal of Freedom* suggested that Rayner had not yet recovered from the "slight disarrangement of his mental faculties" that by his own admission had plagued him during the war and recommended that he not try "to ease his overburdened mind by burdening the public with nonsensical efforts at statesmanship." A visit with Freedmen's Bureau chief O. O. Howard in Washington and the rise of the Radicals in the North soon convinced Rayner to forget about colonization and try to adjust himself to the reality of black freedom. He never went on record in opposition to black suffrage and by the early 1870s had fully acquiesced in it. Experience ultimately convinced him that because black voters supported the Republican party they displayed at least as much intelligence as whites, who blindly followed the despised Democrats.[17]

It seems unlikely that Rayner's flurry of political activity in 1865 and 1866 was motivated by a desire to reenter politics on a full-time basis. If he did harbor such a desire, it was dashed by mid-1866 as the tide turned in favor of the Radicals. Perhaps as early as the war's end he had decided that he would leave North Carolina forever, moving to the Southwest to try to recover his lost fortune in cotton planting. It was not an easy decision. The family, especially Susan, had strong ties to North Carolina and Raleigh. In June 1866, Rayner explained the situation in a poignant letter to his daughter, Sallie. "Go we must, my child. We can't stay there [Raleigh]. None of us have any ties to sever, in leaving there. I know not where our destiny may carry us. An humble home somewhere where we shall all find occupation to employ us, will be most conducive to our comfort and happiness. As to my self, very little will do for me. My great anxiety is for your mother & our children. To see you provided for, so that you will be happy and contented, is all I have to live for, now." [18]

Even while publicly doubting the success of free black labor in the fall of 1865, Rayner had been privately calculating the feasibility of resuming cotton production under the new system. He factored in all the costs of labor and supplies, shrewdly allowing for the likelihood that black women would no longer work in the fields, and that even men could be counted on for no more than an average of five hours per day, half the productivity of slave labor. He estimated an average wage of $12 per month. With such a drastic rise in labor costs, what made cotton planting seem so attractive at the war's end? In October 1865, he speculated that cotton would not "sell for less than 50 cents a pound, during my life. It is more likely to see for 75 cents than for 50." With such astronomical prices, Rayner concluded that he could "make a great deal more money under the hired or paid labor system" than he ever did with slave labor—if the former slaves could be induced to work. [19]

At first he assumed he would simply try his experiment in using free labor to plant cotton on his fine Arkansas plantation. In 1859, he had raised more than five hundred bales on its eight hundred improved acres. His "dwellings and fixtures" there were uninjured by the war, although the property had fallen into disrepair and was bereft of mules and other necessities. His former slaves in Arkansas, some 150 in number, had been sent to Texas for safekeeping during the war. "They have written to me a most touching letter," Rayner explained, "begging me to go after them, and let them come to work, and make cotton for me." But transporting the former slaves, paying their wages, and repairing and resupplying the plantation clearly would require capital that he did not possess. [20]

Soon after the surrender Rayner had traveled to Arkansas to check on his holdings. While there, he learned of a piece of property for sale up river in Coahoma County, Mississippi. With 3,400 acres of land, it was, according to Rayner, "one of the most magnificent plantations I ever saw." An acquaintance of Rayner's, H. C. Chambers, proposed that the two men enter into a partnership to purchase and operate the plantation. The total price of the property was set at $175,000, with each partner contributing $20,000 cash, the balance due in three years. Rayner, however, did not even command the capital needed to resume operations on his own plantation, much less the enormous sum required to enter into the partnership with Chambers. Never one to do things halfway, he decided to try to borrow the entire amount necessary to buy his half of the Mississippi property and plant both it and the Arkansas plantation in cotton. If successful, in a few years he might regain his lost fortune.[21]

Rayner quickly learned that raising such a sum was impossible below the Mason-Dixon Line, but he was widely acquainted with wealthy and influential northern men. In the fall of 1865 he wrote to his old congressional colleagues Robert Winthrop and Hamilton Fish requesting their help in introducing him to prospective investors. It was "no quixotic adventure" in which he was engaging, Rayner explained to Fish. After several trips to the Northeast promoting the scheme, the deal was consummated. Winthrop helped Rayner assemble a group of Boston investors, and Fish did the same in New York. Rayner also sold what he could of his remaining property in Raleigh, and by planting time in 1867 he had raised about $50,000.[22]

The early months of 1867 were busy ones for Rayner. After obtaining his loans in New York in late January, he hurried to Mississippi, where preparations were being made for planting. Rayner and Chambers secured "120 good and efficient laborers" for the Coahoma County plantation and soon began planting 1,200 acres in cotton and 300 in corn. Rayner persuaded the Freemen's Bureau in Raleigh to pay the travel expenses of a handful of his former slaves from North Carolina, and these were joined by former slaves whom he brought back from Texas to work on the Arkansas place.[23] Susan and the children remained in Raleigh until June, when they joined Kenneth in Memphis and set up housekeeping.[24]

Springtime brought disaster. The Mississippi River overflowed its banks, wiping out the young crop in Coahoma County and seriously damaging it in Arkansas. Following the flood, cutworms appeared, requiring the cotton in Coahoma to be replanted four times before a viable stand could be achieved. Even then, only eight hundred acres of very late cotton survived into July. At the Arkansas property, three hundred acres survived the flood, but cultivation was jeopardized by problems with the former slaves. Rayner was dismayed by the "idleness and insubordination" of his former slaves, at whose "own earnest and repeated solicitations" he had brought back from Texas. "What a miserable set of ungrateful wretches they are!" wrote a perplexed and angry Rayner. "The prospect for cotton growers, is dark and gloomy indeed." On the positive side, his health was better than it had been in years, and he tried to be philosophical about his troubles. Reflecting on the horrors of the war, his prolonged depression during the latter stages of the conflict, and the loss of his fortune, Rayner concluded simply "to try and do my duty, and leave the result to a Higher Power. Terrible as was the ordeal of mental suffering, of gloom and despair, through which I passed, yet, I passed through it safely; and I have learn't to submit to what I can not prevent, with resignation, with calmness, and even with hopefulness." [25]

His hopes were dashed in the fall. The caterpillars again appeared, wreaking havoc with the already-short crop. When harvest time came, the final act in Rayner's pecuniary destruction was played out: cotton prices had plummeted to twelve cents a pound. Kenneth Rayner was broke.[26]

He declared bankruptcy the following year. As his fragile planting empire crumbled around him, his health deteriorated to a point even lower than in the dark days of 1864. This time there was no doubting the source of the illness; Rayner himself freely acknowledged that his "spirits" were "crushed." From his Memphis sickbed in July 1869 he wrote a heart-wrenching letter to one of his New York investors to apologize for his inability to pay his debts. The letter, written in a shaky hand, is remarkable for its frankness:

> The pain I suffered, in having to notify those who had kindly aided me, by the loan of money, is beyond description. . . . But I feel that my race is nearly run. . . . I shall die in honest poverty. I have lost every thing through sheer misfortune. It has crushed and overwhelmed me, physically and mentally. The blow is so severe, I can not react from it. For the last 18 months, my nervous system has been so shattered, that I have been powerless for exertion—and for the last 6 months I have been but few times out of doors—and three fourths of my time in bed. . . . But for my sad reflections in regard to my wife and children, death will have no terrors for me.[27]

By late 1869 his condition had not improved. Susan conferred with the doctors, who gave little hope for her husband's improvement as long as Rayner lay in bed in the family's confined quarters in Memphis. In desperation she took an uncharacteristically bold step. After looking at several pieces of property—and without Kenneth knowing about it—she collected the remnants of her personal inheritance and made the down payment on a farm sixteen miles south of Memphis at Nesbitt's Station in DeSoto County, Mississippi. Before he had even seen the place, she had the family's personal effects moved there and set about making the house comfortable. Susan feared that Kenneth would think she had acted unwisely or that he would not like the farm, but as she later told an old Raleigh friend, "it was the wisest thing I ever did in my life." Rayner was "delighted with the place" and soon was puttering about the garden and making plans for planting an orchard. His health gradually was restored. "I am more than repaid for all that I have suffered and all that I have sacrificed," Susan gratefully wrote.[28]

While Rayner had been absorbed with his failed planting venture, Congress had seized control of Reconstruction politics. His hatred of the Democratic party was as strong as ever, but in 1867 he hardly could have looked with approval on the placing of the South under martial law. "I now avoid all reflections upon political questions," he thus told Thomas Ruffin in mid-1867 when they had resumed their friendship. "I care not who is President, or who is King, if I can be allowed to work and to reap the rewards of my honest labor." During his long confinement in 1868 and 1869 the South was gradually restored to civil government under the new rules laid down by Congress. Rayner may have felt ambivalent about black suffrage, and he undoubtedly resented his own disfranchisement under the terms of the Reconstruction Acts, but by the fall elections of 1869 he had decided to cast his lot with the Republican party and acquiesce in its policies.[29]

One reason he could approve of the Republican party was the election of James Lusk Alcorn to the governorship of Mississippi. Alcorn, like Rayner, was an old-line Whig. A native of Kentucky, he had moved to Mississippi in the 1840s and become a successful planter in Coahoma County, the site of Rayner's ill-fated planting partnership. There was nothing in Alcorn's past or present politics of which Rayner might disapprove. "He is a man of great ability and of enlarged & national views," Rayner explained. After Alcorn's election to the governorship in November 1869, Rayner decided to seek appointment as judge of the state circuit court. He evidently was not convinced that his new farm would provide a sufficient living, and a lucrative judgeship would offer an ideal supplement to his income as well as constitute a satisfying return to public life. Hamilton Fish, Reverdy Johnson, O. O. Howard, and many others wrote the governor on his behalf, and Alcorn accordingly nominated him for the position.[30]

Alcorn faced the difficult task of trying to please the disparate groups that made up the Republican coalition in Mississippi. His constituency included virtually all the newly enfranchised blacks, the smaller but powerful group of true Radicals, and an unspecified number of people, mostly old Whigs, who considered themselves moderate Republicans. Rayner clearly fell into the latter group. Exactly what happened to Rayner's bid for the judgeship is unclear, but his nomination for the bench was never confirmed. "I failed of success," he later wrote, "through a covert intrigue, intended not for my injury, but to subserve other ends."[31]

The DeSoto County farm provided a precarious living for the next three years. The Rayners rented their land to former slaves on a sharecropping arrangement and succeeded in meeting the annual installments on Susan's daring purchase. Kenneth professed contentment to devote his "declining days" to the "domestic pursuits of agriculture and horticulture" that he had always loved. At the same time, however, he kept an eye on politics.[32]

Alcorn had not been in office long before the divisions within the state's Republican coalition surfaced. In trying to satisfy everyone he had alienated many on both ends of the political spectrum. Although personally a moderate, he had been forced to share power with the Radicals and thus angered many of those who had once been his supporters. The Democrats were quick to capitalize on the divisions within the ranks of the dominant Republicans. By mid-1871, with Alcorn recently promoted to the U.S. Senate, efforts were made to knit together Democrats and disaffected moderate Republicans like Rayner into an opposition party. In July, DeSoto County's "Opponents of Radicalism" assembled in a mass meeting to organize for the coming fall campaign. They passed resolutions denouncing the carpetbaggers and "earnestly ask[ing] the aid of all good men of all parties and of both races, irrespective of party names or past political associations." Rayner participated in the meeting, but he was obviously uncomfortable with the Democratic tone of the gathering. Seeking to establish more firmly the fact that this was primarily a moderate Republican and not a Democratic movement, he introduced an amendment specifically aimed at black voters. The resolution accused the Radicals of "having so long misled and deceived the colored people by their falsified promises; for having imposed such heavy burdens on the labor of the colored men by their enormously high taxes; for having used the colored men as mere instruments for carrying out their corrupt and selfish scheme of plunder." Rayner also proclaimed the Opponents of Radicalism as "the true friends of the colored people," promising to tell blacks "*the truth,*" to work toward "securing to them all their rights under the law," and to insure that they would receive "the rewards of their honest labor." He concluded his resolution with a call for the black voters to unite with the opposition party in electing "good and true men, who will maintain and defend the rights, privileges, and liberties of all classes, sections, and colors alike." The amendment was adopted, and Rayner later addressed the meeting, giving the Radicals "a most unmerciful castigation" but also "appealing to the honest Republicans among them white and black to come out from among them and range themselves on the side of honesty and economy."[33]

Not surprisingly, Rayner and the Opponents of Radicalism in DeSoto County joined the Liberal Republican movement that nominated Horace Greeley for president the following year. The movement embodied a number of principles that Rayner supported. It called for reform of the corrupt patronage practices of the Grant administration, it was not identified primarily as a Democratic movement, and it might offer a means of wresting the Republican party of the South from the hands of the Radicals and placing it in the hands of moderates. Although it relied heavily upon Democratic support at the polls, Rayner almost certainly would not have supported Greeley if the New Yorker had been strictly a candidate of the Democratic party.[34]

Greeley, however, was badly beaten in the November election, and it became more apparent that moderate southern Republicans like Rayner would either have to cast their lot with Grant and the national party or resign themselves to becoming Democrats. On the surface, the Democratic route might have seemed the most logical for Rayner. He had opposed the rise of the avowedly sectional Republican party in the 1850s; he had voted for secession in 1861; he had seen his fortune, his political standing, and his health shattered by the war the Republicans had waged so fiercely; he had believed in the conservative Reconstruction plan of Andrew Johnson; his bid for a judicial appointment under a Republican state administration had been defeated; and he had opposed the Radicals in the most recent election. But as had always been the case with Rayner, apparent political logic held little sway. If he were ever to reenter politics—and his shaky financial position suggested that he might have to—the decision would be an easy one. He could never be a Democrat.

The time for that decision arrived in February 1873. Rayner concluded that he could no longer support his family adequately on the income from his farm, and he decided to seek an appointive federal office. The position he sought was associated with a famous chapter of American diplomatic history. After the Civil War, the American government had demanded that Britain pay compensation for Union shipping lost to several Confederate raiding vessels built, outfitted, and serviced in England or English ports. The most notorious of these was the C.S.S. *Alabama.* A number of influential Republicans led by Charles Sumner demanded that Britain pay enormous reparations or else risk a war with the United States in which Canada would be the prize. No country—even mighty Great Britain—was foolish enough to risk a war with America at a time when the nation's military forces were so strong and battle-seasoned. Fortunately for both sides, cooler heads prevailed, and the case was submitted to an international board of arbitration, which awarded the United States $15.5 million in damages. In 1873, Congress faced the task of deciding the appropriate method for distributing the money to individual American claimants who had lost shipping to the *Alabama* and her sister ships. Most likely, a special court would be established to adjudicate the claims, and one of these proposed judgeships was the object of Rayner's aspirations.[35]

Rayner sought help from his old friend and benefactor Hamilton Fish, now Grant's secretary of state. In a letter recapping his long record as a Unionist before the war and as a Republican since, Rayner praised Grant and strongly urged the need for native southern Republicans to be identified with the administration. He argued that "a new organization of good and true men, without reference to color or condition—which will ignore and repudiate all the violent factions that are now fighting over the spoils" was the only way to build up the Republican party in the South. "Democracy as an organized entity must be put down and destroyed," he counseled. In short, appointing a conservative southern Republican such as himself would send a signal to the South that the Republicans were ready to put sectional antagonisms behind them and build a truly national party. Rayner also frankly admitted that the position was "very desirable" to him. "It would bring me in pleasant association with the high character and talent of the land, it would enable me to do some service to my country, . . . it would bring relief to my financial affairs, and constitute a pleasant episode in the evening of my days." He conveniently overlooked the fact that he had opposed Grant in the last election.[36]

Acting on Fish's advice, Rayner commenced a massive letter-writing campaign to enlist the aid of prominent men from his political past. The result was gratifying. Dozens of former and present senators, congressmen, governors, supreme court justices, diplomats, generals, and even two Episcopal bishops sent glowing letters to the president urging Rayner's appointment. Former vice-president Schuyler Colfax broke his own rule against interfering in patronage matters to say that "No one in the South deserves it more." America's minister to Great Britain, Robert C. Schenck, cited Rayner's "character, . . . integrity, ability, cultivation & knowledge of law" and suggested that no one "in all the southern states" would be a better choice. William Holden recommended his old antagonist "as not only eminently well qualified . . . but a thoroughly honest man." [37]

When the bill establishing the Alabama Claims Court, officially the Court of Commissioners of Alabama Claims, stalled in Congress, a disappointed Rayner called on Thurlow Weed for help in securing a loan sufficient to pay the final installment on his farm. The loan came through, but by late May of 1874 Congress still had not acted, and without Rayner's knowledge several senators began circulating a petition in the Senate requesting that Grant appoint Rayner U.S. minister to Bolivia. When a horrified Rayner found out about the movement, he quickly wrote to the senators involved and explained that he could not possibly accept such an appointment, even "if it were the proudest court in christendom." In June the Alabama Claims confirmation finally arrived. Almost thirty years after leaving Congress in disgust over the corruption of the Tyler administration, Kenneth Rayner would be returning to Washington.[38]

It had not been an easy road he had traveled in his journey back into government. Pursuing appointive office as he had done violated the republican maxim that the office should seek the man and not the man the office. Furthermore, he had accepted the position under an administration that he himself recognized as corrupt. He admitted that his motives for seeking the Alabama Claims judgeship did not spring entirely from the pure, disinterested desire to render public service that he had long professed as the only acceptable aim of the politician. In his requests to old associates for letters of recommendation he confessed that it was "painful" and "disagreeable" to him to have to do so. But if becoming a federal officeholder under the Grant administration was in many ways a surrender of long-cherished principles, there was one aspect of it that was consistent with his political philosophy and indeed his entire career. In refusing to become a Democrat and perhaps rebuild his political career as a southern Redeemer, he had chosen instead to cast his lot with the tremendously unpopular Republicans. He might have compromised many of his convictions, but he was still a dissenter. A few weeks before his appointment to the bench, he published under his own name a long letter in the Democratic Jackson *Clarion* defending the Grant administration and the Republican party. Sectional issues, he wrote, were dead, and it was "to be regretted" that national politics remained polarized along sectional lines. It had been his "lot to differ with a large majority of them [the southern people] from the agitation of the measures that culminated in war down to the present time." For those southerners who insisted on looking to the past with its shibboleths of white supremacy and the Lost Cause, he had a simple message: "reconstruction will never be complete till public opinion in the South 'realizes the situation,' and adapts itself to the condition of things as it is." That meant accepting blacks as free citizens and turning America's political energies to the task of building a strong and unified nation. "The past can not be undone," Rayner told white Mississippians. "Resignation to the past—duty for the present—and hope in the future, should be the motto of the Southern people."[39]

CHAPTER 9

"A Chequered Life"

◆◇◆

Rayner served with distinction for nearly three years as one of five judges
on the Alabama Claims Court. The court functioned until the beginning
of 1877, when by law it expired. In the meantime the judges acted upon
hundreds of claims by individuals and companies for a share of the $15.5 mil-
lion award paid to the U.S. government by Great Britain. Rayner's opinions
were marked by the almost tedious thoroughness that had characterized his
speeches, letters, and bills during his years as a legislator and politician. At
the end of Rayner's tenure John A. J. Cresswell, a Radical Republican who
served as Grant's postmaster general and counsel for the United States before the court, described the judge as "discriminating, laborious, and faithful
in the discharge of his duties. His judgments were always carefully considered, and his exhaustive opinions, sometimes dissenting and independent,
bear abundant evidence of the great amount of thought and research ex-
pended upon them. But better than all else, a keen sense of justice, and a
conscientious regard for the right, pervaded every act of his official life. His
integrity is unsullied and his personal honor without a blemish."[1]

Rayner's position as a jurist removed him from active participation in
partisan politics, but as an officeholder under the auspices of a Republican
administration he naturally maintained a keen interest in political affairs.
What he saw in Washington troubled him. His only real reason for being a
Republican was his bitter hatred of Democrats. His public and private de-
fenses of President Grant had been half-hearted and unconvincing at best.
He clearly viewed the Republican party not as the representative of hallowed republican principles but simply as the lesser of two evils. He had
succeeded in his own bid for a slice of the federal pie, but he was dismayed

at the crass patronage policies of the administration—especially in the way worthy southerners were passed over. In Rayner's opinion, Republicans were throwing away whatever chance they might have to build up a viable party in the South.

The administration was guilty of transgressions both great and small. Near the end of his tenure, Rayner became involved in one that was small but that well illustrates his attitudes. The case involved one Moses Madry, a black North Carolinian who as a slave before the war had been the property of a family Rayner knew well. While serving in the Union army Madry had suffered an injury that precluded heavy manual labor. He was now living in Washington, but in the campaign of 1876 had returned to his home county in North Carolina and made a number of speeches on behalf of the Republican ticket. Madry had applied unsuccessfully for a position as a watchman in the Interior Department. "If ever any man, black or white, had claims upon the kind consideration of his party," Rayner contended, "this man Moses Madry has." Rayner was acquainted with Madry, could verify his claims of service to the party, and knew that he was "of good character, a sober, honest, and respectable man." "And yet," complained Rayner, "hundreds living here in this District & in the adjoining states of Maryland & Virginia, who did nothing, and many of whom have property, are still provided with good places under the government." Such disregard for the political services of southern Republicans embittered Rayner toward his party.[2]

Eventually he grew so "annoyed and provoked" at the treatment of Madry that he enlisted the aid of Senator John Pool, Judge Thomas Settle, Governor Curtis Brogden, and several other prominent North Carolinians in the effort to procure a place for Madry. When the passage of several months and a personal visit by Rayner and Pool to the Interior Department still failed to produce results, Rayner finally interceded with the new president, Rutherford B. Hayes, on Madry's behalf. It is unclear whether or not his efforts finally succeeded, but Rayner believed that if the Republican party was to fulfill its promise of becoming a national party serving the interests of both races, it could not behave as it had toward Moses Madry and other people like him.[3]

As he had always done, Rayner identified corruption as the root of the party's and the nation's failings. Americans of the Revolutionary generation would be "shocked," he argued in 1876, at how elections were conducted. "Moral vice" and "political vice" went hand in hand, and he believed that the developments of the previous two decades only proved "how rapid has been the decline of political morality, and the reverence for the examples set by the fathers, in a few short years."[4]

When the Alabama Claims Court expired at the beginning of 1877, Rayner was left without employment at the age of sixty-eight. If the electoral imbroglio resulting from the Hayes-Tilden presidential contest could be resolved in Hayes's favor, the Republicans would continue in power for four more years. But still Rayner would have to find support from the incoming Hayes government. In the early months of 1877 his name was occasionally mentioned in connection with a cabinet post, but he was knowledgeable enough to realize that he would not be seriously considered. He hoped for another judicial position, preferably a judgeship on the regular Court of Claims. Rayner pursued it with his usual vigor and had the support of Grant, but an opening on the court did not occur until the new administration was in office. Grant instead nominated Rayner as commissioner to reedit the first volume of the Revised Statues, but an opponent at the head of the Senate committee entrusted with the matter refused to bring his name before the Senate for a vote. On the day after Hayes took office, Grant wrote to the new president stating that he knew "no person better suited" than Rayner for "any judicial position." On April 18, at the suggestion of Secretary of State William M. Evarts, Hayes appointed Rayner as the American commissioner on the United States and Spanish Commission, an international tribunal created to arbitrate claims of American citizens against the Spanish government arising from the Cuban insurrection of 1868.[5]

As it turned out, Rayner attended only one meeting of the United States and Spanish Commission before resigning to accept a different appointment, solicitor of the Treasury. Although disliking it intensely, he occupied the office for the rest of his life. As Rayner put it, the solicitor's office was "anomalous in its character." While its main purpose was to provide legal opinions for the Treasury, it was officially part of the Justice Department. The office was also responsible for collecting all outstanding debts owed to the government, coordinating suits brought against the United States, and administering all lands acquired by the government in payment of debts. With a staff of only fourteen, its employees were burdened with a staggering workload. The solicitor received an annual salary of $4,500.[6]

Rayner's seven years as solicitor of the Treasury were marked by conflict and controversy, although the evidence suggests that he performed his duties with great conscientiousness, ability, and honesty. The Hayes administration, however, in many ways marked the nadir for southern Republicans in the federal government. Following the hotly disputed election in which neither candidate won a clear-cut electoral majority, southern Democrats acquiesced, if not assisted, in Hayes's peaceful inauguration. Hayes soon ended the federal military presence in the South, leaving blacks unprotected in their civil and political rights and effectively pulling the props from beneath white southern Republicans. In the months following his inauguration it became apparent that southern Republicans were politically expendable and would play a very small part in the administration. As James Lusk Alcorn wrote bitterly to Rayner a year after Hayes took office, "The president cares nothing for the endorsement of southern Republicans. He has thrown himself bodily into the embraces of the Democratic party of the South. I would feel no more humiliated in requesting an appointment at the hands of Jeff Davis, if he were President, than I would at the hands of President Hay[e]s."[7]

Rayner quickly came to agree with Alcorn, and it served further to harden his conviction that the Republican party was approaching moral bankruptcy. If the party was not interested in building a permanent, national organization, it could be little better than the hated Democrats. In the spring of 1877, Rayner expressed to Treasury secretary John Sherman his views on how best to "reestablish" the Republican party in the South. He believed that with proper management in 1880 the party *could* be revived in at least five southern states. "To abandon them and surrender them to the enemy, must not be thought of," Rayner told Sherman. "It would be, to abandon the Republican party itself." The main problem, as he saw it, was the continuing sectional animosity of northern Republicans toward the South. Despite Hayes's promises of significant federal aid to rebuild and improve the South physically, little had been done. "Congress, in the bestowal of its bounties, does not seem to know that there is such a country as the Southern States," Rayner complained, "and in the distribution of official patronage our people do not seem to be thought of."[8]

When he spoke of "our people," Rayner meant native-born southerners. What meager patronage that was sent the South's way seemed inevitably to go to transplanted northerners—"that class of men that have destroyed the Republican party, and made the very name of *Republican* odious in the Southern States—I mean the *carpet-baggers*." It was, according to Rayner, "indispensable that the carpet-bag regime be relieved from the cares of office, and native Southerners—or northern born men permanently located there, and who are in affiliation with Southern interests and sympathies be put in their places." Only with intelligent and virtuous natives could the Republicans hope to build a strong and enduring party in the South.[9]

Rayner's ideas about public virtue, honesty, and the national good found few receptive ears in Gilded-Age Washington. He increasingly came to realize that if republican ideals had been threatened in the 1850s, they were virtually foreign in the 1870s. Everyone, in government and out of it, seemed to have some special game to play at the public's expense. And as Rayner learned soon after assuming the solicitor's office, the rules of honor and propriety that he believed governed antebellum conduct no longer applied.

Rayner had been solicitor of the Treasury for a little more than a month when a routine request for an opinion came from Secretary Sherman's office. One John A. Grow had been arrested for forging several drafts on the Treasury. Having been caught, Grow wished to refund the money and have the criminal charges against him dropped. In a clear, forceful, and unequivocal opinion, Rayner rendered the verdict that the Treasury Department had no jurisdiction over the case inasmuch as it was a criminal action brought against Grow not by the Treasury but by the U.S. district attorney. In short, the district attorney should prosecute the case as he saw fit and as the law dictated. What followed next pits Rayner's story against an adversary's, but the overwhelming weight of the evidence indicates that Rayner was telling the truth. Soon after the charges were filed, Grow and A. M. Soltedo, Jr., managing editor of Washington's *National Republican,* called upon Rayner at his residence in hopes of convincing him to intervene on Grow's behalf. Soltedo and Grow apparently were friends. According to Soltedo's account, Rayner told the men not to worry and that Grow's refund of the money would satisfy the authorities. Rayner later contradicted this portion of the story, but whether or not he gave unofficial assurances at his house, the fact remains that in his official opinion as solicitor he later ruled against Grow. In Rayner's account, Soltedo came to the Treasury building and threatened him, saying that "the press would be down upon him" if he refused to submit an opinion favorable to Grow.[10]

Several weeks earlier, at the time of Rayner's appointment to the office, Soltedo had editorialized favorably about the "genuine ability and sterling worth" of the new solicitor. However, a few days after the adverse opinion became known, snide squibs about Rayner's age began to appear in Soltedo's newspaper. "For an old gentleman of eighty-three the Solicitor is remarkably well preserved," read the first. Rayner was sixty-nine. "Hon. Kenneth Rayner denies that he is eighty-three," the paper reported the next day. "He is not more than eighty-one and a half. He is as lithe and chirp as a jay bird, and in the full possession of a brilliant and vigorous intellect. He will live to be at least 150, and it is a sure thing that he will die in office."[11]

This angered Rayner, but the squibs continued. On the third consecutive day, Soltedo wrote, "Solicitor Kenneth Rayner is the oldest in years but the youngest in strength of body and vigor of intellect of any of our statesmen. An old gentleman of South Carolina, who called upon him yesterday, said to him 'Kenneth, how do you manage to preserve your youth? You have not changed a bit during the last eighty years. When first I saw you, seventy-five years ago, you were a member of Congress, and I was a mere boy. Now I look fifty years your senior.' Mr. Rayner smiled complacently, and took a fresh chew of tobacco."

The fourth day brought more of the same: "That famous speech of Patrick Henry's, concluding with the immortal words, 'Give me liberty or give me death!' has been erroneously charged to him. According to 'ye ancient chronicler' it was uttered by our strong and still youthful solicitor of the Treasury, the Right Hon. Kenneth Rayner, who, it is said, was at that time the youngest member of the Virginia House of Burgesses."

By the fifth day, word may have reached Soltedo that Rayner was losing his patience. The squib that day read, "The rumor that Hon. Kenneth Rayner, Solicitor of the Treasury, had killed a newspaper man is without foundation. The learned Solicitor is too young and too handsome to be guilty of such a deed."[12]

On Saturday, September 1, Soltedo mentioned in the paper that Rayner's assistant had left town on business, an occurrence to be regretted inasmuch "as the youthful new Solicitor has not yet fully familiarized himself with the workings of the office." Late in the afternoon on the following Monday Rayner was leaving the office for the day when he happened into Soltedo on the steps of the Treasury building. "You d—d scoundrel, I've caught you at last," Rayner reportedly uttered as he dealt a glancing blow at the editor's jaw with his right fist. The youthful Soltedo answered with a "vigorous left hander squarely on the Solicitor's right eye," and then, "seizing the pugilistic Solicitor by the throat, whirled him around, and, with a sudden jerk, bounced him clear off his feet and landed him upon his back some fifteen steps downward on the granite staircase." Regaining his footing, Rayner cried, "Oh! you s— of a b—h; you d—d scoundrel; d—n your eyes, you son of a b—h" and then "madly rushed up the granite steps" at Soltedo. A bystander tried to restrain him, but Rayner yelled at him to "Get out of the way; I'll knock you down, get out of the way, d—n you." The two combatants again came to blows, with Rayner taking another pounding that sent him tumbling down the steps onto the Treasury lawn. Once more regaining his feet, the enraged Rayner "opened fire in a strain so obscenely and profanely" that it could not be printed. "Let the COARSEST AND MOST REPULSIVE OATHS of an abandoned profligate be imagined, and still truth would lack its measure," Soltedo reported self-righteously.[13]

By this point, two or three hundred spectators had gathered on Fifteenth Street to witness the fight. Rayner's face was smeared with tobacco juice, and his right eye was almost swollen shut, but the fight was anything but gone from him. Reaching into his pocket, he pulled out a clasp-knife and exclaimed, "Let me kill him. Let me rip him up like a dog." The friendly bystander who had earlier tried to separate the two men tried to calm Rayner, who was out of control. " 'He says I'm old. He says I'm old. You saw me strike him in the mouth, didn't you? I did it like a boy, didn't I?' " After further cursing and accusations, watchmen from the Treasury intervened and with great difficulty persuaded Rayner to give up the combat.[14]

In an aftermath reminiscent of his caning incident with William Montgomery in the House nearly forty years earlier, Rayner was summoned before the Police Court to answer assault and battery charges. His closest friend in Washington, Senator John Pool, defended him, but Rayner was clearly guilty. The presiding judge refused to consider any extenuating circumstances, and the fine was $25. Over the following several days rumors circulated in the national press that the president would dismiss the combative solicitor for unseemly conduct, but nothing further was said. Rayner, embarrassed, wrote to Secretary of State Evarts, who had played a large part in securing him the solicitor's post. "If it had been a mere personal quarrel, I would not think of annoying you with any thing of the sort. But this whole trouble grew out of the fact, that I would not prostitute my official functions, to the furtherance of private interests and purposes. In other words, I was assailed for doing my duty." He added that he felt "deeply humiliated, at being under the necessity" of doing what he had done.[15]

The Soltedo incident illustrates how times had changed in Washington and in American public life in the forty years since Rayner had stepped onto the political stage. In the 1840 caning incident, as in his 1856 altercation with Holden, Rayner's conduct in thrashing a slanderous or ungentlemanly political opponent generally had been considered acceptable behavior. Neither of the antebellum incidents seriously diminished the respect that the public or his political friends had for him. Soltedo defended his campaign of ridicule against Rayner as "jokes" that "any sensible man" would have laughed off, and indeed they were—for the 1870s. But Rayner was schooled in the politics and manners of a very different time, when public figures were to be treated with respect and deference. Personal attacks were to be scrupulously avoided, and by Jacksonian-era standards nothing could have been more personal than making fun of a man's age. The offense Rayner felt was compounded by the fact that he truly was being assailed in the paper for doing his duty. Despite Soltedo's weak claims to the contrary, Rayner had unquestionably done the proper thing in clearing the way for Grow's prosecution. But in allowing his outraged sense of honor to lead him to commit what by the standards of the day was considered an improper response, Rayner had succeeded only in making himself a laughing stock. It was a sobering experience.[16]

After the assault on Soltedo it seemed that nothing Rayner did in Washington met with the approval of the press. Much of his trouble arose because few people outside the labyrinthine capital bureaucracy understood the nature of the solicitor's office. The solicitor did not automatically pass judgment on all legal questions confronting the Treasury Department. He only rendered opinions on those questions referred by his superiors at the Treasury or Justice departments. Rayner repeatedly had to explain to aggrieved citizens that "the office of the Solicitor of the Treasury can not assume the function of a judicial tribunal. It acts only on the record, as presented in the papers referred to it." The existence of the solicitor in effect made it possible for his superiors—primarily the secretary of the Treasury—to pass along any particularly abstruse or controversial matter for a decision. When an opinion proved embarrassing or unpopular, the criticism fell into the lap of the solicitor and not that of the Treasury secretary. If the inherent structure of the office subjected Rayner to frequent criticism, his stubborn independence and his almost obsessive commitment to the rule of law only compounded his troubles. After a lifetime as a dissenter, it was far too late for him to change.[17]

In late 1877, Secretary of the Treasury John Sherman sent Rayner a case that presented all of the problems that made the solicitorship such a thankless job and that so often exposed the solicitor to criticism. The case involved a fascinating piece of Civil War history. Sherman asked Rayner to write a legal opinion on a claim submitted to the Treasury Department by Dr. Mary Edwards Walker. Walker had applied to the Treasury for back pay for a clerkship she had been offered but then not allowed to accept. No one in Washington in the 1870s needed to ask who Mary Walker was. She had graduated with honors from Syracuse Medical College in 1855 and was licensed as a medical doctor. In 1862, she volunteered to be a surgeon to the Union army and after a series of alternating acceptances and rebuffs was given the position of contract-assistant surgeon, which carried the rank of first lieutenant. This made her the only female officer in the regular Union army. While attached to the 52d Ohio Infantry in 1864 she acted not only as a doctor but also as a Union spy behind enemy lines and furnished valuable information to her superiors. Ultimately, she was captured and spent four months in a Confederate prison before being exchanged for a southern officer. After the war she received the Medal of Honor for her services.[18]

Her military record, however, was not what made Walker so well known by the late 1870s. Besides being a doctor, soldier, and spy, she had long been a militant women's rights activist. Specifically, she was a dedicated practitioner of dress reform. While in the army she had been allowed to wear a man's uniform that had been modified, and after the war she adopted the practice of always wearing a frock coat, trousers, and a top hat. With her cropped hair and assertive manner she alienated and outraged the greater part of the capital's male population. She was unceremoniously thrown out of public buildings and arrested on the streets for wearing men's clothing. But her greatest problems came when she attempted to claim the pensions or perquisites normally accorded to veterans with distinguished war records. It was one such attempt that brought her case before the solicitor of the Treasury.[19]

In 1873, unable to secure employment as a physician, Walker had applied for a $900 per year clerkship in the Treasury Department. She went through all the proper channels, completing a series of interviews and passing the required written examination. She was formally offered a position in the Treasury—which she accepted—and was told when to report. On the appointed day she was shuffled from bureaucrat to bureaucrat and finally sent home, her clothing apparently having offended the sensibilities of Treasury personnel. The offer of employment was never withdrawn, and for the next year she repeatedly appeared for duty, only to be ignored. For four more years she continued to press her claims until the exasperated Sherman passed her case to Rayner for disposal.

Unlike virtually every other federal officer involved in the Walker matter, Rayner felt obligated to consider the case seriously and "without prejudice." After reviewing her service record and all the facts of the case, which nobody contradicted, he concluded that Walker had been "badly treated" and "should receive the most liberal construction of the law in her favor." From the records he had been furnished, it was plain to Rayner that she had "performed most valuable and meritorious services to her country." Her claim was even more compelling for a simple reason: "She was a woman. She could not take her musket and go into the ranks and fight. But she did what she could. . . . What is the poor pittance of one or two years pay as a clerk, compared with the benefit . . . conferred upon the cause of the Union, in aiding to heal the sick, and hasten their return to the ranks? Is not the life of one soldier thus probably saved by her efforts, worth ten fold the pittance she now asks for?"[20]

As Rayner wrote his opinion, his indignation at the injustice of the situation grew. In trying to report for work, he wrote, Walker had been "put off, and off, and off." She had paid the required twenty-five cents to take the prescribed oath of office, which implied a contractual obligation on the part of the government to give her the position she had been promised. The government, then, in his opinion, owed her one year's back pay. Both the law and justice demanded it. Rayner well knew what had happened in the Walker case, and why. He addressed it forthrightly, explaining that he had "looked at the mere abstract merits of the question" and had "not allowed myself to be swayed, or in any degree influenced, by the sex of the applicant, or by her well-known peculiarities of conduct or of dress. These should not be allowed to prejudice her claim. They involve matters of *taste*, with which I have nothing to do. . . . I regard her as an American citizen, pleading for what she regards as her rights, before a tribunal of her country. As such she is entitled to the same consideration—and no more—as the highest personage in the land."[21]

Once more, an official act of Rayner's brought the condemnation of the press down upon him. The New York *Times* reported on its front page that the opinion "lays down a novel principle," although the story neglected to explain what that principle was. Eight months later the incident was again cited as evidence of Rayner's "eccentricities." According to the *Times*, the opinion in the case of the "notorious female, Dr. Mary Walker," had "caused much ridicule" and was just one of several opinions that proved Rayner to be "a dangerous man with a pen."[22]

The most frequent source of criticism, however, had nothing to do with fistfights with editors or advocacy of women's rights. The most serious allegations seemed inevitably to spring from that great demon of Rayner's life and public career, sectionalism. Every important solicitor's opinion that in any way involved a North-South issue seemed to meet with instant scrutiny in the northern press. And if an opinion ever hinted at favoring a southern claimant at the government's expense, a cry was raised about the unreconstructed rebel in the Treasury Department.

One such instance occurred when the Richmond & Danville Railroad pressed its claim for payment for services rendered to the United States immediately after the war. The railroad, in Confederate hands during the war, had transported large numbers of paroled Union prisoners northward in the weeks after the surrender. In 1866 it filed a standard claim against the government for compensation. Only a portion of the claim was paid, because the company lacked sufficient evidence to prove that the full number of men it claimed to have transported had actually ridden the trains. Later, in 1875, the railroad collected additional evidence to substantiate the earlier claim and resubmitted it. The government approved the claim, but before the compensation was actually paid a new administration took office and the new secretary of war decided to pay a lower mileage allowance than the amount specified in the agreement. The case came to Rayner for an opinion.[23]

In his written statement Rayner pointed out that the issue was not whether compensation was due. The only question put to him was whether the new administration could take it upon itself to reduce the agreed-upon amount. Because the only thing that had changed had been the officials and not the facts of the case, the answer clearly was that the full amount should be paid. To do otherwise was to "violate all faith and confidence." The northern press took a different view. According to a report filed by the Cincinnati *Commercial* and reprinted by the New York *Times,* Rayner had written an opinion "to the effect that Confederate railroads were entitled to payment for transportation of troops and supplies during the war." The *Commercial*'s report, of course, was patently false, but Rayner felt the power of the Bloody Shirt in full force. Not only was his opinion grossly misreported, but Secretary Sherman also overruled his decision. It was not surprising that Rayner felt "his services have not been appreciated."[24]

The press took the same occasion to condemn another Rayner opinion. Again, it involved the last days of the Confederacy. When the Confederate government fled Richmond in 1865, the Virginia state government had $21,000 in gold on deposit at a Richmond bank to be used to pay the regular salaries of state officials. Lieutenant Governor Henry W. Thomas received $500 of this money in payment of his salary before federal troops occupied the city. The federal government was now suing Thomas and other Virginia officials to recover the money, claiming that with the fall of the Confederacy it had become the property of the United States. In a carefully researched twenty-nine-page opinion, Rayner concluded that the government had no claim upon the gold. Legally, he pointed out, the United States had never taken cognizance of the fact that the seceding states had ever been out of the Union. Had the gold belonged to the Confederate national government, or had it been used in the actual prosecution of the rebellion, it would have been subject to confiscation as contraband of war. Such was not the case. If a southern state's coin automatically became federal property in 1865, he reasoned, "why not the state house—the library in it—its statue of Washington—its public works and improvements—its shares in banks, rail-roads, and canals?" Yet none of these had reverted to the federal government in 1865, and no one had ever suggested that they should.[25]

The legal merits of Rayner's argument—and of those, including John Sherman and the U.S. attorney in Virginia, who differed with him—are not particularly important. But there was clearly a measure of logic in his reasoning, and he marshaled an impressive body of international law and other legal precedents and principles to bolster his case. Again, however, he was tried and convicted in the press. The New York *Times* ridiculed the opinion as "State Rights in the Government." A few weeks later the same paper reported the entirely unfounded rumor that "a ring of Southern lawyers and politicians have been trading upon their real or assumed influence with Judge Rayner," and that if Rayner was innocent of "personal corruption" he was nonetheless guilty of "judicial ductility almost equivalent to it." The government lost its cases against Henry W. Thomas and the other defendants in the gold-recovery suits. A U.S. district court apparently saw a good deal more merit in Rayner's reasoning than did John Sherman or the New York *Times*. Summarizing the Mary Walker, Richmond & Danville, and Henry W. Thomas opinions, the *Times* concluded that the combined weight of Rayner's "absurd" opinions would result in his removal from office as soon as Secretary Sherman returned from an out-of-town trip.[26]

Surprisingly, he outlasted John Sherman and three presidents in office. After Hayes retired, both Garfield and Arthur retained Rayner as solicitor. He never relinquished his desire for a return to the bench, but when he was again passed over in 1882 he acknowledged that it was his "last chance." Thereafter he resigned himself to be satisfied with the solicitorship and try to live out his days in peace. But the course of political events in Gilded-Age America profoundly disturbed him. In 1880, he speculated "that the good and the evil elements in man's nature, are the same antagonistic forces, in all ages and all peoples." A life-long lover of things classical, Rayner had recently read two new works on Caesar and Cicero, and they reminded him that "the wicked impulses that sap and ruin human liberty, are the same, under all types of civilization, and under all governmental systems." If anything, the last six years in Washington had confirmed his belief that corruption and placing individual interests ahead of the common good would ultimately undermine the American system of government. He felt convinced "that the time has come in our history—either for our institutions to commence, and in fact have already commenced, on their downward grade to ruin—or for some great man to become the fortunate instrument, for averting the evil to destruction, and of replacing our institutions, where the Fathers left them. Is it too late for the latter! I hope not."[27]

Rayner's status as a reformer in the antebellum years had necessarily made him a dissenter, and in the 1880s, he could still conceive of "nothing so worthy" as the ambition "to reform evils"—evils that he hoped were "not *organic*, but simply *functional.*" But a lifetime spent in futile efforts to reform the evils of corrupt sectional politics had met with nothing but failure. At the most critical moment in the sectional drama—the secession crisis— even he had fallen under their sway. Rayner therefore could not be optimistic that the failures of republican government in America were due simply to "functional" defects. The virtuous republic of Washington and Jefferson was irretrievably gone. Could the liberal state survive and at the same time preserve liberty for its people? He frankly doubted it. "There is no use in attempting to disguise it," he remarked to Hamilton Fish, "but there is an undefined misgiving in the public mind that some danger, some terrible . . . impending calamity . . . threatens our institutions, at no very distant future."[28]

Rayner's faith in the future of America was never restored. On March 6, 1884, he died of a stroke at the National Hotel in Washington. His body was sent back to Raleigh for burial in the Polk-Rayner plot in the Old City Cemetery a few blocks from the state capitol and near the old Polk mansion. The family erected a handsome marble obelisk over his grave, and the Raleigh *Register,* which so many times came to his defense in the bitter party battles of the antebellum years, published an appropriate obituary. "By the death of Mr. Rayner, a lofty niche has become vacant. His was a chequered life, since at different periods he was brought into connection with many parties. But standing by his open grave the differences of the past are forgotten."[29]

Kenneth Rayner's life was indeed chequered. By nature emotional and hot-tempered, he clung tenaciously to Enlightenment concepts of reason, order, and rationality. A self-described "conservative," he repeatedly found himself fighting for reform. A proud member of the southern slaveholding aristocracy, he despised the Democratic party and ultimately made peace with the Republicans. Steeped in the ideology of agrarian republicanism with its emphasis on the rule of "intelligence and virtue," he lived to see the United States embrace liberal democracy and become the bastion of industrial capitalism. In the nineteenth-century South, any of these contradictions might have been enough to cast one in the role of dissenter. Combine them in one man, and dissenter status was assured. Pronounce slavery "an evil to the white race" in 1836, oppose the annexation of Texas in 1845, campaign

for Know-Nothing-Republican fusion in 1856, or endorse black suffrage in
1870, and one would discover the limits of southern dissent. Kenneth Rayner
learned firsthand what it meant to overstep those limits.

Rayner did not live to see the full implications of the revolutionary changes
that had taken place in America during his lifetime. He witnessed the destruction of slavery, the enfranchisement of blacks, and the triumph of the
Democratic Redeemers, but he was spared the spectacle of lynchings, disfranchisement, and formal segregation that swept across the South at the end
of the century. As a national Republican officeholder in the 1870s and 1880s,
he felt the force of Bloody Shirt politics, but he scarcely could have imagined
that the South would remain solidly Democratic into the 1950s. And as a
devotee of republican ideology, little could he have envisioned that a version
of that ideology—in the guise of Populism—would have one last stand in the
South in the 1890s before liberalism and industrial capitalism won their final
victory.

Kenneth Rayner did not live to see these things, but one of his sons did.
John B. Rayner would personify the irony that was southern history. The
young man who had the slaveholder Kenneth Rayner as his father had a
slave woman as his mother. Physically, temperamentally, and ideologically
his father's son, he was—by virtue of birth and tint—consigned to a tragic
life within the severely circumscribed world of the black South. The younger
Rayner's life and career would fully reveal the limits of dissent in the New
South, much as his father's had explored those limits in the Old.

II

John B. Rayner

1850–1918

The civilization that teaches me to think, and then limits my aspiration, will asphyxiate itself with the mephitic breath of its own intolerance.

John B. Rayner, ca. 1917

CHAPTER 10

"The Nominal Continuance of Freedom"

Once during the war, Kenneth and Susan Rayner dined in Raleigh with Susan's niece, Catherine Ann Devereux Edmondston. In her diary that evening, Catherine described the couple. "Susan does not give one the idea of a happy woman," she wrote. "She before whom life was spread out all bright, all prosperous, who had her own way in every thing, despite her property, her position, her children, seems to have some thing which one cannot define present with her. . . . What it is one cannot define, but there is a shadow there." Catherine then criticized Kenneth Rayner and his attitudes toward the war, closing her diary entry with the comment, "I am glad I do not live with such a Raven!" Catherine Edmondston did not directly attribute Susan's undefined sadness to her marriage, but she must have known that her aunt's life as Mrs. Kenneth Rayner was, at times, difficult. One major reason for Susan's unhappiness—perhaps known to Catherine, perhaps not—must certainly have been Kenneth Rayner's sexual infidelity.[1]

Historians who have examined the dynamics of miscegenation in the Old South have shed much light on the nature of master-slave sexual liaisons. Surprisingly, southern society did not apply the usual moral proscriptions against extramarital intercourse to the unions between male slaveholders and their female chattels. The leading historian of the southern moral code has explained that such relationships "posed almost no ethical problems for the antebellum Southern community, so long as the rules, which were fairly easy to follow, were discreetly observed." Those rules dictated that the union be "a casual one in which the disparity of rank and race between the partners was quite clear to any observer" and that "the pairing could not be part of a general pattern of dissoluteness." According to this scholar, "a man should by all means never acknowledge in mixed company his illicit liaison with a woman, black *or* white." Scandal, according to another historian, "was perhaps worse than the deed itself."[2]

Mary Chesnut, an aristocratic southerner who shared much in common with Susan Rayner, confided to her diary an analysis of miscegenation that easily could have described the Rayner household. "Like the patriarchs of old," she wrote in 1861, "our men live all in one house with their wives and their concubines, and the mulattoes one sees in every family exactly resemble the white children—and every lady tells you who is the father of all the mulatto children in everybody's household, but those in her own she seems to think drop from the clouds, or pretends so to think." It comes as no surprise, then, that Kenneth Rayner's illicit affair with at least one slave woman attracted little attention during his lifetime. He did not discuss this union, his white family certainly did not, and political opponents in North Carolina never would have brought up the subject; to criticize a wealthy southern planter-politician on such grounds nearly always would have backfired, so common was miscegenation among Rayner's contemporaries. As one former North Carolina slave recalled, "At dat time it wus a hard job to find a marster dat didn't have women 'mong his slaves. Dat wus a generel thing 'mong the slave owners."[3]

On November 13, 1850, a fifteen-year-old Rayner slave named Mary Ricks gave birth to a son whose father was obviously white. The black descendants of Kenneth Rayner agree that Rayner made no effort to conceal the identity of this and at least one other mulatto child. It is not surprising that he either tacitly or openly acknowledged his mulatto offspring and afforded them special treatment. Given Kenneth Rayner's temperament and the prevailing notions of honor and propriety in North Carolina elite society, it would be surprising had he done otherwise.[4]

The boy, named John Baptis Rayner, was probably born on his father's farm on the outskirts of Raleigh. Either at birth or in early childhood, he was taken from his mother and brought to the mansion in town, where he was placed in the care of his maternal great-grandfather Henry Jett, who raised him. Jett was born a slave, but he had been freed by the provisions of Colonel William Polk's will. He had spent his life in the service of the Polk and Rayner families. Although his ostensible job was that of carriage driver, Jett appears to have fulfilled the dual roles of manager and patriarch of the Polk-Rayner slaves in Raleigh. There were reasons, however, for Jett's privileged status.[5]

Henry Jett's parentage cannot be stated with absolute certainty, but his black descendants agree that he was blood kin to the Polks. In all probability, he was the illegitimate son of Revolutionary War General Thomas

Polk, Susan Rayner's grandfather. Speculation over Jett's mother's identity has ranged from a mulatto slave woman to an Italian mistress. Whatever his parentage, Jett did not possess much Negro blood; in his photograph he appears to be white. With Thomas Polk's death, the family slaves passed to his son. Susan Rayner's father, William Polk, thus found himself in the strange position—not so terribly uncommon in the Old South—of owning his own half-brother. Jett married another Polk slave, Matilda, and they had a large family; he lived to see his granddaughter, Mary, give birth to John Rayner. By this time, the Polk family mansion in Raleigh and the offspring of Henry and Matilda Jett had become the property of Kenneth and Susan Rayner as part of Susan's inheritance. Because Henry Jett's wife and their large family were slaves, Jett continued to live in the servants' quarters and work for Kenneth Rayner, even though he was technically free. Cornelia, also a Jett descendant and a subsequent mulatto child of Kenneth Rayner's, was similarly placed in the care of Henry and Matilda. She and John grew up as brother and sister.[6]

Oral tradition among John Rayner's descendants holds that the boy was brought into Kenneth Rayner's household without much regard for the sentiments of Susan or the other white family members. Whatever Susan thought initially, she, like so many other southern women, had no choice but to accommodate Kenneth's mulatto children. It was no more than her own grandmother had done fifty years earlier when she had been forced to tolerate the special treatment that Thomas Polk accorded Henry Jett. During the Know-Nothing campaigns of the mid-1850s, Kenneth spent many weeks away from home, and Susan would have had to play a large part in the management of the Raleigh household, with its large contingent of both whites and blacks. Even after the decline of Know-Nothingism, Kenneth spent much time visiting his far-flung planting empire. With her husband gone so much, Susan's contacts with her husband's illegitimate children must have been frequent and not altogether pleasant. They were, after all, not only Kenneth's offspring but also her own blood relatives. During the war, Susan managed the Confederate soldiers' hospital in Raleigh. John's sister, Cornelia, told her descendants about Susan Rayner taking the mulatto children with her to the hospital to assist in the care of wounded soldiers. In addition, the Rayners opened their home to a number of wounded Confederate officers, and in later years John Rayner recalled helping to care for them.[7]

When the war began, Kenneth's interstate travels came to a halt. His duties in the secession convention and the location of his plantations near the theaters of war caused him to live primarily in Raleigh through the years of his illegitimate son's early adolescence. It must have been a fascinating environment for the young member of Raleigh's slave "aristocracy." John could not have avoided hearing some of the public speeches that his father made in the 1850s and 1860s, and his own oratorical style would later bear the unmistakable imprint of this exposure. Even for a slave boy, reaching adolescence in the Kenneth Rayner household a few blocks away from the state capitol must have provided unusual opportunities to observe politics. Especially during the secession crisis and the early phases of the war, the Rayners entertained important political figures almost constantly. Chief Justice Thomas Ruffin spent many nights under his friend's roof, and few days passed without the Rayners inviting a visiting legislator, former governor, or Confederate officer into their cordial home. Exactly what impact this environment had on John Rayner, who would have been scarcely seen and never heard, is unclear, but it must have been influential.

In his later years, the younger Rayner vividly remembered the surrender of Raleigh. In 1904, he recalled helping the family hide "cotton and other valuables" from the rapidly advancing Union army. He also related the story of a young Confederate soldier who fired at Sherman's advance troops as they entered Raleigh on the day Kenneth Rayner surrendered the city. Federal authorities quickly apprehended the renegade and after a quick trial sentenced him to hang. "In carrying him to the place of execution they had to pass in front of Judge Rayner's mansion, and my boyish curiosity caused me to follow them." John claimed to have pleaded for the condemned man's life when he realized that the soldier was to be hanged.[8]

John may have received the rudiments of an education even before emancipation. Urban slaves of aristocratic masters enjoyed vastly greater opportunities for education than their counterparts from the cotton fields. Henry Jett probably was literate, for he was chosen in 1868 to lead a secession of two hundred black members from Raleigh's previously racially mixed First Baptist Church, founding the First Colored Baptist Church. If John was not taught to read and write before emancipation, he at least was given religious training, for Jett was described at the time of his death as "a consistent member of the church" for more than sixty years. However, after his father turned Raleigh over to Sherman's army, John Rayner's education really began.[9]

Kenneth Rayner's outlook toward former slaves shifted in the months immediately after the war. First he despaired of blacks being able to function as productive free laborers and whites' refusal to recognize them as free citizens. Thus he advocated colonization as the only practicable solution to the problems posed by emancipation. During 1866, however, Rayner's attitudes changed. He began to realize that both blacks and whites would remain in the South, and as his mental and physical health recovered, Rayner revised his initial pessimistic predictions. He came to believe that, with the proper guidance of whites, freed slaves might be able to adjust to their freedom and become productive citizens much quicker than he had first imagined.

One episode during 1866 helped Rayner make this transition. On one of his postwar trips to the Northeast, he visited his old friend O. O. Howard, the former Union general who, as head of the Freedmen's Bureau, was deeply involved in early experiments with black education. Howard recalled in his autobiography that Rayner, whom Howard "had long known and valued as a personal friend, came to my room to labor with me and show me how unwise were some of my ideas." Howard recalled Rayner's comments about black education: "General Howard, do you not know that you are educating the colored youth above their business? You will only destroy them. Those young girls, for example; they will be too proud or vain to work, and the consequence will be that they will go to dance houses and other places of improper resort." Howard was "astonished" that Rayner expressed such an opinion and set out to prove him mistaken.[10]

Howard took Rayner across the street from his headquarters to the "seminary," where black teen-age girls were being taught. First they visited a music class and heard one black girl sing while another accompanied on the organ. As Howard looked on approvingly, Rayner's "eyes moistened," and he whispered, "They always could sing!" Next the men sat in on a reading class, where the ability of the students and good order of the classroom made a deep impression on Rayner. Howard wrote that his friend "had seldom seen" such an impressive school, "even of whites." As the men left the school and walked back across the street arm in arm, Rayner told Howard, "General, you have converted me!" Before leaving, Rayner promised to support black educational efforts at home.[11]

As his antebellum political career made clear, Rayner had always favored an environmentally determined conception of racial potential over the more popular competing theories that suggested the inherent and permanent inferiority of non-Anglo-Americans. But if he believed that Irish Catholics needed twenty-one years of "training" in the ways of Americanism, then it is not surprising that he entertained certain reservations about the integration of blacks into American society. His rejection of biological determinism, however, meant that Rayner's opinions on black potential could be shaped and revised as new evidence demonstrated that blacks could learn quickly. The same intellectual influences that made him a dissenter during the 1850s again placed him outside his region's mainstream in supporting black education.

Despite considerable opposition from many native whites, a number of schools for former slaves were established in Raleigh in the first years after the war. In 1866 or 1867, young John Rayner enrolled in the Raleigh Theological Institute, later renamed Shaw University. Founded in 1866 by a New England Baptist minister and receiving support from the Freedmen's Bureau, the New England Freedmen's Aid Society, and the American Baptist Home Mission Society, the school's primary mission was to train black ministers.[12]

As the Raleigh Theological Institute was making its first efforts to educate the freed slaves, a group of prominent North Carolina Episcopalians were founding yet another educational institution, St. Augustine's Normal and Collegiate Institute. Incorporated in July 1867 under the auspices of the Episcopal church to train black schoolteachers and ministers, its incorporators included several of Kenneth Rayner's friends. The school opened in January 1868, on land adjoining Rayner's property in Raleigh. St. Augustine's was the institution that he had promised O. O. Howard to help promote, and John Rayner's descendants recalled that Kenneth donated money to the school. Although surviving records are not entirely clear, it seems that when the elder Rayner left Raleigh for Memphis in 1867, he rented the Raleigh mansion to Dr. J. Brinton Smith, first principal of the school. During St. Augustine's first term, some of the female students roomed in the house, while male students lived in the adjoining servants' quarters. Therefore, in the case of John Rayner, the usual practice whereby students leave home for college was reversed—college came home to him.[13]

When Kenneth, Susan, and their children left Raleigh, they took a few of their former slaves with them to Memphis. John and Cornelia, however, stayed in Raleigh. No record survives of communication between the Rayners, although John monitored his father's subsequent political career. Perhaps they did keep in touch, discussing Republican politics and exchanging news about the white and black branches of the family. But it seems unlikely. In the numerous personal letters of Kenneth Rayner that have survived from the Civil War period, he never specifically mentioned his mulatto children. In 1866, he wrote to his daughter, Sallie, that "none of us have any ties to sever" in leaving Raleigh. Kenneth Rayner in 1867 wished to leave behind the life that the war had irrevocably shattered. Ever-paternalistic toward his former slaves, for whom he apparently had sincere affection, he saw to it that his son John received the advantages an education could bring. Having fulfilled what he perceived to be his responsibility toward the young man, the father then turned his back on the son. Such was the legacy of slavery and racism in the South; blacks and whites found their lives undeniably interconnected but ultimately worlds apart.[14]

John probably pursued his education until at least 1870, when the census listed both him and his sister as living in the household of Edward Lane, a thirty-year-old mulatto carriage driver who lived in a predominately black neighborhood. The census-taker did not record an occupation for John, so it is likely that he was still a student, renting a room from the Lanes. The education that Rayner received at St. Augustine's was surprisingly thorough. The curriculum in the mid-1870s included the basics of English, history, and mathematics, although it placed heavy emphasis on the Greek and Latin classics—among them Homer, Plato, Herodotus, Thucydides, Virgil, and Cicero. This formal classical education, so similar to the training his father received fifty years earlier, would be reflected throughout the younger Rayner's life in his writings and speeches.[15]

Although he had not graduated, sometime between June 1870 and November 1872 John Rayner completed his education and left Raleigh. He had taught school briefly in rural schools near Raleigh, but teaching alone did not satisfy his ambitions. Rayner's destination was Tarboro in Edgecombe County, two counties to the east of Raleigh. There, nearly fifty years earlier, his father had attended the academy and begun studying law. John had just turned twenty-one, and a young, educated, black North Carolinian interested in politics could have found no better place to embark upon an exciting political career.

Located in the heart of the most heavily black section of the state, Edgecombe County in 1870 had a population of nearly twenty-three thousand, two-thirds of whom were black. When the Reconstruction Acts of 1867 enfranchised blacks, the Republican party easily gained control of the county's politics and soon established a strong biracial political coalition that moved swiftly and confidently toward securing equal rights for all citizens. As elsewhere in the South, blacks held a minority of the elective offices, but they placed in positions of power white Republicans who were expected to represent black interests. Black elected officials most commonly filled the lower-level local and county offices, which provided valuable grass-roots training for the first generation of southern black political leadership. John Rayner, who grew up in the eye of the political hurricane in North Carolina, naturally was attracted to such an environment.[16]

During Reconstruction, Tarboro in many ways epitomized the deep South. Much more so than either Raleigh or Hertford County, it was the kind of place that William Faulkner would later write about—a place of honor-sensitive, aristocratic planters, struggling poor-white dirt farmers, and masses of oppressed freed slaves. Herds of pigs rooted about the dusty

streets. By night the Union League and the Ku Klux Klan secretly organized. Blacks and the lower classes of whites mingled along the Tar River
waterfront in a district of saloons and brothels known as "Grab All." William
Biggs, the unreconstructed editor of the town's Democratic newspaper, the
Tarboro *Southerner,* proudly quoted Jefferson Davis on the masthead of his
paper: "I AM A SOUTHERN MAN, OF SOUTHERN PRINCIPLES." The local
sheriff jailed Biggs twice in four years to keep him out of duels.[17]

The surviving historical record provides only a meager outline of John
Rayner's life and activities during his years in Tarboro. In keeping with the
rough-and-tumble character of the town, he appears to have sown a few
wild oats as a young bachelor. In November 1872, he was summoned by the
Edgecombe superior court to testify in a bastardy case. The mother, Eliza
Lawrence, claimed that Rayner had fathered her illegitimate child, a charge
he did not deny. The court ordered him to pay court costs and post a bastardy bond that would compensate the county in the event the child became
a public burden. The following spring Rayner again ran afoul of the law and
was found guilty of assault and battery. Neither episode was serious enough
to warrant explanation in the local press, but they suggest he was something
less than the pious man of God that his collegiate theology instructors had
trained him to be. Such indiscretions apparently did little to prevent Rayner's
entry into politics, for in 1873 he was appointed to the first of a number of
local political offices.[18]

The following year Rayner married a fair-skinned mulatto woman, Susan
Staten. Performing the ceremony was Tarboro's white Episcopal priest Joseph
Blount Cheshire, a family friend of the Kenneth Rayners who had been one
of the founders of St. Augustine's University. Clearly, John had not severed
all ties to North Carolina's white elite or to his own past. The couple settled
down to the business of making a living and starting a family, and two years
later their daughter, Mary, was born.[19]

Rayner entered Edgecombe County Republican politics with his appointment as constable of the grand jury for the fall 1873 session of the superior
court. He held the position intermittently for the next five years, serving again
in fall 1874, spring and summer 1876, and spring 1878. Edgecombe County
during Reconstruction was divided into fourteen townships, each of which
elected justices of the peace, school committeemen, and a constable. During
the mid-1870s, a small coterie of Republicans, black and white, shared these
offices, with individuals often holding the county offices concurrently with
state or federal positions. The voters of Tarboro Township elected Rayner
justice of the peace in August 1875 by a straight party vote, and his term
expired in 1877. Under the state's Reconstruction constitution justices of

the peace, or magistrates, enjoyed considerable power. They presided in civil suits involving amounts of $200 or less and in criminal cases punishable by a maximum of one month in jail or a $50 fine. In addition, two magistrates plus a clerk in each township constituted a board of trustees that, under the supervision of the county commissioners, assessed taxes, administered elections, and maintained roads and bridges. As magistrate and trustee, Rayner received invaluable experience in grass-roots politics.[20]

Despite Rayner's and other blacks' success in Edgecombe County politics, the area was no utopia for blacks during Reconstruction. If he had not experienced it already, Rayner's first years in politics provided firsthand exposure to white supremacy in some of its most virulent forms. The county's population was so heavily black that no amount of effort on the part of white Democrats—short of legal disfranchisement—would ever end black political participation. This reality, bleak as it was to whites, did little to encourage a spirit of acceptance or conciliation among the Democrats. Fierce racial animosities in Tarboro never subsided during Rayner's years there. In 1872, the editor of the *Southerner*, William Biggs, echoed the sentiments of the county's unreconstructed white populace when he wrote that "the negro, with some exceptions, in his present state, is depraved, ignorant, brutal, and filled with all the evil depravities to which human nature is subject." Cataloging the many alleged transgressions of freed slaves, including the standard charge that black men had "defiled the chastity and outraged the virtue of thousands of Southern women," Biggs thought it only "natural for human nature to at last give way under such an accumulation of wrongs, and demand redress, even though at the bidding of Judge Lynch." Not surprisingly, Biggs's outspokenness nearly got him killed when he attended a Republican rally and, in his own words, "was fallen upon by a mob of negro and white assassins." Fortunately for the editor, two black men came to his rescue. Such was the political environment that John Rayner entered in 1873.[21]

The Republican grip on the county showed no signs of weakening as Rayner became more deeply involved in local politics, although Democrats went to extraordinary lengths to keep Republicans out of office. These included a campaign mounted in 1874 to prevent Republicans from posting the bonds required of elected officers. The types of rhetoric used in the anti-bond-signing campaign would become the stock-in-trade of Democratic politicians for the next fifty years. The *Southerner* fired the first shots: "*If there is a southern man of southern principles in Edgecombe county who desires Social Equality, . . . Mixed Schools, . . .* [and] *intermarriage between the races, let him put his signature to* [a Republican's] *bond!!!*"[22]

Such demagoguery proved fruitless. Enough financially secure Tarboro citizens were willing to commit "treason to party and race" to enable both white and black Republicans to post bond and take office. The working relationship between blacks such as Rayner and white Radicals such as Sheriff Joseph Cobb proved remarkably durable. In fact, Cobb's and Rayner's association extended to private business dealings, Cobb on one occasion loaning Rayner $250. But the Democrats never gave up. When Republicans again were required to post bonds in 1875, the Democratic press again called on all whites to refuse to sign. Not only were black officeholders a slap in the face of white supremacy, but magistrates like Rayner, who "hardly are able to read and write," were also making "a farce" out of county government. "Oh God!" cried the *Southerner,* "think of the insult you offer your children when you put your signature to the bonds of such men." The campaign again failed, and Rayner won election and posted bond.[23]

The cries of "social equality," "mixed schools," and "intermarriage between the races" proved, in time, to be powerful tools in the hands of southern Democrats. In reality, neither Radical Republicans in the 1870s nor Populists in the 1890s ever seriously advocated the full legal equality that would become the mark of racial liberalism in the mid-twentieth century. What Democrats in Tarboro were really seeking was not to prevent some imagined "social equality," but rather to defeat Republicans by ostracizing anyone who supported them. By Democratic standards, guaranteeing a Republican's bond branded one a traitor to white supremacy. The strategy actually was nothing new; Democrats had employed the same rhetoric in 1856, when they branded Kenneth Rayner an abolitionist for supporting fusion between the Know-Nothings and Republicans.

The ambitious young politician had achieved his first elective office, but over the next two years, things went sour for Rayner in Tarboro. The large Democratic majority elected to the state legislature in 1874 passed a bill calling for a convention to revise the 1868 state constitution. After debating the important question of who was the "original carpetbagger"—Jesus Christ or Judas Iscariot—the 1875 convention eventually passed thirty amendments. One took the election of justices of the peace away from voters and gave the legislature the right to appoint them. As the *Southerner* explained, "we consented to give up our much-loved right of electing Magistrates by the people, so that the incompetent carpet-baggers and negroes would have to stand aside." After his term expired in 1877, Rayner was no longer justice of the peace.[24]

The year 1877 was eventful for Rayner in several other respects. Not only did his tenure as magistrate come to an end, but his private business interests also suffered. In 1875 he had entered into a business partnership with a local political figure, John W. Gant, whom the *Southerner* described as "a white Republican of the blackest description." The men bought a lot fronting the Tar River, adjacent to the Grab All district, and the county commissioners granted a retail liquor license to the firm of "Gant & Rayner." The precise nature of Gant & Rayner cannot be known, however it probably was not a brothel, given the proprietors' status as local political leaders. More likely, Rayner and his partner were running a saloon, restaurant, or general store, any of which might have occasion to apply for a liquor license.[25]

Most of the Grab All district was situated on land owned by the city of Tarboro and leased to assorted "businesses." Gant and Rayner owned their property, but it adjoined the portion of Grab All owned by the city. In 1877, the leases of the district's proprietors expired, and the county commissioners decided to clean up the dens of iniquity. The county moved swiftly and not only evicted the tenants but also demolished the "various tenements defacing the spot." After the commissioners acted, the *Southerner* reported that "Grab All is as silent as some 'banquet hall deserted, whose lights are fled, whose whiskey's dead, and all but the scent departed.' Gant is gone, The others forlorn. Gone to mourn over past glories." Although their privately owned enterprise presumably escaped demolition, Gant & Rayner was a casualty of the successful moral crusade.[26]

The end of his term as magistrate and the demise of Grab All brought Rayner to a crossroads. Three months after the destruction of Grab All, a black Baptist evangelist from Washington, D.C., came to Tarboro and began a series of revivals. On the fourth Sunday of May he baptized thirty-eight blacks in the Tar River. Rayner was among them, and he became a member of the Colored Missionary Baptist Church. Despite his great-grandfather Henry Jett's role in the founding of Raleigh's First Colored Baptist Church, Rayner in his early life apparently had followed the example of his white relatives and was confirmed as an Episcopalian. He was trained in Episcopalian theology at St. Augustine's, and he had been married in the Episcopalian church. Baptism into the Baptist faith opened a new career to Rayner, even as his political career seemed to be drawing to a close. He was ordained to preach, adding the vocation of Baptist minister to his prior occupations of teacher, politician, and merchant. Three months later Rayner sold his interest in the Grab All property. Before long, North Carolina would be a part of his past.[27]

Stripped of his magistrate's office, Rayner served one more appointed term as constable of the superior court in 1878. Edgecombe County and the

Second Congressional District of which it was a part continued to elect black legislators and congressmen, but many local positions that traditionally were springboards to higher offices now were reserved for whites. Perhaps Rayner had not advanced far enough up the political ladder to ever stand a chance of election to a higher post, or maybe financial considerations persuaded him to seek a change. It is also possible that his conversion and the call to preach led Rayner to consider relocating to a region where educated black clergy were in high demand. Most likely, some combination of these factors was at work when he decided to move to Texas.[28]

Rayner was not alone in choosing to leave North Carolina in 1879–80. Conditions for the majority of blacks who were tenant farmers or sharecroppers had deteriorated steadily through the 1870s. The Redeemer legislature of 1876–77 provided for the draconian Landlord and Tenant Act that took away virtually all rights of tenants, including a clause that made violation of tenancy agreements a criminal offense. With such a law on the books and predominately Democratic courts to enforce it, black farmers found themselves hopelessly bound to the land and indebted to white landlords.[29]

In 1879, substantial numbers of blacks began to leave North Carolina and other southern states. Not only had the harsh Landlord and Tenant Act restricted black rights and opportunities, but the loss of the right to elect magistrates, the denial of blacks' right to sit on juries, and the end of black control over their public schools also rankled the former slaves. Radical Reconstruction had sought permanently to secure these fundamental rights for blacks and had failed. Rayner and thousands of other blacks who experienced the promise of Reconstruction spent the next twenty-five years attempting to regain what they lost with Redemption. By late 1879, the exodus from North Carolina had reached such proportions that white planters, fearing the wholesale loss of their black labor force, became truly alarmed. While many blacks emigrated to Indiana and other midwestern destinations, some of the "exodusters" chose the Southwest, including Texas. The flow of blacks attracted national attention and finally resulted in a congressional investigation.[30]

Rayner's search for a fresh start coincided with the mounting exodus. In about 1879, Horatio "Rasche" Hearne, a wealthy planter from Robertson County, Texas, traveled to North Carolina with one of his plantation managers to recruit black laborers. With North Carolina planters working diligently to halt the emigration, men like Hearne would have to find local intermediaries if they hoped to recruit black workers successfully. Although the evidence is largely circumstantial, it is almost certain that Hearne hired Rayner as such an intermediary. As a well-connected local leader who could speak the languages of both blacks and whites, the former magistrate was the perfect choice. His education and legal experience as a justice of the peace enabled him to see that laborers were getting a fair deal, and perhaps most importantly, he was prepared to move to Texas with them. A number of Robertson County planters participated in Hearne's enterprise and secured laborers in North Carolina "in proportion to the contributions they had made toward the expenses of the project." Ultimately, Hearne recruited "several trainloads" of blacks from North Carolina. As one of the county's white old-timers reminisced decades later, "For many years, when a Robertson County Negro was asked if he had been born in Texas, he would answer, 'No sir, Mr. Hearne fotch me out here from North Carolina.'" Oral tradition among Rayner's descendants places the number of exodusters he led to Texas at perhaps a thousand.[31]

When the federal census was taken in 1880, Rayner already had arrived in Calvert in Robertson County. Final arrangements for the emigrants may have involved one or more trips to and from Tarboro to Calvert, but to the knowledge of Rayner's descendants he never returned to North Carolina after 1880. His situation likely resembled that which the New York *Times* described in an October 1879 editorial on the North Carolina exodus: "The negroes who have been sent out to prepare the way before the intending emigrants are notified from home that it would be unsafe for them to return, so violent are the threats made against them by their former masters and present employers."[32] Whether or not Rayner was in Calvert to stay in June 1880, by May of the next year he and his family had settled into their new home. With the money earned from his efforts in the exodus, Rayner bought a comfortable frame house in the black section of Calvert and prepared to start a new life in Texas.

As the black exodus from North Carolina reached its peak in late 1879, the New York *Times* observed that the condition of the black farmers differed "from the old bondage in little beyond the name." White lawmakers and landowners were attempting "to reconcile the nearest possible approach to slavery with the nominal continuance of freedom." Having experienced the promise and the failure of Reconstruction as a grass-roots leader, John B. Rayner could testify to the truth of such a statement. Radical Reconstruction, with its brave experiment in racial equality, had resulted in little more than shattered expectations and new forms of oppression for those southern politicians, black and white, who had embraced its challenge to the South's old order. As his father fumed over the fate of white southern dissenters from the loneliness of an obscure Washington office, John B. Rayner was discovering firsthand the limits of black southern dissent. But at age thirty, he was not yet resigned to a fatalistic acceptance of those limits.[33]

CHAPTER II

"A Shrewd Politician"

John B. Rayner's new Texas home shared much in common with his old one in North Carolina. With 49 percent of the population comprised of former slaves and their families, Robertson County was heavily black by Texas standards. It ranked in the top ten cotton-producing counties in the state. Calvert, located in the western part of the county at the edge of the rich alluvial Brazos River bottom, was the largest town in the county, with a population of 2,280. North and east of Calvert is a brushier region of gently rolling hills interrupted by small rivers and creeks. Cotton grew best in the bottom land, but the soil throughout the county was reasonably good, and farmers outside the bottoms raised a variety of crops, including cotton. Most blacks, however, lived in the southern and western sections of the county where large planters grew cotton on a grand scale.[1]

Rayner's new home also resembled his old one in its postwar political history. When the conflict ended, Robertson County planters who had ardently supported the Confederate war effort experienced the "heavy burden" of Reconstruction. Union troops briefly occupied the county, the Freedmen's Bureau established a station, and following the passage of the 1867 Reconstruction Acts, blacks played an important role in county government. In fact, well into the 1890s the heavily black precincts, including Calvert and Hearne, continued to elect black county commissioners, constables, sheriffs, and four different state representatives. The high degree of opposition to the Democratic party, and the participation of both blacks and whites in that opposition, set the county apart from most others in the South. Moreover, beginning in the 1870s and continuing through the 1890s, Robertson County was a hotbed of third-party activity. Rayner became involved in these movements and eventually came to lead the most important of them.[2]

When Rayner came to Calvert in 1880, the state was in the midst of the second Greenback campaign. The agrarian Greenback party in the county had been heavily black and enjoyed the support of the county Republican organization. Two blacks from the county won seats in the state legislature in 1878 and 1880, and Calvert's own William H. Hamman, a former Confederate general, won the Greenback nomination for governor, evidence of the effective local black-white coalition. But such biracial coalitions were always fragile in the post-Reconstruction South, for they lacked the support of party organizations at the state and national levels. Furthermore, white agrarians as well as black Republicans often balked at the prospect of interracial cooperation. Nevertheless, the tradition of dissent—and of biracial political activism—was already strong in Robertson County when Rayner arrived in 1880.[3]

Rayner maintained a low political profile during his early years in Calvert, concentrating on making a living by teaching school. His family responsibilities grew, for in November 1882, Ivan Edward Rayner was born. John Rayner apparently displayed little interest in again running for an elective position, even though blacks continued to win local offices. He was, after all, a newcomer to a place where established black leaders likely were reluctant to share power. But Rayner had not forsaken politics. As events soon would demonstrate, he was keeping a finger on the political pulse of his adopted state. When the chance came to step onto the public stage once more, Kenneth Rayner's son would be ready.

The opportunity came in 1887. Despite its growing division into what might be termed "Bourbon" and "agrarian" factions, the state Democratic party continued successfully to fend off all serious challenges. But in 1887, a new issue threatened party unity: prohibition. Texans had always dealt with the issue of alcohol by local option. Although Democratic politicians well understood that such "moral" issues as prohibition could seriously undermine unity, by the mid-1880s the small but vocal minority of prohibition activists was proving bothersome. In January 1887, the state executive committee of the Prohibition party petitioned the legislature to frame a constitutional amendment banning liquor. Anxious to rid themselves of the issue and confident that voters would reject any such amendment in a statewide referendum, the legislature and governor agreed to place the measure before the people.

Despite Democratic efforts to portray the prohibition referendum as a nonpartisan issue, it was apparent to Rayner and virtually everyone else in Texas that the election had potentially enormous political ramifications.

Prohibition forced politicians to take sides or else give the impression of being weak or unconcerned. Such prominent Democrats as former Confederate Postmaster-General John H. Reagan and U.S. Senator Sam Bell Maxey announced their support for the amendment, as did the majority of the state's Protestant clergy. Governor Lawrence Sullivan Ross and Congressmen Roger Q. Mills, William H. Crain, and James W. Throckmorton actively opposed prohibition, as did Attorney General James S. Hogg, former Governor Francis R. Lubbock, and Lieutenant Governor Barnett Gibbs. As the campaign heated up in March, the Democrats began to fear that they had underestimated the divisiveness of the question.[4]

Rayner followed the growing controversy with keen interest. The prohibitionists officially commenced their campaign on March 15. They met in convention at Waco and drafted a plan of organization that included the following resolution: "That we make this campaign as citizens of Texas without reference to race, party politics, religious distinctions or temperance societies as such, leaving to all organizations, moral or religious, to adopt their own methods of helping in this great conflict." At home in Calvert, Rayner realized that the delegates had made a crucial error. Although they obviously intended to appeal to black voters, nothing in the prohibitionists' elaborate campaign plan specifically addressed how black votes were to be won. Yet those votes, if delivered in a bloc, could conceivably make the difference in a closely contested race.[5]

B. H. Carroll, Texas's most prominent white Baptist minister, chaired the prohibitionist state executive committee. On March 17, two days after the convention, Rayner wrote Carroll a confidential letter pointing out the oversight made in Waco: "Dear Sir, I know that I am not competent to advise you in theology, doctrine, ethics or any of the sciences that have a tendency to make man pure in purpose and angelic in action, but I know something about campaigning and elections." He explained that he was writing because he was "a prohibitionist from deep religious principle." Rayner reminded Carroll that "the coming campaign will be fought on negroland," and that "the negro vote is quite an item and will play an important part in the coming election." Not being personally acquainted with Carroll, Rayner explained that he had "some little negro in my veins" and knew "the eccentricities of the negro." The little-known black politician had some practical advice for the white prohibition leader.[6]

He laid out his own plan for how the prohibition forces could capture the black vote and bluntly told Carroll something that everybody knew: "money is to be used" in the election by both sides, so prohibitionists had better know how to put it where it would do the most good. In his first piece of advice, Rayner cautioned Carroll about the untrustworthiness of black preachers— a paradoxical attitude for a politician who himself was a black preacher. He warned that "every old worthless Baptist preacher that has no influence or intellect will seek to be appointed a canvasser in this coming election, and if they fail to get the appointment from the prohibitionists they will offer themselves for sale to the whiskey men." Rayner believed he knew "how to get around this class and still keep them our friends." He proposed "to catch the colored men in three traps, viz: The A.M.E. church, the M.E. church and the Baptist church." The first step was for Carroll to ask "the bishop of the M.E. church to come to Texas and call a council of his presiding elders in this matter [and state] that he (the bishop) will appoint no preacher to any work next year that will not take a bold stand for the prohibition constitutional amendment, and have the bishop of the African Methodist church to do the same." Rayner named the state's three most influential black Baptist ministers and instructed Carroll to "have these three men to visit all the Baptist associations that are to be held prior to the election and distribute temperance literature and prohibition sermons, etc." He suggested that the dry forces give L. G. Jordan, editor of the *Baptist Pilot,* "about $200 for the use of his paper, and have Jordan to send a copy of his paper to every Baptist preacher in this state from now until the election." Jordan had access to a list of all the black Baptist preachers in the state, and Rayner was certain that with this financial inducement he would "strongly defend the amendment from a religious standpoint. Be sure to look after the colored papers in the state," Rayner added, noting that if Carroll would follow this advice, he would "silence all the old worthless and characterless Baptist preachers that will annoy you and your committee."[7]

Carroll and the prohibition state committee apparently heeded Rayner's suggestions. In the following weeks the prohibitionists began holding rallies throughout the state for black voters. The black ministers named in Rayner's letter played important roles in these gatherings, and in early June the prohibition press announced the impending arrival of Georgia's Henry M. Turner, bishop of the African Methodist Episcopal Church and one of the most prominent members of the black clergy in America. Encouraged by the implementation of his plan, Rayner himself began stumping Robertson and the surrounding counties in the service of prohibition.[8]

How did he really feel about the issue? He told Carroll that his zeal for the cause sprang from "deep religious principle," but this was the same Rayner who had operated a liquor-selling establishment in Tarboro's Grab All district ten years earlier. Perhaps his conversion and baptism into the Baptist faith had wrought a sincere change of heart. But in spite of his professed religious motivations, Rayner embraced prohibition in 1887 not as a minister of the gospel but as a politician. He wanted to play the liquor question for all it was worth, because in prohibition lay the means for seriously injuring the Democratic party of Texas. From his entry into politics in 1873 until his death forty-five year later, Rayner, like his father before him, spent most of his public life pursuing one political objective above all others—defeating the Democrats.

The prospects looked bright from the prohibitionist standpoint in the early stages of the campaign, but soon there was trouble. In early June, Rayner's letter to Carroll somehow fell into the hands of the opposition, who quickly made its contents public. The *Vox Populi*, a prohibition paper published in Calvert, charged that the letter had been obtained through "foul means," but there was no proof of the charge. The exposure of the letter was "a devil of a mishap" for the drys, and immediately the "Rayner letter" became a major campaign document for the wets. Opponents of prohibition across the state read the letter at antiprohibition rallies, and it received widespread attention in the wet press.[9]

The letter badly embarrassed the drys—not because it was bad advice, but indeed because it was such good advice. Here was a way for the wets not only to associate prohibition with Negroes but also to show the white prohibition leader actually taking advice from a black. Wet newspapers published Rayner's letter under the headlines "Dark Tactics" and explained that Carroll had "'tumbled' to Bro. Rayner's suggestions." "Rayner is an old and astute politician," jeered the Calvert *Courier*, "and Dr. Carroll is but a new hand at the bellows. They are both Baptist ministers, regularly ordained in the service of Christ, and the proprieties, the Courier believes, are not particularly shocked by the doctor's prompt action upon a masterly suggestion from his colored brother." "Rayner is a shrewd politician," added the Waco *Examiner*, "and understands to a dot how to organize a political campaign." When seven black clergymen took to the prohibition campaign trail, the wet press dubbed them "Rayner's Seven." By early July, the *Examiner* could note with considerable accuracy that "the success of the [antiprohibition] cause has never been doubtful for one moment . . . since Parson Rayner came to Parson Carroll's help with advice as to how to run the campaign. The antis should see to it that Rayner has a nice little monument when he dies."[10]

As it became clear that the contest would be fought on both racial and religious grounds, the campaign assumed a character quite different from

its original nonpartisanship. Both sides engaged in demagoguery. A prohibition leader charged that the liquor interests were catering to the "bo-Dutch"
[German immigrants] and "buck niggers" in efforts to keep Texas wet. The
antiprohibitionists, in turn, accused their opponents of being nativists and
racists. The opponents of prohibition also effectively argued that religion
had no place in politics. "That Rayner letter and the presence of Bishop
Turner, apparently carrying out in good faith its recommendations, needs,
nay, demands explanation," wrote an anti editor. "Politics which mix up reli-
gions like that are dark and peculiar, and Dr. Carroll ought not to be in the
business." [11]

Unlike Rayner, many blacks could not see beyond the immediate issue of
prohibition to the larger need to divide the Democratic party. Black Republican leaders such as J. C. Akers of McKinney and Melvin Wade of Dallas
stumped East Texas in the service of the antiprohibitionists, speaking at wet
rallies and meeting Rayner in debate. Their arguments were simple but effective. Drawing upon the natural oratorical ability and keen sense of humor
that would later make him an effective speaker for Populism, Wade told audiences that "he was a Republican because he was built that way, but if it was
necessary in order to secure his personal right to take care of his own stomach to go with the Democrats he would go straight and as quick as a flash
of lightning into the very middle of their camp." Wade and Akers portrayed
prohibition as an attempt to curtail the personal liberties that blacks had only
enjoyed for the few brief years since emancipation.[12]

Perhaps without realizing it, Wade and other wets occasionally touched
upon the real reason for Rayner's ardent support of prohibition. When Wade
made excuses for siding with the Democratic party, he was tacitly admitting
that prohibition struck a blow to the Democrats. Another anti was more ex-
plicit, openly charging Carroll with "doing his best to build up a third party,
which, if established, will destroy the Democracy." The most telling accusation came from the antiprohibitionist editor of the Wills Point *Chronicle*,
who described the typical prohibitionist as a "Prohib-Radical-Greenbacker-
Disaffected-Political-Failure." Whether they knew it or not, the combatants
in the 1887 prohibition campaign were fighting over something of far greater
long-term importance than the right to take a drink. They were fighting over
an issue which, if decided in favor of prohibitionists, could deal a crippling
blow to the Democratic party and thus, hopefully, to white supremacy. If no
one else understood this fact in 1887, John B. Rayner did.[13]

The voters of Texas went to the polls on August 4 and buried prohibition
by a 91,357-vote majority. After the results were known, the jubilant wets

made it clear that those prohibitionists who had thought they could disrupt the Democratic party had been sorely mistaken; destroying the Democratic party was no business for amateurs. As one antiprohibition editor pointedly expressed to B. H. Carroll, "You will greatly oblige us by taking as text for your Sunday sermon: 'Blessed is he that sitteth down on a hot gridiron, for he shall rise again.'" In a more serious vein, the editor of the *Examiner* asked rhetorically where certain prohibitionists would find their future political home and confessed to be unsure. But he predicted that any future movement seeking to divide the Democratic party would "enjoy the embraces" of Rayner, Carroll, and other prohibitionists. In the case of Rayner, that prediction was entirely correct.[14]

Even without a heated political campaign, 1887 would have been an eventful year for Rayner. Sometime before the canvass, probably in 1886, Susan had fallen seriously ill and died. A few days after the prohibition referendum, Rayner was arrested in Calvert on charges that he raped Lizzie Anderson, a black schoolteacher. The assault was alleged to have taken place in mid-July. "The case evicted [*sic*] quite an interest," according to the Galveston *News*, because of the defendant's "notoriety during the late election campaign." Soon after the courts settled the matter in Rayner's favor, he was accosted in a Calvert store by Dennis Anderson, Lizzie Anderson's father. Anderson came at Rayner with a large knife, but as he lunged, the stoutly built Rayner picked up a chair and hurled it at his assailant. The chair struck Anderson in the arm that held the knife, causing a serious self-inflicted wound. Rayner "then ran for dear life, with Anderson a close second." The chase proceeded out of the store and down the busy street, until Rayner ducked into a livery stable. The stable's owner intervened and bravely brought the chase to an end.[15]

The full story of this episode will never be known. The records of the Robertson County district court are complete for the period, but because they contain no mention of charges or a trial, the case almost certainly was dismissed. The "court room," which the press reported was "well filled with spectators," must have been either the preliminary hearing held by the justice of the peace or a grand jury hearing. Rayner, recently made a widower and sharing his father's passionate nature, may indeed have been involved with Lizzie Anderson. But because he was absorbed in the prohibition campaign during the time of the alleged rape, and because the case never came to trial, fairness dictates that his innocence be presumed. This presumption is strengthened by the fact that less than three months after these events, Rayner married his late wife's younger sister, Clarissa, who had come to Calvert from Tarboro to care for Susan. Until Rayner's death more than thirty years later, the marriage would be strong and stable. Clarissa never complained, although she had to shoulder the heavy burdens of children, poverty, an often-exasperating husband, and a society that doubly oppressed black women. She outlived her husband by forty-three years, dying in her Calvert home in 1961 at the age of 106.[16]

Following the prohibition debacle, Rayner temporarily dropped from the political scene. Texas was experiencing some of the hardest economic times in the state's history. The years from 1885 to 1887 had witnessed the most severe drought in anyone's memory. The price of cotton had sunk to 8.6 cents a pound, and farmers found themselves more deeply ensnared in the crop lien system with each passing year. As bleak as prospects looked for white farmers, blacks' prospects seemed even dimmer. The majority of adult black males in Texas were poor tenant farmers, and a gradual hardening of racial attitudes on the part of whites accompanied the deepening agricultural depression. In 1889, the state passed a law allowing separate railroad coaches for blacks, and the next legislature made segregated cars mandatory. Even more disturbing was the escalating rate at which Texas blacks accused of crimes met their fate at the hands of lynch mobs—twenty-two in 1890 alone.[17]

Rayner followed these disturbing developments from his home in Calvert, uncertain of the proper political course to pursue. Blacks in Texas had been more successful than their counterparts in many other southern states in retaining their right to vote, but the traditional champion of black interests, the Republican party, had become a "non-entity," as Rayner so aptly put it. Agrarian discontent lay smoldering just beneath the surface of Texas politics, but the abortive Greenback campaigns of the previous decade provided little cause for encouragement. Rayner realized that political cooperation between downtrodden blacks and whites was not merely desirable; it was a practical necessity if the long reign of the Democrats was to be broken. But how was such biracial cooperation to be achieved when racism was so ingrained in white culture? Most white Texans agreed with the influential Democratic congressman Roger Q. Mills when he stated, "The emancipation of the negro was a merciful, and, we believe, providential, affair; but clothing him with political privileges and power was a thing of satanic origin and consummation." [18]

At the end of the 1880s Rayner could look back over the first forty years of his life and see—as clearly as anyone in America—how white supremacy had disfigured the political life of the nation. He found himself facing a set of circumstances in many ways similar to that which his father confronted in the early 1850s. Kenneth Rayner had grown to political maturity in the two-party South of Jackson and Clay. He had seen that two-party system, despite its shortcomings, bring an unprecedented degree of democracy to America. Fears concerning the future of slavery helped to kill the Whig party, and knowing that a republican form of government could not survive under one-party rule, especially if that party was the Democratic, the elder Rayner had risked his political life on a new party.

John B. Rayner arrived at a similar juncture on the eve of the Populist revolt. Although his role was small, he had participated in restoring the two-party system to the South through the agency of Radical Reconstruction. But the South's determination to preserve white supremacy doomed the chances of the Republicans, as it had the Whigs, to remain viable competitors in the system. As the Democratic party consolidated its hold on the South in the 1870s and 1880s, the black son, like his white father thirty years earlier, was forced to make a choice. He could take a serious political gamble and affiliate with a new party, or he could acquiesce in the rule of a party he knew would bring ruin to his people. For John B. Rayner, as for Kenneth before him, there could be little doubt which choice to make.

CHAPTER 12

"The Silver-Tongued Orator of the Colored Race"

John B. Rayner sensed that he and his people had reached a critical juncture at the beginning of the 1890s. He had shared in the lofty optimism of the Reconstruction years only to see the Redeemer Democrats systematically destroy blacks' hopes for a just biracial society in the South. The Republican party, once the champion of black rights, was impotent without significant white support. Independent politics of the Greenbacker variety had invariably failed to produce lasting reform.

As Rayner sought some avenue that would lead to meaningful change, he noticed the progress of the latest farmers' organization in the South, the Farmers' Alliance. Poor white farmers increasingly found themselves cast into the same dire economic plight as blacks, mired in tenancy and ensnared by the furnishing merchants. Led by a brilliant neighbor of Rayner's from nearby Milam County, Charles W. Macune, the Alliance by 1887 had at least a hundred thousand members in Texas. A parallel organization for blacks, the Colored Farmers' Alliance, also enjoyed rapid growth. Originally a nonpartisan organization, the Alliance recognized the collective nature of rural problems and thus sought to aid farmers by establishing cooperatives. When these private efforts ran headlong into the opposition of powerful business and financial interests, the Alliance began edging closer and closer toward insurgent politics. If such insurgency were to assume a biracial character, it would find an ally in John Rayner.[1]

By 1890, the Alliance was a national organization, and in a series of state and national conventions it framed a series of political "demands" calling for government regulation or ownership of the railroads, abandonment of the gold standard in favor of both paper money and silver, equalization of the tax burden, prohibition of alien land ownership, and a graduated income tax. At the heart of the Alliance program was the Subtreasury Plan, a proposed federal network of warehouses that would store farmers' crops, extend guaranteed low-interest farm loans, and release the crops onto the world market in an orderly fashion, preventing the usual market glut at harvest time. The Subtreasury Plan would go a long way toward solving farmers' most pressing problem, the usurious short-term credit that had previously been available only through furnishing merchants. At the same time, it would increase the money supply, causing inflation and enabling debt-ridden farmers to meet their staggering financial obligations more easily. When the Alliance eventually formed its own independent political movement—the Populist, or People's, party—these demands would form the heart of its platform.[2]

The agrarian movement that produced the Alliance and People's party was an attempt on the part of southern farmers to restore Jeffersonian principles to a rapidly industrializing and urbanizing nation. Populists tended to be small landowners fearful of being driven into tenancy or sharecropping and thus losing the personal independence that Jeffersonian ideology so highly valued. They rarely questioned the concept of private property, the need for commerce and manufacturing, or capitalism broadly defined, but they longed for a return to a simple market economy in which the "producers" of wealth—farmers and other laborers—controlled the marketing of their goods and thus received full value for their labor. It is no coincidence that Populists, including Rayner, consistently described their party as the home of true conservatism, for they saw themselves as the guardians of basic American values that monopolistic combinations had endangered. Because Populists mistrusted banks and large corporations and took as their credo the Jacksonian slogan "equal rights for all and special privileges for none," they also have been portrayed as the ideological heirs of the left, or "Loco-Foco," wing of the Jacksonian Democratic party.[3]

John B. Rayner's attraction to Populism, however, makes more sense if one examines the agrarian movement in the light of the antebellum opposition tradition as exemplified by Whiggery and Know-Nothingism. The parallels are numerous and striking. Whiggery, Know-Nothingism, and Populism each claimed to be the intellectual heirs of Jeffersonian republicanism. All three ran counter to the prevailing American ethos of constant progress; in the eyes of southern Whigs, Know-Nothings, and Populists, the nation had regressed from its golden age of purity and justice and had fallen prey to corruption. They traced that corruption to dangerous concentrations of unchecked power. Whigs had located that power in Andrew Jackson and his

Democratic successors. Know-Nothings continued that theme and grafted onto it the new threat posed by immigrants and Catholics. Forty years later Populists again identified the Democratic party as the source of corruption in the South. When they looked to Washington they discovered that the Democrats had made peace with the Republicans, and both parties had fallen into the hands of monopolistic capitalists. For Texas Populists, the monopolists (variously labeled "plutocrats" or "the money power") posed the same sort of threat to republican institutions as immigrants had to Know-Nothings or Andrew Jackson to Whigs. There was, however, one constant: The corrupt power of the Democratic party lay behind them all.

Those who find the roots of Populism in Jacksonian Democracy have faced one major problem: how to reconcile the negative-government, laissez-faire bias of Jackson with the positive-government program of the Populists. When the focus of comparison is shifted from Jackson and the Democrats to Clay and the Whigs, the contradiction is much less apparent. The Populist advocacy of government intervention to promote and preserve equality of opportunity has much in common with the Whigs' positive-government program as exemplified by Clay's American System. Both sought to take such important economic functions as transportation and finance out of strictly private hands and make them responsive to the will of the people as expressed through their elected representatives.

The nationalistic brand of Know-Nothingism enunciated by Kenneth Rayner also sheds light on intellectual roots of Populism. The Know-Nothings were avowedly against sectionalism and its destructive tendencies in American politics. Southern Know-Nothings, like Populists, usually shared the racial prejudices of their section, but they wished to see racial issues put aside in order to pursue the purification of the government. Both Populists and Know-Nothings believed that a nation preoccupied with the divisive question of race blinded itself to the rapid disappearance of republican freedom, equality, and prosperity. Their perceived need to place social, economic, and political reform ahead of race and sectionalism often made members of both parties more tolerant and open-minded in their racial attitudes. These comparisons between Whiggery, Know-Nothingism, and Populism are not meant to suggest some sort of direct lineal descent, although the examples of Kenneth and John B. Rayner make it tempting to do so. But Populism should be considered as part of the same intellectual tradition of southern opposition as the Whig and American parties.

Rayner was not present in 1891 when a group of fifty Alliance members met at a Dallas working-class hotel to organize the Texas Populist party, but he would soon realize the significance of what they had done. The delegates to that convention endorsed the demands that had been ironed out over the preceding several years by the Alliance. They also debated political strategy, confronting the issue that many must have dreaded but that had to be addressed: How was the party to handle the Negro question? They could not afford simply to ignore blacks, because in close races where the white vote was evenly divided, black votes could mean the difference between victory and defeat. On the other hand, to appear too cozy with blacks would alienate thousands of potential white supporters and subject the new party to the same charges of racial infidelity that had always plagued Republicans. The delegates in Dallas could not have avoided the issue had they wanted to, because a handful of blacks there pressed the issue. Melvin Wade, a black labor leader and Republican activist from Dallas who had been one of Rayner's opponents in the prohibition campaign of 1887, demanded to know whether the new party intended "to work a black and a white horse in the same field." When the whites answered his questions with platitudes, Wade apparently left. But later in the day another black, R. H. Hayes of Fort Worth, continued to press the issue. Hayes, who had been active in independent politics in the 1880s, believed that rural blacks would eagerly "affiliate with any party against monopolies in the interest of the poor man." However, the new party would have to demonstrate good faith by placing blacks in positions of party leadership, "otherwise, as regards the colored vote, the streams would be poisoned."[4]

In immediate terms, this meant black representation on the state executive committee. Chairman Harrison Sterling Price "Stump" Ashby made the most persuasive speech in favor of the proposal. "You are approaching a battlefield in which many errors have been made in the past," the eloquent Ashby told the delegates. "The Democrats have never given those [black] people representation; they have said they would buy enough of their votes with liquor and money. The Republicans have left the negro without a party. If he has a friend it is we, and he can be our friend.... We want to do good to every citizen of the country, and he is a citizen just as much as we are, and the party that acts on that fact will gain the colored vote of the south." Ashby's call for "full representation" brought applause. When one final attempt was made to dodge the issue by appointing blacks to "cooperate" with the whites, rather than electing them outright to the executive committee, Hayes again took the floor. "You will lose in spite of the devil and high water if your do not treat the nigger squarely," he bluntly warned the Populists. Faced with this ultimatum, and having the support of leading whites such as Ashby, the new party took the bold step of electing two blacks, R. H. Hayes and Henry J. Jennings, to the state executive committee.[5]

The 1891 Dallas meeting was small and represented only a fraction of the state's Alliance members. Whether or not it would produce a major third-party movement was still a question in many Texans' minds. Men of both races would have to be educated about the new party—who its leaders were, what its demands meant, and along what lines it was to be organized at the state and local levels. For those who had not closely followed the evolution of the Alliance, it could be confusing even to understand where the order stood in relation to the People's party. Did the Alliance support the third party or did it not? The confusion existing in the fall of 1891 is illustrated in John B. Rayner's initial approach to the new party. Populism apparently had not yet come to Robertson County. A few weeks after the Dallas convention, Rayner wrote Charles Macune a curious letter, explaining that because blacks "will not vote with the Democrats," perhaps "the best thing that we can do is to organize them into Knights of Labor." While there is no evidence that the two men had previously met or corresponded, Rayner clearly recognized that Macune had achieved a preeminent position as the architect of the Alliance economic program, but he apparently mistook Macune, who wished to wage the struggle from within the Democratic party, as a proponent of third-party action. Rayner explained that blacks "are anxious to identify themselves with the labor party." He claimed to have 150 men under his "control" who were "ready for organization" and asked Macune to refer him to the proper authorities who could initiate them into a Knights of Labor chapter. It is important to note that Rayner was not intent upon securing a Knights charter for labor unionism itself, but rather because that seemed the best way to "identify" his people with the new independent political movement. His mention of the "labor party" probably was a reference to the embryonic Populist party, which, although being formed in Texas, at that point was still frequently referred to simply as the "Third Party" and could easily be viewed as a reincarnation of the old Union Labor party. Furthermore, the Knights of Labor and the Farmers' Alliance had enjoyed a cordial relationship. Macune, lagging behind Rayner in his support of a third party, simply forwarded the request without comment to Knights' chief Terence Powderly. Soon the People's party would provide the solution to Rayner's desire for an independent political organization in which blacks could participate.[6]

By the next year no one in Texas had trouble knowing what to call the third party or how to identify its leaders. Rayner began working for the Populist cause among the blacks of Robertson and the surrounding counties, and even Melvin Wade finally turned his back on twenty-five years of Republicanism and affiliated with the new movement. When the state convention of the People's party met in 1892 to choose its first slate of candidates, a few black Populists in South Texas brought encouraging stories of their success in recruiting Negroes to the party. "The colored people are coming into the new party in squads and companies," one reported. The Populists gave their gubernatorial nomination to Judge Thomas L. Nugent of Fort Worth, a quiet, scholarly man with an impeccable reputation as a champion of independent reform politics. The Democrats split into two factions, with the old-line Bourbons nominating railroad attorney George Clark and the more progressive Democrats supporting incumbent Governor James S. Hogg, who had first won election on his promise to regulate the railroads. The fall elections would provide the new party with its first test of how successful it had been in spreading the agrarian gospel.[7]

Rayner and the Populists faced huge obstacles in their first campaign, not the least of which was the resistance of the state's Republican party. In a cynical attempt to defeat Hogg and gain a share of the spoils, the Republicans, led by the eminent black politician Norris Wright Cuney, endorsed Clark. This marriage of convenience between the black Republicans and the Bourbon Democrats embittered Rayner and thousands of other blacks. "The Cuney Republicans," Rayner subsequently wrote, "are 95 per cent negroes and 5 per cent whites. The negroes in this party are hotel flunkies, barbers, dude school teachers, ignorant preachers, saloon waiters, etc." Although a teacher and preacher himself, he had clearly been influenced by the idea, common in Jeffersonian, Whig, Know-Nothing, and Populist thought, that those lacking sufficient intelligence and virtue made poor voters and citizens. His description of black Republicans also suggests that Rayner had imbibed the Populist belief in the special status of farmers and workers—"producers" in Populist parlance—rather than those who earned their living in less socially beneficial ways.[8]

White Populists wanted and needed to win black votes, but they appealed for those votes in a haphazard and halting fashion. Although the Populist program clearly addressed the economic needs of all poor farmers, the 1892 state platform made no specific mention of blacks. Blacks might have been interested in planks that demanded a six-month public school term with state-furnished textbooks, a more equitable lien law, reforms in the notorious convict lease system, and fair elections, but the Populists kept silent on one of the most pressing of black concerns—lynching—and on the many other issues that affected the race. No mention was made of the Jim Crow railroad law, the blatant discrimination in state expenditures for black schools, and the right of blacks to sit on juries. With a platform of this sort, with Hogg on record against lynching, and with Clark enjoying the endorsement of the Cuney Republicans, the Populists stood little chance of success among the masses of Texas blacks. The naming of blacks to the Populist state executive committee and a general appeal to economic self-interest were all that most blacks could see. These gestures, along with the prospect of defeating the Democrats, were sufficient for Rayner in 1892, but not enough to convert the black rank and file to Populism.[9]

The 1892 election returns revealed the failure of Rayner and the Populists to attract black voters as well as the Populists' inability to woo sufficient numbers of whites away from the Democratic party. The state ticket headed by Nugent finished a distant third behind Hogg and Clark. Statistical analysis indicates that at the gubernatorial level the Populists received very little black support. Black voters fell into three roughly equal groups: a third supported Hogg, another third voted for Clark, and the other third stayed at home. Clearly, large numbers of blacks were disgusted with the choice of either Hogg or Clark but could see no good reason to vote for the third option, Nugent.[10]

In the wake of the 1892 debacle, the People's party had to reexamine its strategy. Populist voting was centered in the predominately white frontier farming counties of north-central Texas, with a few pockets of strength in some of the poorer piney-woods regions of the east. The party carried few of the wealthier planting regions where large numbers of blacks lived. In many of these areas the black-dominated Republican party continued to threaten white control, and thus whites were reluctant to split their vote between the Populist and Democratic parties and risk black officeholding. Blacks were just as hesitant to desert the Party of Lincoln and entrust their fate to a group of white southerners. The Populists had to find a way to make both blacks and whites in the Black Belt place reform ahead of racial anxieties. The third party needed to show white Democrats that the desperate financial plight of farmers would never improve under Democratic rule and that whites and blacks could honorably cooperate for the common good without inviting "social equality" for blacks. Populists also had to convince blacks that they were sincere in offering meaningful political participation. There were good reasons to be optimistic about the chances of recruiting more white Populists as the agricultural depression deepened. Cotton prices over the next two years would plummet to less than a nickel a pound, below the break-even

point for even the most efficient farmer. Many whites were already familiar with Populist demands through the Farmers' Alliance and the rapidly
growing reform press. But black "Pop clubs" could not organize themselves,
and few blacks could read (or afford) newspapers that would instill the vital
"education" of Populism. The party needed to address "black" issues more
directly and find more blacks with leadership ability, courage, and dedication
to travel and work tirelessly as organizers and educators.[11]

Rayner had remained inconspicuous during the 1892 election, restricting
his activities to some local speechmaking in the vicinity of Robertson County.
But events there provided a political education that shaped his actions for the
remainder of the Populist revolt. Robertson County in 1892 demonstrated
many of the factors required to bring success to a local Populist organization. First, the local black political hierarchy was already in tune with the
rising agrarian sentiment of the early 1890s. Not only had blacks and whites
achieved an unusual degree of solidarity in the Greenback campaigns of the
preceding decade, but the county also appears to have been a stronghold of
the Colored Farmers' Alliance. Black Alliance members in Calvert inaugurated a newspaper, the *Alliance Vindicator,* in February 1892. Sketchy evidence
suggests that Alex Asberry, the county's leading black Republican politician,
edited it and served as state president of the Colored Alliance. Second, a relatively small but influential group of white Democrats abandoned their party
and proved eager to form a working partnership with blacks. This movement
apparently began with the June 1892 resignation from the Democratic party
of Calvert's E. S. Peters.[12]

Peters, who became one of Rayner's most important white allies in the
People's party, was one of the more enterprising men of turn-of-the-century
Texas. A native of Michigan, he had come to Texas when he was twenty
and married the daughter of James K. Polk Hanna, a successful planter
from Calvert. Peters eventually acquired thousands of acres of land and
served many years as president of the Texas chapter of the American Cotton
Growers' Association. In June 1892, he resigned as chair of the Fourteenth
Senatorial District's Democratic committee. In a public resignation statement he harshly indicted the Democratic party, which he claimed had been
led "away from the fundamental principles of the democracy upon which our
free institutions were founded and [had been] delivered to the oppressive
money and corporate powers which have corrupted its leaders and now control the party." Peters and Hanna, along with Rayner, became the leaders of
the Populists in Robertson County, and in 1892 the party nominated Peters
for state senator and Hanna for presidential elector.[13]

As the fall elections approached, Populists led by Peters, Hanna, and Rayner, and black Republicans such as Asberry began to collaborate. In the first week of September the Populists held a two-day rally at the county fairground in Calvert, where Nugent and lesser Populist personalities spoke. Local black leaders soon were warning blacks about "being made a tool of by designing office seekers" and urging them "to vote for intelligent and respectable men of their own party or else join with the leading white citizens in their efforts in behalf of good government." The Republicans subsequently endorsed Peters and several other local Populist nominees but refused to support Nugent. When election returns were counted, it was apparent what had transpired in Robertson County. The inability of the Republicans and Populists to agree on a joint gubernatorial ticket had resulted in a victory for the Bourbon Democrat, Clark, but in contests such as the congressional race, where the Republicans endorsed the Populist candidate, the third party won with 54 percent of the county's vote. Returns from the entire county are incomplete, but at the Calvert ballot box—the center of fusionist strength with a large black vote—the white Populist candidates for district attorney and district judge swamped their Democratic opponents by a three-to-one margin.[14]

From the vantage point of Robertson County, Rayner could easily read the lesson of 1892; something very new was afoot in southern politics. A party of white native southerners who opposed Democrats of all stripes appeared anxious to allow blacks to participate in shaping party policy. Rayner could look at his home county and see the formula for success: find brave whites like Peters and Hanna who were not afraid to desert the hallowed Democratic party, convert every possible poor white and black farmer to the new cause, and convince the Republicans as a party to enter into an alliance with Populists to defeat the entrenched Democrats. He believed that success at the polls and the realization of justice in government, combined with continuing education and agitation, would soon render Populist-Republican fusion unnecessary. As blacks began to receive a fair break from the Populist state government, they would leave the Party of Lincoln as Rayner himself had done. Blacks could be persuaded to vote a straight People's party ticket, Rayner at one point stated, if only the Populists would "put men on the precinct and county tickets whom he (the negro) likes." The local level was the key. "Kind words and just treatment" from Populists in the precinct and county would eventually translate into statewide victories.[15]

Rayner and the Populists found ample reason for encouragement in the wake of their defeat, despite the fact that they had finished third in the statewide races. The party sent eight of its men to the state legislature in 1892 and, as in Robertson County, scored numerous victories at the local level. In Calvert, E. S. Peters's the *Citizen-Democrat* accurately reported in 1893 that "Populist papers are springing up like mushrooms." Populism was spreading with astonishing rapidity. By the following year the third party was prepared to mount a serious challenge to the now-nervous Democrats, and Rayner was poised on the brink of a remarkable career.[16]

As the 1894 campaign heated up, the state Populist press, metropolitan dailies, and numerous small Democratic weeklies began to note the political activities of a "traveling negro named Rayner." In March of that year the *Texas Advance,* the state paper of the People's party, started publishing speaking schedules of "Rev. J. B. Rayner, colored, our Populist orator." Typically, Rayner would visit a county and speak at black barbecues, picnics, and political meetings or conventions. Sometimes he made his speeches at the county courthouse or a local opera house, sometimes in tiny, off-the-beaten-path black settlements. He publicly offered his services to any county Populist organization that needed them. "I will now gladly visit any part of the state," he proclaimed in the *Advance,* "and organize my people into Populist clubs. Address me at Calvert, Texas." Announcements for his speaking engagements invited "all who favor justice, liberty, a higher price for labor, and a better price for products." [17]

The responses were overwhelming. In April, May, and June 1894 Rayner crisscrossed the eastern half of the state, speaking to crowds of all sizes and descriptions, leaving a trail of black Populist clubs, and consummating local fusion agreements between Populists and Republicans. Driven by the vital issues at stake—or simply curious—rural Texans of both races gathered to see and hear the man who was billed as the "Silver-Tongued Orator of the Colored Race." A report from a Populist partisan in a small town near Austin is typical: "The colored people of Elgin turned out in masse on last Saturday to hear J. B. Rayner of Calvert, our Populist orator. The opera house was filled with white and black, and Rayner made many colored Populists by his address. We are growing in numbers and influence." [18]

Rayner himself frequently took time to report his successes to the Populist faithful. One such letter provides a glimpse into his power as a speaker and the idealism that suffused the efforts of Texas's black Populists:

> "I have fought a good fight and have kept the faith," and by telling the truth converted to our political ideas every colored man and woman in Jasper and Newton counties. I have converted at least fifty per cent of my white auditors. The people in this part of the state are anxious for the truth, and I have told it to them and am proud of my work.

When I first came to these two counties the Democrats tried to hire a little pride-intoxicated colored school teacher to follow and reply to me, and so when I spoke at Jasper he came to reply and commenced to take notes of my argument, and when I had finished my talk, I found that he was nailed to his seat, and from now on he is out of politics.

The people in Jasper and Newton counties are virtuous and brave, and all they need is the light and truth.[19]

Of course, thunderous oratory and "light and truth" alone would not win statewide campaigns. Rayner knew that the poverty of the Populists and the pitfalls inherent in interracial cooperation called for a well-thought-out strategy. Education was a vital part of that strategy. Rayner worked closely with white orators and with the reform press, making recommendations to his white comrades about where their services were needed and helping poor blacks and whites obtain copies of Populist newspapers. He rarely hesitated to instruct his white colleagues on how to run a campaign, giving detailed directions in the *Southern Mercury* for the benefit of county and precinct Populist leaders. Above all, he stressed to white Populists the need to use his own services and enlist local black leaders in the Populist cause. "Our county chairmen in counties where the negro vote is important, should have colored speakers to visit the county, and address and instruct the colored voters," Rayner wrote. "You must reach the negro through a negro. This is possible with the People's party, but impossible with the Democracy. . . . The negro is a silent spectator. He never had any confidence in the Democratic party, and he has lost confidence in the Republican party, and this is written, because I know what must be done to get the negro's vote."[20]

Rayner's activities almost always invited controversy. In Freestone County, he was "circulating among the colored people" two weeks before the local Populist nominating convention. The Democratic Fairfield *Recorder* reported that Rayner led the county's black Republicans to believe "that if they would unite with the Populists they should have two commissioners and a county office." When the convention met and a black delegate allegedly pressed Rayner to make good on the promise, he reportedly denied the existence of any such deal. A local Populist paper gave a very different account of the events. According to the Wortham *Vindicator*, the report of Rayner having promised blacks offices "was emphatically false. . . . But we did offer to seat them in convention and did seat colored delegates from five precincts and allowed them to help us name our ticket."[21]

The *Recorder*'s editor grudgingly admitted the truth of the *Vindicator*'s statement. Then, in a revealing flourish of hypocrisy, he scornfully editorialized, " 'Helped us name our ticket.' How munificent, how noble in the Pops! The colored delegates were not permitted to mention their ticket, but 'they helped us nominate our ticket.' Then, to smooth things over, they gave the colored brother a 'resolution,' allowing them equal right to sit on juries." Rayner obviously had been walking a political tightrope in Freestone County, trying to do justice to his fellow blacks without jeopardizing the party's chances among whites. But whether or not he actually promised Negroes specific offices—which is doubtful—the *Recorder* unfairly charged the Populists with exploiting blacks. Not only did the third party grant them a voice in the nominations, but the resolution favoring blacks on juries also captured the heart of the Populist racial appeal. As long as whites controlled the apparatus of southern courts, they could hold the terrible prospect of the convict lease system over the heads of black sharecroppers, thus maintaining an oppressive labor system that bore an uncomfortable resemblance to slavery. To the white Democratic editor of the *Recorder,* entrenched in a political culture where spoils were the principal object of politics, allowing blacks "equal right to sit on juries" was simply a way "to smooth things over." To blacks, ending Democratic hegemony over the court system was an issue of paramount importance.[22]

In the months following Rayner's initial organization of Freestone County blacks, Populist candidates in the county repeatedly emphasized what Populism could mean to them. Speaking two months later at a black barbecue, L. N. Barbee, the district's white Populist state representative, told the audience, "You all know the Democrats never have allowed you a voice in their conventions and they never will. Because we seated you in our county convention and allowed you a voice in naming our candidates, every Democrat in Freestone county just harped on it." Barbee then asked pointedly, "How many of you have ever sat on a jury? Do you suppose that if I were jerked up down here at Fairfield to be tried before a jury that I would want a jury of lawyers, doctors and highly educated men? No, sir, I would demand a jury of farmers who till the soil as I do, men of my equal. You have the same privilege and ought to be allowed a voice in selecting a jury of your equals." Rayner had brought the word of Populism to Freestone County's black Republicans; it was then up to local white Populist leaders like Barbee to establish a working coalition with them.[23]

Due in large measure to Rayner's work, the profile of black Populism was changing. By the time the 1894 state convention met at Waco, both blacks and whites felt that real progress was being made in attracting blacks to the reform party. Blacks at previous conventions had been conspicuous mainly because of their scarcity, but at the 1894 meeting they participated in Populism in much greater numbers. None played a more prominent role in the convention's proceedings than Rayner.

Rayner and some twelve hundred delegates began converging on Waco on the evening of June 19. The next morning, they made their way to a city park, where the Waco Commercial Club had provided a huge tent for the convention. The charismatic Stump Ashby opened the meeting with a hymn, followed by a prayer. There can be no doubt that many delegates viewed the coming campaign more in terms of a holy war than a political contest. The first hours of the convention were spent in speechmaking by the party's heavyweights, including Ashby and James H. "Cyclone" Davis. But before long, several blacks also addressed the gathering. The total number of black delegates is unknown, but on the convention's first day the Waco *Evening News* reported that "the colored brother was a conspicuous figure and seemed to know what he was there for . . . a hearty welcome was accorded him." [24]

Rayner was among the more conspicuous "colored brothers." On the first day of the convention, Ashby introduced him to the delegates. A correspondent for the San Antonio *Express* reported that few in the audience knew that Rayner was a Negro when he approached the speaker's stand. He commenced his brief address with a joke he frequently used with great effect in his stump speeches. Making fun of white southerners' professed abhorrence of miscegenation, he facetiously explained that the Democratic party "was responsible for his complexion." Rayner then echoed what had become a familiar theme with him; if the Populists meant to help Negroes, they should "let the dude school teachers and long-tailed preachers alone." Rayner recognized that the black political power in the South traditionally had rested in the hands of teachers and ministers. He believed that in paying blind allegiance to the Republican party or kowtowing to Democrats they had too often abused the trust the black masses placed in them. But no more. From now on, black Texans "looked to the third party for their salvation." [25]

Throughout the convention, blacks mounted the podium to proclaim the new gospel of Populism. Their message always revolved around a common theme: the dire economic hardships being endured by both poor blacks and poor whites and the mistreatment of both races at the hands of the old parties. Melvin Wade, now firmly in the Populist camp, echoed this theme when he addressed the convention on the first day. In the 1891 convention Wade had asked whether the People's party intended "to work a black and a white horse in the same field." With characteristic humor, he now told the 1,200 Populists that the "Democratic and Republican parties are just alike. They hitch up the white man and the nigger together and drive 'em together just like the man here in this town I see drivin' a white and a black horse. If one of them stops and don't want to pull—don't make no difference which one it is, white or black—he lays on the whip." The Republican party, Wade argued, had "been treating the nigger just like the hunter treats his dogs. Snaps its finger and they jump and bark, then does this way (motioning down with his hand) and they lay down for four years." With the delegates in stitches, Wade ridiculed the "Young feller [who] says he's a Democrat because his father was one. According to him I ought to want to be a slave because my father was one." [26]

The high point of the meeting came on the second day, when the Populists nominated their candidates for state offices. In a dramatic moment, they placed the name of Judge Thomas L. Nugent in nomination for governor. Then, at the peak of the convention's euphoria, Rayner took the floor to second the nomination. The "colored delegate from Robertson" made an eloquent plea for interracial cooperation. Rayner proclaimed that blacks "had endured 4000 years of savagery and 245 years of slavery, only to find that the white man of the south is the negro's first, best and firmest friend." His voice ringing, he urged Populists to "Nominate Nugent and the negro will be as faithful to your flag as he was to your wives and children when you were fighting the battles of your country." Masterfully appealing to the Confederate tradition without downplaying the fact that slavery was an evil blacks had "endured," Rayner's speech was met with "loud applause" by the enthusiastic delegates, who proceeded to nominate Nugent by acclamation. [27]

On the third morning of the convention, the delegates faced two remaining tasks: selecting a new executive committee for the next two years and adopting an official platform. Rayner, now clearly the chief spokesman for the black Populists, was elected committeeman from the state at-large and took his place on the fifteen-member board. Perhaps equally important, he was named to the platform committee, which met that afternoon from noon until almost 6 o'clock in the evening. Although reportedly "a long war was waged in the committee over the platform," the committee "presented an unbroken front when they entered the big tent." The platform was adopted with near unanimity by the delegates. [28]

No Populist platform ever contained the sweeping civil rights declarations that would come along seventy years later. Yet the platforms of the Texas

People's party in the 1890s contained a number of planks that clearly addressed the interests of blacks. Like its predecessor two years earlier, the 1894 platform included planks demanding major reforms in the brutal convict lease system. The Populists proposed first that "convict labor be taken out of competition with citizens labor," a practice everyone knew held down the wages of common laborers in Texas. If stringently enforced, such a law would also reduce the harshness of the system by reducing the immense profitability of exploiting convict labor. Second, the plank specified "that convicts be given intellectual and moral instructions, and that the earnings of the convict above the expenses of keeping him, should go to his family." Again the plank would go far in humanizing an exploitative institution that all too often victimized blacks and their families.[29]

Both the 1892 and 1894 state platforms included demands for "fair elections and an honest count," measures that would help guard against the fraud that had helped to keep the Democrats in power for twenty years. The 1894 platform also retained earlier planks calling for "an efficient lien law" to protect laboring men, an eight-hour work day for industrial workers, and the creation of a state board of arbitration to hear all disputes between corporations and employees. The 1894 platform, however, went beyond the provisions of the party's 1892 document in addressing blacks' interests. Attesting to the increasing influence of blacks in the party and Rayner's presence on the platform committee, the new platform included two planks that specifically addressed racial issues. One demanded that the state provide "sufficient accommodation for all its insane, without discrimination in color." The other involved public education, an issue many blacks viewed as tremendously important.[30]

The 1892 platform had favored a system of public schools with a six-month academic year, available to all children between the ages of six and twenty, and the adoption of standardized textbooks provided at cost by the state. These demands, modest by modern standards, constituted a major improvement over the existing system of four-month school years and over-priced, inadequate texts. In 1894, however, the Populists went beyond these already substantial proposals by providing that "each race shall have its own trustees and control its own schools." More than any other feature of the platform, this provision bore Rayner's imprimatur; changing the governance of black public schools was an idea he championed for the rest of his life. Because much of the power of white supremacy rested upon the continued ignorance and illiteracy of blacks, taking control of black education away from Democrats was of the utmost importance. The Galveston *Daily News* evaluated the effect of this new plank quite accurately: "This declaration appeals irresistibly to the colored brother. He fairly dotes on schools and the colored delegates enthusiastically declared that 50,000 Republican votes would land in the populist camp next November. They meant it, too. It remains to be seen whether or not they can deliver the goods, but there is no doubt about their sincerity. They will do their best."[31]

Rayner certainly intended to do his best. The black Populists of Texas left the 1894 convention with higher spirits than ever before. A Democratic defeat at the hands of the Populists would not mean sudden equality for blacks; no one, black or white, pretended that it would. But it would mean the defeat of the South's most unequivocal champions of white supremacy and the accession to power of men who seemed honestly committed to improving the plight of the working poor. For Populist leaders like Rayner and Wade, that promise—huge in its significance for blacks in 1894—was enough.

Rayner left Waco and almost immediately commenced a wide-ranging speaking and organizing tour that threatened both his health and personal safety. A week after the convention he made five speeches in Polk County, followed by a thorough canvass of San Augustine, Nacogdoches, and Waller counties. He then ventured two hundred miles to the north—unfamiliar territory for him—and spoke in Lamar, Red River, Bowie, and Morris counties. By early September he was back in the deep East Texas counties of San Augustine and Nacogdoches. Late September found Rayner two hundred miles to the southwest in Bastrop, Hays, and Comal counties, and by the first week in October he had spoken as far south as Jackson County on the Gulf Coast. "I am hard at work day and night for our party," he explained without exaggeration. He was due back in Henderson County near Dallas the following week when the strain of his schedule landed him in a sickbed.[32]

Rayner's experiences on the campaign trail in 1894 dramatically underscore the power of white supremacy and the lengths to which Democrats would go when they believed it to be endangered. He displayed exceptional physical courage when venturing into certain parts of East Texas, literally joking about the threats he encountered. In Morris County, Rayner spoke to a crowd of 450 Populists, both white and black, and reported that later that "night some of the Democrats that worship at the shrine of Bacchus tried to frighten me and make me leave town. One poor little fellow wanted to know who would pay him to run 'that nigger' out of town." Rayner continued undeterred. Although he did not elaborate further on the threat, he did add that "the colored people of Morris county are doing their own thinking and will vote with the Populists. . . . Our party is growing daily and I am cheerful, hopeful and feel that victory is waiting to crown our efforts. My people are . . . developing an individuality that will command the respect of all men. I am working night and day for Judge Nugent and our party."[33]

The emerging biracial alliance tested the resolve of the white members as frequently as it did that of blacks. In Polk County, for example, Populists were "severely criticised" by the local Democratic organ for securing Rayner to lecture in the county. The Democrats accused the Populists of "promising the negroes to elect them to office, and advocating social equality and making fair promises generally in order to get their votes." The local Populist convention simply responded by reminding the public that Democrats had always tried to deceive people, and then they let the matter drop. In doing so, the Populists were in effect refusing to engage in racial demagoguery or to respond seriously to charges of racial heresy. Such refusals took considerable courage in the racially heated atmosphere of the 1890s. In bringing Rayner to organize their county's black voters, the Populists of Polk County had moved about as close to the limits of southern dissent as a body of white southerners would dare go in the late nineteenth century. That they did not cross the line by admitting the Democrats' charges is not so much a measure of the weakness of Populist egalitarianism as it is a testimonial to the grip that white supremacy held on all white southerners.[34]

As Rayner's fame as an orator and proselytizer spread, the chances of racial conflict in the course of his speaking tours increased. In many Black Belt areas, where absolute white solidarity spelled the only hope of preventing the election of black Republicans, Populism threatened to divide the white vote and insure the election of Republican or fusion county tickets. Racial tensions in such areas could boil over during election season. In July 1894, as Rayner was about to visit Waller County in the heart of the southeast Texas Black Belt, such an event took place. A healthy Populist organization in the county was making a strong bid for the black vote and had even placed a Negro on the county ticket. Democrats feared a Republican or fusion victory. On July 10 rumors surfaced concerning a "race war" or "negro rising" in the Brazos river bottom. Soon sixty or seventy armed men formed a vigilante force and rode into the bottom, sending a large number of terrified black families fleeing to the backwoods. For several days all work in the fields came to a halt. The rumors proved entirely false, but Rayner prudently postponed his speaking engagements. The chairman of the county Populist organization directly charged the Democrats with getting up the scare in order to frighten blacks and lay the blame on the People's party.[35]

Ten days later, reports began to circulate on the streets of Hempstead that local Democrats had sent Rayner a telegram threatening his life if he came to town to speak. The threat may have been nothing more than a rumor, because Rayner and the editors of the Hempstead *News* quickly took steps to dispel it. Whatever the case, he took his chances with this volatile situation and made several speeches in Waller County. He spoke at the county courthouse to a large, racially mixed audience, amid rumors that a fusion deal would be consummated between the Populists and Republicans. Every one of the candidates from all parties attended the speech, and Rayner pulled no punches "in abusing the Democratic party." The local Democratic editor admitted the speaker's knowledge of Populist doctrine and his eloquence, comparing him favorably with star orators Stump Ashby and Cyclone Davis. As a prominent local Populist put it, "He is one of the hardest hitters I ever heard."[36]

Except for his appearances at the party's state conventions and at the big summer Populist camp meetings, Rayner spent most of his time working at the grass-roots level. He placed tremendous emphasis on mobilizing a county's black voters on behalf of Populist aspirants for such offices as sheriff or county judge. He understood—perhaps better than many of the party's white leaders—how vital this sort of local organization was. Naturally, he found ample opportunities to promote the candidacy of the party's state and national figures, but usually these races remained secondary in importance. As the 1894 elections drew nearer, however, managers of one congressional campaign recruited Rayner to work specifically in their candidate's behalf. Although historians have despaired over the fact that virtually no major Texas Populist candidate's or organizer's private papers have been preserved, one manuscript collection does survive that provides a rare glimpse into Populist-era Texas politics. The papers of Vachel Weldon uniquely illuminate Rayner's career as well as the inner workings of the Populist revolt in the Lone Star State.

Weldon ran for the U.S. House of Representatives in 1894 as an Independent, supported by a Republican-Populist fusion deal. His twenty-four-county district, the Eleventh, encompassed all of South Texas but extended up the Gulf Coast as far to the northeast as Wharton County, one of the most heavily black regions of the state. The five counties bordering the Rio Grande River contained large numbers of Mexican Americans, and the middle counties varying mixes of whites, blacks, and Hispanics. Five of the upper counties were at least 20 percent black. The only counties with black majorities were Wharton (81 percent) and Jackson (56 percent). The district, like the state as a whole, contained pockets of Populist strength, but in terms of sheer numbers it was traditionally Democratic and was easily expected to reelect the incumbent, William H. Crain. Corrupt Democratic bosses in the Rio Grande River counties always made sure the Democrats won. The Republican party historically garnered support from blacks in the northeastern counties and from German and Anglo-American sheep ranchers in the north-central counties. The best the Independent ticket could hope for in those areas was to keep what few honest Populist or Republican votes there were from being stolen. In the northern counties, however, the prospect appeared bright for enough Independent support to counteract the Democratic advantage in the south.[37]

On October 1, a Populist leader from black-majority Jackson County wrote to Weldon explaining the situation in that locale. "You can carry this county by three fourths, the Republicans and Populists voting for you, but a great effort is being made to induce the negroes to vote the Democratic ticket," he warned. "And of course success in this regard will imperil your success." Here, in its barest form, was the equation that almost always determined Populist success in areas with a significant black population: Neither Populists nor Republicans could expect to win on their own, but if they could combine their votes on one ticket and keep the black vote from landing in the Democratic column, the fusion ticket could win. In the case of the Eleventh District, the first condition—fusion—was accomplished. Populists and Republicans supported Weldon. W. P. Laughler, a white Populist leader of Jackson County, thought he knew how to fulfill the second condition:

> To counteract this [Democratic] influence we have a negro speaker who will hold the colored vote to the Republican [ticket], that he can not turn to the Populist side. I have heard him speak twice in this county, and he is the ablest speaker for the service I have ever heard. He carries such conviction by his appeals and arguments, that few colored men can resist. I am willing to pledge my reputation for a man of judgement upon what I say with regard to him. I am too old a man to allow any temporary enthusiasm to overcome my cooler judgement, and I tell you I have seen and heard him destroy all the effect of a strong Republican [or] Democratic speech in a single sentence, and turn over not only colored Republicans but white Democrats, nor were they slow to acknowledge it. You hear him first, and judge for yourself.[38]

Laughler was referring to Rayner. His letter, written in strict privacy and with great earnestness, indicates not only how devastatingly effective Rayner was as a speaker but also how critically the Populists needed his articulate and skilled black leadership at the grass-roots level. A related problem was that of campaign finance; black leaders could not rely on their own personal wealth as could the white elite. From 1894 to 1898 Rayner labored virtually full-time for the party but received no salary. Apart from the money his wife earned by taking in white people's laundry, he relied entirely upon voluntary contributions from audiences, candidates, and white Populist leaders. The Weldon campaign had to address this problem if Rayner was to do his work. This, according to a Weldon worker, was "the milk in the cocoanut: We want him [Rayner] in Calhoun, Victoria, DeWitt, Karnes, and Goliad counties, and we are as you know not very well equipped financially to employ speakers." Laughler offered to donate his salary as a gin superintendent to pay Rayner during the campaign, and he called upon a neighboring county Populist chairman for added support. These donations, "with voluntary contributions from others," would enable the campaign to keep Rayner "at work until the campaign is ended." Then there would be "no doubt" that Weldon would "carry the counties of this senatorial dis't by so large a majority that the Democratic majorities of the Rio Grande counties will be annihilated." [39]

Weldon did obtain Rayner's services; by October 8 he had delivered eight speeches, with at least seven more scheduled. The Populists needed Rayner to stay longer, and he was willing to stay in the district until election day, but money was short. Weldon had sent $25, but as Rayner argued, "what is this for a traveling speaker[?]" There were times during Populist campaigns when postage stamps needed to answer political correspondence imposed such a financial burden that Rayner had to request that his correspondents enclose stamps in their letters. And when Rayner had fallen ill earlier in the campaign, he publicly thanked his white hometown Populist ally, E. S. Peters, for a $10 donation. "It came at the right time," wrote Rayner.[40]

The Populist-Republican alliance in the Eleventh District stretched its resources to the breaking point to finance Weldon's campaign. But in the dozens of surviving letters that tell of the campaign's financing, the picture emerges quite clearly: Money was a necessity, and the Democrats had most of it. Certainly the Independents knew the game. One Weldon lieutenant in DeWitt County, F. A. Vaughan, described how "two hundred dollars could be used here to a splendid advantage" in "interesting" the county's Negro preachers and a German newspaper editor in Weldon's candidacy. However, such funds were small change compared to what Democrats spent in the Rio Grande Valley.[41]

In the upper counties, success continued to hinge upon Rayner's efforts to swing the black vote Weldon's way. A Weldon supporter in Goliad County reported that the Negroes in his county were solidly in favor of the Independent candidate and added that "Rayner did more good for Weldon than all speakers combined who went to Goliad." But even with blacks firmly lined up behind the Independent ticket, Weldon's forces in such counties had not definitely won the battle. Those black voters who, despite their poverty, refused to be bought were still subject to deception at the polls. Illiteracy ran high among black farmers, and the intricate election laws of the period could confuse all but the most educated and alert voters. Regulations required that ballots be printed on a certain kind of paper, with a specific kind of ink, and folded in a particular way. Otherwise, Democratic election officials could throw the ballot out on a technicality. Democrats practiced the even more common, and probably more successful, tactic of simply passing out Democratic ballots, which they described to blacks as Populist or Republican ballots. Therefore, although Rayner performed his job admirably, the Independents still had to supervise black voting on election day. As Dennis O'Connor, a Weldon supporter, explained, "All the Negroes are unconditional Weldon people but don't know who is to lead them & what I propose to do is to get *men I can rely upon* to give them the Weldon tickets on the day of election." With the election machinery in the hands of the Democrats, it was crucial that the opposition have trustworthy men at every polling place where blacks would be voting.[42]

On the eve of the election, Weldon's backers tried frantically to find ways to counteract the manipulation of black voters in the upper counties and the massive fraud expected in the Rio Grange River counties. "Money is flying," a Hispanic Populist reported from South Texas, and Populists had a mere $33 left in the campaign chest. Despite the efforts of Rayner and his white allies, Weldon faced almost certain defeat.[43]

When the votes were tallied, the fusion ticket had carried sixteen of the twenty-eight counties, nine of them by very large margins. In the five counties with greater than 20 percent black population, all of which Rayner had campaigned in, Weldon won 57 percent of the votes cast. In one of the black-majority counties, Jackson, where Rayner had been especially active, the fusion ticket polled 60 percent. But in the five heavily Hispanic Valley counties—Cameron, Hidalgo, Starr, Zapata, and Webb—Crain defeated Weldon by a margin of nearly three to one. Excluding the five counties along the Rio Grande from the twenty-eight-county totals, Weldon won easily with 55 percent of the vote. In one Valley county, Cameron, the lopsided Democratic majority was enough to prevent what would have been a Weldon victory districtwide.

Even seasoned veterans of the region's politics were shocked at the extent of the fraud. Democratic bosses naturalized large numbers of new citizens the day before the election. Multiple witnesses reported seeing officials at the polls opening ballot boxes and inspecting the ballots after they had been cast. Election judges allowed illegally marked ballots to stand. The Democrats brought hundreds of aliens from Mexico just to vote. Certain precincts voted more than their entire population. At least at one polling place, a man with a gun threatened voters. R. B. Rentfro, an outraged friend of Weldon's, explained that there had been two thousand fraudulent votes cast in three counties, "and the fact can be easily demonstrated. All concealment was thrown aside and Democratic politicians here return Tweed's answer to all remonstrances, 'What in hell are you going to do about it.'" Weldon was urged to "contest and contest vigorously," but despite overwhelming evidence of fraud his lawyer advised against it. Democrat William H. Crain was the next U.S. congressman from the Eleventh District.[44]

Although the Mexican population and international border in many ways make the Eleventh District unique, the Weldon-Crain campaign reveals much about Texas Populism. First, Populist ideological principles under some circumstances could be sacrificed—at least in the short run—in order to achieve the greater goal of defeating the Democrats. Any defeat, even at the hands of a Republican or Independent, loosened the Democrats' grip on the election machinery, the justice system, and patronage, opening the door for future Populist achievements. Second, the black vote *could* be won without resorting to wholesale fraud, but this required black Populist leadership such as Rayner provided and reliable men at the precincts to make sure blacks were not deceived. Finally, the election demonstrates the lengths to which Democrats would go to insure victory. Fraud was easier to perpetrate on the border, but it was widespread across the state.[45]

The 1894 state elections did not bring victory to the Populist state ticket, but in many respects Rayner and his comrades had cause to feel encouraged. With the Democrats reunited behind a single gubernatorial candidate and a Republican ticket again in the field, the election provided the best opportunity yet to gauge Populist strength. Nugent, once more the Populist gubernatorial candidate, finished second to the colorless Democrat Charles Culberson by a vote of 216,373 to 159,676. The Republicans and Prohibitionists polled a combined vote of 83,746. Nugent's vote had increased by more than fifty thousand since 1892. With the help of men like Rayner, Populism was growing in Texas.[46]

Rayner in the fall of 1894 had reached a point remarkably similar to his father's exactly forty years earlier. Following the 1854 elections Kenneth Rayner had found himself in the vanguard of the American party, particularly in the roles of organizer and orator. Now his son occupied the same position in another major reform movement. Kenneth had become the foremost spokesman for a minority within the national Know-Nothing organization—white southerners who wished to participate in a broad national coalition of reformers who would honor southerners' constitutional rights while striving for national political goals. Now John had become the chief advocate of another minority, blacks, within another reform movement. He, too, wished to see the minority he represented cooperate with the majority to pursue common aims, as long as that majority would protect blacks' constitutional rights. In the case of both father and son, success depended on first defeating the sectionally and racially polarized Democratic and Republican parties. The antagonisms bred by slavery, the Civil War, and Reconstruction would have to be put aside if the nation was to have any hope of addressing the other major dangers facing America. If it could not be done, in the end no one would enjoy the promise of freedom, for corruption would continue to prevail over purity, and power would remain in the hands of the few instead of the many.

CHAPTER 13

"All I Ask of You Is Not to Vote for a Democrat"

John B. Rayner had ample cause for optimism as 1894 drew to a close. Although Populists had met defeat in the recent statewide election, the People's party had gained ground. A sizable number of blacks—although by no means a majority—had voted the Populist ticket. Total black voter turnout approached 80 percent, and for the first time in a generation the Democrats polled a minority of all votes cast. Populist gains were especially dramatic in view of the facts that Democrats had patched up the 1892 rift in their party and Republicans had once again fielded their own slate of candidates. The most pressing political reality facing Rayner and the Populists was obvious as they looked to 1896: If all the opposition votes could be combined under the Populist banner, the hated Democrats could be ousted.[1]

This, of course, meant fusion. Texas Populists disagreed over the wisdom of such marriages of convenience. Some took a pragmatic viewpoint, arguing that fusion had been used successfully at the local level and in legislative and congressional races without a significant sacrifice of principle. In this view, defeating the Democrats justified fusion among Populists, Republicans, or Prohibitionists. Others preferred probable defeat over what they viewed as an inevitable dilution of commitment to the Populist platform—a dilution that would be costly in the long run.

National politics greatly complicated the issue of statewide fusion. The problem was that to sanction a fusion between Populists and Republicans in the South was to give tacit approval of comparable agreements between Populists and Democrats in northern and midwestern states, where the minority status of the Democratic party resembled that of the Republicans in the South. If the principle and practice of fusion were thus widely accepted in all parts of the nation, what would happen at the national level? Would it be attempted there, and if so, with what consequences for Populism?

The probable answers to these questions disturbed Texas Populists. By 1895, many, including Rayner, were beginning to fear that fusion might be attempted on the national level. Populists outside Texas and a few other southern strongholds generally considered the monetization of silver as the cornerstone of the third-party program, and as Democrats likewise increasingly favored silver, Populist-Democratic fusion became a more palatable alternative for non-southern Populists. Rayner and other third-party leaders in Texas feared that the national party was surrendering the sweeping reforms of the party as set forth in the 1892 Omaha Platform in favor of one relatively minor concession, silver. The Texans' cry in 1895 and 1896 was to "stay in the middle of the road," that is, to remain steadfast to the Populist demands for fiat money, the Subtreasury Plan, and other antimonopoly reforms. The midroad slogan also carried with it the tremendously important idea that the People's party had to be national rather than sectional. By staying in the middle of the road, Populists—especially those who were black—understood that the party would chart a middle course between the northern Republicans and southern Democrats. Only in this way could racial fears be pushed to the background and constructive government again become the focus of American politics.

The most alarming sign that the national Populist organization might seek an alliance with the Democrats came from the People's party national chair, Herman E. Taubeneck of Illinois, who displayed definite signs of advocating Populist-Democratic fusion in the upcoming presidential election. Despite this disturbing development, the state executive committee in February 1896 passed a resolution expressing confidence in Taubeneck and favoring "an honorable union of all the reform forces of the United States along those lines that will best promote the welfare of all our people." The problem was that the Texans' definition of "an honorable union" could never mean the formal endorsement of a Democrat for president.[2]

No group in Texas was more distressed by national developments than the black Populists. Rayner missed the February meeting of the executive committee because of the shortness of the notice, wiring E. S. Peters to act as his proxy. When he learned that the committee had endorsed Taubeneck, Rayner fired an angry letter to the party's state newspaper. Striking directly to the heart of the issue, he queried: "What do you mean by 'along those lines that will best promote the welfare of all our people?' What lines are these, and why break so suddenly off and indorse Hon. H. E. Taubeneck and the national committee?" Rayner was understandably suspicious. "If you will look deep into this resolution you will see the finger of the silver league or the finger of the bimetal[l]ic league trying to erase the best part of the Omaha platform by

the endorsement of Hon. H. E. Taubeneck." Rayner was undoubtedly dedicated to the midroad Populist program in its entirety. From his perspective,
surrendering the entire Omaha platform in favor of one minor issue, silver,
was to surrender Populism itself. Worst of all, he knew that national Populist-
Democratic fusion would largely end black participation in the third-party
movement. Populists would no longer need black votes, and the avowedly
white-supremacist Democrats would gain control of Populism once and for
all. For Rayner and the other black Populists, staying in the middle of the
road meant not just smart politics but perhaps the last chance blacks would
have to participate meaningfully in politics.[3]

White Populists from all parts of the state concurred with Rayner in his
alarm over possible Populist-Democratic fusion. By April 1896, the pages of
the Populist press bristled with warnings about the intentions of the national
committee. "There is danger ahead," wrote N. A. Gann of Bud, Texas, "I do
not like the utterances of our national chairman. I am afraid there is something wrong." H. C. Howell of Jasper knew exactly what was wrong: "That it
is the purpose of Taubeneck and his co-adjutators to lead the Populist party,
bag and baggage into the camp of the enemy at St. Louis on the 22d day
of next July, is now perfectly plain." To Texas Populists like Howell, who
had spent years battling the Democratic party, the prospect of the upcoming
national Populist convention nominating a Democrat was unbelievable. "Is it
possible," he asked, "that they can succeed in carrying out their treasonable
design?"[4]

Texas Populists realized their worst fears when the national convention
met in July. Elected by local Populists to represent the Seventh Congressional District, Rayner was one of the nearly 1,400 Populists who assembled
in St. Louis, knowing that the Democrats had nominated Nebraska's free
silver champion William Jennings Bryan and Maine banker Arthur Sewall.[5]
With a majority of the Populist delegates supporting Bryan, the best the out-
voted midroaders could do was to engineer the nomination of Georgia's Tom
Watson as vice president, keeping half the ticket in the middle of the road
and possibly forcing Bryan to refuse the nomination. The Texans led the
fight against Bryan, with Rayner and every one of the state's 103 delegates
opposing fusion to the bitter end. Dallas County's Populists reflected the
attitude of the party's members in Texas. In the midst of the convention they
sent their delegate, Jerome Kearby, a message: "Five hundred Populists say
never surrender. Bryan means death."[6]

The Texans, embittered to the extreme, returned home to a hero's welcome and were dubbed "the immortal 103" for having stayed in the middle
of the road. All spring long the political air in Texas had buzzed with rumors

that Populist-Republican fusion on the state level might be consummated, for many Populists would as soon vote for the Republican candidate, William McKinley, as for the Democrat, William Jennings Bryan. As early as March the Austin *Statesman* wrote about "a big political scheme" that had been hatched by Republicans and Populists. It reported that at the February meeting of the Populist state executive committee in Dallas "the Republicans made a proposition to the Populists looking to a fusion during the coming campaign that would be mutually beneficial to both parties." The proposed fusion would, in effect, place the names of Republican presidential electors on the Populist ticket, and in return Republicans would vote for Populist state candidates. Leaders of both parties denied that such an agreement had been reached, but the rumors persisted.[7]

While Rayner was concerned about developments on both the state and national levels, he could not ignore his grass-roots organizational work. Throughout 1895 he had traveled extensively in the eastern half of Texas, making speeches, organizing black Populist clubs, and helping arrange the enormous camp meetings that had become a trademark of the third party. Harrison Sterling Price "Stump" Ashby, the long-time chair of the state executive committee, aided Rayner in scheduling an uninterrupted speaking tour during July, August, and September. He appealed to "all patriotic Populists who can reasonably do so" to send a small donation to help defray Rayner's expenses. "The work I want Rayner to do," Ashby frankly explained, "no white man can do." Published schedules of Rayner's itinerary from the hot summer of 1895 testify to the grueling pace he set himself. In a three-week period in late August and early September he spoke in twelve counties, almost certainly appearing numerous times in each. At camp meetings he shared the spotlight with such national Populist personalities as "General" Jacob S. Coxey, Charles Macune, James H. "Cyclone" Davis, and T. P. Gore.[8]

As 1895 gave way to 1896, Rayner showed no signs of relaxing his relentless crusade. Most politicians campaigned in the summer and fall preceding elections, but not Rayner. Of course, the average white politician was also a planter, lawyer, or businessman, and campaigning took him away from his livelihood; Rayner subsisted on the proceeds from his speeches. Democratic newspaper reporters sometimes commented on the way in which "he converted his speech into silver at its conclusion." "He has evidently been a preacher," another Democrat observed, "judging from his appeal for funds at the close of his argument. The collection was a decided success as was the speech, from a Populist's standpoint." One can scarcely overstate Rayner's power as a public speaker. Twentieth-century Americans, living in the age of microphones, amplifiers, and the electronic mass-media, can never appreciate fully the degree to which nineteenth-century orators could mesmerize a crowd. The surviving descriptions of the forty-five-year-old Rayner's speeches bear an uncanny resemblance to those of his father half a century earlier. Whites and blacks alike marveled at his power over an audience. A third-party partisan captured something of the flavor of an 1896 Rayner speech: "What crowds of people, what throngs of people, by fours, by dozens, on foot, on horses, in buggies, in wagons, above the roars of applause and clapping of hands, you hear the sweet music of the voice of the illustrious Rayner. Now like a wild tornado, now like a summer evening breeze, pointed, logical, severe, yet soft and gentle, the spirit of God is plainly mirrored from his heart, carrying conviction at every breath. God speed his good work!"⁹

When he spoke in the towns and cities, Rayner invariably attracted listeners from both races. From the few surviving accounts, it is possible to piece together the substance of his message as the party reached its greatest test, the 1896 elections. He would commence with a history lesson, Populist-style. The United States was "a great country, a giant with his head lathing in the ice water of the Arctic ocean, his feet in the turbid waters of the gulf, his left hand on the golden gate and his right in the billows of the Atlantic." This giant would rise "with the might of a Hercules and stamp the pigmies"— the Republican and Democratic parties—"into the deep, sad mud of defeat and the deep damnation of retribution." "God put the Democratic party into the world to foster and protect slavery until the savage negro was civilized and Christianized," Rayner theorized. "That accomplished he put the Republican party in motion and built it up to free the negro." "The evolution of parties," he thundered, "must ever proceed." Like most other nineteenth-century Americans, Rayner subscribed to the idea of historical progress, but as a Populist he could not accept the contention that such progress was necessarily continuous and inevitable. His Whiggish belief that freedom depended upon eternal vigilance and that corruption put the survival of the Republic in jeopardy furnished the rhetorical weapons he needed to attack the current state of southern politics. Thus, near the end of a typical public appearance, he proceeded to the audience's favorite part of the speech, roasting the Democratic party:

> The Democratic drag has held back the South, and she is raising a lot of empty-headed and empty-pocketed ninny-heads to vote the same old time-worn ticket of the father and grand-pap. The country [is]

not enjoying the summer excursions and champagne banquets nature provides, for the effluviant corpse of a mission-ended-wet-nurse-of-slavery party obstructs the open sesame to National and individual success. The best elements of the grand old Republican and Democratic parties [are] volunteers to help the Populists clean out the old stables and bury the occupants so deep in mundane mixture that Gabriel will need subsequent assistance to produce power to wind his horn loud enough to call them to resurrection.[10]

Rayner told his 1896 audiences that in the upcoming elections blacks would reverse their traditional loyalty to the Party of Lincoln and vote the People's ticket. Referring to the old parties' all-too-common practice of buying black votes, he contended that "a negro will gladly accept and chuckle over every dollar he can get from boodlers [bribers], but when he goes to the polls he will vote his own way." But Rayner also lectured the blacks in his audiences about their shortcomings as voters. "There is a difference," he chided, "between a negro and a white man: a white man votes from the head; he votes his mind; the negro votes from his heart; he is sentimental on the wrong ocassion." If a black voter "likes a white man he will even vote for a white Democrat solely because he likes him." Then he would turn specifically to the blacks in the crowd and pointedly remind them that "it will be a snowin' in h—l before a white Democrat votes for you because he likes you."

When he addressed white listeners, Rayner would underscore the absurdity of southern whites remaining Democrats solely "to keep down negro supremacy." "A Democrat goes to bed at night and dreams he sees a nigger with the courthouse on his back running off with it. The idea of 8,000,000 blacks, most of them ignorant and nearly all poor, gaining supremacy over 64,000,000 of intelligent whites. Do you white men here believe it?" Rayner then would mount a scathing attack on the corruption of the state and national Democratic administrations, reserving some especially pointed barbs for Governor Charles Culberson and Texas Democrats in Congress. He would emphasize the role black voters had played in the election of past Democratic governors and predict that his people would never again repeat their mistakes. Rayner then closed by reminding blacks that their "only hope for justice" lay with the People's party.

When he "came in like a storm" to deliver this speech at Market Square in Houston, white hecklers tried to disrupt his talk. Undaunted, he "aroused the crowd to numerous applauses by his quick-witted thrusts," telling the hecklers that they were "unmanly" in trying to keep him from exercising the privilege of free speech. That Rayner dared to castigate white hecklers in public bears witness to his courage, and the fact that he could get away with it suggests that white Populists were willing—at least on this occasion—to stand by him. After his appearance a spectator told a reporter, "Houston has felt the storm and may take gracious comfort that a single house is left standing or that one lone official is left to tell the tale of political devastation." [11]

Rayner's outspoken fearlessness in defending Populism and exposing Democratic corruption was also evident in a series of essays he wrote for the Populist press. One such piece appeared prominently on the front page of the *Southern Mercury* under the headline, "The Colored Brother. A Spicy Letter from J. B. Rayner." He spared no faction from biting criticism. The lily-white Republicans, he explained, quit the regular party because the black race "sent too many incompetent and ignorant delegates to Republican conventions, thus making the deliberation in these conventions ridiculous." Rayner believed that with blacks out of the picture the lily-whites would successfully "appeal to complexional prejudices, blue veins, straight hair, and business sentiments." But at least the lily-whites were sincere in their bigotry. In comparison, the black Republicans under Cuney's leadership were "sordid mercenaries in politics," while the few whites in the Cuney faction were nothing but "the mephitic vaporings from a cadaverous carpetbagism." [12]

As hard as he was on Republicans, Rayner was even harder on the Democrats. Although he professed to admire the "boldness and determination" of the Bourbons, their standard-bearer, Grover Cleveland, was "to our American financial system as Benedict Arnold was to West Point." His harshest invective was reserved for the dominant silver, or reform, Democrats. Calling them "chronic office-seekers" with "no political conscience or principle," he charged that they would "accept any platform to get a Democratic nomination, and then jeer and ignore it to get elected." Rayner believed reform Democrats were "Populists in faith, but are too cowardly to confess it." The sooner they went "to pluto's laboratory for the purpose of studying the science of pyrology," the better it would be for the South. He knowingly predicted that the so-called reformers in the Democratic party would write a "boustrophidon platform and fill it with platitudes and ambiguous terms," and in the next election would "use bribes, deception and shotgun intimidation to capture negro votes." Time would prove him entirely right. "The only rights we negroes will ever enjoy," he concluded, "will be the right the southern white man gives us." The only whites in Texas who were prepared to grant those rights were Populists. "Vote the People's Party ticket," Rayner instructed his readers. "We will get better wages for our work and we will have better times in the south." [13]

Rayner's writings in the Populist press in 1896 also betrayed his growing class consciousness. In an April editorial he chronicled the rise of reform Democrats in Texas and explained how former governor Hogg had ridden his towering ambition into the governor's office. The "piney wood's parvenu," as Rayner sarcastically called Hogg, early on had "discovered that his path to the gubernatorial chair would have to be a hiatus between the laborer and the capitalist; and, "On either side of this hiatus was to be a granite wall, spiked on top with hatred, bitter and lasting, that he (Hogg) would engender between the farmer and the railroads." The problem, as Rayner viewed it, did not lie in a Marxian conflict between labor and capital; America had grown undemocratic because the government had erected unnatural barriers and brought unnecessary antagonism between the classes. Nor did Populists such as Rayner question the sanctity of private property. Indeed, they were motivated largely by the perception that small landowners were rapidly losing their land and being driven into dependency and peonage, and that once there (as most blacks and many whites already were), no amount of hard work would ever allow them to escape. Populists criticized a government that granted special privileges to large corporations like railroads, enabling capitalists to exploit average farmers or mechanics. Rayner saw James Hogg as typical of the selfish professional politician about whom republican ideology so often warned. Hogg represented the interests of neither capital nor labor. As a classic example of a corrupt politician, he had simply taken advantage of the deplorable "hiatus" between the railroads and farmers to win the governorship: "Down this dismal sewer, with his true character hid from an expectant people, he walked into the gubernatorial office."[14]

Explaining current political and class cleavages, Rayner argued that in normal times Americans would not be politically divided along class lines; presumably, he would have said that partisan differences should be over means and not ends. However, "the greed, rottenness and incivism of the two old parties" had disturbed the natural state of American politics and divided citizens into two antagonistic classes. The lower class "pleb[e]ians" supported the Populist cause. The upper class "patricians" clung to the two old parties and were "secretly together on all vital issues."

Rayner then analyzed the upper class in a way that might lead casual observers to see his opinions as somewhat Marxian. He arraigned the old parties for their alliance with "a simony pulpit, the daily mendacious press, [and] all the bankers and corporations of the world." But to Rayner neither capitalism nor wealth were inherently evil. He criticized Democrats and Republicans not so much because they were in league with capitalists, but rather because of the ways the corrupt parties' leaders had perverted the proper economic relationships in America, pitting one economic group against another. In order "to carry out their fiendishness, the two old parties . . . will make the banker intimidate the merchant and manufacturer, and the merchant will intimidate the small farmer, and the farmer will bribe or intimidate the laborer and tenant farmer." Put in these terms, no single economic class was innately bad; the blame lay with the political forces that caused one group to exploit the other. Republicans like Wright Cuney and Democrats like Jim Hogg lacked the necessary civic virtue to represent the organic interests of all the people. When faced with the choice of promoting their own interests or those of the American people, such politicians chose the selfish route.[15]

Because of Republican and Democratic bosses' self-interest, Rayner predicted that in the upcoming elections the old parties would undoubtedly avoid real issues. Men fighting for office rather than principles would choose instead to harp on the danger to white supremacy and make emotional appeals to party loyalty. Republican and Democratic moral bankruptcy would thus force them to "ignore civilized warfare, and . . . do only bush fighting." Rayner optimistically predicted that the old parties' "dishonorable methods" would fail to save them, "for the leaven of the People's Party has permeated all the people, except the incorrigible." In this analysis, "all the people" included businessmen, planters, yeoman farmers, and manufacturers, as well as propertyless sharecroppers and laborers. It also would have to include blacks as well as whites.[16]

With Rayner and other midroad Populists holding such views, the reasons are apparent for their serious reservations about fusion with either of the major parties in statewide elections. To combine with either of the old parties was to join forces with the enemy. In precinct or county races it was different, because party ideology counted for relatively little. Fusion at the local level between Republicans and Populists had proven successful not only in bringing victory at the polls but also in securing greater justice for blacks. A few third-party county officeholders such as sheriffs Garrett Scott of Grimes County and A. J. Spradley of Nacogdoches County seemed remarkably dedicated to protecting the lives and property of their black constituents. When Rayner, by his own account, "broke up the Democracy" in Nacogdoches, he felt it worth public mention that "not an unkind word was said" to him while in the county. He considered the Populist lawman Spradley "brave as a lion" and pronounced him "the best sheriff in Texas." But a fusion agreement at the state level involved more than just pragmatic politics. It was a matter of principle. Moreover, such a sacrifice of principle could also backfire at the polls; a formal alliance with either the Democrats or the Republicans could alienate thousands of dedicated Populists. Any formal statewide fusion arrangement would be extremely risky.[17]

In late summer 1896, Rayner and the other party leaders began to focus on the upcoming state elections. Texas Populists held their state convention in Galveston two weeks after the National People's party fused with the Democrats in St. Louis. During the short time between the two meetings, renewed talk of a deal between Populists and Republicans at the state level reached a fever pitch. The Populists continued officially to deny any such intentions, but their anger at their party's actions in St. Louis, combined with their unceasing animosity to the Texas Democratic party, lent credence to the fusion talk. On the eve of the state convention, influential Populist editor Milton Park of the *Southern Mercury* angrily wrote that there was "no possibility of the Peoples party of the south fusing with any other party," but then qualified the statement, saying that the Populists "might join forces with . . . the Republican, Prohibition or Union Labor party, but never with the Democratic party. . . .That sort of a fusion is too disgusting to be thought of." [18]

In reality, Rayner and the more radical leaders of the party had already determined that a fusion between Texas Populists and Republicans was a necessity. All political eyes in Texas were focused on Galveston as the first of nearly two thousand delegates began assembling on August 4. Rayner was among the first to arrive, probably to engage in some private discussions with Cuney and several other Republican leaders, all of whom conveniently appeared in Galveston the day before the convention began.[19]

The ensuing convention was a stormy affair. Nominating a state ticket was uncontroversial; with the death of the beloved Nugent, labor attorney Jerome Kearby of Dallas had become the consensus choice for governor. The real fight revolved around the issue of fusion—whether to endorse Bryan, McKinley, or neither, and whether or not to seek a fusion arrangement with Republicans at the state level. Everyone had his own opinion and believed it represented the genuine middle-of-the-road position, but the truth was plain: the middle of the road had been destroyed at St. Louis.

For Rayner, there was never any question about the necessity of repudiating the national convention's nomination of Bryan. On the second day of the meeting, thirty-five black delegates responded to Rayner's call for a caucus in order to "find out where they stand." He closed the session both to whites and to the press, but allowed one Dallas *Morning News* reporter, whom the blacks trusted, to attend. The delegates sensed that they had arrived at a crucial moment not only in the life of their party but also in the long struggle for black rights in Texas. Their discussions, recorded in detail by the lone reporter, capture mixed feelings of optimism and anxiety.[20]

Rayner called the caucus to order with a blunt statement of fact: "The Democratic party can not be trusted with the finances of the country and they can not be trusted with the rights of the negroes." He then turned the meeting over to L. N. Sublett of McLennan County, leaving at least one of the delegates confused. Nelson Polleyman of Caldwell immediately complained "that the negroes had been advised not to support W. J. Bryan for president, but Rayner had left them right there without telling them who they should vote for." Of course, no one seriously believed that Rayner was finished. "We'll reach that soon," knowingly replied Sublett.

Some informal discussion followed, with the blacks seemingly no more united on a course of action than their white counterparts. One thing, however, was clear: Black Populists found any fusion deal with Republicans extremely distasteful. Exerting his independence, a delegate from Columbus argued that "J. B. Rayner has been my political orator for four years, but he can't lead me into anything I don't know all about.... I take the position that even if Bryan is a stanch Democrat and I can get a part of what I want I will do it and wait for the rest. We must act carefully and not on an impulse." At this point Rayner quietly defended his position: "There has been no talk of any Republican [fusion] or of any vote. All I ask of you is not to vote for a Democrat."

A short discussion followed, whereupon Rayner introduced a series of resolutions he had written for consideration. After endorsing the Omaha Demands and dismissing free silver as a Democratic "panacea," the resolutions addressed the real issue at hand, fusion. Both major parties were "evils," Rayner's document stated, but of the two, the country had "more power to endure" McKinley than Bryan. Thus, if the Populist national committee would not repudiate Bryan, then "we will lead our state with the name of William McKinley and the Republican state electors and we will give the state to McKinley if the Texas Republicans will vote for [Populist Gubernatorial nominee] J. C. Kearby."

The chair allotted each delegate five minutes to state his views on Rayner's resolutions, and again the delegates debated earnestly. One argued that the Republicans could not be trusted to uphold their end of a fusion bargain. Another hoped the resolutions would be voted down, saying, "If the negro is to be used as a purchasable commodity, no wonder the white people have no confidence in him and no use for him."

But Rayner knew all these men well, and he had anticipated the divisions in their ranks. Thus his resolution had wisely supported first the replacement of Bryan with a new midroad presidential ticket, reserving fusion with the Republicans as a second choice. If Bryan could not be removed from the top of the Populist national ticket, this would allow black Populists to save face with their white comrades at home by making Populist-Republican fusion appear to have been forced on them. As a black delegate from Wilson County argued, "If you don't adopt this resolution my county is going Democratic. This resolution is what we need." Another concurred, saying, "I left the Republican party and joined the Populist party because I believed that the Populist party is the one for the negroes. I canvassed my county before I came here, and if the Populists stick to the Democratic nominee, there are many there who are not going to vote for him. I don't say, mind you, that I'm going to vote for McKinley, but never will I vote for Bryan."

This last Populist concluded his remarks by suggesting that he would sit out the presidential election rather than vote for Bryan *or* McKinley. Again Rayner felt that things were getting out of control. He chastised his fellow delegates: "I called you here for consultation, and it's not treating me right that there should be such insinuations that I have tried to lead you astray— that I am trying to sell you to the enemy." Rayner's "hurt feelings" elicited cries of "No, no; nothing of the kind meant." So he continued. "What my object in this is I will tell you plainly: I want the negro Populists to get together and agree, that we may show that we do not intend to support any Democrat; so that fact may be very apparent. We want a straight Populist [ticket] and don't want anything to do with anything else—that's what I want to show." But of course Rayner was not really talking about a "straight Populist" ticket at all; the clear intent of the resolutions was to show black support for fusion with the Republicans. Informed observers knew that the national Populist committee was not about to repudiate its nomination of Bryan at this late date.

Thereafter, the tide of the caucus shifted in Rayner's favor. The closing arguments of two more delegates revealed their understanding of the political realities facing black Texans at the climax of the Populist revolt. The first said, "When I go out to make a speech in this campaign the first thing that is going to be thrown at me is that the Populist party has indorsed the Democrats. And how am I going to answer them? I can't answer it. Then what kind of an argument can I make? Nothing." The second added, "We are tired of Democratic supremacy and tyranny, and we can't get rid of it by voting for and electing Bryan, himself a Democrat, inculcated with Democratic doctrine. Of two evils choose the lesser—and at this time McKinley is the lesser. We are never going to get rid of Democratic tyranny by voting for a Democrat, I tell you. We are here to do something, ought to do something, so let's do it." Rayner's resolutions passed, eighteen to thirteen. The divided vote illustrates the sincerity with which blacks held their midroad Populist principles. Fusion with the Republicans was as distasteful to many of them as it was to the whites, and Bryan was equally unacceptable. The black Populists of Texas understood that their dream of a national party that would put aside sectionalism was in dire danger. Like their white counterparts, blacks found that St. Louis had eliminated the middle of the road. But despite the defeat of Populist principles on the national level, some comfort lay in the idea that maybe Democrats were finally to be defeated in Texas. With this goal in mind, the black Populists were not afraid to go on record as supporting fusion. Most understood that they had nothing to lose.

The convention did not follow Rayner's lead in openly endorsing a political trade with the Republicans, but behind the scenes the groundwork was laid for exactly such a deal. With the support of such party heavyweights as Kearby, Ashby, Harry Tracy, Marion Williams, Barnett Gibbs, and, of course, Rayner, the pro-fusion forces succeeded in appointing a three-man "campaign committee" to meet with the Republicans and work out the details of fusion. Officially, the Populists endorsed neither Bryan nor McKinley, but it was clear that Texas Republicans would support the Populist state ticket in return for Populist votes for McKinley. It would be up to state and local Populist leaders to make sure that the rank and file went along with the plan on election day.[21]

Because of lengthy speechmaking and parliamentary maneuvers, the convention ran into an unplanned fourth day. By Saturday morning, only a corporal's guard of about 150 delegates remained, but they still had to elect a new state executive committee and adopt a platform. Although only a fraction of the original delegates were left, the departing Populists apparently had arranged for proxies, because the full voting strength of the convention was registered on the various roll calls. The executive committee, as usual, was chosen by congressional districts and consisted of thirteen white men. When the time came to elect the two delegates-at-large, Rayner and two whites received nomination. Rayner said he would prefer to withdraw from the race, deferring to the two white nominees, but he expressed concern that his absence from the committee would lead Democrats to say, " 'Oh, yes, since the Pops have gotten to the point where they can elect a ticket they deny the negro any representation.' " Rayner's supporters "would not allow him to withdraw." The chair told him he was out of order, and the election proceeded. "Votes came to Rayner right and left" and were divided between the two white candidates. When one of the white nominees withdrew, the delegates elected Rayner by acclamation.[22]

The 1896 platform differed little from the 1894 document. One new feature was a plank that declared the party to be "in favor of equal justice and protection under the law to all citizens without reference to race, color or nationality." This was a significant statement, but the platform committee had balked at a resolution that would have "recognized" the Negro "in such positions as his capacity fits him to fill." This veiled reference to black office-holding proved too much for white Populists. Once again, the Populists had traveled further toward racial equality than the major parties, but still they had gone only part of the way. It was, however, about as close as southern blacks would come for the next sixty years.[23]

Rayner and the Populists left Galveston and commenced what was perhaps the most acrimonious campaign in Texas history. As planned, the Texas Republican convention placed no state ticket in the field, thus indicating their acceptance of the fusion plan. The Populists' main task—in addition to the usual efforts to convert the adherents of the old parties to Populism—was to try to convince Populist voters to support the fusion deal. Although Populists continued to deny that any formal agreement had been struck to trade McKinley votes for Kearby ballots, Democrats missed no opportunity to lambaste the Populists for their alliance with black Republicans. Rayner and the black Populists, of course, had no such qualms, nor did the bulk of the adamantly anti-Bryan white Populists. But the Democrats' charges of racial treason and their appeals to white solidarity were difficult for many white Populists to ignore.

As the campaign progressed and the fusion plan became more widely known, white Populists from across the state registered their refusal to support McKinley. One diehard reportedly said that "if the Republican electors are put on the populist ticket I will not vote for them nor any candidate who is a party to such a fusion." Some Populist candidates for local offices withdrew rather than join "one of the most unholy political coalitions ever conceived by the mind of man." The words *unholy, disgraceful, dishonorable,* and *unseemly* pepper white Populist utterances from the period. To make matters worse, many who denounced fusion said that they would not only refuse to support McKinley, but that they would also vote for Democratic Bryan-Sewall electors in preference to the Populist Bryan-Watson ticket. Among these were the old Alliance national lecturer Ben Terrell and W. M. "Buck" Walton, who declined his Populist nomination for state attorney general and published a scathing public exposure of the fusion arrangement. Such was the opposition of white southerners to the idea of uniting with the party of Radical Reconstruction and alleged Negro domination.[24]

No Populist struggled harder to lay to rest potentially destructive racial tensions than Rayner. Arguably, no Populist leader had more at stake. His December 1895 editorial in the *Southern Mercury* had opened with the explanation, "I am glad the time has come when the monster breath demagogues will have to quit talking about 'social equality,' 'negro supremacy' and the 'solid south.'" Rayner dismissed these terms as "slang phrases" left over from Reconstruction, terms that had no significance in the 1890s. Throughout the campaign of 1896 he used this same line of reasoning on the stump. In September, Rayner made his standard stump speech in Cherokee County. The Democratic Houston *Post* reported that "his discourse, from beginning to end, consisted of a frantic appeal to the colored voters to vote the Populist ticket in the hope of securing social equality." He held out the "tempting bait" of black participation on juries in the event of a Populist victory and "was interrupted at frequent intervals by the cheers of white Populists present." Of course, Rayner never advocated "social equality" any more than did white Populists, but for the Democratic correspondent covering the speech, his advocacy of Negro jury service implied just that. In the eyes of the reporter, the white Populists' cheers of the speech branded them as traitors to white supremacy.[25]

In addition to their charges of racial treason against white Populists, Democrats also tried to deceive black voters. The Populist state platform provided that "each race shall have its own pro rata proportion of the school fund," meaning that equal per capita funding should go to both black public schools and white. The Democrats issued a circular, "scattered broadcast across the state," that told blacks that the plank meant that they would receive an unfair portion of the fund. This was demagoguery at its worst, because under Democratic rule most black schools never received more than a fraction of the funding that white schools did. By comparison, the Populist planks on black education had been among the party's most liberal and just racial pronouncements.[26]

Democrats scored a major coup a month before the election when a leading black Republican, William M. "Gooseneck Bill" McDonald, bolted the fusion arrangement and pronounced for Culberson. McDonald would later become one of the richest blacks in America through his astute business, fraternal, and political activities. Populists charged that the Democrats bought McDonald, but nothing was ever proven. He actively campaigned for the Democratic state ticket, and his defection caused serious damage to the fusion cause among black Republicans.[27]

Finally, Democrats did not fail to invoke another time-honored racial tradition in the South, physical intimidation. On the eve of the election, L. N. Sublett, who had chaired the black Populist caucus at the Galveston convention, spoke at Willis, Texas. After his speech, a mob gathered at the home of the local black family where Sublett was staying and demanded that they surrender their guest. A lynching appeared imminent, but "the conservative element" in the mob overruled it. Instead, the mob forced Sublett to leave the county "on foot, with his grip in one hand and his overcoat on his arm." Shots were fired as he hurriedly left, but Sublett escaped unharmed. Local Democrats later justified their actions, claiming Sublett had used "violent and incendiary" language in his speech when he called "the entire [Democratic] party a set of — — —, an epithet too vile to print." [28]

Rayner continued to campaign vigorously. The week after the state convention, Dallas Populists invited him to join Kearby and other party notables for a grand rally. Rayner was unable to attend, but at the conclusion of the event Judge E. L. Wood read a statement from him. "I am sorry I can not attend your ratification meeting on the 22d instant, but if our Savior continues my life, I and 65,000 other negroes will be at J. C. Kearby's ratification meeting in November next, at which time Texas at large will ratify the action of our state convention." Rayner predicted that Texans would elect Kearby governor "because he is a friend to right, justice and the common people" and "we want our state capitol to be the temple of justice and charity, and not an Augean stable, to house a lot of political vampires." Rayner promised to keep "speaking and making converts for Populism and votes to help elect my ideal man, the Hon. J. C. Kearby." With that, the rally adjourned. [29]

Rayner did work furiously until the election. As soon as the Galveston convention adjourned in August, he had taken the first train back to Calvert to confer with Robertson County's Populists. He told his hometown allies that 85 percent of the county's blacks would vote the Populist ticket. Robertson County Democrats were greatly interested in the actions of Rayner and the Populists. Blacks had held offices in the county since Reconstruction, and Democrats had not carried the entire county in thirty years. As the Populists, Republicans, and Democrats held their local nominating conventions, the Houston *Post* correspondent in Robertson County reported that "county politics is almost at white heat now." Little was being said about the national races; all eyes were focused on local affairs. [30]

By the end of August, partisans in the county were formulating their campaign strategies. On August 30, the Galveston *News* published a report from Calvert, announcing that "J. B. Rayner, the Populist leader in this county, will be a candidate for the legislature." The *News* failed to elaborate on the report, except to say that "Rayner is well educated, a fluent speaker and a shrewd political wire worker, and will be hard to beat." Nothing more was ever said about Rayner's alleged candidacy. The story may have been nothing but a rumor, or perhaps Rayner discovered that his name had been suggested for office and quickly put a halt to the talk. At any rate, in mid-September the county's Populists met in convention and immediately appointed a committee to confer with local Republicans. After two days of negotiations the two parties agreed on a joint county ticket in which four of the nominees were Populists and the balance Republicans. Several of the fusion candidates were black, including Jesse Smith for county commissioner from Calvert precinct and the long-time Republican leader, Alex Asberry, for state representative.[31]

The Democrats soon announced their ticket as well. Among their number was O. D. Cannon, the incumbent Democratic county judge. Cannon was something of a legend in Robertson County. First elected county judge in 1890, he enjoyed a well-deserved reputation for violence. By 1896 he already had killed three men. In the most celebrated incident, a black lawyer, Hal Geiger, who had served a term in the state legislature as a Republican, was arguing a case in Cannon's court. A witness recalled years later that Geiger made an insolent remark and was promptly corrected by the judge. When Geiger "refused to show the judge the proper respect," Cannon calmly raised his revolver and put five bullets into Geiger. In this case, as in the other two murders he committed, the jury refused to convict the hot-tempered judge. Presumably, black insolence justified homicide in Robertson County. When he was not standing trial for murder, Cannon found other ways to flaunt the law. The county's district court records are sprinkled with cases involving Cannon not as county judge but as the defendant in gambling cases and other minor offenses. Earlier in 1896 he had been tried (and cleared) on extortion charges when he allegedly took payoffs to dismiss cases.[32]

Cannon and like-minded Democrats had begun to despair of ever putting an end to black officeholding in Robertson County. As an old-timer recalled years later, "the conservative white voters were beginning to realize that severe measures would have to be taken to assure the election of white people to office." On election day they put those measures into motion. The county seat, Franklin, was crowded with armed men all day. Democrats "quietly deposed" the black town marshal before the polls opened, and forty men with Winchester rifles stationed themselves at the courthouse to turn away all but Democratic voters. In the lower end of the county, a large company of black voters marched from their homes in the Brazos bottoms, accompanied by a brass band, to cast their votes in Hearne. An armed delegation of Democratic horsemen accosted them on the Little Brazos River bridge, threw the band instruments into the river, and dispersed the crowd. At Hearne, "a great number of pistol shots were fired in front of the polls when the negroes from the bottom came in to vote," and subsequently the box polled six hundred fewer votes than in the previous election. In one rural precinct that traditionally gave the fusion ticket a ninety-vote majority, the presiding officer reported that "a masked man took the box and returns away from him." In another, the Democratic candidates for sheriff and tax collector stood at the door of the polling place, one with a gun and the other with a club, and held off black voters. About mid-afternoon, word reached Judge Cannon that in spite of these countywide efforts the election might hinge upon his home precinct. "I went down to the polls and took my six-shooter," he recalled. "I stayed there until the polls closed. Not a negro voted. After that they didn't any more in Robertson County." Cannon boasted that he personally stood off a thousand blacks that day. When asked many years later about his violent role in bringing white rule back to the county, he explained that "I only shot when I thought I had to. I know God pulled me through."[33]

In spite of these extreme measures, the election was close. Initial returns gave the black fusion candidate for state representative, Asberry, a sixty-five-vote majority out of nearly five thousand votes cast. When election officials blatantly counted him out, Asberry made the mistake of threatening to contest the election. Cannon confronted him in a Franklin saloon and shot him. The bullet entered Asberry's arm, and he fled on foot for Calvert, ten miles away. Democrats put the county bloodhounds on his trail, and tradition in Robertson County holds that the wounded Asberry beat the hounds back to Calvert. Only Smith, the black candidate for county commissioner, won a victory so clear-cut that it could not be stolen. He quietly declined to accept the office, and his Democratic opponent was duly sworn in. Thus white supremacy returned to Robertson County.[34]

The Populist defeat in Rayner's home county was reflected in the statewide results. Amid great excitement and widespread fraud, intimidation, and violence, the Populist gubernatorial candidate, Jerome Kearby, lost to Charles Culberson by a vote of 298,528 to 238,692, and the Bryan-Sewall presidential ticket carried the state with 54 percent of all votes cast. Populist or fusion congressional candidates ran strong races in five districts but won none of them. The radical Populist leadership's high hopes for statewide victory were shattered, and the fault rested largely with the Populists themselves. Fusion had failed. Analysis of the election indicates that more than forty thousand of those who had supported the Populists in 1894 returned to the Democratic party—enough defections to cost Kearby the election. Estimates reveal that black votes were almost evenly divided between Culberson and Kearby. Although this was enough to indicate the considerable success of Rayner's efforts, it also underscores the effectiveness of the Democrats in controlling the black vote.[35]

The national convention's nomination of Bryan had driven Texas Populists to the desperate expedient of trying to support McKinley without appearing to do so, and that ill-fated maneuver had guaranteed the destruction of Populism on the state level. If the attempt to form a political coalition with blacks had been a radical step, the need to disguise the arrangement underscores how unprepared white Texans were for such radicalism. Few white Populists could countenance such an "unholy alliance" unless they held rather advanced views on black political rights. However, white Populist leaders in Texas had surpassed the majority of their rank-and-file constituents in their desire to defeat the state Democratic ring and in their willingness to join hands with black Republicans in order to accomplish it. If fusion was radical, then it is clear that the average Texas Populist had not been radicalized to the same extent as party leaders. Democratic race-baiting was successful in persuading thousands of wavering Populists that the Democratic party was the only guarantor of white supremacy. In later years, Rayner would come to understand this with great clarity, and it would embitter him toward poor whites for the rest of his life. As both Rayner and his white fusionist allies in the Populist movement learned, to threaten white supremacy was to exceed the limits of southern dissent.

Back in Robertson County, E. S. Peters sold his Populist newspaper in Calvert and gave up on politics for a number of years. In a spiteful mood, the county's Democrats voted to prohibit anyone who voted for the fusion ticket in 1896 from participating in future Democratic primaries. Rayner may or may not have returned from his last campaign appearance in time to witness the violent overthrow of Populism in his home county; he may well have been at the head of the company of blacks who were terrorized on the Little Brazos River bridge. The lack of surviving information on his whereabouts is not surprising; in subsequent years he understandably kept quiet about the election of 1896. For the next two years, as one Populist editor put it, the People's party of Texas "drifted with no firm hand upon the helm." When the state convention met in July 1898, the "colored brother" was "conspicuously absent." Various accounts in the state press of executive committee meetings fail to mention Rayner's name, and papers took no notice of whether he appeared at the state convention or won reelection to his place on the committee.[36]

Yet, amazingly, he returned to the campaign trail in one final, futile effort to salvage some vestige of independent politics in Texas. In July 1898, Rayner announced that he would be holding "colored People's party campmeetings" during the next two months if local Populists would help him with the arrangements. "This is the time for action, and there is no place in human endeavor for the idle and lukewarm," he trumpeted in the *Southern Mercury*. A week later his spirits remained high as he anticipated another campaign: "Past defeat has not discouraged me; I am again ready for the onset." In August, Rayner announced one of the most extensive speaking tours of his career, a punishing twenty-four-stop canvass of the south-central Texas Black Belt. Gone, however, were the days of statewide campaigning in every East Texas county, converting blacks to Populism, and trying to bring local Republican and People's parties into agreement on a fusion ticket. His call for aid in holding black camp meetings apparently went largely unanswered, and Rayner ultimately directed his efforts toward the one lone congressional candidate in the state whom he thought might stand some chance of defeating a Democrat. The campaign would provide a poignant postscript to his years as a Populist.[37]

The contest pitted one of the promising newcomers of Texas politics against a political veteran. The young Albert Sidney Burleson was a prototype of the new "progressive" southern Democrat. With the backing and assistance of the wily political manager Edward M. House, Burleson was conducting his first congressional race, promising to support an income tax, denouncing imperialism, and speaking harsh words against monopolies. No one needed to point out that he also stood for white supremacy. George Washington "Wash" Jones opposed him in the contest. Jones was a unique personality in Texas politics. A unionist before the Civil War, the Bastrop County native had served as a colonel in the Confederate army and won the lieutenant-governorship in 1866 under Presidential Reconstruction. He soon renounced his allegiance to the Democratic party and embarked upon a quixotic thirty-year career as the leading independent politician in the state. Endorsed at various times in his long career by Republicans, Greenbackers, Independents, Union Laborites, and Populists, the awkward, folksy, sincere Jones won election to Congress in 1878 and 1880 and lost two consecutive races for the governorship in 1882 and 1884. He was so politically independent that he refused even to affiliate formally with the People's party, although he held Populist views and the party endorsed him. Jones had always appealed for Negro votes, and black Texans genuinely respected him. A decade earlier, in the wake of the 1887 prohibition campaign, a Waco editor had written that those seeking to defeat the Democratic party in the future would "enjoy the embraces" of both Rayner and Jones. Now, at the very end of the Populist era, that prediction proved accurate.[38]

Following a two-week campaign swing in September that took him through eight of the district's nine counties, Rayner returned to Bastrop County to spend the last days of the race marshaling black support for Jones. A local newspaper reported that Jones was "standing up well in a hopeless race for congress" and expressed surprise "that a man of his age could endure the fatigue of a campaign against a young and brilliant man like Albert Burleson." Rayner met with his usual success on the stump, and even the Democratic press reported that a speech he made in Jones's behalf was "witty and at times almost eloquent." When the returns came in, however, it was apparent that young Burleson had buried Jones, who carried only Bastrop County, where a devoted personal following gave him a lopsided two-to-one margin. By contrast, in Washington County—with one of the largest black populations in the state—the Independent ticket polled only 724 votes to the Democrats' 5,296. The day had passed when a black majority in a Texas county spelled trouble for Democrats. Burleson was to serve eight successive terms in the House of Representatives, followed by eight years as postmaster general. In one of his first acts in Woodrow Wilson's cabinet, he put into motion a plan that helped to accelerate the segregation of federal government offices and facilities. With Burleson on his way to national fame, Wash Jones accepted defeat for the final time, and John B. Rayner's career in insurgent politics came to a dreary end.[39]

CHAPTER 14

"There Is No Relief in Politics"

◆◇◆

Throughout history, dissenters who have tried to reform repressive political systems have often faced long years of exile when their efforts to change their societies failed. Such was the fate of John B. Rayner at the dawn of the twentieth century. Although he did not leave Texas, he lived in exile just the same. The events of the late 1890s not only dealt a mortal blow to southern dissent as personified by the People's party, but they also effectively ended Rayner's participation in politics. His reform movement utterly destroyed and his people terrorized, Rayner disappeared almost completely from the public view for four years.

The magnitude of the Populist defeat can be gauged by the tenor of public affairs in and around Robertson County. The Populists in Rayner's home county had been so cowed by the violent events of 1896 that the party's candidates two years later would neither accept nomination nor campaign. "This is as it should be," noted a local Democratic editor. "The white people of the county should stay together from this [point] on and forever do away with the colored politician." The week after the election, a Democratic newspaper in Calvert rejoiced that "The last nail was driven in the coffin of Robertson county Populism last Tuesday." The white people of the county were "at last of one mind, politically speaking," and were finally united in favor of "white supremacy and good county government economically administered. Today the white people are in the saddle," explained the editor of the Calvert *Chronicle*, "and they are determined to stay that way." [1]

In nearby Grimes County, Populism met with a later, but equally dramatic, demise. The Populist-Republican coalition in that county had succeeded in electing a number of county officials, including a black county clerk and a white sheriff, Garrett Scott, who employed black deputies. With the coalition firmly in control, supported by the county's blacks and poor whites, the party managed to survive intact to 1900. Perhaps inspired by the example of Robertson County, Democrats in Grimes formed a White Man's Union that systematically harassed and terrified Populists of both races. The political confrontation culminated in the assassination of the black county clerk and a five-day siege by the White Man's Union of the county jail, where the sheriff and his deputies were barricaded. The critically wounded Scott relinquished his office and retired from Populism when state troops arrived to escort him from the county.[2]

In less dramatic fashion, old Populist leaders one by one said their good-byes to the party. For most, however, it meant more than just a change of occupation. Rayner's friend A. J. Spradley, the Nacogdoches sheriff who had courageously defended blacks from the lynch mob, released his farewell statement to the press. Rayner had called Spradley "the best sheriff in Texas," and he had become famous throughout the state. Communicating something of the spirit that, at its best, Populism had embodied, Spradley wrote that he was relinquishing the sheriff's office "for life." Addressing his notice to "those who have been my friends, white or black, rich or poor, and to those who have been otherwise," he could only take comfort in "the satisfaction of knowing that I have tried to do my duty." Spradley and some other Populists eventually returned to the Democratic party, justifying it on the grounds that the Democrats had endorsed many Populist demands. Compromise, they believed, was better than surrender. Even these Populists, however, felt ambivalent about their return to the Democracy. Joe Eagle, the young, dashing, former Populist congressional candidate from the Houston district, regretted the party's defeat but could "see no good to come from keeping up the populist party organization. . . . I prefer, right or wrong, to fight in the open," he wrote. "I am not ashamed of the part I have played—it has, I hope, been open and manly."[3]

By the turn of the century the party lay in such shambles that even prominent Populists often did not know where their erstwhile colleagues stood politically. In July 1900, Populists in the northeast Texas town of Paris tried to organize a party encampment for the following month. The chair of the encampment committee, well-known third-party man James W. Biard, drew up a list of speakers to be invited to the gathering. His list included Jerome Kearby, Joe Eagle, Stump Ashby, and Rayner. Kearby, his health rapidly fading after years spent pursuing losing causes, had retired from public life and in a few years would be dead. The youthful Eagle had announced his return to the Democratic party three weeks earlier. Rayner's friend Ashby, who had refused a Democratic bribe to withdraw from the lieutenant governor's race in 1896 and who had spent most of his personal savings in the Populist cause, wrote Biard a frank private letter declining the invitation. Ashby's letter, like Spradley's and Eagle's, captures the strong emotions the old Populists felt in the wake of the party's defeat: "I will say in reply to the invitation of your committee that I have spent the best years of my life in defence of the people, as I believed it. I did it largely at my own expence. Now I am old & poor, and I cannot leave my only hope of a livelihood—that is work on my farm, & go out to make speeches for my expences. I am sorry that I am not younger & in better financial condition, so that I might again go out on the free list, but I *cannot*."[4]

There is no record that Rayner ever replied to the committee's invitation. If he had answered, the response likely would have echoed Ashby's, for Rayner had also spent the best years of his life in defense of the people, as he believed it. There was, however, one major difference; while Ashby was poor and disillusioned, he was white. Biard was asking Rayner to come to one of the most rabidly anti-Negro sections of the state to speak on the virtues of biracial cooperation. Paris was the same town in which several years earlier Henry Smith, a black man accused of a crime, had been brutally tortured with a hot poker before being burned alive before thousands of white onlookers. Under the circumstances, it is not surprising that Rayner chose not to accept the invitation.[5]

Rayner not only had dropped from the political scene, but he also thought it best to withdraw from Calvert at times during these years. As if addressing Rayner personally, a Robertson County editor in 1900 asked, "Pop[ulist], where art thou? Art thou asleep or gone visiting? I never hear from you. . . . If you don't show up I don't know what will become of Mr. Negro." Where Rayner had gone was Victoria, Texas, one-hundred fifty miles to the south of Calvert. He had secured a part-time pastorate with a church in the South Texas city and, although his home and family remained in Calvert, he spent much time preaching in Victoria. It is, in fact, the only record that survives of Rayner actually being formally identified with a congregation. Perhaps he had to remove himself far from his home region—where the people had not so often heard him denounce "worthless and characterless" Negro preachers—in order to find a church that would have him. It is not known how long Rayner maintained this long-distance affiliation, but during his long years of exile from public affairs it not only provided subsistence for him and his family, but it also served as a safe harbor from the smoldering racial and political animosities of Robertson County.[6]

Rayner no doubt needed the extra income during the first years of the new century, for he suffered a serious financial and emotional setback in 1901. The *Southern Mercury* reported on April 18 that the Rayner home in Calvert had been "nearly destroyed" by a fire that damaged the kitchen and house-hold furniture. Losses were estimated at $600, an enormous sum for a family of meager means. Reminding readers that Rayner was "an old-time middle of the road Populist," *Mercury* editor Milton Park requested that "the old Populists who know personally of his faithfulness to the Populist party, would do well to remember him in a substantial way now in his loss." Whether any assistance materialized is not known, but given the poverty of so many Populists, the contributions could not have been great.[7]

Although 1898 had seemingly made it clear that Populism was dead and that Rayner's place in politics would be severely circumscribed in the future, it was not easy for him to cut all ties to his beloved cause. In 1902 the corporal's guard of old midroad Populists who refused to countenance surrender attempted a reorganization of the state and national parties, along with socialists and other reform groups, under the new name of the Allied People's party. Milton Park led the movement in Texas, and Jo A. Parker of Louisville, Kentucky, became the chair of the national executive committee. In the spring of 1902, Parker put out a call for "one thousand true men to work for the National Committee at reasonable compensation." These so-called "national organizers" presumably would be given authority to organize Allied People's party clubs, and the compensation would probably be a percentage of the dues. Breaking a public silence that had lasted nearly four years, Rayner wrote Parker in May to offer his services, to which Parker quickly assented. The *Mercury* applauded Rayner's commission, commenting that "the people of his race . . . above all people, should be eager to free themselves from the imperialism of combined capital." In his letter to Parker, Rayner had proudly proclaimed that his "fervor [for] Populism grows with my age," and that he was "getting ready for the coming political onset." Rayner reminded the *Mercury*'s readers that he needed financial support if he was to "write, and speak and work" for the movement. But he claimed to be "in the discussion and agitation to stay until the people will think wisely and act righteously." His name began to appear in the paper on lists of available Populist speakers.[8]

The *Mercury* soon reported that Rayner was renewing his efforts to spread the word of Populism among blacks and was even planning to travel to Houston County to speak and organize Populist clubs. In August, Rayner published the schedule of a proposed eleven-stop speaking tour through Henderson, Anderson, Leon, Madison, Montgomery, and Burleson counties. However, the campaign never materialized. The Allied People's party proved ephemeral, and it was unrealistic to expect that either blacks or whites in East Texas would have lent any assistance to Rayner's efforts to recruit black voters. To have followed through with his campaign plans would not only have proven futile but also probably dangerous.[9]

While Rayner faded from the public memory, the triumphant white Democrats of Texas moved to consolidate their power and finalize the subjugation of blacks. Throughout the Populist revolt, voter turnout among black Texans had steadily risen, reaching a high of 85 percent in the presidential election of 1896. By the fall 1902 elections, black turnout had fallen to a pitiful 23 percent through a combination of fraud, intimidation, terror, the establishment of local white-primary rules, and a general demoralization of black voters. That same year the state legislature submitted a poll tax amendment to voters. The measure, which did not affect the 1902 general elections, passed easily with 65 percent of the vote. The voters had simply written into law and given permanence to what in reality had already been accomplished: the disfranchisement of most blacks, along with many of the poor whites who had cooperated with them in the Populist revolt.[10]

Although Democrats led the movement for the poll tax, it would be a mistake to blame them exclusively for disfranchisement. White Populists also contributed significantly to the passage of the poll tax. As early as 1896 the *Southern Mercury*'s Milton Park had suggested that blacks were "miserably to be blamed to let the Democrats use them in such a way." Park advised blacks to "learn from experience, and develop their manliness" so Democratic "rascals cannot handle them in that way." Park issued an ominous—and prophetic—warning: "If the negro does not qualify himself to be a freeman, and act like one, the American people will become so thoroughly disgusted with this sort of thing after a while, that they may rise in their might and take the ballot away from him. Therefore, let the negro consider and be forewarned." Thus when voters went to the polls in 1902 to decide the poll tax issue, twice as many old Populists supported it as opposed it. Rayner was fully aware that large numbers of his former white Populist allies had supported the measure that would help curtail black participation in politics.[11]

A month after the poll tax was approved, Rayner wrote an editorial that seemed to signal a new direction in his political thought. Published in the Houston *Post* and reprinted by the *Southern Mercury*, the essay endorsed the tax. The new amendment, according to Rayner, "virtually eliminates the worthless negro from politics and the ballot box; but its adoption will not disfranchise the negro who respects his citizenship, but will awaken to patriotic activity every negro in Texas whose spark of manhood is still alive." Whatever he may have thought about the poll tax before its adoption, no advantage could be gained by opposing it after the fact.[12]

However expedient it may have been, Rayner's decision to endorse the tax was not necessarily inconsistent with his long-held beliefs. Throughout the 1890s he had been critical of blacks who, like "Gooseneck Bill" McDonald, had voted Democratic, and of the thousands of others who either had sold their votes or refused to vote other than a straight Republican ticket. For years he had been telling blacks that a black man "has to have some sense before he can become a populist." Therefore, after the downfall of Populism Rayner was critical of the role he believed blacks had indirectly played in causing its defeat and their own disfranchisement.[13]

"The great number of ignorant and mercenary voters among my people has compelled white people in the South to resort to the white man's primary and the white man's union," Rayner wrote in 1904. His whiggish political ideology probably also influenced his decision. As a believer in the principles of Revolutionary-era republicanism, he held that virtue and intelligence were the sine qua non of political participation. For more than a decade he had battled against poor blacks' stubborn attachment to the Republican party and had seen their votes corrupted by Democratic liquor and money. Likewise, he could not have so soon forgotten how many poor whites had responded favorably to the racial demagoguery of the Democrats, helping them put down the Populist experiment in biracial politics. If restricting suffrage to those possessing the wherewithal to pay a poll tax would eliminate corrupt or ignorant voters of both races, so much the better. As a black southerner in the early twentieth century, Rayner felt no constraints in criticizing the conduct of blacks. He opened fire on everyone—of whatever color—whom he believed had prevented the realization of a republic governed by virtuous citizens, both black and white.[14]

Rayner's indictment of ignorant voters thus forms a central theme of his writings on disfranchisement in the years after 1900. "The South acted wise and patriotic when it required the black voter to prepare himself to vote," he wrote in a characteristic statement. He frequently argued that "as long as ignorance goes to the ballot box imbeciles will go to our legislative halls." Although he believed that "all men have worth and hold fee simple title to justice," Rayner firmly held to the conviction that "there is no place in a democracy for the ignorant and immoral." The poll tax, if fairly administered, would restrict suffrage to those taxpaying citizens of both races who held steady jobs and fixed residences in a community. Rayner may have supported the poll tax in 1902 hoping to forestall a statewide white primary and arrest the progress of the countywide white primary. Perhaps by this show of good faith, white Texans eventually would restore suffrage to worthy blacks in those counties where they had lost it.[15]

Although Rayner's endorsement of the poll tax sounds like Booker T. Washington-style accommodationism, it must be compared to his harsh condemnation of the other principal means of disfranchisement, the white primary. He pulled no punches in attacking the primary, for it was a disfranchising method that discriminated solely on the basis of skin color, without regard to education, character, property ownership, taxpaying, or any of the standards that republican ideology traditionally used to measure intelligence and virtue. In effect, the white primary accomplished the exact opposite goal of the poll tax; it gave the ignorant and vicious members of the white race the ability to govern the intelligent and virtuous representatives of the black race.

Rayner's bitterness toward the white primary is evident throughout his political essays of the post-Populist period. If the South had "acted wise and patriotic" in restricting the suffrage of ignorant blacks, he wrote, it "acted otherwise when it failed to require all white men to do the same." He harshly criticized the "ignorant poor white men in the Democratic party in the South, who dominate the white man's primaries" for their ignorance "of the mission of republics and democracies." Racism and republicanism were antagonistic because "As long as any state in the union allows the vote of an ignorant, worthless man to kill the vote of an intelligent, worthy man, just so long will problems multiply, and progress be retarded." Rayner repeatedly argued that "intelligence and virtue are the only certificates that can give a right to vote," and he stated flatly that "the color of a man's epidermis is no prima facie evidence of political competency or incompetency." "There is no relief in politics," explained a frustrated Rayner, "as long as the white man's primary names the officers who are to be elected to preserve the peace and dignity of the state, and if there was no white man's primary there would be no relief as long as the majority of the negro voters did not comprehend the import of their votes."[16]

Rayner's attitudes toward suffrage help explain his public course after 1903. As his positions on the poll tax and white primary demonstrate, that course embodied a confusing and often inconsistent mix of accommodation and militancy. Even throughout the Populist era, Rayner had understood that the realpolitik of the turn-of-the-century South required that black activists like himself defer to white leadership. His Populist stump rhetoric had always contained an acknowledgment that the white people of the South were the

"Negro's best friend." But following the traumatic events of the late 1890s and early 1900s, accommodationist rhetoric and actions assumed a far more prominent role in Rayner's public life. It galled him, but he could see no alternative.

For Rayner, living in the changed atmosphere of the early 1900s, one overriding goal assumed precedence over all other considerations. That goal was securing some recognition, however small or symbolic, that all blacks were not inherently and permanently inferior to all whites, and therefore certain blacks deserved a meaningful voice in government. It was obviously a greatly diminished goal compared to the high hopes of the Populist period. "My class of Negroes," he contended in a Jeffersonian tone, "have race love and race pride and are very ambitious to form among ourselves an aristocracy of virtue and esthetical and industrial intelligence." He was willing to sacrifice the votes of the majority of blacks, if only the tiny class of educated, property-owning, taxpaying Negroes would be allowed to participate in politics on an equal basis with whites. On one hand, that meant endorsing poll taxes, literacy tests, voter registration rules, property requirements, or any other restrictions as long they were to be applied equally to blacks and whites. On the other hand, it meant fighting the white primary and other forms of strictly racial discrimination, including extralegal forms of physical intimidation. Rayner was prepared to acquiesce in white leadership as long as some qualified class of blacks could freely and independently participate in the selection of those whites. The experiences of the Populist revolt had proven the folly of hoping that all black adult males would be allowed this right, or that they would exercise it intelligently and honorably. The stuffed ballot boxes, bartered votes, gunplay, demagoguery, and sheer ignorance of voters in the 1890s not only had contributed to the undoing of Populism, but had also led to a racist white backlash unparalleled since the darkest days of Reconstruction. This backlash convinced Rayner that Populism, however noble its intentions or pregnant with democratic possibilities, had been a tragic mistake for blacks. Populism had promised all black men meaningful suffrage, but its defeat had rendered it infinitely harder for even the most intelligent and virtuous blacks to achieve political equality.[17]

Securing truly free voting rights, if only for a handful of the most worthy black citizens, became one of the chief motivating factors in the last fourteen years of Rayner's life. Until intelligent and virtuous blacks could cast a ballot unimpeded and uninfluenced by white laws, violence, or chicanery, the entire race would be denied the simple promises of life, liberty, and the pursuit of happiness set forth in the Declaration of Independence. The elaborate economic reforms so central to Populism seemed rather esoteric and visionary compared to what had become the cold reality of the twentieth century: Most blacks could not go to the polls on election day and vote at all. It was now clear to Rayner that Populism had been a gamble with much higher stakes than he had imagined, and the price of defeat was enormous. By moving too fast to secure sweeping reforms, blacks lost whatever political gains they had made since the end of Reconstruction. They would have to start over. If "bad white men" had destroyed Populism, as Rayner believed, it was because they were successful in "exploiting the credulity of my ignorant race." [18]

Because education was obviously vital in remedying the ignorance that had so handicapped blacks in politics and elsewhere, it comes as no surprise that in the post-Populist years Rayner directed much of his attention to black education. He long had worked for the betterment of black public education in Texas. As a member of the committee that framed the Populist state platform, he had been instrumental in drafting provisions calling for an equitable division of the public school funds and for black control of black schools. He also had frequently criticized the quality of the state's black schoolteachers and advocated better training and higher standards for educators.

Rayner's first recorded public statements after his five-year exile from public life focused on the current state of public education. Writing to the Houston *Post* in May 1904, he began his essay, "Solution of Negro Problem," by praising the generosity of whites. In a style reminiscent of Booker T. Washington, Rayner stated that "the South is the best place on earth for the negro, and the Southerner is the negro's best friend." This friendship existed because "the Southerner is taxing himself to help educate the negro." Rayner painted a verbal picture that would have given most white southerners little with which to disagree. He commended the South's generosity in employing black laborers, in helping blacks with their church work, and in knowing "how much length to give the political tether which is to hold the negro until his citizenship is superior to his ambition." Having paid lip service to white supremacy, Rayner then got down to specifics. "It is the duty of the State to educate the negro to do the work which the business interests of his country will call on him to do," he proclaimed. "The negro needs a moral education rather than a book education, for the negro's sense of gratitude has no memory in it, and his conscience needs culture. The Southerner in his effort to solve the negro problem is making some sad mistakes." Those "mistakes," upon which Rayner blamed the current "Negro Problem," lay not in the fact of tax-supported public education, but rather how common schools were managed. He identified poorly qualified teachers and an inappropriate curriculum as the two sources of trouble. Fearing that the legislature might soon act on proposals to eliminate all public funding for black schools, Rayner offered a startling alternative: "I would close all the negro free schools in Texas for two years." [19]

Closing the schools for two years would "enable the race to slough off the pride-intoxicated aphrodisiacal pedagogues who are now sucking the moral strength from the negro race." It would also "cure the school-teaching mania, now an epidemic among the young negroes." The hiatus would force "the best negroes" to "quickly organize themselves into independent school communities and employ only the best teachers, and thus draw the line between the good negro home and the bad negro home, and this will help the good negroes to become more self-dependent and independent, and the good negroes would soon build up among themselves an aristocracy of virtue and intelligence." During the two years that the schools were to be closed, the state government was to "keep separate and intact the unused money belonging to the negro schools, and at the end of the two years apportion the money to the use and benefit of the negro schools." Rayner's proposal essentially would have privatized black education. It also would have removed the schools from white control, a goal Populists had supported. At the same time, however, the plan retained some public funding for black education. [20]

Rayner's proposal was ignored, but his new role as educational theorist apparently created a new opportunity in late 1904. The previous year a black educator, Dr. James Johnson, had laid the plans for a Negro "normal and industrial" college to be located at Conroe, about forty miles north of Houston. The school was to be modeled on the Tuskegee plan, stressing vocational training. As it began to take shape, Johnson realized that the success of a private black college would require someone with extraordinary ability in fund-raising, a skill he apparently did not possess. Toward this end, in October 1904 the school's board appointed Rayner as financial agent. [21]

Conroe College had modest beginnings, but there was cause for guarded optimism about its chances for success. When Rayner became financial agent, the institution owned eight acres of donated land, one four-story building with twenty-three rooms, two smaller buildings, and enough lumber for the construction of another "commodious" building. In the fall 1904 term the school boasted forty boarding students and about a hundred others. Perhaps even more important for such an enterprise, the school enjoyed the formal blessing of local white leaders. Several of Conroe's leading citizens, including a banker, a judge, and the city's mayor, sat on the school's advisory board. In an era when some whites criticized the very idea of black education, it would be vital for the institution to have white approval. [22]

It would take more than nods of approval, however, for a new black college to survive. Conroe College needed money. Tuition and contributions from the state's poverty-stricken blacks would never be enough to provide more than a fraction of the required funds. State aid was a possibility, but a remote one in the prevailing atmosphere of distrust and resentment between the races. Church-supported colleges could draw upon the collective resources of whatever convention or association they were affiliated with, but Conroe College was to be secular. The school's only chance of survival lay in Rayner's ability to tap potential sources of white philanthropy. The strategy had worked for Booker T. Washington at Tuskegee; maybe it could do so at Conroe.[23]

The new financial agent wasted no time in unveiling his scheme to raise money. If Populism had taught Rayner anything about conducting a successful crusade, it had taught him the importance of publicity. For the next two-and-a-half years, Rayner kept Conroe College almost constantly in the press, filling the columns both of large urban dailies and small country weeklies with glowing reports of how the school was helping to solve the race problem in Texas. The goals of the institution were identical to those he had recommended for the state's public school system. "Scholars" at Conroe College were to be taught:

1. The science and art of politeness.
2. How to obey law and respect for public sentiment.
3. How to resist temptation and be virtuous.
4. That idleness is sin—all labor is honorable.
5. That a good character is the greatest wealth.
6. That the white people in the South are the negro's best friends.
7. That Christianity means love and service.[24]

Two weeks after his appointment to the fund-raising post, Rayner began to publicize his most ambitious project at the school. He proposed that the white people of Texas donate money for a large, four-story, fireproof brick building, dedicated "to the memory of the faithfulness of the slaves to their masters' families during the war between the States from 1861 to 1865." The building would be dubbed the "Hall of Faithfulness," and over the main entrance would be placed an appropriate commemorative marker. Rayner in no way equivocated about his goals: "This school must be made to Texas what Tuskegee is to Alabama."[25]

Although this accommodationist philosophy differed markedly from his old Populist militancy, Rayner's appointment allowed him to resume the activities he had long relished: travel, speech-making, and agitation. Besides the long-term objective of raising money to erect the Hall of Faithfulness, the school needed an immediate $2,000 to repair existing buildings and complete projects already underway on campus. Rayner immediately took to the road, criss-crossing the eastern half of Texas and cultivating his old Populist contacts in both the black and white communities. In January 1905, D. C. Tharp, a Conroe bank president who sat on the college's advisory board, assured Rayner that "the board has full confidence in you." Tharp observed that "the School is rapidly becoming a state more than a local institution" and reminded Rayner that blacks as well as whites would have to be forthcoming with their support. By late March, Johnson and the white board had rewarded Rayner with the additional title of president of the college. It is doubtful that the honor involved any change in Rayner's status as chief fundraiser. Johnson's official title became secretary and founder, and he appears to have continued as chief administrator. However, the title of president gave Rayner additional status in his high-profile mission. The white press was soon describing him somewhat inaccurately as "the moving spirit in the school" and calling him "the Booker T. Washington of Texas." [26]

Rayner's efforts on behalf of Conroe College placed him in some unusual situations. If politics makes strange bedfellows, raising money for the Conroe Normal and Industrial College created even stranger ones. In April 1905, Rayner traveled to Palestine, Texas, and appeared before the reunion of the John H. Reagan Camp of the United Confederate Veterans. The old rebels were impressed and passed a resolution endorsing the Hall of Faithfulness. Rayner later repeated this performance at the annual national meeting of the Confederate Veterans in New Orleans. He clearly understood the strong emotional attachment that white southerners felt for the Lost Cause, which by the early 1900s had become a kind of secular religion in the South. Rayner appeared ready to assume any posture—no matter how accommodating—to raise funds for his new cause. [27]

Promoting the school among Democratic politicians also created some strange bedfellows. The same month that he appeared before the Confederate veterans in Palestine, he paid a visit to Alexander Watkins Terrell. The seventy-five-year-old Terrell had been an officer in the Confederate army, U.S. minister to Turkey, and a leader of the state Democratic party for forty years. He introduced the first poll tax measure in the Texas legislature in 1879 and had been one of the state's leading proponents of suffrage restriction ever since. Firm in his belief that "the foremost man of all the world is the Anglo-Saxon American white man," Terrell sponsored legislation in 1903 and 1905 that brought sweeping reforms in Texas election laws. As a leader of the progressive wing of the party, he had done as much as any man in the state to disfranchise blacks. It is no small irony, therefore, that Terrell sponsored a resolution in the state house of representatives endorsing Rayner's efforts to build the Hall of Faithfulness at Conroe College. Resolutions and letters of endorsement soon followed from the state senate, justices of the supreme court, and members of the railroad commission. But as in the case of the Confederate veterans, resolutions did not pay teachers' salaries or construct campus buildings. If Conroe was to become the Tuskegee of Texas and John B. Rayner its Booker T. Washington, applause and resolutions had to be backed by dollars. Although he must have been disappointed that donations failed to keep pace with public displays of approval, Rayner knew from the first that his school's prosperity would depend largely upon his success in cultivating white philanthropists. And from the start he cultivated them with a vengeance.[28]

Whatever his contemporaries may have thought of Rayner, nobody could accuse him of timidity. If one sought money from rich white Texans, he reasoned, what better place to begin than with one of the richest white men in the state? Exactly one week after being appointed financial agent of Conroe College, Rayner addressed a letter to the Houston businessman John Henry Kirby. Thus began a remarkable relationship between an often-reactionary white millionaire capitalist and a black former agrarian reformer that continued for the rest of Rayner's life.

Using his best handwriting, Rayner addressed Kirby: "Sir: I beg you to forgive me for intruding upon your valuable time. I do so, because I believe you to be greatly interested in all endeavors for human amelioration." In a blatant refutation of Populist doctrine, Rayner explained that he believed "the rich people of every country, to be the custodians of the people's happiness." Assuming the most accommodating stance possible, he made his pitch for Kirby's aid:

The altruistic and unrequited work which I am now doing for human amelioration, would be greatly emphasized, and made more effective, if you will condescend to acquaint yourself with the purposes and work of the Conroe-Porter Industrial College, at Conroe, Texas. I am the financial agent for this school, and if the Lord will permit me, I shall go North among your millionaire associates next Spring, and try to raise some money for the school, and before I start, I shall ask you for a recommendation, and in the interim, I beg you to con[de]scend to inquire about the school, and see if it has merits and purposes which you can approve. . . . I do hope that all true chivalrous patricians like yourself, will take some interest in this school and help make its work more effective.

Yours in much humility, and for
Human Amelioration,
J. B. Rayner.

Rayner had played his cards well, for Kirby was immediately receptive to the idea and took a sincere interest in the work being done at Conroe.[29]

At the turn of the century, Kirby's career was a classic American success story. Rising from modest beginnings to become the unrivaled king of the East Texas lumber industry, he later expanded into railroads and oil. As a subscriber to Andrew Carnegie's Gospel of Wealth philosophy, Kirby cultivated a reputation as a philanthropist and model employer. During hard times, however, he responded to labor unrest by suspending paychecks, blacklisting, and hiring strikebreakers. Unfortunately, Rayner had caught his potential benefactor at a bad time. The "Prince of the Pines" had overextended himself through complex oil dealings, and his main endeavor, the Kirby Lumber Company, had suffered in the process. Payrolls went unpaid, millworkers walked off the job, and by early 1904 Kirby's lumber and oil companies were both placed in receivership. He was by no means broke, but the next five years proved trying.[30]

In light of his dire financial straits as of December 1904, it is all the more surprising that Kirby took an interest in Rayner's appeal. Yet he not only replied promptly and positively to Rayner's initial request for letters of introduction, but he also invited his new acquaintance to Houston, expressing a wish "to confer with you personally before hand as I think I can make some suggestions that may be of value to you." Throughout the remainder of Rayner's association with Conroe College, the two men corresponded frequently, with Rayner asking Kirby's aid in obtaining letters of recommendation, securing appointments to speak to white business groups, and determining the best strategies for promoting the school. Kirby loved flattery, and Rayner was practiced at the art. "I know your powerful influence in the social, commercial, financial, and political world," he told Kirby, "and I know that your public spirited, broad[,] liberal, and resourceful mind . . . can evolve some effect[ive] plan, which will give me the ear of Houston, and I beg for it." Nor could Kirby's paternalism fool Rayner into believing that he was free from the usual notions of white supremacy. In a typical statement designed to appeal to his patron's racism, Rayner wrote, "I know that

I have more respect and reverence for Southern taste, Southern customs, and Southern sentiment, and Southern traditions, than Booker T. Washington has, and I am no obsequious sycophant; but I am man and philosopher enough, to honor and reverence those racial esthetics, of the superior race, which centuries of thought, energy, patriotism, education, and religion have established immovable and indestructable in this country, for the immaculate preservation of the superiority of the Anglo-Saxon race."[31]

Rayner's careful courtship finally bore fruit, although doubtless not as richly as had been hoped. Kirby ultimately contributed $250 to Conroe College. That sum, although not great, was nevertheless a considerable help to the cash-strapped institution. Considering the donor's seriously embattled finances at the time, it testifies to his sense of paternalism. It also likely appealed to his personal vanity and soothed a conscience that may or may not have been bothered by the low wages and poor conditions endured by both black and white laborers in the Kirby mill towns. Perhaps he felt that the money might also pay dividends later by promoting his reputation as a friend to blacks, who might in turn serve as convenient scabs in some future strike.

Whatever the personal motives of either man, the relationship between Rayner and Kirby says much about the state of race relations in early-twentieth-century Texas. Kirby, ultra-conservative on most political issues, represented the opposite end of the political spectrum from Populism. He not only believed the People's party to have championed "heresies in questions of policy and no principle," but he also opposed William Jennings Bryan as a dangerous liberal. However, Democratic progressivism was the wave of the political future in the South, and progressive Democrats now supported many of the more moderate Populist demands. Yet those same progressives were unrivaled champions of the most severe forms of racism. Rayner faced a cruel dilemma. He could support the progressives, or he could join forces with those white southerners who stood for monopoly, the gold standard, political cronyism, laissez-faire government, and demon rum. White Populists could easily choose the former, but when Rayner reentered public life in 1904, he made the only choice he could make. If blacks had any remaining allies among whites, those allies were the reactionaries, not the progressives. They were men like John Henry Kirby. It comes as no surprise that during the last fourteen years of Rayner's life—in his hundreds of surviving essays, editorials, and letters—the word *Populism* never appears. The reformers were now the enemy, and if he hoped to survive among the reactionaries, he had to try to forget that the Populist revolt had ever happened.[32]

It is difficult to assess Rayner's overall ability as a fund-raiser, for the glowing reports in the press undoubtedly give an exaggerated picture of his success. Still, the school made major progress. By March 1906, near the end of Rayner's tenure, the college was reported to be "in a flourishing condition." The number of boarding students had grown to 320, and Rayner believed that the school could easily have an enrollment of 2,500 if facilities were available. He and Johnson employed a Tuskegee graduate to head the Agricultural Department, and student carpenters were productively occupied building a house for a private individual. Equally encouraging reports came from the Home Economics Department, where young women were learning the fine points of cooking, sewing, and managing a household. In early 1907 a number of important Texas business and political leaders were listed as contributors to the school, including George W. Brackenridge and Otto Wahrmund of San Antonio; George W. Littlefield and Edward M. House of Austin; and John H. Kirby, H. B. Rice, S. F. Carter, and James A. Baker, Jr., of Houston.[33]

The most notable achievement came in late 1906, when Rayner secured $100 cash and a $1,000 loan to purchase about a hundred acres adjacent to the school. The benefactor was Bertrand Adoue, a prominent banker and commission merchant of Galveston. A French immigrant, Adoue had gotten his start in New Orleans and for a while had settled in Calvert, where Rayner made his acquaintance. The addition of the land—assuming the loan could be repaid—would enable Conroe College to conduct real agricultural training and at the same time raise a cash crop to defray expenses. In a letter to Rayner, Adoue proffered his best wishes for the school's success, along with some stern advice: "I hope that your proteges will appreciate what is being done for them by assisting you to liquidate the debt. They must be made to understand they are 'men,' and not 'wards.' As men, they will command the respect and even the admiration of the white race; as wards, they must be objects of contempt, and should not expect anything else." Relatively few white Texans in 1906 were willing to admit that blacks might "command the respect and even the admiration of the white race." Adoue was one of them; Kirby was another. Neither had much respect for the progressive wing of the Democratic party. And as a wealthy banker and merchant, Adoue—like Kirby—represented most of the things that Populists had once despised.[34]

Adoue also occupied a high position in the ranks of the Texas antiprohibition forces. Liquor had become an increasingly important and divisive issue in the state ever since the Democratic party succeeded in squelching the Populist revolt and "reforming" the electoral process. Many of the politicians who had first taken sides on the issue in 1887 were still in the fight twenty

years later, trying either to banish John Barleycorn from the state or to preserve Texans' right to imbibe whatever they pleased. Although Rayner had
been in the thick of the 1887 campaign, stumping the state to speak against
the evils of strong drink, when the wets and the drys renewed their contest
in the early twentieth century he found himself on the opposite side of the
political fence. In prohibition, as in so many other things, Rayner was forced
to reckon with the new reality of the twentieth century. And the reality was
that reformers—in this case prohibitionists—were the group most dedicated
to segregation and disfranchisement.[35]

There were practical reasons, having little to do with racial liberalism,
why the antiprohibition forces recruited Rayner. The poll tax effectively had
disfranchised a majority of blacks, but those who paid the tax could still officially vote. The white primary in most East Texas counties barred them from
voting in the Democratic primary, which normally was the only election that
mattered. But prohibition elections were different because they were decided
in the general elections rather than primaries. Furthermore, whites often
were fairly evenly divided over prohibition. In counties with significant black
populations, Negroes could serve as a "swing" vote much as they had during Populism. The opponents of prohibition thus found natural allies among
blacks.

Like oppressed laborers in other places and times, black Texans in the
early twentieth century sought a measure of solace in alcohol. Under normal
conditions, a majority probably would eagerly go to the polls to fight prohibition. But the early 1900s were not normal times. The wets rapidly realized
that it would take extraordinary efforts to induce blacks to pay their poll taxes
and go to the polls in prohibition elections. Hard times continued to take
their toll on blacks' pocketbooks, and fraud, intimidation, and plain disillusionment discouraged even those who could pay the poll tax from exercising
their right to vote. If the wet forces were to keep Texas from eventually going
bone-dry, they would have to find ways to induce blacks to pay their poll
taxes and vote to defeat prohibition.

During the years of Rayner's retirement from public life, the drys had
been organizing. The Texas Local Option Association was founded in 1903
to encourage calling local-option elections. The Women's Christian Temperance Union and, later, the Anti-Saloon League, stepped up their agitation.
To counter the growing dry sentiment, the liquor industry created an organization of its own, the Texas Brewers' Association. The association provided
the structure for a cartel of the state's major breweries, the guiding force of
which was St. Louis-based Anheuser-Busch. Over the next decade the asso-

ciation fixed prices, divided territories, and spent hundreds of thousands of dollars combating prohibition in Texas. Brewers fought a losing battle against the adoption of the poll tax in 1902, and beginning in 1905 they employed Rayner to get out the black vote in local-option elections across the state.[36]

Rayner plunged into the prohibition wars with his typical energy and dedication. If, as a former prohibitionist, he entertained doubts about the intrinsic worthiness of the wet cause, the surviving historical record does not communicate those misgivings. For seven years beginning in 1905, he kept in almost constant contact with representatives of the Texas Brewers' Association, individual brewery officials, and representatives of local antiprohibition organizations, ready on short notice to travel to the scene of the next local-option contest. From 1905 to 1907, he kept a grueling schedule reminiscent of the Populist campaigns, splitting his time between his fund-raising activities for Conroe College and campaigning against prohibition. The tactics were also similar to those used in the 1890s. Rayner typically would travel to a county in which a local-option election had been called and meet with leaders of the county or precinct antiprohibition forces. For support in the new cause, he would seek out leaders in the black community, drawing on the huge network of friends and acquaintances he had made during the Populist years. Finally, he would arrange to make a series of speeches—often midnight rallies in backwoods black settlements—and try once again to work the oratorical magic of the past. No one could have been better suited to the purposes of the brewers.[37]

Rayner's arrangement with the Brewers' Association was informal; he was never salaried. Other than expenses, he allowed the brewers to pay him whatever they deemed him worth in a given situation. Part of this strategy stemmed from the need for a black to avoid appearing "uppity." Part of it may have been merely a wise ploy on his part to make his employers feel beholden to him rather than vice-versa. However, much of his reasoning came from Rayner's own scruples about being perceived as a hireling. After spending years as a Populist answering charges that blacks in the third party were nothing more than tools of ambitious white men, and after making precisely the same charge against blacks who voted Democratic, he could hardly justify his actions on grounds other than disinterested patriotism. He gained a reputation among many antiprohibition leaders as a man who was "patriotic enough not to make any specific charges." "I am satisfied," wrote another wet official, "that Mr. Rayner will do our cause a world of good! He is intelligent, has great weight with his people, and is not a 'paid' anti, but one from principle and at heart!" Patriotic or not, Rayner felt strongly compelled to work against prohibition. The chief goal of the wets was to persuade blacks to pay their poll taxes and then vote against prohibition. Because prohibition was closely identified with the progressive Democrats, it was natural for him to oppose the drys. But at the practical level, antiprohibition held even more fundamental significance for Rayner: it simply kept blacks involved in politics. Almost any movement intent upon registering black voters and getting them to the polls would have gained his endorsement. Virtually any group— even monopolistic beermakers—would have constituted acceptable allies in the struggle to preserve black voting rights.[38]

Correspondence of the Brewers' Association provides a fascinating glimpse into the inner recesses of early-twentieth-century black politics. Apart from the considerable light these records shed on the local-option fights, they also offer a more detailed examination of the techniques Rayner no doubt used in the Populist era. A 1907 local-option election in Travis County illustrates many of these techniques. In February, he wrote to brewers' representative Otto Wahrmund of San Antonio, apprising him of the probability that an election would soon be called in the county. "I was in Austin last week, and while there I unearthed the purposes and plans of the pros." He went on to explain that the pros had already raised $3,000 cash for the campaign. Soon they would circulate the petition needed to call an election. Rayner told Wahrmund that as soon as the election was approved, the pros were to conduct a house-to-house campaign in the black community, employing women to spread literature. The money was to be used to buy prohibition literature and pay black speakers. "If I had the money I would meet you in Austin," Rayner offered, "and we could do some effective work, and overthrow the purpose, and thwart the plans of the pros."[39]

Six weeks passed, and the wets had done nothing. Rayner again wrote Wahrmund, cautioning the brewers to "prepare for a battle in Travis County." He asked his associate point blank, "Do you want me to manage the colored vote in that county during the coming campaign?" Always the optimist in the midst of an election, he assured Wahrmund that he had "full charge of the colored vote" in Travis County. Often this sort of request was all it took for the brewers to dispatch Rayner to a county, but this time they thought Rayner was mistaken about the strength of dry sentiment.[40]

On the verge of being left out of the campaign, Rayner again wrote to Wahrmund. "I know the conditions in Travis County well, and I tell you now if the anti campaign is not wisely managed our side will suffer loss. I want to help win the victory in Travis. Again, let me warn you that danger is ahead, and we must not blunder." If the brewers would finance his activities in Austin, he would "find out all the plans of the pros and make some speeches, [and] silence all the negro preachers" who had enlisted in the prohibition cause. By this time it was becoming apparent that Rayner had been right about prohibitionist strength in Travis County. A third brewery official, R. L. Autrey of the Houston Ice and Brewing Company, suggested to Wahrmund that he reconsider sending Rayner. Autrey reminded Wahrmund that Rayner not only was the "manager of a negro college at Conroe," but also that he was "a particular friend of the president of the negro college at Austin. I think he can truly close the negro church doors to the prohibitionists in Austin." Wahrmund finally acknowledged that what his fellow brewer said was accurate. "I know from personal experience that all you say of the gentleman referred to is only too true, and I am confident that he could help out a whole lot." He promised to recommend Rayner to the local anti committee in Austin.[41]

As the Travis County campaign unfolded, it became clear that the drys were indeed well organized. On May 8, local antiprohibition chair George W. Littlefield reported that the capital city was seriously divided on the question and that it would be "a hard fight." By the fourteenth, Rayner was "on the ground at work." He found to his dismay that the wets had done nothing at all to court the black vote. In contrast, the colored prohibitionists were "shelling the woods." The brewers gave him $50 to commence the campaign, and soon Rayner had "used that money and created a confusion and fight among the colored prohibition leaders" that enabled him to "take the zeal and rabid fanaticism out of the leaders of the colored pro campaign committee." He wisely did not elaborate in writing exactly what that meant. He and his white counterpart quickly devised a satisfactory working arrangement. Littlefield furnished Rayner with "a full supply of refreshments" that he used to open his campaign headquarters. Soon he had the black vote in line, and when election day came the antis carried Travis County by a comfortable margin.[42]

In the prohibition wars of the early twentieth century, as in the Populist campaigns, Rayner constantly had to harass his white political associates for adequate compensation. Although they almost always acknowledged his invaluable contribution to the cause, few antiprohibitionists were as honest as Rayner's friend Bertrand Adoue. "Mr. Rayner has rendered valuable service," the Galveston businessman told one brewery official, "for which we have paid regularly, not very liberally, it is true, and he has gotten additional small sums from other parties." Despite the usual tactic of leaving the amount of his compensation to the discretion of the brewers, they still occasionally grew impatient with his not-always-gentle reminders that he had to live off what they paid. After recommending Rayner to an official of Anheuser-Busch, one Texas brewer suggested that Rayner had "one very, very serious drawback, however, and that is his mania for money. He will everlastingly and eternally be after you for the sinews of war." The "sinews of war" in reality did not amount to much. After the Travis County campaign Rayner billed the brewers $5.90 for railroad fare, $1 a day board, and $7.10 "for treating the boys down in the city, away from headquarters." For the six days' work he performed, Rayner told the brewers, "You can pay me what you please for the time." The brewers appear to have paid a total of $50, including expenses, for his work in Austin. Even this sum was higher than usual, the normal reward being about half that amount. Brewers' Association records indicate that the most Rayner ever received in a year was $230 for an almost unbroken summer of campaigning in 1907.[43]

Campaigning against prohibition both helped and hindered Rayner in his efforts to promote Conroe College. On one hand, most of the meaningful contributions to the school appear to have come from white antiprohibitionists. On the other hand, these contributions were never large, and time spent in politics was time that might have been devoted to fund-raising. In the spring of 1907, after less than three years in his position at Conroe, Rayner's association with the school ended. Fire has claimed the college's records, so the exact circumstances of his departure are uncertain. It is clear, however, that at about the time Rayner left Conroe the school underwent a dramatic change, abandoning its original mission as a vocational college modeled after Tuskegee and becoming instead a theological school for the training of black ministers. The college affiliated itself with the one of the black Baptist associations and hired Dr. David Abner, Jr., former president of Guadalupe College in Seguin, to replace Rayner as president. Abner brought with him a corps of faculty members to teach religion.[44]

Rayner may have resigned his position because of the accelerating rate at which prohibition elections were being called, or James Johnson may have decided that his fund-raiser's increasingly high profile in politics was injurious to the school's interests. But the change in Conroe College's mission almost certainly played the major role in Rayner's departure. Since the 1880s the "Reverend" Rayner had shown little but contempt for black preachers and organized religion. Near the end of his tenure at Conroe, he wrote that the "army of bigots and fanatics" who comprised the forces of "religious conservatism" were so "vigilant in watching and guarding their creeds and traditions that they have no time to do good to any one. God never authorized any man or class of men to compile a creed." Drawing a curious

analogy (given the writer's former status as a Populist platform committeeman), Rayner suggested that "creeds are to religion, what platforms are to
political parties, a baited trap to catch the thoughtless, and increase the number of adherents." True Christians had only two creeds: "'Thou shalt love
the Lord thy God with all thy heart, and with all thy soul, and with all thy
mind'. . . . [and] 'Thou shall love thy neighbor as thyself.'"[45]

Throughout the rest of his life Rayner fought a one-man crusade against
religious denominationalism. "Suppose I declare that the life and character of a Christian is God's only church on earth," he proposed in 1909. "A
Christian can not be a sectarian, because a sectarian is a devotee to some
ecclesiastical concoction boiled in the crucible of religious intolerance by
high caste hierarchs." Striking blow after blow at the resurgent Protestant
fundamentalism of the Progressive Era, Rayner articulated a philosophy of
religion that reflected older, antebellum concepts of human perfectionism.
He argued that there was "no such condition as human depravity; what we
call depravity is simply the good spot in man concealed, and the true science
of salvation is to know how to find this good spot and develop it." He contended that "the evolution of thought is the revelation of God, and I believe I
can be the son of God, just like Jesus the Christ was while he was in flesh."[46]

Protestant Christianity historically had placed its greatest emphasis upon
personal salvation. Although Rayner declared that humans could gain salvation by achieving perfection, such individual perfection was made possible
only by working to reform society. The church, he wrote in 1909, should be
"a corporation of givers and altruistic workers, who co-labor with Christ for
the redemption of humanity." He was convinced that the time had come "for
the people to know the great difference between Christianity and religion. . . .
Christianity means personal service first, last, and all the time." Traditional
black religion had placed much emphasis on the afterlife, and Rayner frequently argued that "Christianity is not a ticket to admit man into heaven, but
an antidote for the love for sin. The heaven we create here is as beatific as the
heaven hereafter." He acknowledged that blacks were making progress, but
that progress was occurring "in spite of the churches." Continuing his life-
long criticism of the black clergy, he declared that "the preachers in my race
talk too much about heaven, golden slippers, diamond crowns and long white
robes, when they should be preaching about duty, means to make the best
use of all industrial opportunities, and that efficient service means honesty,
politeness, and obedience."[47]

Formulating this secular, reformist theology enabled Rayner to reach into
his own past and resurrect many of the old Populist doctrines without having

to place them in a political context. As he had done in his Populist days, Rayner forcefully criticized the excesses of American capitalism. He saw nothing inherently wrong in American democracy, private enterprise, or material wealth, but when democracy prostituted itself before the corporations, when pursuit of private interests impinged on the common good, and when love of money was placed before love of family and other human beings, something had gone terribly wrong. So although Rayner accepted money from the brewers' cartel and pandered to John Henry Kirby in order to keep blacks voting and preserve their educational opportunities, he also issued public indictments of capitalism, materialism, and greed.

"The dollar mania," Rayner warned, "is now a national epidemic," and he believed that churches were largely to blame. Noting the frequent conflict between capitalism and Christian values, he lambasted the hypocrisy of pious monopolists: "The rich people make the church a large donation and then go out and organize a combine to corner the necessities of life, and expect God to help them rob the poor because of their gift to the church. Is this civilization? Is this Christianity?" America, her individualistic values reinforced by organized religion, had given the corporations carte blanche to exploit the poor. In the process, the nation's political institutions had been corrupted. "Commercialism," Rayner explained, "has made religion its 'cat's paw' in its effort to be created an individual, and a demi god. When any human government gives a charter to any body of men to do business, to sue and be sued, these charter institutions will be exploited by chimerical politicians and ignorant voters, and for self preservation, these chartered institutions will be forced to lobby legislative bodies, suborn courts for the privilege of being individualized, and will obsequiously cower before hierarchal power to hallucinate the people for the purpose of being apotheosized and immuned."[48]

Rayner had sought and failed to translate his beliefs about service into action through the agency of Conroe College. The college's metamorphosis from a secular vocational school to a training ground for old-fashioned Baptist ministers must have come as a severe personal affront to the man who believed that "church power is the most sublime, the most drastic, the most intolerant and the most destructive of human liberties." For the four years following his departure from Conroe, Rayner was forced to rely on his political activities and journalistic efforts as outlets for reformist urges. In 1911, however, the chance to do something concrete to help his race again arose, and once more he seized the opportunity. In August of that year Rayner was appointed financial agent for the Farmers' Improvement Agricultural School at Ladonia in northeast Texas. Perhaps this time he would be able to realize his own vision of how the black race was to effect its own salvation.[49]

The Farmers' Improvement Society (F.I.S.), which sponsored the school, was in 1911 the largest and most influential black self-help organization in Texas and perhaps the South. Founded in 1890 by Robert Lloyd Smith, a native of Charleston, South Carolina, and organized at a time when the Colored Farmers' Alliance was in decline, the F.I.S. was intended to encourage black solidarity and cooperation, teach black farmers to be more efficient and self-sufficient, and offer affordable insurance and burial benefits. It grew slowly at first, but by the time Rayner became affiliated with it the society boasted eight hundred branches with twelve thousand members.[50]

It was natural that Rayner and Smith would be attracted to one another, because the two men shared similar philosophies of black uplift. As a devoted friend and adherent of Booker T. Washington, Smith had faithfully sought to emulate Washington's strategies of self-help and accommodation. Yet, like Rayner, Smith was at the same time an active politician. Avoiding Populism, he had served as Texas's last black Republican state legislator from 1895 to 1899. At Washington's urging, Theodore Roosevelt had appointed Smith deputy to the U.S. marshal for eastern Texas in 1902, a position he had held until William Howard Taft removed him in 1909. Thus, like Rayner and many other black leaders in the early twentieth century, Smith seemingly espoused the accommodationist philosophy while striving to preserve a measure of black political influence and working behind the scenes for racial justice.[51]

Smith had long dreamed of an agricultural school as a natural complement to the other functions of the F.I.S. When the institution finally opened its doors in 1909, its stated purpose was threefold: "First: To give the student a practical training in correct methods of farming. Second: To give him a good, well-trained mind by pursuing a fair course of instruction at least as far advanced as the high school. Third: To train him up to true family life where habits of order, system, and thoroughness prevail." In other words, Smith's ideas about the kind of training blacks needed almost exactly matched those Rayner had enunciated in 1904, which he had sought to implement at Conroe College. Although Smith referred to the school as a college, it was really a boarding school for children from grades one through twelve. Like Conroe in its earlier days—and indeed like Tuskegee—the F.I.S. school combined basic academic and vocational training with a strong dose of moral instruction. Conroe College and the Farmers' Improvement School had another thing in common—shaky finances. Local F.I.S. branches were supposed to contribute to the school's upkeep, but impoverished black farmers could never adequately support the institution. When Smith hired Rayner to oversee fund-raising, the school owned eighty-two acres of sandy farmland with three buildings. Rayner immediately set out to publicize the cause and, hopefully, convince white Texans to contribute.[52]

During the next three years Rayner dusted off all of his old techniques and renewed his former contacts in what was essentially a replay of his experiences with the Conroe school. He traveled far and wide across the state, lecturing before both black and white audiences, cultivating the goodwill of anyone with money. He bombarded newspapers with stories about the F.I.S. and its innovative program for black uplift. The school was crowded and desperately needed more buildings and equipment, but after reading the first of Rayner's publicity pieces in the Galveston *Daily News*, Smith seemed confident "that at last we have found a man who can let the world know what we are trying to do." To this he soon added, "I hope that you will hustle as never before in all your days."[53]

If possible, Rayner went to even greater lengths than in the Conroe days to ingratiate himself with powerful whites. One of his first acts as financial agent was to write to J. S. "K. Lamity" Bonner, editor of *K. Lamity's Harpoon*, a bitingly satirical newspaper published in Austin. Bonner enjoyed a well-deserved reputation as the preeminent race-baiter in Texas, yet Rayner addressed him respectfully, agreeing that he had "well advertised the derelict negro" and meekly asking him to put in "a good word of commendation for the worthy negro." Bonner responded by defending his extreme racism and then presenting Rayner to his readers as "a worthy example for the negro race." What Rayner or the F.I.S. school gained from such an endorsement is at best questionable, but it no doubt came at a great psychological cost to the once-proud Rayner.[54]

Soon after accepting the F.I.S. position, Rayner reintroduced the idea of a Hall of Faithfulness to be financed by white donations in commemoration of the steadfast services rendered by southern slaves during the Civil War. If R. L. Smith objected to such a degrading tactic, he must have swallowed his pride, as Rayner had done long ago, and agreed that the end justified the means. Once again, whites throughout the state applauded Rayner's accommodationism. One admirer declared that "Rayner is the most unselfish negro I ever knew" and pronounced him "the greatest negro on the American continent." Another wrote, "Not 200 miles from Houston an aged ex-slave resides. He is frequently called 'the white nigger.' At the risk of his life he stood by the whites during the crucial period of reconstruction, his work being like that of a mediator between the two races. To respect all in their several places and relations as superiors, inferiors, or equals is the solution of any social or race problem." [55]

Years of telling whites what they wanted to hear were beginning to exact a toll on Rayner's dignity. In 1904 he had told stories about helping Kenneth Rayner hide valuables from the approaching Yankees; by 1912 these stories had become tales about "standing with the whites" during Reconstruction. Although there was perhaps some truth in his "faithful slave" stories, Rayner was simply lying about his course during Reconstruction. At times he stooped even lower, telling various whites that he was "no admirer" of the social-equality-seeking Booker T. Washington, and that he considered Thomas Dixon, author of such racist novels as *The Clansman*, to be "a wonderful writer and a deep and profound thinker." In trying to appeal to the rapidly disappearing paternalism of upper-class whites by emphasizing the class differences among blacks, he succeeded primarily in making himself appear elitist. The black masses who idolized Rayner as a Populist orator must have wondered how he could be so critical of average blacks, and other Negro leaders often thought he went too far in trying to placate whites. A black newspaper editor seriously questioned Rayner's accommodationist course. "The southern whites are not fools. They know every negro desires every right which the laws of the land guarantee him. They know the only reason he is not in possession of them is because he can not take them, and it is our opinion that they are without respect for the negro who talks to them contrarywise. Negroes of the Rayner brand should receive a welcome in neither race. The brave white men of the South, like brave men everywhere, loathe a coward, who, instead of battling for his liberties, whines like the whipped dog, or who, like a grinning jackass, declares that he deserves none." [56]

The editor was mistaken about the "brave white men" who "loathed" a black sycophant; in reality, the more sycophantic a black man was, the more whites applauded him. Rayner's stature among whites testifies to this. Another of Rayner's black critics, Dallas minister A. S. Jackson, placed his condemnation in a different context, however. Referring to the proposed Hall of Faithfulness, Jackson reportedly said that "no kind of building and school was worth the sacrifice of manhood that Raynor was making and that he would find that in trying to satisfy the white supremacists of Texas, he was

attempting to feed a wolf—'the more you give him, the more he wants.'"
Rayner gradually was discovering the cruel truth in Jackson's analysis. The
more concessions he made to white supremacy, the more strident it became.
For black leaders in the Progressive Era, temporary sacrifices of principle had
a way of becoming permanent. Nothing illustrates this better than Rayner's
role in party politics in the twentieth century.[57]

CHAPTER 15

"I Am a Man"

In 1912, John Rayner sat down to write an essay for the Houston *Chronicle*. Apparently reflecting upon his own political career, he made what seemed to be a disarming confession:

> Since some of the colored race have attempted to be protagonist in politics, we (negroes) have been deceived by irridescent visions of political power and idle ease, and misled by utopian promises, and we (negroes) as a race became so hallucinated . . . that we could not see the red flag of danger ahead, and when we came to our senses we found our political opportunities circumscribed, and our manhood proscribed, and what our fatuous presumption did in the past, our meekness and general moral worth must undo. The negro of today is not the negro of yesterday. Man must make himself worthy and admirable before he attempts by his vote to shape the policy and fix the destiny of states. . . . Politics has nothing to offer the negro.

Yet as Rayner's campaigning against prohibition demonstrated, his public statements eschewing politics cannot always be taken at face value. Indeed, his political interests after the turn of the century had not ended with local option elections. He was still desperately searching for some meaningful way to play the role of black dissenter in the South.[1]

When Rayner reentered public life in 1903, he not only went to work for Conroe College and campaigned against prohibition, but he also sought once again to influence party politics. For all practical purposes, the People's party was gone by this time, and the state's Republicans had been almost as successful as the Democrats in purging their ranks of black participants. Disfranchisement had reduced the number of black voters in general elections from about 160,000 to somewhere between 15,000 and 40,000. Only in certain very close elections could blacks hold the balance of power as they had often done in the 1890s.[2] Confronted with this set of circumstances, Rayner had concluded that he would simply support the best candidate in any given race, regardless of party affiliation. That candidate might be an old Populist-turned-Democrat who had been a friend in the 1890s. He might be a Democrat who, if elected, would perhaps prove friendly to Rayner's school projects. Rayner sometimes supported a candidate who on racial issues was merely the lesser of two evils in a two-man race. Occasionally he lent his political weight to a campaign out of sheer self-interest. Usually several of these factors combined to convince him to support a certain candidate.

Such was the case in a 1903 congressional race, Rayner's first recorded political activity following the defeat of Populism. He campaigned in Houston's sizable black community on behalf of J. M. Pinckney, who had been nominated to fill the unexpired term of Thomas H. Ball. A Confederate veteran from Waller County, Pinckney had earned a reputation as a friend to blacks while serving as district attorney and county judge. His anti-lynching utterances apparently canceled any objections that Rayner might have entertained because of Pinckney's stance as a prohibitionist. Blacks still held the balance of power in Houston because of unusual circumstances. In an effort to effect the repeal of a municipal ordinance that had recently segregated the city's streetcar system, a surprising number of Houston blacks had paid their poll taxes and registered to vote; consequently, they could also vote in the congressional election. A month before the election, it appeared that the white Republican candidate would give Pinckney a hard fight, but as the election approached, "a number of representative negroes," among them Rayner, "espoused the cause of the Democratic nominee." With black support, Pinckney carried Harris County by a slim margin, 974 votes to his opponent's 950. In campaigning for Pinckney, Rayner relinquished what had been his overriding goal in the Populist years: defeating the Democratic party at all costs.[3]

This congressional race demonstrates Rayner's willingness to support whomever he deemed the best candidate, regardless of party. But Pinckney's mild anti-lynching stance and the unattractiveness of the Republican candidate fail to account entirely for why Rayner campaigned for Pinckney. A letter written after the election provides a clue. In April 1904, the chair of Pinckney's campaign committee in Harris County, Wharton Bates, wrote to Governor S. W. T. Lanham on Rayner's behalf. Bates told the governor that he was writing "at the earnest solicitation of the numerous good Democrats of the 'Black Belt' " who thought Rayner should be rewarded for the "valuable service" he had rendered in the recent election. Rayner wished to be appointed superintendent of the State Colored Blind Asylum. Bates, who apparently was a former Populist, explained that he had known Rayner for fifteen or twenty years and that there had "never been a time in politics when it was to the interest of the white people but that he has been strictly identified with them." Rayner's election would "have a good effect on the negro race in the entire State," and Bates urged the governor to make the appointment.[4]

The governor remained unconvinced and did not name Rayner to the post, but the episode suggests that Rayner had determined to use his political connections to further his own interests as well as those of his race. If that meant supporting a Democrat, so be it. On at least two other occasions he tried to secure the superintendency of the Colored Blind Asylum. In 1910, he procured the endorsement of the brewer Otto Wahrmund, who told the antiprohibitionist Governor O. B. Colquitt that Rayner had been the governor's "friend, politically speaking." Again the effort came to naught. In 1914, under yet another gubernatorial administration, Rayner tried once more. He requested John Henry Kirby's intercession with the new governor, James Ferguson. Unfortunately, Kirby had opposed Ferguson's candidacy in the primary, so the patronage door was shut for a third time.[5]

Rayner campaigned for a few other white Democrats over the years, most notably Kirby when the lumber baron ran successfully for the state legislature in 1912. Often they were potential contributors to Rayner's schools or men who would perhaps use their political influence to send some patronage his way. But in the two decades following the defeat of the Populists, Rayner more often than not supported the Republican party. As was the case with Kenneth Rayner, John cooperated with Democrats only under the most unusual circumstances. He publicly proclaimed that "in religion and politics" he was an independent, contending that "the man who is so conservative that he can boast that he has always voted an unscratched [straight party] ticket indirectly acknowledges that he allows others to do his own thinking." Rayner's independence naturally stemmed from his long-held antipathy toward the two major parties, and no doubt it reflected the reality that blacks possessed few palatable political options after the turn of the century.[6]

By the early 1900s, the division of the Republican party into "lily-white" and "black-and-tan" factions had grown more pronounced, with the white faction emerging dominant. The white Republicans often rivaled Democrats in their devotion to white supremacy. The victory of the lily-whites served as salt in Rayner's already-smarting political wounds. He seems to have wanted to wash his hands of partisan politics altogether, but a lifetime of political activism was hard to forsake. Of one thing, however, he was sure. "The negro," he wrote in a 1908 essay, "if he has self-respect and racial pride, will repel with disdain every effort to make him the protege of any political party." Rayner went on to explain that blacks were naturally Republicans because they were grateful for the party's traditional championing of black rights. However, "office seekers and politicians" had been making blacks "a political stepping stone, to the negro's disadvantage, long enough." Pro-Negro planks in any party's platform were useless, he declared, because platforms did not produce justice. Neither Democrats nor Republicans stood any longer as "sponsors for man's inalienable rights." Instead, they were "panderers for great commercialism, and the man with influence who can exploit voters and who can not subscribe very bountifully to campaign expenses will find the elephantine and asinine ears of the two old parties closed when he clamors for man's inalienable rights."[7]

Despite his independent public stance, Rayner frequently favored Republicans, invariably doing so in presidential elections. But as usual in his erratic political career, he did not behave as one might expect. Rather than support the black-and-tan faction of the Texas G.O.P., Rayner urged acquiescence in lily-white control of the state party. Employing the same line of reasoning that many white Republican strategists, including his father, had used since Reconstruction, Rayner suggested that the only way to build up the party in the South was to place it under the leadership of native whites. "Some facts must be admitted even if they are painful, and one fact is: That the white man who associates with the negro on terms of political equality in Republican conventions in the South will not in these days be able to induce other white men to unite with the Republican party."[8]

There was much truth in this analysis. The great stumbling block for the Republican party in the South always had been its reputation as the party of blacks. Indeed, time has shown that the establishment of the two-party system in the South depended on the reconstitution of the G.O.P. as a conservative probusiness party controlled by whites. The problem for Rayner was not that he misunderstood what must be done to revive the Republican party; the problem was that his solution depended upon the permanent removal of blacks from positions of party leadership. Was bringing two-party politics to the South worth such a sacrifice? Rayner concluded that it was. Thus in politics, as in education, he tried to "feed the wolf" of white supremacy by his willingness to support a lily-white Republican party. Instead of the party being thankful for black acquiescence in white leadership and in return championing basic black rights, Republicans, now free of Negro influence, simply ignored black interests. The more Rayner fed the wolf, the more it wanted.

Rayner remained aloof from Republican politics until the elections of 1908. With the lily-white faction now dominant, in August of that year he advised blacks that "there is nothing for the political negro to gain by opposing the political methods of the white Republicans in Texas." In May 1908, he contacted Cecil Lyon, a moderate white Republican leader supported by the lily-whites, offering his services as a stump speaker in the fall presidential campaign. Rayner wished to make a speaking tour of Illinois, Indiana, New York, Pennsylvania, and Maryland—states where a mobilized Negro vote might play a decisive role in bringing a Republican victory. Lyon believed that Rayner had "absolutely the right idea" about the need for blacks to consent to white leadership of the party and promised to do anything he could to help arrange the tour. He explained, however, that any action would have to wait until the national committee met and devised a campaign plan. Lyon denied wanting "to run the negro out of the party" but pointed out that even if every black in Texas voted Republican, the party still could not carry state elections.[9]

With his views now in consonance with those of the state party's white leader, Rayner was ready to work for the election of William Howard Taft. The Taft campaign apparently never availed itself of his services, but Rayner continued to turn his pen and influence to the task of supporting the national Republican party. As time went by, however, Republicans at the state level moved even beyond Lyon in their willingness to proscribe blacks. By 1910 Rayner had had enough. J. O. Terrell, the G.O.P. gubernatorial nominee, opened his campaign by proclaiming that "the Republican party in Texas would never again be dominated by an 'alien race.'" Rayner lashed out at Terrell's "ingratitude and prejudice," reminding his readers in the Houston *Chronicle* that despite "persuasion, intimidation, bribe and persecution," blacks had continued to vote Republican. Now the party was repaying black fidelity by branding them as aliens. Rayner could accept Republican support for suffrage restriction; he could endure white control of the party's conventions; he could concede the fruits of patronage to white Republicans; but he would never countenance the party's standard-bearer questioning the Americanism of blacks. "How can the negro be an alien," he asked angrily, "when he has been in America 291 years?" Furthermore, the Negro had been "a brave soldier and a faithful servant in every war this country has engaged [in] from the 'Boston massacre' to San Juan Hill." Rayner concluded this public outburst by telling blacks that they would be better off if the South remained Democratic. "There is a duty which the negro owes to his self-respect, greater than any duty he owes to any political party, and before he can vote for Mr. J. O. Terrell he will have to dishonor his self respect and the love he has for his race. The negro has made many political mistakes because he followed bad white men, but 'never more.' " [10]

For the next two years Rayner felt so discouraged that he often recommended that blacks eschew politics altogether. In early 1912 he stated that "the negro farmers in Texas have no confidence in political promises; they do not care if Hon. J. K. Vardaman secures the repeal of the thirteenth, four-teenth and fifteenth amendments to our national constitution, nor do they care if Mr. Vardaman repeals the ten commandments and burns up all the Bibles—God lives, and the negroes are trusting in righteousness of an all-wise and all powerful God." However, the key question facing Texas Republicans in the spring of 1912 was not the Mississippi demagogue, Vardaman, but rather the question of who was to be the party's presidential nominee. Taft and Roosevelt had parted ways, bitterly dividing the party nationally and in Texas. By this time Rayner's essays in the *Chronicle* had acquired something of a cult following among readers of both races. One reader submitted a series of questions to him, requesting for the benefit of other readers that Rayner state his public position on current issues facing blacks. [11]

In his reply Rayner voiced his clearest warning to date about the futility of black participation in partisan politics. Although he acknowledged that his words would cause many blacks "to misunderstand and mistrust my council," Rayner nevertheless advised blacks "to keep out of the fight" and let the warring Republican factions " 'stew in their own grease.' " With an indictment reminiscent of his harangues from the Populist era, Rayner charged that "the Republican party of today is simply sponsor for the powers that prey upon labor." The one-time Party of Lincoln, he contended, now believed "in the autocratic centralization of power in the national government, and believes that corporations are great individuals with immunities and greater privileges to do as they please." Republicans had "apotheosized the dollar, and made the voter an obsequious worshiper." Rayner's verdict echoed that of his early Populist days: "The Republican party in the South has nothing for the negro." [12]

Despite these strictures concerning black participation in partisan politics, Rayner in 1912 made yet another exception to his own advice. Far from letting the Taft and Roosevelt factions "stew in their own grease," he vigorously took sides. When Roosevelt failed to gain the Republican nomination, the former president founded the Progressive party and deliberately set out to capture the lily-white Republican vote in the South. In Texas he was aided by Cecil Lyon, who despite lily-white proclivities had previously enjoyed Rayner's support. As it became clear that blacks would have to choose between Taft and Roosevelt, Rayner composed an impassioned letter to his people bitterly denouncing Lyon, branding Roosevelt a "political maniac" who was "trying to organize a white man's Progressive party out of the Negro haters of the North and South," and urging blacks to vote for Taft. Assuming the persona of the Great Emancipator, he framed his otherwise anonymous appeal as "The Spirit of Abraham Lincoln Calling His Colored Children Whom He Emancipated." Speaking through the persona of Lincoln, he reminded blacks that citizenship and the right to vote had "cost this Country streams of tears and blood; and great national pain and suffering." Failure to go the polls would be a sign of ingratitude; in effect, blacks would be saying that they wished "to return to a slavery more debasing than chattel slavery." Rayner ordered blacks to vote a straight Republican ticket. "The whole world is watching you," he stated. "The spirits of John Brown and Abraham Lincoln will be at every ballot box in Texas on the day of election in next November to see if the colored man is true to the party that gave him liberty, the right to vote, and the free school. God save the colored people from Democratic hate and wicked persecution is the prayer of Abraham Lincoln." [13]

The "Spirit of Abraham Lincoln" essay was anonymous, and in his signed, public essays—especially those in the white press—Rayner continued to advise blacks to shun politics. In 1912 such advice included warnings against black participation in the prohibition issue. "There once was a time," he wrote, "when the question of prohibition could be discussed without passion," but now "both sides have exhausted their store of reason and facts, and have also exhausted their patience, and from now on all local option elections will be force meet force, and it will be best for all negro voters to keep away from the polls on all local option elections." The man who had spent years urging blacks to vote against prohibition now told them to "let the white people settle this question among themselves." It had grown "too dangerous for the negro voter to dive into." [14]

Rayner clearly felt embittered about the failure of white men from both parties and from both sides of the prohibition question to further the cause of black rights. But it must be remembered that he was writing for a newspaper with a large white readership and that his main public cause at the time was fund-raising for the F.I.S. school. In fact, Rayner's private actions again directly contradicted his public advice to blacks in the *Chronicle*. A few weeks

after his essay appeared, he was in Beeville at the behest of the brewers, holding a "secret caucus" with black leaders, showing them how to mark their
ballots in the upcoming local option election, and laboring to "set in motion
some subtle forces which would get the colored voters to the polls." [15]

Over the next two years Rayner's public political utterances grew increasingly erratic and contradictory. He adhered to his belief that blacks should
"keep out of conventions and let the white people manage the political campaigns," but beyond this he appeared unable to decide what they should do.
At times he advised blacks "to vote with the Southerner on all questions" and
praised Democrats such as John H. Kirby and Joe Eagle, but then he turned
around and complained that there was "no relief in politics." He wrote in the
Chronicle that blacks should be "neutral in political campaigns" and "vote for
the best man," and then he proceeded to inform his readers that he would
"vote that Republican ticket of the Old Abraham Lincoln stamp." Rayner had
tested virtually every political option since the demise of Populism, and none
ultimately seemed to hold any promise for betterment of the race. The limits
of dissent for a black southerner in politics had been reached in the 1890s.
It is true that much of the apparent irrationality of his course stemmed from
the need to stay in the good graces of the brewers and to appear apolitical in
his role as financial agent of the Farmers' Improvement School. But even as
a spokesman for these causes he fell far short of consistency.[16]

Rayner's years in the public spotlight were rapidly drawing to a close by
1912. When his benefactor Bertrand Adoue died in late 1911, he knew he had
lost his "most substantial friend" from the ranks of the antiprohibitionists.
Rayner's relationship with the brewers had always been stormy, for although
he left his pay to their discretion, the beermakers considered him greedy.
While alive, Adoue had played the peacemaker, pointing out Rayner's value
to the cause and reminding the brewery officials that Rayner's pay was not
very generous. In July 1912, however, when Rayner approached Otto Wahrmund for a F.I.S. donation following a successful local option election, Wahrmund turned him down, claiming to be too busy. Rayner's quick temper,
which he normally held in check when dealing with white people, overruled
his patience. He fired an irate letter back to Wahrmund:

> You say you have not the time to help me is a sad surprise. I am a
> protagonist in the cause of anti-prohibition. I have done more anti-
> prohibition than all the other ___ combined. I have placed the iron
> hand of Machiavel[l]ian diplomacy upon the religious, educational and
> business gatherings of my people and kept them from making campaign

thunder for the intolerant and fanatical prohibitionists. I have wet a score of dry counties in Texas or kept them from drying. I merit the highest consideration from the patriotic antis. I represent the colored farmers of Texas, and I tell you their votes saved the State from the blighting hand of the prohibitionists. . . . How can you . . . ignore my importunities? Every saloon in San Antonio should donate to my school. I have stood undaunted before the frowns of religious women and endured the imprecations of mad prohibitionists and have been forced to lose personal property and mortgage the best of my property . . . and my endurance and suffering has been your material progress. I am now doing all I can to make the colored pastors of your city your political friends. You say "you will have to excuse me," I will do so but when you need a colored vote and call on me I shall need tell you to excuse me. . . . I am not a renegade; but if you all want success you can have it through my labors. I am a man, and I am as proud of my influence as you are of your great wealth and prosperous business. Can you forgive a slight or ignore it? I know my powers, and you know yourself, and when you slight my powers it proves that you don't need mine. Don't trouble to answer this letter. You "have not the time to spare." [17]

Rayner thus parted ways with the brewers amid great resentment on both sides. Ironically, less than three years later the state attorney general hauled the Texas Brewers' Association and the individual breweries who composed the cartel into district court and charged them with antitrust violations and illegal interference in elections. The beermakers were resoundingly defeated, fined $281,000, and forfeited their charters to conduct business in Texas. The state's case rested primarily on subpoenaed records of the brewers, and among the most damning of the evidence (in the eyes of whites) was the extensive correspondence between brewery officials and their black political organizer. Rayner must have felt a certain satisfaction as the brewers' empire collapsed around them. [18]

The brewers' refusal to contribute to the F.I.S. school indicated Rayner's general failure to produce the major donations the institution needed. In a replay of his experiences at Conroe, the considerable publicity Rayner achieved for the school was never matched by financial support from those who applauded the loudest. Attempts to tap northern philanthropy via Booker T. Washington and Tuskegee met with only limited success. Sometime in mid-1914 Rayner left the Farmers' Improvement Society. Records of the circumstances surrounding his departure have not survived, but it is likely that declining health, personal financial difficulties, and the lack of major fund-raising successes prompted the move.[19]

With his final retirement from active public life, Rayner found it increasingly difficult to support himself and his family in the middle-class style to which they were accustomed. It is true that by 1914 the Rayners had managed to accumulate eight lots in the Negro section of Calvert, on which John maintained rented houses. In addition, the family purchased a small tract of farmland in the country, also rented to a tenant. After his retirement Rayner and his sons maintained the property, and from time to time he collected rents on land owned by white absentee landlords in return for a percentage of the rents. When these sources of income proved insufficient, he fell back on his long-time patron, John H. Kirby, for employment. Kirby's East Texas lumber mills employed both black and white laborers, and from time to time Kirby needed additional hands. With his considerable powers of persuasion and far-flung contacts in the black communities of Texas, Rayner could easily procure all the millhands Kirby needed. In the last several years of his life Rayner performed this service on an irregular basis, and at one point he was said to have recruited Mexican peasants. Perhaps the most tragic aspect in a career filled with irony was how Rayner was forced to make a living during his last years. As a Populist, he had spent years championing tenant farmers and denouncing landlords, absentee owners, and greedy corporations. Now, in his old age, Rayner himself was something of a landlord, he assisted absentee owners, and his recruitment efforts sent hundreds of poor blacks into the hands of a large corporation.[20]

As Rayner's reliance upon Kirby grew, he adopted an increasingly conservative political posture in his dealings with the lumber magnate, partly because Kirby himself had gradually gone from conservative to reactionary in politics. The "Prince of the Pines," however, remained paternalistic in his dealings with Rayner, who felt he had no choice but to cultivate the relationship. Kirby's feelings about Rayner were unquestionably sincere; he never failed to answer letters from Rayner promptly and personally, and he wrote privately to a white friend of his "abiding respect" for the "colored preacher, teacher and scholar." [21]

How much of Rayner's conservatism in his letters to Kirby was genuine—and how much was a sham—cannot be determined for sure. But clearly the two men sincerely concurred in their mutual hatred of the "reformers" in the progressive wing of the Democratic party, albeit for different reasons. "We are living in an inauspicious age," Rayner confided in a July 1915 letter. "The greed of labor unions, and the prolific growth of mushroom demagogues who are laboring to become exponents of this insatiate greed is a dire menace." In other letters he elaborated on the same theme. "Thoughtful conservatism is tired of reformers, political innovations, and utopian promises," he stated, telling Kirby that it would be "dangerous for you to demur" when the country called on Kirby's leadership. He observed that "since the political negro is not in the white man's way, the white voter is becoming more thoughtful, more conservative, and more independent, and reason and conservatism must organize against thoughtlessness and chimerical innovations, and the anarchy of agrarianism." Those who had "apotheosized the word 'progressive'" had "hallucinated the thoughtless with its meaning." Rayner allowed himself only one indulgent hope that hearkened back to the Populist period. "The white man's insatiate greed is the white man's danger," he predicted, "and some day the Negro vote will be called upon to save the South." [22]

Even Kirby's sponsorship fell short of providing enough income for Rayner to meet his financial obligations. In 1914 his troubles were compounded by a fire that completely destroyed one of his rental houses. When the fire broke out, Calvert's new fire truck "made a record run" to the scene, but the city had not bothered to extend water mains into the Jim Crow neighborhood. The house was a total loss. As he fell behind in his taxes, Rayner resorted to more desperate measures. He approached wealthy Houston businessman Harris Masterson for an $800 loan. A former Republican judge who had amassed a fortune in land, Masterson assumed a mortgage on Rayner's eight town lots, including the family's home. The debt was to be paid with interest in six months. When the due date arrived, Rayner could not produce the sum. He pleaded for more time, which Masterson granted. By January 1915, four months after the payment was due, the money still had not materialized, and Masterson foreclosed. [23]

When the sheriff of Robertson County publicly auctioned off the lots to satisfy the debt on January 5, Harris Masterson was the only bidder. He paid a total of $25 for the eight pieces of property, obviously a minute fraction of their total worth. Whether or not something illegal had transpired between Masterson and the sheriff, Rayner was faced with losing nearly everything he owned, including the roof over his head. Unbeknown to John, Clarissa had written a desperate letter to Masterson: "Dear Sir, My husband had you to take up some notes here in the bank on our property and the notes would have been paid but we did not get enough rent on our farm to pay the notes. I worked so hard to buy the property that you have a mortgage on and I don't want to lose my property and beg you to have mercy and patience with us and give us more time. If you please, let me know if you will give us some more time. We will pay you interest for all the time we use you[r] money. I am the wife of J. B. Rayner. Will you please let me hear from you?" Three more months passed, and Masterson neither had sold the property nor evicted the Rayners. His agent wrote to Rayner, offering him a chance to buy back the property despite the fact that Rayner "acted very bad" and showed himself "to be ungratefull and unapreciative and unreliable." At the last moment, Rayner somehow managed to buy back his own house, and the lot on which it stood, for an undisclosed amount. It is safe to say that Masterson lost no money on the transaction. In the wake of this near-disaster, Rayner ruefully told Kirby that "I have been too zealous to get my people to '*think*,' and today my family is paying the tax for my past zeal."[24]

Despite the financial troubles that occupied much of his attention in his last years, Rayner still found time to satisfy his insatiable appetite for reading, especially contemporary sociological and scientific works. In the early teens, Rayner's curiosity about history, race, and social reform brought him into contact with the flourishing eugenics movement that had emerged in the United States in the early twentieth century. Extensive studies in criminal anthropology and a simplistic understanding of modern genetic theory convinced many reform-oriented Americans that crime, vice, feeblemindedness, alcoholism, poverty, and disease were hereditary rather than products of a faulty environment. Racists pressed the new theories into service to explain the alleged deficiencies of Negroes, and nativists did the same for immigrants. By about 1910, various societies and individuals were promoting such eugenics-inspired measures as immigration restriction and sterilization of the unfit.[25]

Eugenics attracted Rayner for several reasons. First, it was "scientific," which appealed to his belief in the primacy of reason over emotion. Second, the emphasis on heredity helped him explain why reform seemed to have failed in improving the moral and material progress of his people. However, eugenics was not just a negative movement aimed at preventing the unfit from outnumbering the fit; eugenicists also sought to facilitate the careful selection of biologically compatible mates, to encourage health, hygiene, and morality among parents, and to promote better prenatal care and child-rearing practices. The new pseudoscience doubtless explained much to Rayner about why, as a descendent of white statesmen and soldiers, he seemed to differ so much from other blacks.[26]

Eugenics could be pressed into service by conservatives, much as social Darwinism had been, to underscore the futility of efforts to improve the condition of humanity. Yet it also attracted reformers; for example, many clergymen with social gospel beliefs employed its more positive aspects as an adjunct to their other reform programs. The movement's dualistic nature accommodated itself easily to Rayner's own complex mix of conservatism and reform-mindedness. Leaving further and further behind the egalitarianism of his Populist years, he began to stress the innate inequality of humanity but refused to let that belief diminish his fervor for reform. "All men are worthy," he pronounced, "but men are not equal, and the inequality of man is the axle upon which the restless wheel of evolution turns man continually toward the perfect and sublime." Elaborating upon this theme, Rayner proposed in 1914 that "the mission of law is to adjust the inequality of man, and give to the weak and the humble an aegis of protection and a palladium of defense, and to the ignoble the nobility of protection and to the criminal justice." But eugenic theory confirmed in Rayner's mind his growing suspicion that reform had severe limits. One could "take the red neck and hillbilly of the Georgia crackers," he speculated, "and give him an immaculate and empyrean family and give him the most polished education, and when he reaches manhood he will be only a parrot—he can only repeat what he has learned from books, but cannot initiate nor originate."[27]

In his writings on eugenics Rayner reflected the competing strains of thought within the movement as well as his own inner conflict between hereditarian and environmentalist beliefs. Although he believed "that man can obtain the transcendental perfect," he nonetheless thought that "civilization must have a base, a sure foundation, and this base must be uncontaminated blood corpuscles whose purity will be ambrosial food for the brain cells. When the blood is sin poisoned with filth the brain cells will be paralyzed and the will power destroyed." As a consequence, Rayner urged that "all diseased people and children of drunkards must be sterilized and the saloons closed up forever."[28]

While he was associated with the F.I.S. school, Rayner claimed that eugenic principles were being taught there. In this regard his beliefs in eugenics typified the positive rather than the negative aspects of the movement. When publicizing the school, he explained that "the girls are taught a knowledge of eugenics, how to understand prenatal influence, and the constructive and destructive influence of environment in motherhood." It was an odd combination of hereditarianism and environmentalism, therefore, that led him to recommend that pregnant women "see nothing but beauty, hear nothing but music and lovable truths, and [be] treated with immaculate reverence and celestial kindness." All the education in the world would be for naught if these influences were missing. After leaving the school, Rayner tried to convince Kirby to send him to East Texas milltowns to lecture on eugenics to black millworkers. Kirby agreed that it would be a good idea but claimed he was unable to finance the effort.[29]

Rayner's growing skepticism about human ability to adapt and improve ultimately manifested itself not only in eugenics but also in nativism. In a truly ironic twist of fate, the same ideology that had so enamored Kenneth Rayner now captivated his son sixty years later. Twentieth-century blacks had greater justification for their resentment of immigrants than did antebellum white southerners. It was understandably difficult for blacks to see the logic, or the justice, in allowing recently arrived non-English-speaking immigrants—some of whom were illiterate—to take their seats in a first-class railroad car while southern-born, college-educated blacks had to make their way to the second-class Jim Crow compartment. As Rayner put it, "the majority of the negroes may be incompetent voters, but when it comes to pure devotion to Americanism and an inextinguishable love for the South . . . the negro will be given the first place of honor by all who are competent to think."[30]

One must be careful not to compare too closely the Know-Nothing movement of the 1850s and the nativist sentiments of black Americans in the Progressive Era, but clearly the younger Rayner came to share attitudes in many ways similar to those his father held a half-century before. Designing politicians—primarily Democrats—might advocate easy naturalization laws in order to gain the votes of immigrants, but, according to Rayner, one could "never Americanize these people by congressional enactments in the corporations' cathedral at Washington." Like his father, Rayner was concerned about the ability of foreigners to exercise intelligently the rights and responsibilities of American citizenship, but he used his background in eugenics to help explain the problem. "Our American civilization is very rapidly becoming Europeanized," he warned in 1914, "not from the castles of Europe, but from the hovels. . . . People whose ancestors never raised their hands in defense of liberty can not teach the sons of patriotic heroes lessons in freedom." Rayner argued that the "political stomach of a republic is a very delicate organ," and it could not easily "digest the naturalized voter." He went to great lengths to point out that the first bloodshed in the American Revolution was that of a black, Crispus Attucks, and that Alexander Hamilton's mother was a mulatto. The solution to the immigration problem was clear: "Every man coming to this country should be required to pay $1,000 for his citizenship and remain for 21 years a good citizen before he is allowed to vote or hold office." After all, "the children of the people who founded this great republic can not vote nor hold office until they are 21 years old." The son thus embraced the same remedy that his father had endorsed. However, John B. Rayner's nativism resulted not so much from his fear of the impact that immigration was having on American institutions but rather from the way that immigration underscored the blatant denial of meaningful citizenship to blacks. If his words sounded harsh, it should be remembered that Rayner—himself a tax-paying grandson of a Revolutionary veteran—was barred from voting in the Democratic primary in his own hometown.[31]

When in 1917 the United States entered World War I, Rayner sensed a new opportunity for blacks. He long had opposed imperialism and war in general, but like other Americans he patriotically supported the war once it had been declared. Rayner guessed that if blacks could be placed in combat roles, they would return from Europe with enhanced leverage to bargain for civil rights. Military service also would provide steady employment and encourage savings among young black males—goals he had spent years promoting. A week after Congress declared war on Germany, Rayner wrote to Kirby, expressing his opinion that blacks should be urged to serve. Apparently he wanted the lumber baron to send him to the milltowns to encourage enlistments. Rayner's letter has not been located, but Kirby's answer survives. "I do not agree with you that they [blacks] can render the best service to their country at this time by seeking military positions. What our Republic needs and what the world needs is more producers." Kirby suggested that Rayner could serve the country best "by encouraging industry and patient and energetic toil in the lines for which your people are best qualified," and he refused to finance Rayner's lectures in the milltowns.[32]

Rayner replied by telling his benefactor that although Kirby had "righteous" motives, "the truculent enemies of the colored people say just what you say." Kirby would never do anything to intentionally hurt blacks, Rayner believed, but he had to disagree with his analysis of the situation. "Now when it comes to war," Rayner contended,

> I don't believe in its "*hell.*" . . . I truly hope and pray that this country will never be forced to place a gun or sword in the colored man's hands. The sword is the sceptre of tyran[n]ical autocracy, the instrument of religious intolerance, and fanaticism, and I am perfectly willing for the white man to have a fee simple title to use it as long as the fatherhood of the Devil prevents the brotherhood of man. I believe in peace, virtue, toil, and plenty; and I truly desire all colored people to be Christlike in character, and to serve in truth and love all humanity. . . . I am still

preaching, lecturing, and writing about the beauty, utility, peace, and prosperity of the farm life, and the hellish horrors of modern warfare: but I will not teach my people an unpatriotic lesson. I tell my people if the country calls for you to go on the battle field, to go, and face the enemy and never retreat and never surrender.[33]

Rayner did not live to see the end of the war, and the great majority of blacks served not in combat roles but in support capacities as stevedores, cooks, and manual laborers. He did survive long enough to read the news from Houston in September 1917, where, after continually being harassed by police and insulted by white citizens, black troops from Camp Logan staged a riot in which seventeen whites died. In the aftermath, thirteen black soldiers were hanged and forty-one given life sentences. Black participation in the war effort—far from bringing progress in civil rights—seemed instead to be fanning the flames of prejudice. It was the same story that had been being replayed since Emancipation; black hopes were built up, only to be torn down. And the end result always was that whites rededicated themselves to keeping blacks "in their place."

America's entry into World War I coincided with the onset of serious physical problems for Rayner. Over the years his naturally stout physique, like that of his father's, had given way to overweight; the grueling years on the campaign trail and lecture circuit, with the inevitable bad food and insufficient rest, had taken their toll. Now sixty-seven, he confided to Kirby that he still had "to hustle for bread when not laboring for others," but hustling was growing more difficult. All of his children were grown and gone from home. Despite Rayner's public efforts to keep blacks out of the cities and down on the farm, two of his sons had gone to Chicago—a move Rayner had encouraged. His youngest daughter, Susie, was attending the colored normal school eighty miles away at Prairie View. Although he was a loving husband and a proponent of women's suffrage, he could be dictatorial around the house, demanding that his meals be served on time and hot. He had always maintained an office in his home, and interruptions while he worked, wrote, and thought were strictly forbidden. Declining health increasingly restricted his travels, and his sources of income were more uncertain than ever. He and Clarissa took as many as five black children into their home as boarding students, with John as teacher.[34]

In 1918 Rayner began to exhibit signs of what was probably either kidney or liver failure. Diagnosed as "dropsy," the illness resulted in edema, which manifested itself as a massive swelling of the hands and feet. Confined mostly to his home, Rayner could do little besides give his boarding students their lessons, help his less literate neighbors write letters and untangle minor legal affairs, and reflect on a lifetime spent battling white supremacy. Rayner never kept a diary, and almost no truly personal letters survive, but it seems that he had few genuinely close friends. His light skin, refined manners, polished speech, and close associations with whites had always set him apart from the majority of the blacks in Calvert. His last days apparently were lonely.[35]

Fortunately for biographers, Rayner did bequeath one remarkable group of private writings to posterity. In the final years of his life he began compiling a collection of his own "Wise Sayings." This group of aphorisms, totaling more than a hundred manuscript pages, appears originally to have been intended for publication, just like the rest of his essays. Indeed, certain of the sayings did find their way into print. Clearly, however, the majority of the adages were never published. They took the form of aphorisms because they undoubtedly were meant to be instructive and easy to remember. Never a philosopher in the sense of one who develops pure theory, he had always intended that his essays, letters, and speeches educate and motivate his audiences to direct action. The "theorist" who never tried to put ideas into practice had "exploited humanity from time immemorial," Rayner believed. Such a person was no better than the "practical man" whose only question was, " 'Will it pay?' " What appears to have happened is that as he tried to put his innermost beliefs onto paper, Rayner found that many of those beliefs expressed much more radical ideas than were permissible in the public press. Therefore, he collected only the most "inoffensive" of the sayings for publication but continued to write whatever he felt, strictly for his own benefit.[36]

These adages cover a wide range of topics. Religion, education, war, money, marriage, and music all receive attention. Aphorisms are by definition simplistic, but they are nevertheless convenient ways to summarize the writer's beliefs. The maxims display Rayner's continuing interest in eugenics and his dedication to nativism, but even stronger is his undying commitment to a Populistic conception of economics and materialism: "Commercialism is a euphemistic word for artful preying: its motive is lustful covetousness, and it deals and exploits without a conscience or compunction." The religious emphasis so prominent in the thought of southern Populists emerges clearly in these writings: "The inordinate love for money, and ambition for power, are twin evils; whose father is Satan, and whose mother is selfishness." A number of the sayings were derived directly from the Populist diagnosis of American economic ills: "When wealth concentrates, misery radiates"; "no man can be charitable with money for which he did not give value received"; "interest on money invalidates the principal in man"; "the man who takes usury from his fellow man, gives the devil a mortgage on his soul"; and "Carnegie has erected many mausoleums for dead thought, and our economic system which enabled him to erect these sepulchral monuments keeps the people who produced his wealth from having time to read the books in the Carnegie Library."

The most prominent theme in the aphorisms, however, is not materialism. Not surprisingly, Rayner devoted much of the private thought of his last days to the question that had occupied his life—the relationship between the black and white races in America. These writings were never published and could not be published in the South of 1918. He straightforwardly posed the main theme of the racial aphorisms: "God does not intend for one part of his people to feel that they are superior to another part." A number of the adages attack the hypocrisy of whites and the irrationality of racism. Rayner was particularly frustrated by the unending stream of white criticism of black intelligence and character. He pointed out that "the man or men who take from me the responsibilities of a full fledge citizen, take from me the opportunity to prove the true mettle of my virtues." He continued in this vein by calling the white southerner "the most unreasonable of all men," because he "teaches the Negro to believe himself an inferior being, and at the same time requires of the Negro a character par excellent." If whites were superior, how was miscegenation to be explained? "A superior race never mixes their blood with the blood of an inferior race," Rayner reasoned. "How can you boast of your superiority when the world sees every day in the variegated complexion of the so called inferior race, the fruits of your most intimate social equality association with your so called inferior race?"

Since the Populist period, Rayner frequently had indulged in speculation about the future. In these private writings, his predictions become ominous and at times apocalyptic. As a point of departure, he noted that "time will prove whether the white man's civilization is *igni fatuus* or promethean fire whose celestial heat welds humanity into Christian solidarity." Yet he never completely relinquished his faith in republicanism as the ideal form of human government. As badly as things had turned out for blacks in the South, the root values of American civilization nevertheless were "all the light the Negro has in the night of intolerance." It was "dark now," but perhaps "the hideous and horrible travail of the Negro through the valley of political and industrial intolerance" would signal "the birth of the day." However, Rayner was terribly pessimistic about the coming days, and he issued some dire warnings to whites. "The white race can only save itself by saving the black race," he cautioned. "If the Southerner keeps his sentiments, he will be sure to lose his land, his political power, and be eliminated from the commercial affairs of the country." He believed that white supremacy would "finally be his [the white man's] undoing, because the Southern white man is impinging a law that no man wrote, and no legislative body enacted." If whites continued to nurse the "hallucinated idea of race superiority," they would awake one day to find that they were watching "through a retrospective kaleidoscope [their] superiority in the past."

The very words *superiority* and *inferiority* took on new meanings in Rayner's sayings. The superior man was merely "he who does his duty because he fears God and loves man." Conversely, "the most inferior man in the world is he who can not see his opportunity to do good." "The superior man," Rayner proposed, "labors to make all men superior, and the inferior man is he who is afraid to divide his opportunities with others. Again, the superior man is he who makes a righteous use of power." He felt that whites clearly had failed to use their power righteously. The unreasoning prejudice that sanctioned the lynching and burning of blacks would discredit southern whites in the eyes of future generations. "The white people who say the most cruel things about the Negro," argued Rayner, "are not morally nor mentally competent to write or express a thought that the future will pay any attention to." He reminded himself "never to listen to the counsel of the man who is too cowardly to contend for you to have equal political and industrial opportunities." Only when whites developed "intelligence and virtue enough to have mutual confidence in each other, respect for law, and a profound reverence for our course of justice," would mobs cease to "organize to murder and burn human beings." White southerners had forgotten one simple truth: "Only the tried are convicted, or cleared."

Turning his attention to the political institutions that undergirded the system of white supremacy, Rayner indicted the Democratic party in a manner that surely would have pleased his father. White southerners had imbued the party with a near-sacred infallibility, with tragic results. "The faith the South has in the Democratic party," Rayner bitterly noted, was "stronger than the faith the South has in God." Throughout American history, every time whites had faced a struggle, blacks had been there "with strong arm and obedience, striking for the same." Each time whites "had resisted tyranny and fought for liberty the Negro was there with his gun, fireing at every opportunity." Now whites had "monopolized all the good in the civilization which the Negro helped to build up," and it seemed to Rayner that blacks' only justice would come in some distant time and place, "where the 'Tree of Life' will not be guarded with Democratic sentinels."

But the Democratic sentinels would not even allow him to die in peace. Sometime during the last months of his life, Rayner collided one last time with the local symbol of white supremacy, Calvert's town marshal. Ailing from dropsy and barely able to get around, Rayner had failed to comply with a town ordinance requiring that pets be tagged. The white sheriff demanded that he tag his dog, and Rayner stubbornly refused. The angry sheriff resorted to a time-honored southern remedy for dealing with dissenters: physical violence. The beating he administered to Rayner was not particularly severe, but the victim was a sick man approaching sixty-eight. After the incident, Rayner continued to see to his teaching duties as best he could, but gradually his condition deteriorated. In the "wise sayings," he had noted that as "our bodies gro[w] old, ugly, full of pains, and decrepted, the soul is in travail, and will soon throw off its body and re-appear more like its Creator." On July 14, 1918, Rayner died of congestive heart failure. In keeping with his wishes, there was no church funeral, but rather a simple service at the Rayners' home. Few of the newspapers for which he had once written bothered to note his passing. The next day he was buried in the Jim Crow cemetery on the outskirts of Calvert.[37]

Epilogue

The story of Kenneth and John B. Rayner underscores the pervasive influence of racism and issues related to race in American politics. In the South, racial considerations were usually paramount, yet there were always those who for a variety of reasons wished to see race removed from the political equation. One did not have to be what we today would call a "liberal" in order to desire this result. As the case of the Rayners has shown, one could in many ways be quite conservative and still (to use their phraseology) deprecate the "agitation" of the "Negro question." It is curious—and significant— that both Kenneth and John B. Rayner used the word *conservative* to describe themselves throughout their lives. Kenneth believed that the Whig, American, and Republican parties were the conservative parties of his time. His son used the same adjective to describe a party that has often been termed "radical," the Populists. What was the common denominator? To belong to each of these parties in the nineteenth-century South was to be a dissenter. But it was to be a dissenter in the manner of Thomas Jefferson, a southerner who founded the region's dissenting tradition when he wrote that "all men are created equal."

The tradition that Jefferson and his generation of southerners transmitted to Kenneth and John B. Rayner was one the nineteenth-century South lost somewhere along the way. Jefferson and many of the other Founding Fathers realized the long-term incompatibility of republican government and slavery, and for that reason they did what they could to set the institution of racial slavery on the path to extinction. The political battles that their ideological heirs had to fight in the nineteenth century are a measure of the Founders' failure to deal effectively with the problem. The reasons for their failure are ironic. Although they knew that the continuing presence of slavery made achieving the promise of freedom problematic, they also understood that the American republic itself could not become a reality if the question of slavery were not pushed to the background of public debate. Thus the Founders allowed slavery to persist in the new United States while at the same time realizing its incompatibility with the nation's theory of freedom.

This ironic legacy was bequeathed to the nineteenth century. The need to defend white supremacy imposed strict limits on political dissent and made constructive public careers for men like Kenneth and John B. Rayner nearly impossible. To a much greater degree than the Revolutionary generation, the Rayners were forced to confront the issue: would America be a republic where all were created equal or would the presence of slavery continue to frustrate the efforts of statesmen to perfect republican government? Before the Civil War, Kenneth Rayner, like Jefferson before him, could see no way around the dilemma but to try to relegate the issue of slavery to the background. When slavery was destroyed in the bloody conflict that both Rayner and Jefferson foresaw, Rayner believed that the dilemma might be resolved. With slavery gone, the nation could put racial issues behind it and proceed with the business of realizing Jefferson's dream. Sectionalism could be ended. With this end in mind Kenneth Rayner became a Republican. But the failure of the Republicans themselves to obliterate sectionalism led him by the time of his death to feel nothing but disillusionment and fear for the future of republican government.

John B. Rayner followed in his father's footsteps in striving for a political system not predicated on race. As a "black" man, the personal stakes were higher for him, but his understanding of the nation's promise and of its reality was the same as Kenneth's. The younger Rayner saw clearly the incompatibility between republicanism and racism. In his early career he joined the only party in the South that seemed committed to resolving that problem, the Republicans. But like his father, John B. Rayner by the 1880s came to realize that the party of Lincoln had surrendered the goal of eliminating the racial problems that kept the nation's politics sectionally polarized and undemocratic. The People's party offered the potential solution to this dilemma by promising to erase the sectional and racial obstacles to true republican government. But Populism, too, proved unequal to the task. Futile efforts to divide the triumphant Democrats and a resignation to the slow process of education was all Rayner had left.

As a unique American family, the story of the Rayners did not end with the death of Kenneth in 1884 or of John in 1918. Kenneth's white sons did not inherit his abilities in politics, agriculture, or law, but they did lead interesting lives. In another classic case of southern irony, all three ended up in Texas along with their black half-brother. The eldest, Kenneth Jr., moved to Dallas, where he served as chair of the county's Republican party in 1884. At a time when local Republicans were dividing into warring black and white wings, he led the white faction. He died the year after his father.[1]

William Polk Rayner, the second son, led a troubled life. While serving as deputy United States revenue collector in Fort Worth, he killed the proprietor of a gambling hall in a conflict over a woman of dubious character. He was tried, pleaded self-defense, and was acquitted. After serving for a time as deputy United States marshal in Dallas, he moved to El Paso, where he again met with trouble. He was gambling in a saloon with Wyatt Earp late one night in 1885 when an argument arose among the saloon's patrons. In the ensuing brawl Rayner was shot in the arm and the abdomen. He lingered near death for more than a month. His mother and brother came to care for him, but he died of his wounds.[2]

Hamilton Polk Rayner, the youngest son, likewise had no shortage of excitement in his life. He entered the field of law enforcement as the town marshal of Hunnewell, Kansas, a rough cattle town where at the age of twenty-three he cleaned out a gang of ruffians, six-guns blazing. He subsequently served as deputy sheriff in Tarrant and Hood counties, Texas, before moving to El Paso to become special agent for the Southern Pacific Railroad and a Texas Ranger. He dabbled unsuccessfully in local Republican politics and died in 1932. Hamilton's son, Kenneth, became a respected lawyer in Memphis and served one term in the Tennessee state legislature, dying in 1966.[3]

The daughters of Kenneth and Susan Rayner led somewhat more respectable, if less exciting, lives than their brothers. Sallie, the eldest, married Joseph H. Hyman of Edgecombe County, North Carolina, who served as colonel of the 13th North Carolina Regiment in the Confederate army and sat with Kenneth Rayner in the 1865–66 state legislature. She died in 1905, leaving six children. Her younger sister Susan lived with her parents after their return to Washington and married assistant surgeon-general Arthur H. Glennan in 1881. Susan had five children and died in 1910.[4]

Kenneth Rayner's black descendants also led interesting lives. His black daughter, Cornelia—John B. Rayner's sister—married and lived most of her adult life in New York. When her son-in-law found employment as a railroad worker she was able to travel extensively by train at reduced rates. A relative recalls that with her light complexion Cornelia delighted in "passing" as white and riding in the white people's cars.[5]

John B. Rayner and his wives Susan and Clarissa had five children. The daughters, Mary and Susie, married and lived their lives in Texas. All three sons, Ivan Edward, Loris Melikoff, and Ahmed Arabi, moved to Chicago in the great black migration before 1920. Ahmed and Loris became undertakers, and the firm Ahmed founded still remains in the family. A. A. Rayner & Sons performed more than 1,600 funerals in 1986.[6]

One Rayner descendant did inherit the political proclivities of his ancestors. A. A. "Sammie" Rayner, Jr., the grandson of John B. and great-grandson of Kenneth Rayner, entered the political arena in Chicago in the early 1960s. Fiercely independent in politics, he mounted serious but unsuccessful races for Congress four times and mayor of Chicago once. He also ran as an independent candidate for city alderman in 1963 and 1964, losing by narrow margins. But as the black activist Stokely Carmichael noted, "he was building an image in the black community as one who could and would speak out. The black people were getting the message." Rayner's difficulty in winning his first two aldermanic races was attributable to the fact that he was running in opposition to the machine politics of Mayor Richard Daley and against machine-backed candidates.[7]

In 1967, Sammie Rayner mounted one final race for the city council. Chicago's Sixth Ward was an inner-city black neighborhood that had always been controlled by the Democratic machine. Rayner campaigned day after day, door to door, attending black civic functions and talking with youth gangs on their own ground. On election day he won handily, becoming the first black to win a seat on the council by opposing the Daley machine. The tradition of dissenting politics in the Rayner family had come full circle from the campaigns against Jackson to the battles of the People's party to the streets of Chicago. But as Sammie Rayner remarked when asked about his opposition to Richard Daley, "I wasn't anti-Daley; I was pro-people." His grandfather and great-grandfather would have approved.[8]

Notes

Abbreviations Used in the Notes

BTP   *Brewers and Texas Politics*
DAB   *The Dictionary of American Biography*
DMN   Dallas *Morning News*
SM   Dallas *Southern Mercury*
DUP   Daniel Ullman Papers
GDN   Galveston *Daily News*
GP   Governors' Papers
HC   Houston *Chronicle*
HP   Houston *Post*
JBRP   John B. Rayner Papers
JHKP   John Henry Kirby Papers
KRP   Kenneth Rayner Papers
LC   Library of Congress
NA   National Archives
NCC   North Carolina Collection, University of North Carolina, Chapel Hill

NCDAH   North Carolina Division of Archives and History, Raleigh
NCS   Raleigh *North Carolina Standard*
RR   Raleigh *Register*
PTR   *Papers of Thomas Ruffin*
PWAG   *Papers of William Alexander Graham*
PWMP   *Papers of Willie Person Mangum*
RG   Record Group
SHC   Southern Historical Collection, University of North Carolina, Chapel Hill
WDVD   William D. Valentine Diaries

Introduction

1. The literature on republicanism is extensive and growing rapidly. The following works have been particularly valuable in shaping the ideas on republicanism and liberalism found in this study: Bailyn, *Ideological Origins;* Wood, *Creation of the American Republic;* Appleby, *Capitalism and a New Social Order;* Hartz, *Liberal Tradition;* Pocock, *Machiavellian Moment;* McCoy, *Elusive Republic;* Appleby, "Republicanism and Ideology"; Kerber, "Republican Ideology"; Baker, "From Belief into Culture"; Oakes, "From Republicanism to Liberalism."

2. Throughout this book, I have attempted to retain the spelling and punctua-

tion used in original quoted sources. When misspelled words could be corrected by placing omitted letters in brackets, I have done so. Original capitalization has been retained, with the exception of the words *Democrat/democrat, Republican/republican, Populist/populist,* and variations thereon. Nineteenth-century Americans used these words both as party names and political concepts, but they followed no consistent rules of capitalization to differentiate between the two. Therefore, I have sometimes deemed it necessary to change the capitalization in these quoted words to reflect the meaning intended in the original.

3. Degler, *The Other South,* 1. On page 345 of his study, Degler remarks that "It is fascinating to speculate that [John B.] Rayner, who came from North Carolina, was related to the North Carolinian Whig-Unionist Kenneth Rayner, perhaps even his natural son."

Chapter 1

1. Counihan, "Convention of 1835," 340; J. G. de Roulhac Hamilton, "Kenneth Rayner," undated manuscript, Van Noppen Papers. Kenneth Rayner's birthdate is variously given as June 20, 1808 or May 2, 1810. Rayner himself usually gave his age to correspond with the 1810 date, and that is the date recorded on his grave. However, 1810 cannot be correct, because he is named in his father's 1809 will. Thus June 20, 1808, will be assumed to be correct for the purposes of this study.

2. Moore, *History of North Carolina;* J. G. de Roulhac Hamilton, "Kenneth Rayner," *DAB,* 15:416–17; Winborne, *Colonial and State History,* 147–48; Hamilton, "Kenneth Rayner"; Will of Amos Rayner, 1809; land plat, October 8, 1789, both in KRP, SHC; Sixth Census, 1840, Hertford County, N.C., Population Schedule.

3. Turner and Bridgers, Jr., *History of Edgecombe County,* 362–64. Rayner's library passed down to his great-granddaughter, Ruth Matlock, who upon her death left the books to the Incarnate Word College Library in San Antonio, Texas, where I examined them.

4. K. R. to Thomas Ruffin, April 27, 1830, *PTR,* 2:10. Although Rayner was admitted to the North Carolina bar, there is no evidence that he ever practiced the profession.

5. Ibid.

6. For election returns, see *RR,* November 23, 1832.

7. Hamilton, "Kenneth Rayner," *DAB; Appendix to the Congressional Globe,* 27 Cong., 2d sess., 404 (quotations).

8. Hamilton, "Kenneth Rayner," *DAB;* K. R. to John Branch, July 28, 1834, Branch Family Papers (quotations).

9. Ibid. (quotations). For the two major parties' ideologies, see Howe, *Political Culture;* and Meyers, *Jacksonian Persuasion.*

10. K. R. to John Branch, July 28, 1834, Branch Family Papers.

11. Counihan, "Convention of 1835," 335–36; Connor, "Convention of 1835," 91–92; Kruman, *Parties and Politics,* 12.

12. Counihan, "Convention of 1835," 337–40; *Statement of the Number of Votes;* Moore, *History of North Carolina.*

13. Hamilton, "Kenneth Rayner" (first quotation); Moore, *History of North Caro-*

lina (second quotation); Amos Rayner Pension Application, Records Relating to Pension and Bounty Land Claims, NA.

14. Counihan, "Convention of 1835," 336–37. The Convention Act passed by the legislature dictated that the lower house be apportioned by federal population and the upper house by the amount of taxes paid. The convention was allowed to set the size of the senate and house and to change the borough system that gave certain towns their own representative. Ultimately, the convention decided upon the maximum allowable membership for both houses, and the borough system was abolished altogether. The new constitution can be found in *Journal of the Convention*, 95–101.

15. Counihan, "Convention of 1835," 347 (first quotation); *RR*, June 23, 1835 (second quotation); Rayner, *Speech of Hon. Kenneth Rayner in the Convention of 1835* (subsequent quotations).

16. Connor, "Convention of 1835," 105 (first quotation); Rayner, *Speech of Hon. Kenneth Rayner in the Convention of 1835* (subsequent quotations).

17. *RR*, December 22, 1835 (quotation). For a perceptive analysis of the importance of republican ideology and the interplay between national, state, and local issues, see Kruman, *Parties and Politics*.

18. Hoffman, *Andrew Jackson and North Carolina Politics*, 90–101 (first quotation); *RR*, December 22, 1835 (subsequent quotations).

19. *RR*, December 22, 1835.

20. Ibid., January 24, 1837 (quotations); K. R. to James H. Hammond, April 11, 1836, Hammond Papers.

21. *RR*, March 15, 1836, September 17, 1838.

22. Norton, *Democratic Party*, 74–82; *RR*, March 15, 1836; K. R. to R. C. Borland, November 19, 1838, Borland Family Papers; *RR*, December 10, 1838 (quotations).

23. *RR*, December 17, 1838 (quotations). For a sampling of reactions to the resolutions, see Willie P. Mangum to Thomas D. Bennehan, December 9, 1838, K. R. to Willie P. Mangum, December 31, 1838, both in *PWMP*, 2:534–38; James Graham to William A. Graham, December 14, 1838, January 4, 1839, William A. Graham to Susan W. Graham, December 23, 1838, January 6, 1839, all in *PWAG*, 2:24–33; K. R. to Edward B. Dudley, July 14, 1840, GP. Also see Walton, "Elections," 173–76. Although presented in December, Rayner's speech defending the resolutions was published in an extra edition of the *RR*, March 4, 1839, and concluded in the regular edition.

24. *RR*, March 4, 1839.

25. Ibid., July 6, 1839.

26. Ibid., August 24, 1839.

Chapter 2

1. Adams, *Memoirs*, 10:168.

2. *Appendix to the Congressional Globe*, 26 Cong., 1st sess., 66–70.

3. Ibid. (quotations). On Jackson's use of executive power, see Remini, *Andrew Jackson*, 138–40. For a discussion of the ideological antecedents of Whiggery in the "national" wing of the Democratic-Republican party, see Howe, *Political Culture*, 90–91.

4. K. R. to William A. Graham, April 5, 1840 (first and second quotations), *PWAG*, 2:79–80; *Appendix to the Congressional Globe*, 26 Cong., 1st sess., 412–18 (third and fourth quotations).

5. This entire series of letters was published in the Washington *Globe*, May 30, 1840.

6. J. D. Ward to Edward B. Dudley, May 30, 1840 (first quotation), GP; James Graham to William A. Graham, *PWAG*, 2:94–95; The Washington *National Intelligencer*, June 2, 1840, gives Rayner's version of events. The Washington *Globe*, May 30, 1840 (second quotation), offers Montgomery's story.

7. K. R. to Edward B. Dudley, June 25, 1840, GP.

8. WDVD, June 20, 1840 (first and second quotations); K. R. to Edward B. Dudley, June 25, 1840 (third quotation), GP.

9. For Rayner's efforts to promote this project, see K. R. to Edward B. Dudley, May 1, May 20, June 25, 1840, January 29, 1841, all in GP.

10. K. R. to Edward B. Dudley, June 25, 1840, GP (first quotation); K. R. to William A. Graham, April 5, 1840 (second quotation), *PWAG*, 2:79.

11. K. R. to William A. Graham, April 5, 1840, *PWAG*, 2:80.

12. WDVD, July 27, 1840.

13. Ibid.

14. *RR*, September 1, October 9, 30, November 13, 24; WDVD, August 16, October 22, 1840 (quotation).

15. *RR*, September 1, 1840 (first and second quotations); WDVD, October 26 (third quotation), October 29, November 4, 1840. The spectacular voter turnout of 1840 is perceptively analyzed in McCormick, "New Perspectives." For Harrison's success in North Carolina, see Hamilton, *Party Politics*, 53–68.

16. Adams, *Memoirs*, 10:366.

17. K. R. to Edward B. Dudley, December 22, 1840, GP.

18. *Appendix to the Congressional Globe*, 26 Cong., 2d sess., 306.

19. *RR*, May 25 (quotation), June 1, 1841.

20. Ibid., June 15, 1841; Simms, *Emotion at High Tide*, 146–50. Tyler's position on Whig policies, especially the issue of a national bank, was not entirely clear. Although he represented the anti-bank, states' rights wing of the party, he had nevertheless supported Clay for the nomination. His message to Congress at the beginning of the special session did little to clarify his position. If vague, the message nevertheless did embrace issues connected with banking, public lands, and federal revenue—the general topics about which Whigs were most concerned. Rayner wanted to keep congressional attention focused on these areas. For Tyler's message, see the extra edition of the Washington *National Intelligencer*, June 1, 1841.

21. *Appendix to the Congressional Globe*, 27 Cong., 1st sess., 46–50.

22. Ibid. (quotations). This is one of the central themes of Holt, *Political Crisis*.

23. *Appendix to the Congressional Globe*, 27 Cong., 1st sess., 46–50.

24. Adams, *Memoirs*, 10:480 (first quotation); K. R. to Stephen Elliott, June 17, 1841 (second quotation), Elliott Papers; Simms, *Emotion at High Tide*, 149–52. For reasons that are not entirely clear, Rayner voted against the rules as they were eventually adopted, even though they were only slightly different than his own proposal. Introduced by Virginia Whig Alexander H. H. Stuart, the successful resolution re-

adopted the gag rule and prohibited the chance for further discussion. It thus was even more sweeping than Rayner's alternative. Rayner may have voted against Stuart's resolution because it barred even the reception of petitions from the inhabitants of slaveholding regions themselves—a right Rayner believed those inhabitants possessed. Such a proposition had been introduced by Pennsylvania Democrat Charles Brown, and Rayner may have supported it. On balance, however, he was pleased that the matter had been settled as it was.

25. For the breach between Tyler and congressional Whigs, see Brown, *Edward Stanly*, 75–93; Chitwood, *John Tyler*, 217–36; Cooper, *Politics of Slavery*, 149–66; Schurz, *Henry Clay*, 2:199–220; Seager, *and Tyler too*, 147–63; Simpson, *A Good Southerner*, 45–55.

26. Washington *National Intelligencer*, September 15, 1841.

27. Seager, *and Tyler too*, 283 (quotation); Simpson, *A Good Southerner*, 55.

28. *RR*, July 15, 1842 (quotations); K. R. to James A. Pearce, October 18, 1843, Miscellaneous Papers, NCDAH; K. R. to Leverett Saltonstall, January 21, 1844, Saltonstall Papers.

29. *Appendix to the Congressional Globe*, 27 Cong., 2d sess., 404–7.

30. Thomas S. Hoskins to William A. Graham, May 8, 1842, *PWAG*, 2:306–307 (first quotation); *RR*, May 26, 1843 (second quotation).

31. *RR*, May 26, 1843.

32. Moore, *History of North Carolina* (second and third quotations); K. R. to James A. Pearce, October 18, 1843, Miscellaneous Papers, NCDAH (quotations one, four, and five); *RR*, July 28, 1843. Although his father was a Baptist minister, Rayner had joined the Episcopal church upon reaching adulthood.

33. *RR*, August 8, 13, 1843.

34. *Appendix to the Congressional Globe*, 27 Cong., 3d sess., 187–90.

35. K. R. to Willie P. Mangum, December 31, 1838, *PWPM*, 2:536 (first and second quotations); *RR*, July 15, 1842 (subsequent quotations).

36. *RR*, April 19, 1844; Washington *National Intelligencer*, April 18, 19, 27, 1844; Murray, *Wake*, 2:395; Waugh, *North Carolina's Capital*, 68–69; Eaton, *Henry Clay*, 173–74; Peterson, *The Great Triumvirate*, 360. Rayner's house no longer stands, but the tree in the first block of East North Street, today estimated to be more than four hundred years old, bears a marker identifying it as the Henry Clay Oak.

37. *RR*, April 19, May 3 (quotations), 1844; Murray, *Wake*, 1:394. The *RR* stated that Clay was the guest of Governor John M. Morehead.

38. K. R. to Leverett Saltonstall, January 21, 1844, Saltonstall Papers; K. R. to Joseph B. G. Roulhac, March 19, 1844, Ruffin-Roulhac-Hamilton Papers (quotation). On Clay's defeat, see Kirwan, *John J. Crittenden*, 293–94; Eaton, *Henry Clay*, 177–79; *RR*, November 15, 19, 22, 29, 1844; Schurz, *Henry Clay*, 2:267–68.

39. For a similar interpretation, see Brown, *Politics and Statesmanship*, 146–47; also see Holt, *Political Crisis of the 1850s*.

40. Washington *National Intelligencer*, December 4, January 27 (first quotation), 1845; K. R. to William A. Graham, February 5, 1845 (second quotation), *PWAG*, 3:23. Rayner used a February 17 debate on a bill to reduce the pay of the army as the occasion for his speech on Texas annexation. His hour expired, and on February 26 he used a debate on river and harbor improvements as the occasion to conclude

the speech; see Washington *National Intelligencer,* February 19, 28, 1845; *Appendix to the Congressional Globe,* 28 Cong., 2d sess., 410–12, 358–63.

41. *Appendix to the Congressional Globe,* 28 Cong, 2d sess., 410–12.

42. This and those in the following five paragraphs are from ibid., 359–63.

43. Rayner, *Speeches of Mr. K. Rayner, of North Carolina . . . Prefaced by an Address to His Constituents,* 3–7. All the quotes from the following two paragraphs are from this same letter.

Chapter 3

1. *RR,* March 14 (quotation), 21, April 11, May 20, 1845.

2. Parks, *Leonidas Polk,* ch. 1; "William Polk," *DAB,* 15:43–44.

3. A number of Susan's schoolgirl letters can be found in the Polk-Yeatman Papers; for example, see Susan Polk to Sarah Polk, May 1, 1835, February 15, 26, 1836.

4. William A. Graham to Susan Washington Graham, August 1, 13 (first quotation), 16 (second quotation), 1841, all in *PWAG,* 2:224–29.

5. Charles L. Hinton to William A. Graham, July 12, 1842, ibid., 2:352.

6. Lucius J. Polk to Mary Polk, October 25, 1842, Polk-Yeatman Papers. Susan's inheritance had been held in trust for her until her marriage, when it passed into joint possession of herself and Kenneth. Future sales of the property could be effected only with the legal approval of both spouses, although there is no record that Susan ever disapproved of any transactions Kenneth made. On inheritance practices among the North Carolina elite, see Censer, *North Carolina Planters,* 104–18.

7. K. R. to Sarah Polk, December 20, 1842, Polk-Yeatman Papers; K. R. to James A. Pearce, October 18, 1843, Miscellaneous Papers, NCDAH; K. R. to Leverett Saltonstall, January 21, 1844, Saltonstall Papers.

8. K. R. to James A. Pearce, October 18, 1843, Miscellaneous Papers, NCDAH (quotation). Mary Brown Rayner was born on June 5, 1843, in Raleigh, notation in Rayner Family Bible, in possession of Rayner's great-great-granddaughter, Sallie Savage, Midland, Texas.

9. K. R. to Leverett Saltonstall, January 21, 1844, Amos Rayner to K. R., February 8, 1842, n.d. (ca. 1842), K. R. to Amos Rayner, January 31, 1843, all in KRP, SHC; will of Sarah Hawkins Polk (probated 1844), Wake County Wills, NCDAH; will of Amos Rayner (probated 1843), Hertford County Wills, NCDAH.

10. For more detail on Susan's land inheritance, see John Houston Bills to Sarah Polk, October 17, November 18, 1842, January 18, March 9, 1843, John Houston Bills to K. R., November 25, December 30, 1843, May 31, 1844, February 5, 1846, all in John Houston Bills Letterbook; K. R. to Sarah Polk, December 20, 1842, Polk-Yeatman Papers; certification of receipt of stock shares and city lot by K. R., September 27, 1843, Polk-Yeatman Papers; wills of Colonel William Polk (probated 1834) and Sarah Polk (probated 1844), Wake County Wills, NCDAH. Some of this property only passed into Kenneth's and Susan's hands upon the death of her mother in 1844.

11. K. R. to Duncan Cameron, December 7, 1845, Cameron Papers.

12. Ibid.

13. Ibid.

14. Ibid. (quotations); land deed from James Dick to K. R., December 20, 1845, Chicot County Land Records.

15. Rayner, *Speech . . . in the Hall of the House of Commons,* December 8th, 1856.

16. New York *Times,* October 29, 1865. The lengthy letter from Rayner in this issue of the *Times* summarizes his practices and views on slavery and slaveholding from the vantage point of a few months after Appomattox.

17. For a discussion of the critical attitude that southern Whigs like Rayner held toward slavery, see Brown, *Politics and Statesmanship,* 179. The few southerners who sought to ameliorate harshness of the peculiar institution by proposing legal safeguards for slave marriages and family life seem to have been Whigs; see Nevins, *Ordeal of the Union,* 1:532; Taylor, "Humanizing the Slave Code," 323–31; *RR,* April 18, 1855.

18. New York *Times,* October 29, 1865 (first and second quotations); *Appendix to the Congressional Globe,* 27th Cong., 1st sess., 437 (third quotation).

19. New York *Times,* October 29, 1865 (quotations); Sixth Census, 1840, Hertford County, N.C., Slave Schedule; Seventh Census, 1850, Hertford County, N.C., Slave Schedule; Eighth Census, 1860, Hertford County, N.C., Slave Schedule; Eighth Census, 1860, Wake County, N.C., Slave Schedule; Chicot County Tax Rolls, 1861, Chicot County Courthouse, Lake Village, Ark. On inheritances of slaves by daughters of elite families, see Censer, *North Carolina Planters,* 105.

20. New York *Times,* October 29, 1865.

21. K. R. to Thomas Ruffin, July 12, 1862, *PTR,* 3:253 (first and second quotations); New York *Times,* October 29, 1865 (third quotation).

22. Birth dates recorded in Rayner Family Bible.

23. *RR,* January 16, 1846.

24. Jon. H. Jacobs to Willie P. Mangum, July 20, 1846, *PWPM,* 4:460 (quotation); Norton, *Democratic Party,* 144; WDVD, June 4, July 28, 1846.

25. *RR,* August 14, September 11 (quotation), 1846.

26. *RR,* December 22, 1846. Rayner was chair of the Joint Select Committee on Redistricting.

27. For Rayner's speeches defending the redistricting bill, see ibid., December 22, 1846, January 8, 1847. For Democratic replies, see *NCS,* December 30, 1846, January 6, 13 (first, second, third, fourth, and fifth quotations), 1847; Jeremiah Pearsall to Willie P. Mangum, February 12, 1847, *PWPM,* 5:41 (sixth quotation).

28. Pegg, *Whig Party,* 152; Brown, *Edward Stanly,* 106; Tolbert, *Papers of John Willis Ellis,* 1:lii–liii. Maps of the pre- and post-"Raynermander" districts can be found in Parsons et al., *United States Congressional Districts,* 28–30; also see Raleigh *Star,* January 13, 1847.

29. Charles L. Hinton to Willie P. Mangum, January 22, 1847 (first quotation), *PWPM,* 5:17; Richard Hines to Willie P. Mangum, January 19, 1847 (second quotation), *PWPM,* 5:16.

30. *RR,* March 21, 1843, October 30, November 17, December 11, 1847; WDVD, September 7, 1847; Pegg, *Whig Party,* 121.

31. *RR,* November 27, 1847 (first and second quotations); Kruman, *Parties and Politics,* 33 (third quotation).

32. *RR,* November 27, 1847.

33. Ibid.

34. *RR*, February 2, 9, 1848; William A. Graham to James W. Bryan, January 11, 1848 (quotation), *PWAG*, 3:212; David Outlaw to Emily Outlaw, February 10, 1848, David Outlaw Papers.

35. Brown, *Edward Stanly*, 106–11.

36. Ibid. (first quotation); David Outlaw to Emily Outlaw, March 3, 1848 (second quotation), David Outlaw Papers; *RR*, July 13, 1853 (third quotation). In 1836 Susan Polk had expressed displeasure with Badger's rapid remarriage after Mary Polk Badger's death; see Susan Polk to Sarah Polk, February 26, 1836, Polk-Yeatman Papers.

37. WDVD, March 7, 1848 (quotation); Hamilton, *Party Politics*, 124.

38. Hamilton, *Zachary Taylor*, 96; *RR*, June 14, 1848; Cooper, *Politics of Slavery*, 244–45.

39. *RR*, June 28, 1848.

40. *RR*, August 16, September 9, 20, October 11, 1848; WDVD, May 20, October 7 (quotations), 1848.

41. *RR*, January 17, 1849 (quotation). For a more detailed explanation of the southern critique of the Proviso, see Thornton, *Politics and Power*, esp. 220–21. Rayner's critique of the Proviso bears an uncanny resemblance to that delineated by Thornton.

42. *RR*, October 31 (quotations), November 7, 14, 1849. The articles did not carry Rayner's name but were simply signed "R." Beyond the slightest doubt, Rayner wrote them; the style as well as the arguments are unquestionably his, and the editor identified the author as "one of the leading and most gifted public men in the State,— formerly a Member of Congress." One should not attach too much significance to the fact that they were published anonymously, however, because any politically knowledgeable person in North Carolina would have easily deduced their authorship. Taylor did not formally enunciate his proposal until his message to Congress in December 1849. However, those who followed politics closely were already aware of its basic contours early in the year. See Hamilton, *Zachary Taylor*, 175–80; Holt, *Political Crisis*, 76–77.

43. Cooper, *Politics of Slavery*, 276–84.

44. David Outlaw to Emily Outlaw, May 31, 1850, David Outlaw Papers (first, second, and third quotations); *RR*, August 28, 1850 (subsequent quotations). This rebuke to northern "fanatics," like Rayner's 1849 "Communications," was published in the *Register* and simply signed "R." Like the earlier articles, the style and arguments mark it unquestionably as Rayner's.

45. Rayner, *Resolutions on the Subject of Slavery*, 255–60.

46. Land deed from Mary W. W. Ashley, executrix for Chester Ashley, to K. R., December 3, 1850, Chicot County Land Records. Rayner paid $4,800 for the land.

47. On the importance of internal improvements in North Carolina politics, see Jeffrey, "Internal Improvements," 111–56; Kruman, *Parties and Politics*, 55–85.

48. *RR*, February 21, 1849.

49. Ibid. Rayner also reported favorably on a system of memory improvement known as "phreno-mnemotechny," lectured upon in Raleigh by one Professor Pliny Miles; see *RR*, August 21, 1847.

50. A number of the books in Rayner's library carried inscriptions to his children.

51. *RR*, November 3, 1852; McLaurin, "State Fair," 213–29; Cathey, *Agricultural*

Developments, 81–88. Rayner performed a signal service for the society when in 1855 he helped to mediate a divisive conflict over which journal would be adopted as the organization's official organ; see Wallace, "Agricultural Journals," 275–306; K. R. to Thomas Ruffin, April 28, 1855, *PTR*, 2:465–66.

52. Johnson, *Ante-Bellum North Carolina*, 484–85. Rayner's letters to Thomas Ruffin during the Civil War offer the best look at Rayner's agricultural interests. See K. R. to Thomas Ruffin, July 18, 1861, February 16, March 28, June 24, November 26, 1863, February [?], August 26, September 29, 1864, in *PTR*, 5:174, 291, 310, 318, 345, 373, 420, 424; also see undated note in folder 489, manuscript Ruffin Papers, beginning with "I sent you cuttings"; Raleigh *Southern Advertiser*, September 29, 1853; *RR*, May 16, 1855, October 29, 1856, August 24, 1859; Rayner, *An Address Delivered Before the North Carolina State Agricultural Society*.

53. Rayner, *An Address Delivered before the North Carolina State Agricultural Society*. All the information in the following three paragraphs comes from this speech.

54. Quoted in Foner, *Free Soil, Free Labor, Free Men*, 12. Rayner's ideas on the status of labor—particularly his adherence to the labor theory of value—also placed him in accord with northern political nativism; see Laurie, " 'Nothing on Compulsion'," 1820–50, 357–58.

55. Rayner, *Speech of Hon. Kenneth Rayner in the House of Commons, on The Bill to provide for establishing a Hospital* (quotations). For a brief sketch of Dix, see Tyler, *Freedom's Ferment*, 304–7. For an analysis that places the national asylum movement in the context of antebellum social history, see Rothman, *Discovery of the Asylum;* McCulloch, "North Carolina Asylum," 185–201. Rayner displayed similar sympathy for the deaf, dumb, and blind, and supported the movements for state schools for them; see Kruman, *Parties and Politics*, 82; *RR*, December 13, 1848, January 10, 1849.

56. Knobel, "Nativists and Indians," 175–98.

57. Ibid.; Raleigh *Star*, November 29, 1848 (quotation).

58. K. R. to George Copway, March 21, 1849, in Copway, *Organization of a New Indian Territory*, 27.

Chapter 4

1. WDVD, April 28, 1852.

2. Ibid.

3. *RR*, June 23, 1852. For an overview of the 1852 presidential campaign in North Carolina, see Morrill, "Presidential Election of 1852," 342–59.

4. WDVD, July 19 (first quotation), 21 (second quotation), 22, 1852; Wilmington *Daily Journal*, October 2, 1852 (third quotation). On Scott and the 1852 election, see Holt, *Political Crisis*, 123–26; Morrill, "Presidential Election of 1852."

5. WDVD, July 19 (first quotation), 21 (second, third, and fifth quotations), 24 (fourth and sixth quotations), 1852.

6. WDVD, July 22 (first quotation), August 2, November 4, 1852; *RR*, March 16, 1853 (second quotation).

7. Walton, "Elections," 168–92. Walton states that Rayner fell only one vote short of election, but all the contemporary sources agree that eighty-one votes were required and that Rayner received only seventy-nine; see *RR*, December 8, 1852; *NCS*,

December 8, 1852; Wilmington *Daily Journal,* December 8, 9, 1852; Fayetteville *North Carolinian,* December 11, 1852.

8. *RR,* January 12, 1853.

9. Fayetteville *North Carolinian,* December 11, 1852 (first quotation); *NCS,* December 8, 1852 (second quotation).

10. *RR,* January 12 (first quotation), 19, February 2, March 2, 16, April 6, May 11, July 13, 1853; *NCS* (quoting the *North State Whig*), December 29, 1852 (second quotation). There was, beyond doubt, a degree of truth in these accusations. Rayner had been flattered by the near-unanimous support he received in the senatorial balloting, and he experienced great trouble in answering many of the charges that Miller and others leveled at him. Perhaps the most damning evidence was eyewitness testimony that Rayner's "friends" had counseled him to chart a noncommittal course in the presidential campaign as a strategy for obtaining bipartisan support in the senate election; see especially the correspondence involving Henry W. Miller and William H. Tripp, *RR,* February 2, March 16, 1853.

If Stanly himself ever sensed that Rayner was motivated by anything other than political jealousy, it cannot be found in his correspondence. Stanly was convinced that Rayner was simply an unprincipled scoundrel. When he discovered that Rayner had been privately critical of his actions during a controversy in which Stanly and Henry A. Wise nearly fought a duel, Stanly stated that Rayner's conduct "*had been anything but what a gentleman and a friend had a right to expect!*" See Edward Stanly to Thomas Sparrow, April 16, 1855, Thomas Sparrow Collection. On the Rayner/Polk-Stanly/Badger feud, see Brown, *Edward Stanly,* 108–11; William A. Graham to James Graham, April 5, 1848, *PWAG,* 3:217; David Outlaw to Emily Outlaw, February 10, March 3, 1848, David Outlaw Papers.

11. *RR,* December 29, 1852.

12. For Rayner's land acquisitions, see land deed from Andrew J. Polk to K. R., March 25, 1848, Wake County Land Records, NCDAH; land deeds from Duke Brantly to K. R., May 26, 1853, and Nathan S. Hoggard to K. R., May 24, 1853, both in KRP, SHC; land deed from Silas Craig to K. R., April 13, 1853, Chicot County Land Records. In 1850, Rayner owned fifty-two slaves in Hertford County, N.C., seventy-one in Chicot County, Ark., and nineteen in Wake County, N.C.; see Seventh Census, 1850, Slave Schedules for Hertford County, Chicot County, and Wake County. For Rayner's agricultural production, see Seventh Census, 1850, Agricultural Schedules for Hertford County, N.C., Wake County, N.C., and Chicot County, Ark.; Eighth Census, 1860, Chicot County Agricultural Schedule.

13. Rayner, *Address Delivered Before the Graduating Class;* Rayner, *Address of the Hon. Kenneth Rayner at the Examination;* Rayner, *An Address Delivered Before the North Carolina State Agricultural Society; RR,* April 27, 1853; WDVD, August 3, 1854.

14. Rayner, *Speeches of Mr. K. Rayner . . . Declining a Re-Election* (quotations). On the origins of the nativist political movement of the 1850s, see Beals, *Brass-Knuckle Crusade;* Billington, *Protestant Crusade;* Curran, *Xenophobia and Immigration;* Knobel, *Paddy and the Republic;* Overdyke, *Know-Nothing Party;* Scisco, *Political Nativism.*

15. *Kruman, Parties and Politics,* 160; *NCS,* September 20, 1854 (first quotation), November 19, 1856; Rayner, *An Address Delivered Before the North Carolina State Agri-*

cultural Society, 5 (second, third, and fourth quotations); K.R. to Daniel Ullman, November 29, 1854, DUP (fifth quotation).

16. K.R. to Andrew Johnson, ca. June 1865, Civil War Collection, NCDAH (quotation). Texts of the order's degrees can be found in Scisco, *Political Nativism*, 135–37.

17. Washington *National Era*, November 30, 1854; Cincinnati *Enquirer*, November 28, 1854; Scisco, *Political Nativism*, 134–38; Beals, *Brass-Knuckle Crusade*, 156–57; Wilson, *History of the Rise and Fall of the Slave Power*, 2:420–22. Wilson's account of Rayner's activities in Cincinnati must be considered the most reliable, because in writing the book he consulted Rayner himself; see Henry Wilson to K.R., April 8, 1873, KRP, SHC.

18. Beals, *Brass-Knuckle Crusade*, 135–36; Scisco, *Political Nativism*, 136–37; *NCS*, May 26, 1855. Scisco and the *NCS* both carried copies of the degree.

19. K.R. to Andrew Johnson, ca. June 1865, Civil War Collection, NCDAH; Rayner, *Life and Times*, 104–5; Wilson, *Rise and Fall of the Slave Power*, 2:422; K.R. to Daniel Ullman, January 22, 1855, DUP.

20. Kruman, *Parties and Politics*, 159–79; Overdyke, *Know-Nothing Party*, 69–70.

21. WDVD, November 11, 1854 (first, second, and third quotations), January 27, 1855 (fourth and fifth quotations).

22. On the Catholic church's aggressive campaign of the 1850s, see Billington, *Protestant Crusade*, 289–321.

23. Rayner, *Reply to the Manifesto of Hon. Henry A. Wise*. All the information in the following five paragraphs comes from this document.

24. For a more complete explanation of the connection between nativism, republican ideology, and the environmentalist conception of American nationality, see Knobel, *Paddy and the Republic*, esp. 129–64.

25. Rayner, *Reply to the Manifesto of Hon. Henry A. Wise*.

26. *RR*, June 7 (first quotation), July 26, August 9, 1854; *NCS*, August 16, 1854 (second quotation).

27. *RR*, December 13, 1854, January 17, 24, 31, February 7, 1855; K.R. to Daniel Ullman, November 29, 1854 (first quotation), January 22, 1855 (second and third quotations), DUP; Kruman, *Parties and Politics in North Carolina*, 161–62.

28. These notices were all republished in the Raleigh newspapers. See *NCS*, November 29 (first quotation), December 13, 1854; *RR*, May 23 (second quotation), February 7, April 25, February 14 (third and fourth quotations), 1855.

29. K.R. to Daniel Ullman, March 7, 1855, DUP.

30. Ibid. (quotations). For a biographical sketch of George Law, see Curran, *Xenophobia and Immigration*, 63–64; Curran identifies Rayner as a Law supporter, but the evidence does not support such a claim. Rayner did support the bid of James W. Barker, who backed Law, for reelection as president of the national council in 1855, but this should not be construed to mean that Law was Rayner's first choice for president of the United States. Law not only had done little to merit the nomination, but his background was also that of filibusterer and a Democrat—credentials that would not have endeared him to Rayner.

31. K.R. to Daniel Ullman, February 17 (first, second, third, and fourth quotations), May 4, 1855 (fifth and sixth quotations), DUP.

32. K. R. to Daniel Ullman, January 22, 1855, DUP.

33. K. R. to Daniel Ullman, February 17, 1855, DUP.

34. K. R. to Daniel Ullman, January 22, 1855, DUP.

35. Overdyke, *Know-Nothing Party*, 91–95; WDVD, May 24, 1855; K. R. to Daniel Ullman, May 8, 1855, DUP.

36. *RR* (copying story from the Petersburg *Intelligencer*), May 16, 1855 (quotations); K. R. to Daniel Ullman, May 4, 1855, DUP.

37. *RR*, May 21, 23, 30, 1855; K. R. to Daniel Ullman, May 8, 1855 (quotation), DUP.

38. K. R. to Daniel Ullman, May 8, 1855, DUP.

39. New York *Tribune*, June 4, 7, 8, 1855 (quotations).

40. New York *Times*, June 8, 1855.

41. Ibid., June 9, 1855.

42. Ibid.

43. Ibid.

Chapter 5

1. New York *Tribune*, June 12, 14 (quotations), 1855.

2. Ibid., June 13 (first and second quotations); the text of Rayner's resolutions is quoted in *RR*, July 4, 1855.

3. New York *Tribune*, June 14, 1855.

4. Rayner, *Speech of Hon. Kenneth Rayner in the Hall of the House of Commons, December 8, 1856*, 3 (quotations). The New York *Times*, June 16, 1855, published a table containing each delegate's name and his votes on the three sets of resolutions. In the text of its article, the *Times* mistakenly reported that Rayner's substitute received only forty-four votes, but the table itself shows forty-six. The same table was reproduced in the *NCS*, June 27, 1855.

5. New York *Tribune*, June 15, 1855.

6. Ibid., June 19, 1855; Baltimore *Sun*, June 21, 1855.

7. *RR*, June 27, 1855 (quotations); *NCS*, July 4, 1855.

8. *NCS*, July 4, 1855 (quotations); Harris, *William Woods Holden*, 52. Evidence of Holden's campaign against Rayner can be found in numerous issues of the *Standard* in 1855; cf. the issues of February 7, March 3, June 13, July 11, 25, August 22, September 5, 12, 1855. The attacks were renewed with vigor in the late fall of 1856. The tale of the papal nuncio blossomed into a national controversy in the fall of 1855. Sam Houston made the same charge as Rayner, and both sides spent an inordinate amount of time and energy trying to prove or refute the accusations. Finally, Barringer published a letter basically substantiating the content of his and Rayner's conversation concerning the nuncio's statement, but Barringer claimed that Rayner had misunderstood him—that he had not meant to imply that a bargain had existed between Rome and the Pierce administration. Rayner promptly produced letters from a number of other witnesses who had also heard Barringer's story and had similarly "misunderstood" him. The Know-Nothings eventually backed off somewhat from the charge of an actual "corrupt bargain," but they maintained that the nuncio's early knowl-

edge of Campbell's appointment and his undeniable interest in the make-up of the cabinet was strong evidence of the Vatican's involvement in American politics; see *NCS*, August 1, 8, 18, 22, September 5, 12, 1855; *RR*, August 1, 25, 29, September 5, 12, 19, 26, October 3, 1855; New York *Times*, August 7, 1855; numerous clippings from the Washington *American Organ*, Boston *Post*, and Washington *Evening Star*, all in Barringer Papers.

9. *RR*, July 4, 1855.

10. *NCS*, July 4 (first and second quotations), 11 (subsequent quotations), 25, 1855.

11. Ibid., July 25, 1855 (first quotation); K. R. to Daniel Ullman, August 21, 1855, DUP (second quotation).

12. K. R. to Daniel Ullman, August 21, 1855, June 2, 1856, DUP; K. R. to Anna Ella Carroll, May 12, 1856 (first quotation), March 7, 1856 (second quotation), Carroll Papers.

13. K. R. to Daniel Ullman, August 21, 1855 (quotations), June 2, 1856, DUP.

14. K. R. to Daniel Ullman, August 21, 1855, June 2, 1856, DUP; K. R. to Anna Ella Carroll, March 7, 1856, Carroll Papers.

15. K. R. to Anna Ella Carroll, March 7, 1856, Carroll Papers (quotations); New York *Tribune*, February 19, 21, 22, 23, 1856.

16. New York *Tribune*, February 26, 1855.

17. There has been a great deal of confusion over the exact timing and size of the northern delegates' bolt from the 1856 convention. Some apparently withdrew after the failure of their resolution calling for restoration of the Missouri Compromise. Most, however, left only after Fillmore's nomination. The total number of the bolters has been put as low as forty-two and as high as seventy-one. For a sampling of these conflicting accounts, see Curran, *Xenophobia and Immigration*, 69–70; Gienapp, *Origins of the Republican Party*, 261–62; Kirwan, *John J. Crittenden*, 303–4; Overdyke, *Know-Nothing Party*, 136.

18. *RR*, April 2, 1856; K. R. to Daniel Ullman, June 2, 1856, DUP (quotations); K. R. to Anna Ella Carroll, May 12, 1856, Carroll Papers.

19. K. R. to Daniel Ullman, June 2, 1856, DUP (quotations). Gienapp, *Origins of the Republican Party*, 330–34, provides a detailed portrayal of the free soilers' secret machinations at the New York convention.

20. New York *Times*, June 17 (quotations), 18, 1856.

21. *RR*, July 9, 1856.

22. Ibid., August 6, November 5, 1856; Rayner's letter, originally published in the New York *Times*, October 31, 1856, can also be found in the *RR*, November 19, 1856, *NCS*, November 19, 1856, or Greensborough *Patriot*, December 19, 1856. Lengthy excerpts were also published in the New York *Tribune*, November 4, 1856. John M. Botts of Virginia published a similar letter in the October 31 New York *Times*.

23. For example, if 50 percent of the Union ballots cast were those with Fillmore as one of the electors and 50 percent were those with Frémont, thirteen of the electors would vote for Fillmore and the other thirteen for Frémont in the electoral college (assuming the ticket won a statewide plurality). The twenty-seventh elector, of course, would be a Buchanan elector because Fillmore and Frémont had occupied that position, splitting the Union vote. In the event that the state's electoral votes

would actually mean the difference between national victory or defeat for either candidate, the division of votes was to be dispensed with and the entire electoral vote cast for that man; see Gienapp, *Origins of the Republican Party*, 407.

24. *NCS*, November 19, 1856; Isaac Hazlehurst to Millard Fillmore, August 12, October 30, 1856 (with accompanying clippings), Fillmore Papers.

25. Alexander Cummings to Thurlow Weed, October 28, 1856, Weed Papers (quotation). The dozens of letters from Pennsylvanians to Fillmore will not be cited individually here; see Fillmore Papers, July 25-October 29.

26. K. R. to Millard Fillmore, November 27, 1856, Fillmore Papers; Alexander Cummings to Thurlow Weed, October 31, 1856, Weed Papers (first quotation); *NCS*, November 19, 1856 (subsequent quotations).

27. Alexander Cummings to Thurlow Weed, October 31, 1856, Weed Papers (first quotation); Isaac Hazlehurst to Millard Fillmore, October 30, 1856, with Fillmore's notation of his telegraphed reply on the back, dated November 1, Fillmore Papers (second quotation); K. R. telegraph message to Millard Fillmore, November 3, 1856, with Fillmore's notation of his telegraphed reply on the back, Fillmore Papers (third and fourth quotations). Fillmore's initial reply to Rayner was to have read, "Success alone can justify any union with Republicans—but that may my friends there determine," but Fillmore crossed out "with Republicans" and sent to Rayner only the message as quoted in the text.

28. Rayner, *Speech . . . in the Hall of the House of Commons, December 8th, 1856*, 11. Rayner's contention was, in a sense, true. The term *fusion* most commonly refers to an arrangement whereby one party agrees to vote for another party's candidate. In the Pennsylvania case, Know-Nothings voting for the Union ticket actually would have been electing Fillmore electors. It was, in fact, the only way to elect *any* Fillmore electors (as well as any Frémont electors). Therefore, the arrangement was fusion depending strictly on one's definition of the term.

29. New York *Times*, November 10, 1856; *NCS*, November 19, 1856 (first quotation); Rayner, *Speech . . . in the Hall of the House of Commons, December 8th, 1856*, 9; Hamilton, *Benjamin Sherwood Hedrick*.

30. *NCS*, November 5, 12, 19 (first quotation); Rayner, *Speech . . . in the Hall of the House of Commons, December 8th, 1856*, 9 (second quotation).

31. Ibid., 9 (quotations); *NCS*, December 3, 1856.

32. *RR*, December 3, 1856; *NCS*, December 3 (first, second, third, and fourth quotations), November 26, (fifth and sixth quotations), 1856.

33. *RR*, December 17, 1856; *NCS*, December 17, 1856. The physical description of Rayner is based on an 1856 engraving made for Anna Ella Carroll's American party campaign book, *The Great American Battle;* see also K. R. to Anna Ella Carroll, March 7, 1856, Carroll Papers. The only other antebellum likeness of Rayner is a formal oil portrait probably painted in 1849, now in the possession of Rayner's great-grandson, Kenneth Rayner Hyman, Jr., San Antonio.

34. Rayner, *Speech . . . in the Hall of the House of Commons, December 8th, 1856*, 1 (first quotation), 3 (second, third, and fourth quotations), 6–7 (fifth quotation).

35. Ibid., 13 (first quotation), 15 (second quotation).

36. Ibid., 16 (first quotation); *NCS*, December 17, 1856 (second quotation).

37. *RR*, July 9, 1856.

Chapter 6

1. *NCS*, December 1, 1858.

2. K. R. to Anna Ella Carroll, April 6, 1857, Carroll Papers.

3. *RR*, November 17, 1858 (reprinted from the Philadelphia *North American*).

4. Rayner never relinquished his nativist convictions. In 1860, he still was complaining bitterly in private about foreign and Roman Catholic influence on national politics, but he was forced to acknowledge that the issues emphasized by the American party were "no longer living issues." See K. R. to Anna Ella Carroll, February 12, 1860, Carroll Papers; Murfreesboro (N.C.) *Citizen*, September 6, 1860.

5. K.R. to Anna Ella Carroll, November 23, 1859, Carroll Papers (quotation); *RR*, October 12, 1859.

6. On the ad valorem issue, see Butts, "The 'Irrepressible Conflict,'" 44–66; Kruman, *Parties and Politics*, 189–96.

7. K. R. to Thomas Ruffin, March 20, 1860, *PTR*, 3:76.

8. K. R. to Thomas Ruffin, March 6, 1860, *PTR*, 3:72.

9. *NCS*, March 28, 1860.

10. *RR*, March 28, 1860 (quotation). Also see the *RR*'s editorial of April 4 and the *NCS*'s response of April 11.

11. Kemp P. Battle to William A. Graham, April 16, 1860, *PWAG*, 5:156–57; also see *RR*, April 18, 1860.

12. Murfreesboro (N.C.) *Albemarle Southron*, July 26, 1860.

13. *RR*, August 8, 1860.

14. K. R. to Anna Ella Carroll, November 23, 1859, Carroll Papers; Thomas Corwin to K. R., April 20, 1860, KRP, SHC.

15. *RR*, February 29, 1860.

16. Rayner's letter appeared in the *NCS*, August 22, 1860, and the Murfreesboro (N.C.) *Citizen*, September 6, 1860. All quotations in the following four paragraphs are from this letter.

17. K. R. to Thomas Ruffin, December 25, 1860, *PTR*, 3:109.

18. For example, see William Badham, Jr. to K. R., December 30, 1860, William Badham Papers.

19. *NCS*, October 24, 1860 (the *NCS* copied the *Press*'s story); K. R. to Thomas Ruffin, December 25, 1860, *PTR*, 3:109 (first quotation); William H. Seward to Abraham Lincoln, December 25, 1860, Lincoln Papers, series 1, LC (second quotation); Abraham Lincoln to William H. Seward, December 29, 1860, in Basler, *Works of Abraham Lincoln*, 4:164 (third quotation); Hamlin, *Life and Times*, 369; Carman and Luthin, *Lincoln and the Patronage*, 12; Nicolay and Hay, *Abraham Lincoln*, 3:362; Seward, *Seward at Washington*, 487. Lincoln ultimately decided to tender an offer to Rayner's Know-Nothing colleague in North Carolina, John A. Gilmer. Gilmer considered the offer and then declined, as Rayner doubtless would have done.

20. K. R. to Thomas Ruffin, December 25, 1860, *PTR*, 3:109 (first and second quotations); K. R. to Andrew Johnson, ca. June 1865, Civil War Collection, NCDAH (third quotation).

21. *RR*, March 6, 13, 1861; K. R. to Andrew Johnson, ca. June 1865, Civil War Collection, NCDAH.

22. K. R. to Andrew Johnson, ca. June 1865, Civil War Collection, NCDAH. The North Carolina legislature apparently considered naming Rayner as one of the delegates to the Washington Peace Conference, but his Unionism may have been seen as too conditional for him to be an appropriate choice. The delegation that finally was chosen consisted of five of Rayner's long-time associates: George Davis, Thomas Ruffin, David S. Reid, Daniel M. Barringer, and John M. Morehead. See Rufus S. Tucker to Thomas Ruffin, January 24, 1861, *PTR*, 3:114; Gunderson, *Old Gentlemen's Convention*, 106; Boykin, *North Carolina in 1861*, 153–56.

Chapter 7

1. K. R. to Andrew Johnson, ca. June 1865, Civil War Collection, NCDAH (quotation); *RR*, May 15, 1861; K. R. to Thomas Ruffin, May 15, 1861, *PTR*, 3:156–57.

2. K. R. to Andrew Johnson, ca. June 1865, Civil War Collection, NCDAH.

3. Ibid. (quotations); Sitterson, *Secession Movement*, 245–47; *Journal of the Convention of the People*, 6, 14–15.

4. K. R. to the Worshipful Justices of the Peace, of the County Court of Hertford County, August 21, 1861, KRP, NCDAH; K. R. to William A. Graham, June 25, 1861, *PWAG*, 5:274–77; K. R. to Thomas Ruffin, July 9, 1861 (first quotation), July 18, 1861 (second quotation), February 15, 1863, George W. Mordecai to K. R., November 21, 1861, all in *PTR*, 3:171, 173, 291, 192–93; *RR*, December 18, 1861.

5. *War of the Rebellion*, Official Records, series 1, 9:193–94; K. R. to Thomas Ruffin, July 12, 1862, *PTR*, 3:253; Barrett, *Civil War in North Carolina*, 48–148. Rayner's observations on the military progress of the war are sprinkled liberally throughout *PTR*, vol. 3.

6. K. R. to Jefferson Davis, December 8, 1862, War Department Collection.

7. K. R. to Thomas Ruffin, December 25, 1862, *PTR*, 3:282 (first and third quotations); *RR*, April 4, 1860 (second quotation).

8. K. R. to Thomas Ruffin, March 8, 1863, *PTR*, 3:302–4.

9. Birth and death dates recorded in the Rayner Family Bible; funeral announcement for Henry Albert Rayner, August 20, 1859, KRP, SHC; K. R. to Thomas Ruffin, June 24, 1863, *PTR*, 3:318–19.

10. K. R. to Thomas Ruffin, May 30, 1863 (first quotation), manuscript in Thomas Ruffin Papers [one of the few Rayner letters not included in the published edition of the Ruffin Papers]; K. R. to Thomas Ruffin, July 12, December 25, 1862, December 31, 1863 (subsequent quotations), *PTR*, 3:253, 282, 359.

11. K. R. to Thomas Ruffin, July 12, 1862, *PTR*, 3:253–54.

12. Kruman, *Parties and Politics*, 222–70; K. R. to Thomas Ruffin, November 23, 1862, *PTR*, 3:271–72 (quotations).

13. Leonidas Polk to K. R., August 14, 1863, Leonidas Polk Papers (quotations); Raper, "William W. Holden," 493–516; Harris, *William Woods Holden*, 107–55.

14. K. R. to Thomas Ruffin, January 12, 1864, *PTR*, 3:362–63 (quotation); Raper, "William W. Holden," 507–8.

15. K. R. to Thomas Ruffin, January 23, 1864, *PTR*, 3:365.

16. The editorials were published under the pseudonym "Amicus" in the Raleigh *Confederate*, February 18, 22, March 9, 1864. Rayner identifies himself as their author in K. R. to Thomas Ruffin, February 18, 1864, *PTR*, 3:369–70 [the editor of the published Ruffin Papers mistakenly transcribed "Amiens" instead of the actual "Amicus"].

17. K. R. to Thomas Ruffin, June 15 (first, second, third, fourth, fifth, and sixth quotations), July 4 (seventh quotation), July 18 (eighth quotation), September 29 (ninth quotation), 1864, all in *PTR*, 3:391–94, 400, 404, 424–25.

18. K. R. to Andrew Johnson, ca. June 1865, Petitions for Pardon, 1865, Civil War Collection, NCDAH.

19. Ibid. (first and second quotations); Harris, *William Woods Holden*, 182–83; Harvey M. Watterson to Andrew Johnson, June 29, 1865, in McPherson, "Letters From North Carolina," 354–55 (third and fourth quotations).

20. George B. Simpson to William A. Graham, May 21, 1866, *PWAG*, 7:103–4.

21. William A. Graham to George B. Simpson, June 2, 1866, *PWAG*, 126–27 (first quotation); Max R. Williams, editor of the Graham Papers, in a footnote to the letter from George B. Simpson to William A. Graham, May 21, 1866, *PWAG*, 104 (second quotation); K. R. to William A. Graham, September 4, 1865, *PWAG*, 6:351.

22. George B. Simpson to William A. Graham, May 21, 1866, *PWAG*, 7:103 (quotation). For evidence of Rayner's and Holden's friendship, see W. W. Holden to K. R., August 1, 1877, KRP, SHC. The prominent North Carolina Unionist John Pool, who in 1864 introduced a resolution in the North Carolina state senate calling for peace negotiations, wrote a letter of recommendation to President Grant for Rayner in 1873. Pool stated that "in 1864, he [Rayner] sustained the Union men in North Carolina, in their efforts to urge the Confederate authorities into a peace with the general government on the best terms attainable." See John Pool to Ulysses S. Grant, November 11, 1873, Applications and Recommendations; Harris, *William Woods Holden*, 154.

23. The events related in this and the following paragraphs are compiled from Barrett, *Civil War in North Carolina*, 372–77; *War of the Rebellion*, series 1, 37:180–96; and typescripts of correspondence between Rayner and Moore, dated May 10, 13, 20, 1867, KRP, SHC. Moore mistakenly identified Thursday, April 13, as the date of Samuel Mordecai's funeral and the day that Rayner urged Vance to surrender the city. The actual date had to be April 11.

24. Typescript of letter from K. R. to B. F. Moore, May 13, 1867, KRP, SHC.

25. Rayner, *Speech of Mr. Rayner, of North Carolina, on the Question of the Reception of Abolition Petitions*, 20.

Chapter 8

1. New York *Times*, October 29, 1865; K. R. to Hamilton Fish, October 30, 1866, Fish Papers; land deed from K. R. to Cornelius B. Riddick, May 30, 1863, Hertford County Land Records; K. R. to Andrew Johnson, ca. June 1865, Civil War Collection, NCDAH. On prewar slave prices, see Stampp, *Peculiar Institution*, 415–17.

2. New York *Times*, October 29, 1865.

3. Ibid.; K. R. to Hamilton Fish, October 30, 1866, Fish Papers; K. R. to Hamil-

ton Fish, February 12, 1873, Applications and Recommendations; K. R. to Andrew Johnson, ca. June 1865, Civil War Collection, NCDAH.

4. Endorsement of Rayner's amnesty application by Holden, July 6, 1865, attached to K. R. to Andrew Johnson, ca. June 1865, Civil War Collection, NCDAH; K. R. to Andrew Johnson, July 8, 1865, in McPherson, "Letters from North Carolinians," 355–56.

5. R[ichard]. H. B[attle]., Jr., to Kemp Battle, October 31, 1865, Battle Family Papers (quotation); Wilmington *Daily Journal,* November 30, 1865; Hamilton, *Reconstruction,* 142–47; Alexander, *North Carolina Faces the Freedmen,* 38–39.

6. Gavin Hogg to his daughter, November 28, 1865, Hogg Papers.

7. Rayner, *Life and Times,* title page (first quotation), 363 (subsequent quotations).

8. Ibid., 74 (first quotation), 193–94 (second quotation).

9. Ibid., 103–6.

10. Ibid., 194–95.

11. Ibid., 230 (first quotation), 232 (second quotation). This interpretation is the central theme in Holt, *Political Crisis.*

12. Rayner, *Life and Times,* 223–26.

13. Ibid., 224.

14. K. R. to Hamilton Fish, March 3, 6, 1866, Fish Papers; K. R. to Andrew Johnson, April 6, July 2, 1866, Johnson Papers.

15. Rayner, *Life and Times,* 218–29.

16. New York *Times,* October 29, 1865.

17. Raleigh *Journal of Freedom,* October 28, 1865 (quotations); the *Journal* quoted passages from the *National Republican.* On Rayner's visit with Howard and his changing views toward black potential, see chapter 10. For evidence of Rayner's support for black suffrage, see Hernando (Miss.) *Press,* July 6, 1871; K. R. to Hamilton Fish, February 12, 1873, Applications and Recommendations. In the second session of the 1865–66 North Carolina legislature, Rayner chaired the "committee of the whole" in the house of commons that passed the state's "black code." The code as finally adopted was aimed at keeping blacks "in their place" and establishing a workable labor system. Most of the features of the code technically applied to both blacks and whites, although it obviously was aimed at blacks. Although restrictive, the North Carolina code was not as harshly repressive as its counterparts in most other southern states. For example, a provision that would have prohibited black testimony even in cases involving blacks was defeated by the legislators. Rayner's role in the passage of the code is curious. Although he chaired the committee of the whole, he apparently took no part in the debates. Furthermore, his name never appears in the various roll calls as the legislators debated the provisions of the code. Perhaps he was absent on the days that votes were taken, or as chairman he saw fit not to vote, but his total lack of participation suggests that he was adhering to the sentiment he expressed in the Johnson biography: all matters concerning the status of blacks should be avoided for the present. On the code's provisions, see Alexander, *North Carolina Faces the Freedmen,* 39–51. For the debates on the code and Rayner's silence, see *NCS,* February 7, 14, 28, March 7, 1866.

18. K. R. to Sallie Rayner, June 29, 1866, original in possession of Mr. and Mrs. Hyman H. Kirkpatrick, Weslaco, Tex.

19. K. R. to Hamilton Fish, October 23, 1865, Fish Papers.

20. Ibid., October 30, 1866.

21. Ibid., October 30, 1866 (quotation); Eighth Census, 1860, Agricultural Schedule, Chicot County, Ark.

22. K. R. to Hamilton Fish, October 23, 30 (first quotation), 1867, Fish Papers; K. R. to Henry A. Smythe, February 3, 1867, Barlow Collection. Winthrop acted as trustee for William Amory, Nathaniel Thayer, John L. Gardner, Henry J. Gardner, and Josiah Bardwell, who collectively loaned Rayner $20,000. In New York, Samuel L. M. Barlow, Leonard W. Jerome, Henry A. Smythe, and Marshal O. Roberts each contributed $5,000. John R. Richards of Baltimore contributed $7,800; details of these transactions can be found among the Kenneth Rayner Bankruptcy Papers. Rayner was personally acquainted with Marshall O. Roberts, a New York shipping magnate and the associate of the former Know-Nothing leader George Law. He also likely knew Henry J. Gardner, former Know-Nothing governor of Massachusetts, and Leonard W. Jerome, who served in the diplomatic service under Fillmore and edited a Know-Nothing newspaper in Rochester. For information on Barlow, Roberts, and Thayer, see *DAB*, 1:613–15, 16:11–12, 17:409–10. On Jerome, see *National Cyclopaedia of American Biography*, 42:448–49.

23. K. R. to Henry A. Smythe, February 3, 1867, Barlow Collection (first quotation); K. R. to Nelson A. Miles, June 12, 16, 1867, Records of the Assistant Commissioner for the State of North Carolina, Bureau of Refugees, Freedmen, and Abandoned Lands, 1866–70, RG 105, NA.

24. K. R. to Henry A. Smythe, February 3, 1867, Barlow Collection (first quotation); K. R. to Nelson A. Miles, June 12, 16, 1867, Records of the Assistant Commissioner. Rayner apparently maintained residences on the Mississippi and Arkansas plantations as well as in Memphis, where he made his base of operations. Before the war Susan had always refused to come to her husband's plantation in swampy Hertford County, and now she also balked at living on the Mississippi River in the hot months. She appears to have spent the cool months of 1867 and 1868 in Memphis and the summers with Polk relatives in Maury County, Tennessee. In mid-1867, Rayner also set up a sawmill on a two-thousand-acre tract of wooded land north of Memphis that was part of Susan's inheritance. The venture was short-lived; see K. R. to Thomas Ruffin, July 5, 1867, *PTR*, 4:221–25 (date of this letter mistakenly printed as 1869 in published edition of the Ruffin Papers).

25. K. R. to Thomas Ruffin, July 5, 1867, *PTR*, 4:221–25.

26. K. R. to William H. Seward, January 31, 1870, Seward Papers; K. R. to Hamilton Fish, January 31, 1870, Fish Papers.

27. K. R. to Hamilton Fish, January 31, 1870, Fish Papers (first quotation); K. R. to Samuel L. M. Barlow, July 2, 1869, Barlow Collection (second quotation).

28. Susan Polk Rayner to Ellen [Mordecai?], undated letter, Cameron Papers (box 27, undated correspondence) (quotations); K. R. to William H. Seward, January 31, 1870, Seward Papers; K. R. to Thurlow Weed, September 19, 1872, Weed Papers.

29. K. R. to Thomas Ruffin, July 5, 1867, *PTR*, 4:221–25.

30. K. R. to Hamilton Fish, January 31, 1870, Fish Papers (quotation); Hamilton Fish to James L. Alcorn, February 28, 1870, George W. Culberson to James L. Alcorn, February 18, 1870, T. J. Wheat to James L. Alcorn, February 28, 1870, O. O.

Howard to James L. Alcorn, February 24, 1870, Reverdy Johnson to James L. Alcorn, February 7, 1870, all in KRP, SHC. On Alcorn's life and career, see Pereyra, *James Lusk Alcorn.*

31. K. R. to Hamilton Fish, February 12, 1873, Applications and Recommendations (quotation). On Alcorn's patronage policies and his appointments to the circuit court, see Harris, *Day of the Carpetbagger,* 302–3. The fact that Rayner's political disabilities had not yet been removed by Congress might have had some bearing on his failure to be confirmed, although he knew as early as February 8 that his pardon was imminent. By March the pardon had been granted. See Schuyler Colfax to K. R., February 8, 1870, KRP, SHC; Hernando (Miss.) *Press,* March 24, 1870.

32. K. R. to Thurlow Weed, September 19, October 1 (quotation), 1872, February 24, 1873, Weed Papers.

33. Hernando (Miss.) *Press,* July 6, 1871.

34. Ibid., June 27, 1872.

35. On the *Alabama* arbitration, see Cook, *Alabama Claims.*

36. K. R. to Hamilton Fish, February 12, 1873, Applications and Recommendations.

37. For Fish's advice, see Hamilton Fish to K. R., February 17, July 28, 1873, Fish Papers. The letters from Colfax, Schenck, and Holden, dated respectively December 12, 1873, December 9, 1873, and January 8, 1874, can be found in Applications and Recommendations. Other recommendations in the same file include those written by Hannibal Hamlin, Millard Fillmore, Reverdy Johnson, R. W. Thompson, John Pool, R. C. Powers, O. O. Howard, Thomas Atkinson, William M. Evarts, Isham G. Harris, W. M. Green, James L. Alcorn, William B. Hayes, C. T. Quintard, Tod R. Caldwell, and Nathan Clifford.

38. K. R. to Thurlow Weed, February 24, 1873, Weed Papers; J. L. Alcorn, A. Ramsey, H. Hamlin to Ulysses S. Grant, May 27, 1874, F. K. Frelinghuysen, H. B. Anthony, Z. Chandler to Ulysses S. Grant, May 28, 1874, Applications and Recommendations; K. R. to H. B. Anthony, June 10, 1874, Miscellaneous Manuscript Collection, LC (quotation); Hamilton Fish to K. R., June 23, 1874, Fish Papers.

39. K. R. to Hamilton Fish, July 14, 1873, Applications and Recommendations (first quotation); Rayner's letter in the *Clarion* was published in two issues, April 30 and May 14, 1874 (subsequent quotations).

Chapter 9

1. John A. J. Cresswell to Rutherford B. Hayes, March 10, 1877, KRP, SHC (quotation). For information on the Court of Commissioners of Alabama Claims and a sampling of its decisions, see Hackett, *Geneva Award Acts.* Transcripts of decisions that Rayner wrote can be found in Records of the Court of Commissioners of Alabama Claims, 1874–76, Memoranda and Decisions, ca. 1874–76 (no. 15), Records of Boundary Claims Commissions.

2. K. R. to Thomas Settle, December 3, 1876, Settle Papers.

3. K. R. to Thomas Settle, January 1, 1876 [1877], Settle Papers, (quotation); K. R. and John Pool to Rutherford B. Hayes, undated note, Hayes Papers.

4. New York *Times*, May 5, 1876 (quotations). Rayner's comments were expressed in public and private letters that he wrote urging Hamilton Fish, his old Whig colleague, to seek the presidency. Also see K. R. to Hamilton Fish, April 11, April [May] 5, 1876, Fish Papers; Hamilton Fish to K. R., April 14, May 6, 1876, KRP, SHC.

5. W. D. Bickham to Rutherford B. Hayes, February 14, 1877, Hayes Papers; Washington *National Republican*, June 19, 1877; Ulysses S. Grant to Rutherford B. Hayes, March 6, 1877, KRP, SHC; K. R. to Hamilton Fish, March 7, 1877, Fish Papers; K. R. to John Sherman, March 12, 1877, KRP, NCDAH; K.R. to William M. Evarts, Evarts Papers; Synopsis of Claims Decided, March 31, 1883 (no. 343), Records of Boundary and Claims Commissions. The KR Papers at the SHC contain dozens of letters related to his efforts to obtain an appointment to the Court of Claims. Eventually the letters of recommendation numbered several hundred.

6. K. R. to J. D. C. Atkins, February 14, 1878, Letters Sent, Records of the Solicitor of the Treasury.

7. James L. Alcorn to K. R., February 6, 1878, in KRP, SHC. The best work on the Compromise of 1877 is still Woodward, *Reunion and Reaction.*

8. K. R. to John Sherman, March 12, 1873, KRP, NCDAH (first, second, and third quotations); K. R. to William J. Clarke, May 28, 1878, KRP, SHC (fourth quotation).

9. K. R. to Charles Devens, June 6, 1877, Anthony Collection.

10. For the conflicting accounts of Soltedo's conversations with Rayner, see Washington *National Republican*, September 4, 1877. For Rayner's opinion in the Grow case, see K. R. to [Acting Secretary of the Treasury] R. C. McCormick, August 13, 1877, Letters Sent, Records of the Solicitor of the Treasury.

11. Washington *National Republican*, June 18 (first quotation), August 23 (second quotation), 24 (third quotation), 1877.

12. Ibid., August 25 (first quotation), 27 (second quotation), 28 (third quotation), 1877.

13. Ibid., September 1 (first quotation), 4 (subsequent quotations), 1877. The account of the brawl is Soltedo's. Rayner's version was somewhat less colorful but did little to contradict Soltedo's.

14. Ibid., September 4, 1877 (quotations); Washington *Evening Star*, September 5, 1877.

15. Washington *National Republican*, September 6, 7, 10, 19, 1877; K. R. to William M. Evarts, September 8, 1877, Evarts Papers (quotations).

16. Washington *National Republican*, September 4, 1877.

17. K. R. to W. W. Gordon, January 5, 1878, Gordon Family Papers, W. W. Gordon Series.

18. For Rayner's opinion, see K. R. to John Sherman, December 6, 1877, Letters Sent, Records of the Solicitor of the Treasury. Walker's career can be traced in great detail in Proceedings of the Army Board and Medical Officers File.

19. For a sampling of Walker's quixotic crusade against male chauvinism, see New York *Times*, March 24, December 8, 1877, March 4, 20, December 6, 1878.

20. K. R. to John Sherman, December 6, 1877, Letters Sent, Records of the Solicitor of the Treasury.

21. Ibid.

22. New York *Times*, December 8, 1877 (first quotation), August 18, 1878 (subsequent quotations).

23. K. R. to John Sherman, July 14, 1877, Letters Sent, Records of the Solicitor of the Treasury.

24. Ibid. (first quotation); New York *Times*, August 18, 1878 (second and third quotations).

25. K. R. to John Sherman, May 1, 1878, Letters Sent, Records of the Solicitor of the Treasury.

26. New York *Times*, June 28 (first quotation), September 27 (second, third, and fourth quotations), August 18 (fifth quotation), 1878. For the final disposition of the federal suits against Henry W. Thomas and ten others, see U.S. Attorneys' Reports, vol. 21, Virginia, Eastern District, 1873–80, Records of the Solicitor of the Treasury.

27. K. R. to B. M. Beck, January 4, 1882, KRP, SHC (first quotation); K. R. to Hamilton Fish, May [26?], 1880, Fish Papers (subsequent quotations).

28. K. R. to Hamilton Fish, May [26?], 1880, Fish Papers.

29. Washington *Post*, March 7, 1884; New York *Times*, March 6, 1884; Raleigh *Register*, March 12, 1884 (quotation).

Chapter 10

1. Crabtree and Patton, *"Journal of a Secesh Lady,"* 108.

2. Wyatt-Brown, *Southern Honor*, 307–8 (first, second, third, and fourth quotations); Clinton, *Plantation Mistress*, 214 (fifth quotation). Also see Genovese, *Roll, Jordan, Roll*, 413–31.

3. Woodward, *Mary Chesnut's Civil War*, 29 (first quotation); Rawick, *North Carolina Narratives*, pt. 2, 15, of *American Slave*, ed. Rawick, 97 (second quotation).

4. John B. Rayner's birth date is given in a clipping of his obituary, JBRP, available on microfilm from the Schomburg Center for Research in Black Culture, New York, N.Y. The originals are in the Barker Texas History Center, University of Texas, Austin. Black descendants of Kenneth Rayner who have shared their families' oral traditions include Ahmed A. Rayner, Ann Rayner Childs, Sammie Rayner, and Ivan Rayner, all of Chicago, and Arlene Carrington, Washington, D.C. Ahmed A. Rayner is the son of John B. Rayner and grandson of Kenneth Rayner. The other Chicago Rayners are grandchildren of John B. Rayner. Arlene Carrington is a relative of Cornelia Rayner Keeling, the mulatto daughter of Kenneth Rayner and either a sister or half-sister of John B. Rayner. I am indebted to all of these Rayner descendants for their generous assistance.

5. Most of the following information on John B. Rayner, Henry Jett, and slaves in the Kenneth Rayner household was provided by Arlene Carrington, whom I interviewed in April 1987. She related her family's oral traditions and shared the extensive research that she has conducted into the genealogy of the interrelated whites and blacks in the Polk and Rayner families. She furnished copies of William and Sarah Polk's wills, which provide for Henry Jett's manumission upon William's death and a small inheritance upon Sarah's. These wills also are on file at the NCDAH.

6. The Italian mistress story appears to have originated with Susie Rayner Roligan, daughter of John Rayner; see Jack Abramowitz, "John B. Rayner," 162. According to Rayner's descendants, she was the authority on family history and had done extensive research into her father's background. Another black Rayner descendent, Arlene Carrington, was not aware of the Italian mistress story, but in most other respects the information Susie Rayner Roligan gave Abramowitz agrees with that given me by Arlene Carrington and appears reliable. Ms. Carrington possesses a photograph of Henry Jett. Jett's obituary can be found in the Raleigh *News and Observer*, April 26, 1890. He was more than a hundred years old when he died. It is not certain whether Mary Ricks gave birth to John and Cornelia, but there is little doubt that Kenneth Rayner was father to both. The descendants of John Rayner believe there was another mulatto son, but he is a shadowy figure in the family's oral tradition.

7. Ivan Rayner (one of John Rayner's grandsons) specifically recalled hearing the story of Kenneth Rayner's open acknowledgment of the mulatto children from his father, Loris Melikoff Rayner. For Susan's hospital work, see documents in War Department, Collection of Confederate Records; and interview with Arlene Carrington, Washington, D.C., April 17, 1987. For John B. Rayner's recollections, see Houston *Chronicle*, August 19, 1904.

8. Houston *Chronicle*, August 19, 1904 (quotation). Rayner told this anecdote in 1904 for the benefit of a white reading audience, so it is quite possible he invented or at least embellished the part about begging for the soldier's life. However, his story about the soldier firing into the Union troops and being captured and hanged is accurate; see Murray, *Wake*, 1:507–8.

9. First Baptist Church Minutes; Murray, *Wake*, 1:617; Raleigh *News and Observer*, April 26, 1890 (quotation).

10. Howard, *Autobiography*, 2:391–93.

11. Ibid. (quotations); O. O. Howard to J. L. Alcorn, February 24, 1870, KRP, SHC.

12. Murray, *Wake*, 1:607–10; Carter, *Shaw's Universe*, 2–5. The school's early enrollment records have not survived, thus rendering it impossible to ascertain the exact dates on which Rayner attended. Rayner told a reporter in 1896 that he attended Shaw and went from there to St. Augustine's College, graduating from neither; see *GDN*, August 9, 1896.

13. Abramowitz, "John B. Rayner," 162–63; Halliburton, *History of St. Augustine's*, 2–7; Murray, *Wake*, 1:612–13. Bishop Thomas Atkinson, Reverend Joseph B. Cheshire, and Dr. Kemp P. Battle were among Kenneth Rayner's friends who incorporated St. Augustine's.

14. K. R. to Sallie Rayner, June 29, 1866, photocopy of original in the possession of Hyman H. and Genie Kirkpatrick, Weslaco, Tex.

15. Ninth Census, 1870, Wake County, N.C., Population Schedule. One of Rayner's contemporaries at St. Augustine's was Anna J. Cooper, who later earned a doctorate in French from the Sorbonne in Paris and became president of Frelinghuysen University in Washington, D.C. She recalled the curriculum. Another contemporary of Rayner's who studied at St. Augustine's was Charles N. Hunter, who became a leader in black education in North Carolina; see Hutchinson, *Anna J. Cooper*, 32; Haley, *Charles N. Hunter*.

16. Anderson, *Black Second;* Mobley, "Princeville"; Turner and Bridgers, *History of Edgecombe County;* Watson, *Edgecombe County.*

17. Anderson, *Black Second,* 6–7.

18. Edgecombe County Superior Court, Minute Docket 2 (1872–76), 67; Tarboro *Southerner,* May 1, 1873.

19. Marriage Register in Calvary Church Records, marriage date May 27, 1874; Tenth Census, 1880, Robertson County, Tex., Population Schedule.

20. For John Rayner's elections, see Edgecombe County Superior Court, Minute Docket 2 (1872–76), 169, 365, 528; 3 (1876–79), 35, 147; Edgecombe County, Commissioners' Minutes 2 (1871–76), 479, 492; 3 (1876–82), 13, 26, 42, 68, 139, 153. For duties of the magistrate's office, see *Hand-book for County Officers,* 2–3.

21. Tarboro *Southerner,* January 11 (first, second, and third quotations), July 11 (fourth quotation), 1872.

22. Ibid., August 7, 1874.

23. Ibid., September 4 (first quotation), September 11, 1874, July 9 (second and third quotations), August 13, 1875 (fourth quotation); Edgecombe County Land Records, Deed Book 39, 572.

24. Hamilton, *Reconstruction,* 604–6, 640–43 (first quotation); Tarboro *Southerner,* March 30, 1877 (second quotation).

25. Tarboro *Southerner,* July 19, 1877 (quotation); Edgecombe County Commissioners' Minutes 2 (1871–76), 432; land deeds from John B. and Susan Rayner to John W. Gant, December 29, 1875; agreement between John B. Rayner and John W. Gant, March 6, 1876, Edgecombe County Land Records.

26. Tarboro *Southerner,* February 9 (first quotation), February 16, 1877 (second quotation).

27. Ibid., June 1, 1877; land deed from John B. Rayner and wife to Richmond Lawrence, Jr., September 1, 1877, Edgecombe County Land Records.

28. Edgecombe County Superior Court, Minute Docket 3 (1876–79), 147; Anderson, *Black Second,* passim.

29. Anderson, *Black Second,* 20.

30. Ibid., 80; Logan, *Negro in North Carolina,* 119–25; Logan, "Movement of Negroes," 45–65. Emissaries from Tarboro-area blacks took a petition to Washington, D.C., in September 1879 seeking aid in emigrating West; see New York *Times,* September 23, 1879 (two separate articles). The actual number of North Carolina "exodusters" is unknown.

31. Parker, *Historical Recollections,* 30 (quotations), 34. In early 1880, the Tarboro *Southerner* repeatedly criticized out-of-state labor agents and the black "exodusters," arguing that blacks were being deceived by the outsiders; for example, see March 4, 1880. Information on John Rayner's role in the migration is from my interview with Ivan Rayner, Chicago, Ill., January 1987. Ivan Rayner is the son of Loris M. Rayner and the grandson of John Rayner. He acknowledges that his father might have exaggerated the thousand-person estimate. However, if Rasche Hearne indeed recruited "several trainloads" of laborers, the estimate might be accurate. U.S. Census data also indicate that the county experienced a large influx of blacks from North Carolina; for an analysis of the census, see McMillan, "Calvert," 120–21, 142–44.

32. Tenth Census, 1880, Robertson County, Tex., Population Schedule; New York

Times, October 6, 1879 (quotation); interview with Ivan Rayner; land deed from George Burck to John B. Rayner, May 9, 1881, Robertson County Land Records.

33. New York *Times,* September 23, 1879.

Chapter 11

1. *Compendium of the Tenth Census,* pt. 1, 54, 306, 374, 819; McMillan, "Calvert," 17–24; Parker, *Historical Recollections,* 32–33, 46; Baker, *History of Robertson County,* 1–5; Garner, "Calvert," 140–45.

2. Baker, *History of Robertson County,* 160–65 (quotation); Parker, *Historical Recollections,* 45–47.

3. Barr, *Reconstruction to Reform,* 371–83; Martin, "Greenback Party," 161–77; Rice, *Negro in Texas,* 53–67, 197.

4. Barr, *Reconstruction to Reform,* 85–92; Hazel, "Prohibition Campaigns," 14–53.

5. Quoted in Hazel, "Prohibition Campaigns," 24.

6. J. B. R. to B. H. Carroll, San Antonio *Express,* July 27, 1887. This letter appeared in a number of antiprohibition newspapers in the state.

7. Ibid.

8. San Antonio *New Era,* June 2, 1887; Waco *Examiner,* June 10, 18, 1887; *DMN,* June 18, August 17, 1887.

9. Waco *Examiner,* June 19, 1887 (quotations). The only extant copy of the *Vox Populi,* an issue dated August 5, 1887, can be found in the Hamman Papers. John Rayner's letter was published in papers such as the San Antonio *Express,* July 27, 1887; Wills Point *Chronicle,* July 7, 1887; Waco *Examiner,* June 14, 1887; and Waco *True Blue,* July 1, 1887. For examples of the commentary the letter inspired, see Waco *Examiner,* June 26, 28, July 2, August 28, September 2, 1887.

10. Waco *True Blue,* July 1, 1887 (first quotation); Calvert *Courier,* quoted in Waco *Examiner,* June 18, 1887 (second quotation); Waco *Examiner,* June 18 (third and fourth quotations), July 2, 1887 (fifth quotation).

11. Waco *Examiner,* May 26 (first quotation), June 10 (second quotation), 28, 29, July 7, 1887; San Antonio *Express,* July 7, 1887.

12. Waco *Examiner,* May 12 (quotation), May 27, 31, 1871; *GDN,* June 18, 1887; Victoria *Advocate,* July 9, 1887.

13. Waco *Examiner,* June 7, 1887 (first quotation); Wills Point *Chronicle,* July 21, 1887 (second quotation).

14. Hazel, "Prohibition Campaigns," 52; San Antonio *Express,* August 6, 1887 (first quotation); Waco *Examiner,* September 2, 1887 (second quotation).

15. *GDN,* August 17, 1887.

16. Interview with A. A. Rayner, Chicago, January 1987; Robertson County Marriage Records, Death Records.

17. For the agricultural situation and the plight of black farmers, see Spratt, *Road to Spindletop,* 141, 292, 295; Rice, *Negro in Texas,* 165, 178. On segregation, see Barr, *Reconstruction to Reform,* 108. On lynching, see Cutler, *Lynch-Law,* 183; Raper, *Tragedy of Lynching,* 123–38; SoRelle, "'Waco Horror'," 517–36.

18. J. B. R. to C. W. Macune, November 12, 1891, Powderly Papers (first quotation); Bryan *Eagle,* October 31, 1889 (second quotation).

Chapter 12

1. On the Farmers' Alliance, see Barnes, *Farmers in Rebellion;* Goodwyn, *Democratic Promise;* Hicks, *Populist Revolt;* McMath, *Populist Vanguard;* Mitchell, *Political Education.* On the Colored Alliance, see Abramowitz, "Negro in the Agrarian Revolt," 89–95; Gaither, *Blacks and the Populist Revolt,* 3–25; Goodwyn, *Democratic Promise,* 278–81; McMath, *Populist Vanguard,* 45–47.

2. Goodwyn, *Democratic Promise,* esp. 154–76; McMath, *Populist Vanguard,* 90–109; Palmer, *"Man over Money,"* esp. 104–10. The 1890 Alliance Demands framed at Ocala, Florida, can be found in Tindall, *A Populist Reader,* 88–89.

3. Works on Populism emphasizing the Jeffersonian nature of the movement include Miller, *Oklahoma Populism;* and Mitchell, *Political Education.* The Jacksonian roots of Populism are stressed in Palmer, *"Man over Money,"* 17, 114.

4. *DMN,* August 18, 1891 (quotations). Historians have disagreed considerably on the nature of the Populist approach to blacks. For generally flattering portrayals of the Populists' racial attitudes, see Abramowitz, "Negro in the Populist Movement," 257–89; Goodwyn, "Populist Dreams," 1436–56; Hair, *Bourbonism and Agrarian Protest;* Goodwyn, *Democratic Promise;* Woodward, *Tom Watson;* Woodward, *Origins of the New South;* Woodward, *Strange Career;* Woodward, "Populist Heritage." Those who tend to emphasize the limitations of Populist racial liberalism include Chafe, "Negro and Populism," 402–19; Gaither, *Blacks and the Populist Revolt;* Hackney, *Populism to Progressivism;* Hart, *Redeemers, Bourbons, and Populists;* Palmer, *"Man over Money";* Saunders, "Southern Populists"; Shapiro, "Populists and the Negro," in Meier and Rudwick, *Essays in Negro Life,* 2:27–36; Shaw, *Wool-Hat Boys;* Simms-Brown, "Populism and Black Americans."

5. *DMN,* August 18, 1891 (quotations); also see Goodwyn, *Democratic Promise,* 285–91. The proposal to place blacks in an appointive advisory role came from delegate Samuel Ealy Johnson, grandfather of Lyndon Johnson. In his account of the 1891 meeting, Lawrence Goodwyn takes special note of the fact that Hayes and Jennings, rather than Melvin Wade, became the first two black Populist committeemen. In Goodwyn's view, this was due to the fact that the party's organizers were wary of Wade's "racial militancy" and were thus more comfortable with the more moderate tone of the other black aspirants. This may be true, but the conclusion is debatable. Wade apparently left the hall after the morning session; had he stayed he almost certainly would have participated in the afternoon discussions and, as a well-known Dallasite, would have caught the attention of the *DMN* reporter. He might well have been elected instead of Hayes or Jennings. In addition, Hayes's repeated forceful insistence that blacks then and there be voted a place on the executive committee can hardly be described as submissive; he may not have wielded quite as sharp a tongue as Wade, but Hayes was no Uncle Tom. Finally, although little is known about Jennings, it is likely that men like Ashby, Sam Evans, Thomas Gaines, S. O. Daws, and William R. Lamb would naturally favor Hayes as a black ally in the party's leadership, for Hayes already had rendered valuable service under the Independent banner in the 1880s. Although Melvin Wade had genuine credentials as a labor agitator, his continued allegiance to the Republican party may have made him appear not too radical in the eyes of the Populists, but rather too conservative.

6. J. B. R. to C. W. Macune, November 12, 1891, Powderly Papers.

7. *GDN*, June 24, 1892 (quotation). On Nugent, see Alvord, "T. L. Nugent," 57, 65–81; Nugent, *Life and Work;* Pollack, *Just Polity*, 266–307. For John Rayner's first recorded campaign activity as a Populist orator, see *GDN*, September 13, 1892.

8. *SM*, December 12, 1895.

9. The 1891 and 1892 Populist state platforms can be found in *DMN*, August 18, 1891, June 24, 1892. For the 1892 Omaha Platform of the national People's party, see Tindall, *Populist Reader*, 90–96.

10. Cantrell and Barton, "Texas Populists," 662–63.

11. Martin, *People's Party in Texas*, 60–65. For the Populist educational campaign and the role of the reform press, see Mitchell, *Political Education*.

12. *HP*, February 5, 18, 1892, noted the birth of the *Alliance Vindicator* in Calvert. In the *Post* of December 13, 1891, it was reported that one "A. Alsbury" was president of the Colored State Alliance of Texas. This is probably Alex Asberry of Calvert, who had long been a leader of Robertson County's black Republicans. He served in the state legislature in 1888, was defeated in 1890 and 1894, and lost again by fraud in 1896; see St. Clair, "History of Robertson County," 152–54. For Asberry's obituary, see Franklin *Central Texan*, January 5, 1900.

13. Telephone interview with Margaret Peters (granddaughter-in-law of E. S. Peters), Beaumont, Tex., June 1987; Hempstead *News*, June 2, 1892 (quotations); *HP*, September 6, 24, 1892; "Col. E. S. Peters," *Collin County Historical Scrapbook No. 6*, May 18, 1898, Wilson Collection. In 1892 or 1893, Peters began publishing a Populist newspaper in Calvert, the *Citizen-Democrat;* the only two extant issues can be found in the Texas Collection, Baylor University. Rayner described Peters as "a rich farmer and a true Populist, and always a friend to the poor," *SM*, October 4, 1894.

14. *HP*, September 1, 18 (quotations), 1892. Official election returns in the gubernatorial and congressional races from Robertson County can be found in the Texas Elections Archive of the Public Policy Laboratory, Texas A&M University. Returns from the Calvert precinct, showing the Populist-Republican fusion in three races, are from *GDN*, November 10, 1892. Both Peters and Hanna were defeated because their districts included several counties in which Populists were greatly outnumbered. However, they almost certainly carried Robertson County by comfortable margins.

15. *SM*, June 26, 1896.

16. Martin, *People's Party*, 210; *HP*, August 4, 1893 (quotation).

17. *DMN*, July 30, 1894 (first quotation); Dallas *Texas Advance*, March 24, April 7, 1894 (second and third quotations); *SM*, July 5, 1894 (fourth quotation).

18. Beeville *Bee*, October 19, 1894 (first quotation); Dallas *Texas Advance*, April 7, 1894 (second quotation).

19. Dallas *Texas Advance*, May 19, 1894.

20. Ibid.; *SM*, August 11, 1898.

21. *HP*, April 22, 1894; Fairfield *Recorder*, May 18, 1894 (quotations) (*Vindicator* quoted in the *Recorder*). The *Recorder* is available on microfilm, but portions of this issue had to be pieced together from fragments of the original hard copies in the Texas Collection, Baylor University.

22. Fairfield *Recorder*, May 18, 1894 (quotations); Goodwyn, *Democratic Promise*, 118–19; Rice, *The Negro in Texas*, 242–44. The importance of black participation in

the judicial system of one Texas county is dramatically illustrated in Nieman, "Black Political Power."

23. Fairfield *Recorder,* August 3, 1894 (quotations). In Freestone County, Populists never gained control and Barbee's support for black jury service was never translated into action. It is not known to what extent white Populists supported the calling of black jurors. There is no clear proof of blacks actually serving on juries in any Populist county. However, white Populists did go on record as supporting black jury service in Robertson, Cherokee, Nacogdoches, and Jasper counties. See *HP,* February 26, 1892, September 17, October 19, 1894; *DMN,* May 14, 1894; Jacksonville *Banner,* November 9, 1894; Ross, "Andrew Jackson Spradley, 'A Texas Sheriff,' " 48–49; Jasper *News-Boy,* June 13, 1894. The situation in Houston illustrates Populists' ambivalence on the issue; in June 1894, a Populist convention rejected a resolution favoring black jurors, but in September a similar resolution was passed by a vote of 11–10. See *DMN,* June 11, 1894; *HP,* September 19, 1894. In most of the Populist strongholds of East Texas such as Grimes and San Augustine counties, where one would expect to find support for black jurors, the sources for examining this question have not survived.

24. *DMN,* June 20, 1894; Waco *Evening News,* June 20 (quotation), 21, 1894.

25. San Antonio *Express,* June 21, 1894.

26. *DMN,* August 18, 1891 (first quotation); Waco *Evening News,* June 21, 1894 (subsequent quotations).

27. *GDN,* June 22, 1894.

28. Ibid., June 23, 1894. The original 1891 executive committee was a thirty-two-man board; in 1892 it was reduced to fifteen members. The two original blacks on the committee, Hayes and Jennings, disappeared entirely from the political scene.

29. Waco *Evening News,* June 22, 1894. This issue contains the complete text of the party platform.

30. Ibid.

31. Ibid. (first quotation); *GDN,* June 23, 1894 (second quotation).

32. *SM,* July 5, September 20, October 4 (quotation), 1894; Dallas *Texas Advance,* July 28, August 18, 25, 1894; Livingston *East Texas Pinery,* August 2, 1894; *HP,* August 23, September 8, 1894; Edna *Jackson County Progress,* October 5, 1894.

33. Dallas *Texas Advance,* August 25, 1894.

34. Livingston *East Texas Pinery,* August 2, 1894.

35. Hempstead *News,* July 12, 19, 1894; Dallas *Texas Advance,* August 25, 1894.

36. *HP,* July 29, 1894; *DMN,* July 30, 1894 (first quotation); Dallas *Texas Advance,* August 25, 1894 (second quotation); Hempstead *News,* August 2, 1894.

37. For the boundaries of the district, see *Biennial Report of the Secretary of State of the State of Texas, 1894,* 246–47. Racial composition is calculated from the 1890 population statistics in U.S. Census Office, *The Twelfth Census of the United States, 1900, Population,* Vol. 1, pt. 1, 557–60. The Eleventh District was 18 percent black, not far from the state average of 22 percent. It contained larger than average numbers of Mexican Americans and white Republicans, which makes the district somewhat atypical demographically. However, there was no such thing in Texas as a "typical" congressional district. The six districts in which fusion was attempted range from 4 percent black to 53 percent black, the average being 32 percent. In the Hill Country

of central Texas, white Republicans (often Germans) were predominant enough to elect a Republican congressman. Therefore, without claiming "typicality" for the Eleventh District, it is possible to argue that it is a composite of Texas's racial and ethnic diversity.

38. W. P. Laughler to Vachel Weldon, October 1, 1894, Weldon Papers.

39. Ibid. (quotations). On the Rayners' financial situation, see *SM*, September 20, 1894; Beeville *Bee*, October 19, 1894.

40. J. B. R. to Vachel Weldon, October 8, 1894, Weldon Papers (first quotation); *SM*, September 20, October 4, 1894 (second quotation), March 5, 1896.

41. F. A. Vaughan to Vachel Weldon, October 5, 1894, (quotations); R. B. Rentfro to A. S. Crisp, October 14, 1894, both in Weldon Papers.

42. Dennis O'Connor to A. S. Crisp, October 16, 1894, Weldon Papers. For an excellent contemporary example of how ballots were fraudulently manipulated, see *GDN*, November 1, 1896.

43. V. F. Carvajal to A. S. Crisp, October 26, 1894, Weldon Papers.

44. A. J. Carothers to Vachel Weldon, November 8, 1894; R. B. Rentfro to Vachel Weldon, November 12 (quotations), 14, 1894; Benjamin Kowalski to Vachel Weldon, November 27, 1894; Frank Feuille to Vachel Weldon, November 25, 1894, all in Weldon Papers.

45. In the other five congressional races where fusion occurred—the Second, Third, Seventh, Eighth, and Ninth districts—the fusion tickets also lost. In the Eighth District race, fusion candidate C. H. Jenkins was defeated by only 376 out of over thirty-two thousand votes cast. Like Weldon, Jenkins could have contested the election but chose not to. Neither of the two Populist congressional candidates who did contest their narrow defeats, Jerome Kearby and J. H. "Cyclone" Davis, were successful in their contests. See Martin, *People's Party*, 221.

46. "Regular" Republican W. K. Makemson received 57,147 votes; "lily-white" Republican John B. Schmitz, 5,304; Prohibitionist J. M. Dunn, 21,295. See Barr, *Reconstruction to Reform*, 157.

Chapter 13

1. Among eligible black voters, about 17 percent voted for the Populist gubernatorial candidate. The Democrats and Republicans each polled about one-third of the black vote, with the rest not voting. The final election results showed the Democratic state ticket with 49 percent of all votes cast. Populists, Republicans, and Prohibitionists combined polled 51 percent of the vote. For a more detailed analysis of the election returns, see Cantrell and Barton, "Texas Populists," 663, 672–73.

2. Goodwyn, *Democratic Promise*, 437–63; *SM*, March 12, 1896 (quotation).

3. *SM*, March 26, 1896.

4. Ibid., April 16, 1896 (quotations). For other expressions of Populist opposition to Taubeneck and Democratic fusion, see ibid., April 2, 9, 23, 30, 1896.

5. Rayner and E. S. Peters were chosen as Robertson County's delegates to the convention; see *GDN*, July 14, 1896. While there is no clear proof that Rayner attended the St. Louis gathering, it is safe to assume that he did. The convention was very large, and only a handful of the most nationally prominent delegates received

mention in the press. Rayner's name was missing from Texas newspapers during the convention, indicating his probable absence from the state.

6. *HP,* July 23, 1896 (quotation). The best accounts of the St. Louis convention can be found in Durden, *Climax of Populism,* 23–44; Goodwyn, *Democratic Promise,* 477–92; Hicks, *Populist Revolt,* 359–67; and Stanley L. Jones, *Election of 1896,* 250–63. The delegate formula gave each state a delegate for every senator and representative it had in Congress, plus a delegate for every two thousand Populist votes cast in any statewide election since 1891. This clearly gave disproportionate representation to heavily populated states and to states in which fusion had been used successfully. For example, New York, with a mere eight thousand Populist voters, was allotted fifty-four delegates, whereas Texas, with twenty times that many Populists, got only twice as many delegates. The best gauge of fusionist versus midroad strength in the convention was in the vote on a permanent chairman, in which Nebraska's William V. Allen defeated Maine midroader James Campion by a vote of 758 to 564. Among those who agree that the delegate formula discriminated against the heavily midroad South are Hicks, *Populist Revolt,* 361; and Goodwyn, *Democratic Promise,* 459–63. For other views, see Barnes, *Farmers in Rebellion,* 177–83; and Durden, *Climax of Populism,* 31.

7. Austin *Statesman,* March 30, 1896. For other expressions of this theory, see ibid., March 25, 1896; and Austin *Evening News,* March 24, 1896. Fusion rumors were rife at the time of the Republican convention held in Austin in March.

8. *SM,* June 13, (first and second quotations), July 25, August 15, 1895; *DMN,* August 18, 1895; Cameron *Herald,* August 29, 1895.

9. Beeville *Bee,* October 19, 1894 (first quotation); Smithville *Transcript,* October 31, 1898 (second quotation); *SM,* January 9, April 23, June 25, (third quotation), 1896.

10. These quotations and those in the next two paragraphs are compiled from three accounts of two separate 1896 speeches: Austin *Statesman,* March 24, 1896; *SM,* April 9, 1896; and *HP,* October 22, 1896. Rayner's mixture of humor with overblown diction made him one of the state's most entertaining speakers. In his October 21, 1896, speech in Houston, for example, he commented on the controversy surrounding a $2,500 retainer paid by the state government to former governor Hogg for legal services Hogg rendered in an anti-prizefighting case. Rayner told his audience that Governor Culberson "gave Hogg $2500 to root a couple of minutes to prevent two bruisers from beating the faces off each other and making their concave dorsal vertebrae convex." Nineteenth-century audiences loved such oratory, whatever their political affiliation.

11. *HP,* October 22, 1896.

12. *SM,* December 12, 1895.

13. Ibid.

14. Ibid., April 9, 1896.

15. Ibid., June 26, 1896.

16. Ibid.

17. Fuller, *"A Texas Sheriff"*; Goodwyn, "Populist Dreams"; Ross, "Andrew Jackson Spradley, 'A Texas Sheriff'"; *SM,* September 20, 1894 (quotations). For an example of Spradley's protection of blacks while Populist sheriff of Nacogdoches County, see Bryan *Eagle,* August 12, 1897.

18. *HP*, August 2, 3, 4, 5, 1896; Austin *Statesman*, August 1, 6, 1896; *SM*, August 6, 1896 (quotations).

19. The following account of the 1896 convention is compiled from these sources: *HP*, August 5, 6, 7, 8, 9, 12, 1896; *DMN*, August 7, 8, 9, 1896; *SM*, August 13, 1896; San Antonio *Express*, August 7, 8, 9, 1896; Austin *Statesman*, August 6, 7, 8, 9, 1896; *GDN*, August 9, 1896. Where specific information could be found in only one of these sources, the location will be cited individually.

20. *DMN*, August 8, 1896. The following account of the black caucus is taken entirely from this issue.

21. For the activities of the Populist and Republican campaign committees and their efforts to arrange fusion, see *GDN*, August 16, 23, September 29, October 3, 9, 31, 1896; *HP*, August 15, 19, September 2, 11, 14, 16, 28, 1896; Beeville *Picayune*, October 30, 1896. Martin incorrectly suggests that fusion was the brainchild of the Republicans, and that "history does not record" the Populist response to the overtures of the Republicans; see Martin, *People's Party*, 243. Durden believes that the Populist condition for fusion required the fielding of a McKinley-Watson electoral ticket, and "the deal never came off"; see Durden, *Climax of Populism*, 75–76. In 1900 the most famous of all the Texas Populists, J. H. "Cyclone" Davis, clearly explained what had happened four years earlier: "In Texas in 1896 we fused with the Republicans or undertook to on both state and national matters. The mixing was notorious in many ways. Our 'plenary committee' met often with their committee." See Rockdale *Messenger*, February 1, 1900.

22. *HP*, August 9, 1896 (first quotation); *GDN*, August 9, 1896 (second quotation); San Antonio *Express*, August 9, 1896 (third quotation).

23. *SM*, August 13, 1896 (first quotation); *DMN*, August 8, 1896 (second quotation).

24. *HP*, August 10 (first quotation), 26, September 3, 13, October 11, 17, 21, 24, 1896 (second quotation), October 15 (third and fourth quotations), 1896; *GDN*, August 22 (fifth and sixth quotations), October 5, 6, 1896. See also *HP*, September 2, 9, 1896; *GDN*, August 20, 26, 1896; Beeville *Picayune*, October 9, 16, 1896.

25. *SM*, December 12, 1895 (first and second quotations); *HP*, October 1, 1896 (subsequent quotations); also see Austin *Statesman*, March 24, 1896.

26. *SM*, October 29, 1896. As the party's official organ, the *SM* went out of its way to explain the school-fund plank in an unequivocal manner: "It [the plank] means that the colored people shall have that proportion of the school fund the number of colored children entitles them. It means that the colored children shall be counted the same as the white children, and that the school funds shall be paid out equitably and no distinction made on account of color in the distribution of the school money. . . . The expression in the People's party platform has no reference to the amount paid into the fund by colored people, but only refers to the equitable distribution of the funds for the purpose of maintaining the schools."

27. *HP*, October 4, 1896; Barr, *Reconstruction to Reform*, 170; Rice, *Negro in Texas*, 84. On McDonald's overall career, see Glasrud, "William M. McDonald," in Barr and Calvert, *Black Leaders*, 82–111; Bundy, *Life of William Madison McDonald*.

28. *GDN*, November 2, 1896 (first quotation); *HP*, November 3, 1896 (second quotation).

29. *DMN*, August 23, 1896.

30. *GDN*, August 11, 1896; St. Clair, "History of Robertson County," 148; *HP*, August 13, 1896 (quotation).

31. *GDN*, August 30 (quotations), September 17, 1896; *HP*, September 20, 1896; St. Clair, "History of Robertson County," 155.

32. Baker, *History of Robertson County*, 164–65 (quotation); St. Clair, "History of Robertson County," 155–56; Lockhart *Register*, April 6, 1887; Robertson County District Court Records, esp. Books B, D, and P; clipping from Houston *Press*, February 18, 1931, original in possession of Otis D. Cannon. I am indebted to Otis D. Cannon, Houston, grandson of the judge, for sharing this newspaper clipping and his own recollections of his infamous grandfather. In 1899 Judge Cannon eventually murdered a fourth man, former county school superintendent W. A. Gray. Gray, having taken office in 1893, probably was a Populist or Republican. This time Cannon was tried and convicted of the murder and sentenced to life imprisonment in the state penitentiary. His defense in the case rested on a claim that he was addicted to drugs. After serving thirteen years, Cannon won a pardon under unusual circumstances, regained his license to practice law, and began writing a book about the Bible.

33. St. Clair, "History of Robertson County," 154 (first quotation); McCarver and McCarver, *Hearne on the Brazos*, 27 (second quotation); *GDN*, November 7, 1896 (third quotation); Bryan *Eagle*, November 12, 1896 (fourth quotation); clipping from Houston *Press*, February 18, 1931, original in possession of Otis D. Cannon (fifth, sixth, and seventh quotations).

34. *GDN*, November 7, 1896; *HP*, November 11, 1896; St. Clair, "History of Robertson County," 154–55.

35. On the election outcome, see Barr, *Reconstruction to Reform*, 171–72. For statistical estimates and a more complete explanation of their meaning, see Cantrell and Barton, "Texas Populists," 685–89.

36. Kosse *Cyclone*, September 23, 1897; *SM*, January 27 (first quotation), February 10, March 17, August 4, September 15; *HP*, July 26, 27, 28 (second quotation), 1898; Austin *Tribune*, July 27, 1898. On June 9, 1898, the *Southern Mercury* published a brief notice saying that a black military company had been organized at Calvert, with Rayner as captain. No other record of this survives and apparently nothing ever came of it.

37. *SM*, July 7 (first quotation), 14 (second quotation), August 11, 18, 1898.

38. Barr, *Reconstruction to Reform*, 35–36, 51–76, 214; Bastrop *Advertiser*, November 5, 1898; Rice, *Negro in Texas*, 62–66; Waco *Examiner*, September 2, 1887 (quotation).

39. *SM*, August 18, 1898; Smithville *Transcript*, November 4, 1898 (quotations); *GDN*, November 12, 1898; Tindall, *Emergence of the New South*, 143–44.

Chapter 14

1. Franklin *Central Texan*, October 7, 1898 (first and second quotations); Calvert *Chronicle*, November 11, 1898 (subsequent quotations).

2. Goodwyn, "Populist Dreams."

3. *SM*, September 20, 1894 (first quotation); Navasota *Plaindealer*, December 1,

1898 (second, third, and fourth quotations); *HP*, June 24, 1900 (fifth and sixth quotations).

4. Encampment committee minutes, July 14, 1900; H. S. P. Ashby to James W. Biard, July 14, 1900 (quotation), both in Biard Papers. Biard apparently had already sent the invitation to Ashby before the encampment committee officially met on July 14.

5. On the lynching of Henry Smith in Paris, Texas, see *HP*, February 2, 3, 15, 1893.

6. Franklin *Central Texan*, May 4, 1900 (quotation). A. A. Rayner distinctly recalled his father's frequent trips to preach in Victoria, although he was unsure of the exact years. During 1900, however, Rayner was a frequent enough resident of Victoria to be enumerated on the federal census both in Victoria and Calvert; interview with A. A. Rayner, Chicago, January 1987; Twelfth Census, 1900, Victoria County, Tex., Population Schedule.

7. *SM*, April 18, 1901.

8. Ibid., June 19, (quotations), August 14, 1902.

9. Ibid., August 21, 1902.

10. For estimates of black turnout in 1892, 1894, and 1896, see Cantrell and Barton, "Texas Populists," 663. The estimate of black turnout in the 1902 gubernatorial race is from Kousser, *Shaping of Southern Politics*, 207. The idea that blacks had already stopped voting before legal disfranchisement was enacted is the "fait accompli" theory first proposed by political scientist V. O. Key, Jr., in *Southern Politics*, 533–39.

11. *SM*, May 28, 1896. Most of those who were still calling themselves Populists as of 1902 opposed the poll tax, but they were only a fraction of the number who had once been Populists. Among those who had been Populists at the party's peak in 1894, half simply sat out the election; see Cantrell and Barton, "Texas Populists," 691–92. Miller reaches a similar conclusion, see "Progressive Coalition."

12. *SM*, December 18, 1902.

13. Ibid., April 9, 1896.

14. *HC*, August 19, 1904.

15. Ibid., December 19, 1909 (first quotation), June 11, 1911 (second quotation), June 16, 1912 (third quotation).

16. Ibid., December 19, 1909 (first and second quotations); fragment of essay in JBRP, beginning with "sure to respond with Colt's Automatic" (third and fourth quotations); clipping in JBRP from Galveston *News*, August 18, 1912 (fifth, sixth, and seventh quotations); *HC*, February 23, 1913 (eighth quotation).

17. Rayner, "Southern Chivalry and the Negro," undated manuscript, JBRP. Rayner never explicitly recanted Populism. In fact, in his voluminous writings after the turn of the century he never again mentioned the People's party by name. But he repeatedly discussed the political "mistakes" of the past, and these clearly were references to Populism.

18. Ibid.

19. *HP*, May 22, 1904 (quotations). In voicing this proposal, Rayner was probably responding to C. W. Gordon's calls to change state law so that public school funds would be allocated to the races according the taxes paid by each. Gordon, a newspaper editor and Democratic politician from Rayner's home town, based his campaign on a similar proposal put forward by Mississippi governor James K. Vardaman, an arch-

racist. Such a law would effectively abolish public support for black education; see Calvert *Chronicle*, March 4, April 1, July 8, 1904; Holmes, *White Chief*; Kirwan, *Revolt of the Rednecks*, 144–240, passim.

20. *HP*, May 22, 1904. Despite Rayner's fears, the Texas legislature never curtailed its meager support for black education. Black schools continued to receive "the crumbs that fall from the white man's table." In 1901, black school property was valued at slightly less than one-tenth of white property, and by 1922 that percentage had dropped to about 5 percent. Black teachers in 1910 earned on the average 74 percent of what white teachers made. See Brophy, "Black Texan," 42, 35.

21. Articles of incorporation for Conroe-Porter Industrial College, filed March 9, 1904 in Texas Secretary of State's Office, JBRP; appointment papers naming Rayner financial agent of Conroe-Porter Industrial College, October 22, 1904, JBRP. The college was co-founded by Professor D. Porter, hence the first official name of the college was Conroe-Porter. However, Porter appears to have had only a very brief connection with the school, for all mention of him disappears in 1905, and his name was dropped from the name of the school. For a brief discussion of Rayner's activities for Conroe College, see Abramowitz, "John B. Rayner," 168–73.

22. Clipping in JBRP from *HP*, November 7, 1904.

23. Abramowitz, "John B. Rayner," 168–69. On Washington, see Harlan, *Booker T. Washington*.

24. Clipping in JBRP from *HP*, November 7, 1904.

25. Ibid.

26. Ibid.; D. C. Tharp to J. B. R., January 27, 1905, JBRP (first quotation); clipping in JBRP from *HC*, April 6, 1906 (second quotation); clipping in JBRP from Victoria *Advocate*, March 25, 1907 (third quotation).

27. Clipping in JBRP from *HP*, April 15, 1905; clipping in JBRP from *HC*, April 8, 1906. There is no record of the former Confederates backing up their ringing endorsements with donations. On the emotional significance of the Lost Cause in the early-twentieth-century South, see Wilson, *Baptized in Blood*.

28. A. W. Terrell, quoted in Barr, *Reconstruction to Reform*, 204; clipping in JBRP from Texas *House Journal*, April 26, 1905; clipping in JBRP from Galveston *Tribune*, May 9, 1905; clipping in JBRP from Galveston *News*, May 10, 1905.

29. J. B. R. to John H. Kirby, November 29, 1904, JHKP. The Kirby Papers, including the records of his various business concerns, are a massive, mostly uncatalogued collection.

30. On Kirby, see Morgan, "No Compromise—No Recognition," and "Gospel of Wealth," 186–97; Maxwell and Baker, *Sawdust Empire*, 98–105. Lasswell, *John Henry Kirby*, is adulatory, but contains much useful information. A scholarly biography of Kirby is much needed.

31. John H. Kirby to J. B. R., December 1, 1904, JBRP (first quotation); J. B. R. to John H. Kirby, January 4, 1905, JHKP (second and third quotations).

32. "The Perils of Democracy," speech delivered by Kirby to the Southern Pine Association, February 1918, JHKP (quotation). For Kirby's opposition to Bryan in 1896, see *HP*, September 1, 1896.

33. Clipping in JBRP from *HP*, April 15, 1906; clipping in JBRP from Victoria *Advocate*, March 25, 1907 (quotation).

34. B. Adoue to J. B. R., November 14, 1906.

35. For Adoue's activities in the antiprohibition campaign see *BTP*, passim. On the close relationship between Democratic progressivism and prohibition in Texas, see Gould, *Progressives and Prohibitionists.*

36. Barr, *Reconstruction to Reform,* 230–32; Gould, *Progressives and Prohibitionists,* 43–44; *BTP*, 1:534.

37. For Rayner's activities on behalf of the Texas Brewers' Association, see *BTP*, 1:55, 68–69, 249–52, 263–64, 267, 513, 534; 2:563, 602, 638, 681–82, 697, 718–19, 731–32, 749, 767–68, 796, 905–6, 908, 921, 925, 950, 1055–62, 1453, 1479.

38. Ibid., 2:658, 796.

39. J. B. R. to Otto Wahrmund, February 25, 1907, ibid., 2:1055–56.

40. J. B. R. to San Antonio Brewing Association, April 17, 1907, ibid., 2:905–6 (quotations); San Antonio Brewing Association to J. B. R., May 5, 1907, ibid., 2:1058; George W. Littlefield to San Antonio Brewing Association, May 8, 1907, ibid., 2:1060; J. B. R. to Ormond Paget, April 20, 1907, ibid., 2:1058; San Antonio Brewing Association to Ormond Paget, April 20, 1907, ibid., 2:1057–58.

41. J. B. R. to Otto Wahrmund, May 4, 1907, ibid., 2:1058 (first and second quotations); R. L. Autrey to Otto Wahrmund, May 5, 1907, ibid., 2:1058 (third quotation); Otto Wahrmund to R. L. Autrey, May 6, 1907, ibid., 2:1058–59 (fourth quotation).

42. George W. Littlefield to the San Antonio Brewing Association, May 8, 1907, ibid., 2:1060 (first quotation); J. B. R. to Otto Wahrmund, May 14, 1907, ibid., 2:1061 (second, third, and fourth quotations); J. B. R. to Otto Wahrmund, May 17, 1907, ibid., 2:1061 (fifth and sixth quotations). For results of the Travis County election, see Austin *Statesman,* June 2, 1907.

43. Bertrand Adoue to Texas Brewing Company, November 27, 1908, *BTP*, 1:264 (first quotation); Otto Koehler to E. S. Clauss, May 6, 1910, ibid., 1:55 (second quotation); J. B. R. to Otto Wahrmund, May 17, 1907 (subsequent quotations), ibid., 2:1062. Also see 1:143, 188, 190, 193, 197, 206.

44. On contributions from white antiprohibitionists, see clipping in JBRP from Victoria *Advocate,* March 25, 1907. On the school's change of direction, see "Program for the Eighteenth Annual William A. Johnson Memorial Institute, held on April 28–30, 1964, at Conroe Normal and Industrial College." This pamphlet contains a brief historical sketch of the college and was given to me by the school's current president, J. P. Daviss. It deals primarily with Abner's accomplishments and makes no mention of Rayner.

45. *HC,* March 17, 1907.

46. Ibid., May 9, 1909 (first and second quotations), November 28, 1909 (third quotation), February 4, 1912 (fourth quotation).

47. Ibid., May 9, 1909 (first quotation), August 15, 1909 (third quotation), December 1, 1912 (fourth quotation), January 4, 1914 (fifth quotation); Rayner "The Travail of the South in Its Travel from Imperfection Back to Perfection," undated manuscript, JBRP (second quotation).

48. *HC,* November 19, 1905 (first quotation), November 8, 1914 (second quotation); Rayner, "The Travail of the South" (third quotation).

49. *HC,* February 18, 1912 (quotation); R. L. Smith to Whom It May Concern, August 31, 1911, JBRP.

50. On Smith and the F.I.S., see Carroll, "Robert Lloyd Smith"; Carter, "Robert Lloyd Smith"; Smith, "An Uplifting Negro Cooperative Society"; *Constitution and By-Laws*, Farmers' Improvement Society Papers.

51. On Smith, his political activism, and his relationship with Washington, see Robert Lloyd Smith to Booker T. Washington, June 9, 1897, *Washington Papers*, 4:305–6; Booker T. Washington to Theodore Roosevelt, October 7, 1901, *Washington Papers*, 6:232; Booker T. Washington to Theodore Roosevelt, December 14, 1901, *Washington Papers*, 6:346–47; Theodore Roosevelt to Booker T. Washington, April 4, 1902, *Washington Papers*, 6:434–35; Emmett Jay Scott to Booker T. Washington, June 23, 1902, *Washington Papers*, 6:448; Booker T. Washington to William Howard Taft, June 18, 1909, *Washington Papers*, 10:138–39; Booker T. Washington to Jacob Henry Schiff, September 18, 1909, *Washington Papers*, 10:176. On politicians, including Smith, who espoused the Washington philosophy, see Meier, *Negro Thought in America*, 248–55.

52. Smith, "An Uplifting Negro Cooperative Society," 10466 (quotation); Carroll, "Robert Lloyd Smith," 85–93. For a summary of the school's assets, income, academic program, and enrollment, see U.S. Office Department of Education, *Negro Education*, 2:575.

53. R. L. Smith to J. B. R., August 31, 1911; R. L. Smith to J. B. R., September 11, 1911 (first quotation); R. L. Smith to J. B. R., November 9, 1911 (second quotation), JBRP.

54. *K. Lamity's Harpoon*, clipping dated December 1911 (quotations), clipping dated December 1912, both in JBRP. Also see R. L. Smith to J. B. R., December 9, 1911, JBRP.

55. *HC*, December 3, 1911 (first quotation), January 14, 1912 (second quotation).

56. Unidentified black editor quoted by Rayner, ibid., August 19, 1904 (quotation).

57. A. S. Jackson quoted in Banks, "Pursuit of Equality," 40.

Chapter 15

1. *HC*, October 20, 1912.

2. On black turnout, see Gould, *Progressives and Prohibitionists*, 48–49; Kousser, *Shaping of Southern Politics*, 240–46.

3. *HC*, October 14, 19, 23, 30, 1903; November 2, 5, 17, 18 (quotation), 1903; Wharton Bates to S. W. T. Lanham, April 26, 1904, all in JBRP.

4. Wharton Bates to S. W. T. Lanham, April 26, 1904, JBRP.

5. Otto Wahrmund to O. B. Colquitt, November 13, 1910, *BTP*, 2:1479 (quotation); John H. Kirby to J. B. R., October 12, 1914, JHKP.

6. *HC*, April 17, 1910 (first quotation), March 17, 1907 (second quotation). For Rayner's occasional support of Democratic candidates, see J. B. R. to John H. Kirby, October 31, 1912, JHKP; and Joe H. Eagle to J. B. R., November 20, 1912, JBRP.

7. *HC*, August 9, 1908 (first and second quotations), December 19, 1909 (third and fourth quotations). Following the death of the long-time black Republican leader Norris Wright Cuney in 1897, William M. "Gooseneck Bill" McDonald and his white ally E. H. R. Green controlled the "black-and-tan" faction into the early years of the twentieth century, but black influence in Republican conventions continued to diminish with each passing election. In 1902, the two factions achieved an uneasy peace,

united under the state chairmanship of Cecil A. Lyon. The black-and-tans staged abortive bolts in the next three elections, but each time the now-dominant lily-whites were easily able to control the state party; see Casdorph, *History of the Republican Party*, 70–94.

8. *HC*, April 17, 1910,

9. Casdorph, *History of the Republican Party*, 78–79; *HC*, August 23, 1908 (first quotation); Cecil A. Lyon to J. B. R., May 22, 1908 (second and third quotations), Cecil Lyon to J. B. R., June 20, 1908, J. B. R. to William H. Taft, June 30, 1908, all in Taft Papers (series 3).

10. *HC*, November 6, 1910.

11. Clipping from *GDN*, February 10, 1912, JBRP (quotation). A. A. Rayner recalled that many readers of the *HC* subscribed to the paper for no other reason than to read his father's essays; interview with A. A. Rayner, January 1987, Chicago.

12. Clipping from *HC*, March 17, 1912, JBRP.

13. Rayner, "The Spirit of Abraham Lincoln Calling His Colored Children Whom He Emancipated," undated manuscript (ca. fall 1912), JBRP. There is no notation on this manuscript indicating where, or if, it was published. Most likely it appeared in the black press, without Rayner's name affixed to it. On Roosevelt and the black vote, see Link, "Theodore Roosevelt and the South"; and Mowry, "The South and the Progressive Lily White Party."

14. Clipping from *HC*, March 16, 1912, JBRP.

15. J. B. R. to Otto Wahrmund, June 1, 1912, *BTP*, 1:68.

16. Clipping from *GDN*, August 18, 1912, JBRP (first quotation); *HC*, October 20, 1912 (second quotation), February 23, 1913 (third quotation), October 20, 1912 (fourth and fifth quotations), August 23, 1914 (sixth quotation).

17. J. B. R. to Otto Wahrmund, July 9, 1912, *BTP*, 1:68–69.

18. *BTP*, 1:1.

19. Rayner assiduously courted Emmett J. Scott, the young Texan who was Washington's secretary at Tuskegee. Scott had been John H. Kirby's "office boy" and was later editor of a black newspaper in Houston before joining Washington in Alabama. In 1912 Rayner finally secured a promise of $1,000 from Scott, provided the F.I.S. could match the sum. There is no record to indicate success or failure; see Emmett Scott to J. B. R., December 5, 1912, January 13, 1914, both in JBRP. A report of the U.S. Office of Education compiled in 1914 indicated that the Jeanes and Slater Funds had contributed $620 that year to the school. See U.S. Office of Education, *Negro Education*, 2:575.

20. Rayner's acquisition of these lots can be traced in the Robertson County Land Records and Tax Rolls. Rayner acquired his first lot in 1881, and in 1895 he purchased the adjacent lot. The other six lots were purchased between 1904 and 1910. The "farm" referred to is probably a twenty-five-acre tract registered in Ahmed Rayner's name, but which John and Clarissa apparently managed. Ahmed moved to Chicago in 1914. For information of Rayner's work as a rent collector, see Friench Simpson to J. B. R., August 29, 1913, JBRP; and interviews with Howard Williams, November 1986 and June 1987, Calvert. Williams was a student of Rayner's in the last years of Rayner's life. He recalled that Rayner also collected rents on lands in Robertson County that comprised part of the Rice Institute (now Rice University) endowment.

For Rayner's work as a recruiter for Kirby, see J. B. R. to John H. Kirby, March 29, April 3, November 24 1913, John H. Kirby to J. B. R., November 22, 1913, July 9, 1915, all in JHKP; Goodwyn, *Democratic Promise*, 303–4.

21. John H. Kirby to James M. Barclay, December 11, 1913, JHKP.

22. J. B. R. to John H. Kirby, July 7, 1915 (first, second, eighth and ninth quotations), September 7, 1915 (third, fourth, and fifth quotations), all in JHKP; *HC*, January 18, 1914 (sixth and seventh quotations).

23. Calvert *Picayune*, April 23, 1914. See deeds dated February 6, 1914 and January 5, 1915, Robertson County Land Records; J. B. R. to Harris Masterson, August 3, 31, 1914, Masterson Papers. Rayner appeared on the county's delinquent tax list in mid-1914; see Calvert *Picayune*, April 9, 1914.

24. For Masterson's acquisition of Rayner's property, see deed dated January 5, 1915, Robertson County Land Records. For the Rayners' efforts to prevent foreclosure, see Clarissa Rayner to Harris Masterson, January 15, 1915 (first quotation), T. L. Larkin to J. B. R., April 16, 1915 (second and third quotations), both in Masterson Papers; J. B. R. to John H. Kirby, September 22, 1915, JHKP (fourth quotation). At this time Rayner also attempted unsuccessfully to secure an appointment as steward for the black state college at Prairie View through Kirby's influence; see John H. Kirby to Paul Waples, September 6, 1915, JHKP.

25. Haller, *Eugenics*, 3.

26. Ibid., esp. 58–94.

27. Ibid., 83; *HC*, November 15, 1908 (first quotation), October 18, 1914 (second quotation); clipping from San Antonio *Express*, May 24, 1912, JBRP (third quotation).

28. *HC*, February 15, 1914.

29. Clipping from Fort Worth *Record*, August 19, 1912, JBRP (first quotation); *HC*, April 13, 1913 (second quotation); J. B. R. to John H. Kirby, July 7, 1915, John H. Kirby to J. B. R., July 9, 1915, both in JHKP.

30. *HC*, December 19, 1909.

31. Ibid., June 11, 1911 (first quotation), February 15, 1914 (second quotation), June 16, 1912 (fourth and fifth quotations); Rayner, "The Federal Government's Best Asset," undated manuscript addressed to Editor of *Home Defender*, JBRP (third quotation); Rayner, "Southern Chivalry, and the Negro," undated manuscript, JBRP. On blacks and nativism, see Shankman, *Ambivalent Friends*.

32. John H. Kirby to J. B. R., April 18, 1917, JHKP.

33. J. B. R. to John H. Kirby, April 19, 1917, JHKP.

34. Ibid.; interviews with Lawrence Goodwyn, March 1987, Durham, N.C.; A. A. Rayner, January 1987, Chicago; Howard Williams, November 1986 and June 1987, Calvert, Tex.; Jessie Yepp, June 1987, Calvert, Tex. Rayner argued that "when the woman gets the ballot God will get into politics," see *HC*, January 18, 1914.

35. Interviews with Howard Williams; interview with Jessie Yepp. Captain William H. Bradshaw III, M.D., of Brooke Army Medical Center, San Antonio, explained "dropsy," the edema that afflicted Rayner. Eventually it results in cardiac decompensation, or the inability of the heart to maintain effective blood pressure.

36. This collection of "wise sayings" are in the JBRP. Among the manuscript aphorisms are several clippings, showing an example of the sayings that appeared in print. It is impossible to know over what time span these manuscripts were written,

and some may date from as early as 1912. However, it is safe to say that many of them were written in the last year or two of Rayner's life, when declining health caused the deteriorating penmanship and occasional lapses in his train of thought displayed in the writings. The quotations in the following six paragraphs are scattered throughout the "sayings" and are not cited individually.

37. Interviews with A. A. Rayner, Howard Williams, and Jessie Yepp. Williams and Yepp both recalled the incident with the town marshal; Williams explained that the conflict over the dog was "a front"—the real source of the quarrel was "political," although he was unable to elaborate on the true nature of the disagreement. Rayner's obituary from the [San Antonio?] *Inquirer* is in JBRP; it was written by W. P. Mabson, Jr., son of the black legislator from North Carolina. The younger Mabson wrote that his father and Rayner "attended school together and fought many a political battle that brought recognition to the Negroes of their native state."

Epilogue

1. Dallas *Herald*, December 8, 1881, April 3, 1884.

2. Ibid., December 29, 1881, January 5, February 16, 1882, April 5, 1883, April 16, 1885; El Paso *Times*, April 15, 16, 18, 19, 1885.

3. Raleigh *News and Observer*, January 8, 1928; Texas Ranger Appointment Papers, Texas Adjutant General's Office, May 17, 1899; Resolution on the Death of Kenneth Rayner, in *Bench and Bar;* Last Will and Testament of Kenneth Rayner, Will Book 8, DeSoto County, Mississippi Wills.

4. Information on Sally Rayner Hyman and Susan Rayner Glennan comes from Rayner genealogy papers, KRP, SHC; the Rayner Family Bible in possession of Sallie Savage, Midland, Tex.; and interviews with Kenneth Rayner Glennan, Jr., Dallas, Tex., January 1987, Sallie Savage, Midland, Tex., August 1987, Kenneth Rayner Hyman, Jr., San Antonio, Tex., May 1987, and Genie Kirkpatrick, Weslaco, Tex., January 1987.

5. Interview with Arlene Carrington, Washington, D.C., April 1987.

6. Abramowitz, "John B. Rayner," 163–64; interviews with A. A. Rayner, Sammie Rayner, and Ann Rayner Childs, Chicago, January 1987.

7. Carmichael and Hamilton, *Black Power*, 174; interviews with Sammie Rayner, January 1987, Chicago, and July 1988, College Station, Tex.

8. Interview with Sammie Rayner, July 1988.

Bibliography

Archival Manuscript Collections

Anthony Collection. Manuscripts and Archives Division, New York Public Library.

Badham, William, Papers. Manuscript Department, William R. Perkins Library, Duke University, Durham, N.C.

Barlow, Samuel L. M., Collection. Huntington Library, San Marino, Calif.

Barringer Papers. Southern Historical Collection, University of North Carolina, Chapel Hill.

Battle Family Papers. Southern Historical Collection, University of North Carolina, Chapel Hill.

Biard, James W., Papers. Barker Texas History Center, University of Texas, Austin.

Bills, John Houston, Letterbook. Southern Historical Collection, University of North Carolina, Chapel Hill.

Borland Family Papers. Swem Library, College of William and Mary, Williamsburg, Va.

Branch Family Papers. Southern Historical Collection, University of North Carolina, Chapel Hill.

Cameron Papers. Southern Historical Collection, University of North Carolina, Chapel Hill.

Civil War Collection. North Carolina Division of Archives and History, Raleigh.

Elliott, Stephen, Papers. Perkins Library, Duke University, Durham, N.C.

Evarts, William M., Papers. Library of Congress, Washington, D.C.

Farmers' Improvement Society Papers. Texas Collection, Baylor University, Waco, Tex.

Fish, Hamilton, Papers. Library of Congress, Washington, D.C.

Gordon Family Papers. Southern Historical Collection, University of North Carolina, Chapel Hill.

Governors' Papers. North Carolina Division of Archives and History, Raleigh.

Hamman, William H., Papers. Rice University, Houston, Tex.

Hayes, Rutherford B., Papers. Rutherford B. Hayes Presidential Center, Fremont, Ohio.

Kirby, John Henry, Papers. Houston Metropolitan Research Center, Houston, Tex.

Masterson, Harris, Papers. Fondren Library, Rice University, Houston, Tex.

Miscellaneous Manuscript Collection. Library of Congress, Washington, D.C.

Miscellaneous Papers. North Carolina Division of Archives and History, Raleigh.

Outlaw, David, Papers. Southern Historical Collection, University of North Carolina, Chapel Hill.

Polk-Yeatman Papers. Southern Historical Collection, University of North Carolina, Chapel Hill.

Powderly, Terence, Papers. Catholic University, Washington, D.C.

Rayner, Kenneth, Papers. Southern Historical Collection, University of North Carolina, Chapel Hill.

Rayner, Kenneth, Papers. North Carolina Division of Archives and History, Raleigh.

Rayner, John B., Papers. Barker Texas History Center, University of Texas, Austin.

Ruffin, Thomas, Papers. Southern Historical Collection, University of North Carolina, Chapel Hill.

Ruffin-Roulhac-Hamilton Papers. Southern Historical Collection, University of North Carolina, Chapel Hill.

Saltonstall Papers. Massachusetts Historical Society, Boston, Mass.

Settle Papers. Southern Historical Collection, University of North Carolina, Chapel Hill.

Seward, William H., Papers. Department of Rare Books and Special Collections, University of Rochester Library, Rochester, N.Y.

Sparrow, Thomas, Collection. East Carolina Manuscript Collection, East Carolina University, Greenville, N.C.

Ullman, Daniel, Papers. New-York Historical Society, New York, N.Y.

Van Noppen, Charles Leonard, Papers. Manuscript Department, William R. Perkins Library, Duke University, Durham, N.C.

Weed, Thurlow, Papers. Department of Rare Books and Special Collections, University of Rochester Library, Rochester, N.Y.

Weldon, Vachel, Papers. Barker Texas History Center, University of Texas, Austin.

Wilson, Walter B., Collection. Barker Texas History Center, University of Texas, Austin.

Published Correspondence

Anti-Saloon League. *The Brewers and Texas Politics.* 2 vols. San Antonio, 1916.

Hamilton, J. G. de Roulhac, ed. *The Papers of Thomas Ruffin.* 4 vols. Raleigh, 1918.

Harlan, Louis R., and Raymond W. Smock, eds. *The Papers of Booker T. Washington.* 14 vols. Urbana, 1972–89.

McPherson, Elizabeth Gregory, ed. "Letters from North Carolina to Andrew Johnson." *North Carolina Historical Review* 27 (July 1950): 336–63.

Shanks, Henry Thomas, ed. *The Papers of Willie Person Mangum.* 6 vols. Raleigh, 1950–56.

Tolbert, Noble J., ed. *The Papers of John Willis Ellis.* 2 vols. Raleigh, 1964.

Williams, Max R., ed. *The Papers of William Alexander Graham.* 7 vols. to date. Raleigh, 1957- .

Microfilm Manuscript Collections

Calvary Church Records. Tarboro, N.C., Southern Historical Collection, University of North Carolina, Chapel Hill.

Carroll, Anna Ella, Papers. Maryland Historical Society, Baltimore.

Fillmore, Millard, Papers. Buffalo and Erie County Historical Society, Buffalo, N.Y.

Hammond, James H., Papers. Library of Congress, Washington, D.C.

Hogg, Gavin, Papers. Manuscript Department, William R. Perkins Library, Duke University, Durham, N.C.

Johnson, Andrew, Papers. Library of Congress, Washington, D.C.

Lincoln, Abraham, Papers. Series 1. Library of Congress, Washington, D.C.

Polk, Leonidas, Papers. Southern Historical Collection, University of North Carolina, Chapel Hill.

Rayner, John B., Papers. Schomburg Center for Research in Black Culture, New York, N.Y.

War Department Collection of Confederate Records. Confederate Papers Relating to Citizens or Business Firms. Record Group 109. National Archives, Washington, D.C.

Memoirs, Diaries, Speeches, and Contemporary Accounts

Adams, Charles Francis, ed. *Memoirs of John Quincy Adams*. 12 vols. Rpt. New York, 1969.

Carroll, Anna Ella. *The Great American Battle*. New York, 1856.

Copway, George. *Organization of a New Indian Territory East of the Missouri River*. New York, 1850.

Crabtree, Beth G., and Patton, James W., eds. *"Journal of a Secesh Lady": The Diary of Catherine Ann Devereux Edmondston, 1860–1866*. Raleigh, 1979.

Howard, Oliver O. *Autobiography of Oliver Otis Howard: Major General United States Army*. 2 vols. New York, 1908.

Moore, John W. *History of North Carolina with Special Reference to the Annals of Hertford County and the Albemarle Country; Extracts from the Murfreesboro Inquirer, 1877–8*. Collection of clippings in North Carolina Collection, University of North Carolina, Chapel Hill, n.p., n.d.

Nugent, Catherine, ed. *Life Work of Thomas L. Nugent*. Stephenville, Tex., 1896.

Rayner, Kenneth. *Address Delivered Before the Graduating Class of the United States Military Academy*. New York, 1853.

———. *Address of the Hon. Kenneth Rayner at the Examination of the Students of Union Academy*. Murfreesborough, N.C., 1854.

———. *An Address Delivered Before the North Carolina State Agricultural Society*. Raleigh, 1854.

———. *Life and Times of Andrew Johnson*. New York, 1866.

———. *Reply of Hon. Kenneth Rayner to the Manifesto of Hon. Henry A. Wise*. Washington, 1855.

———. *Resolutions on the Subject of Slavery*. Raleigh, 1850.

———. *Speech of Hon. Kenneth Rayner in the Convention of 1835*. Raleigh, 1855.

————. *Speech of Hon. Kenneth Rayner in the Hall of the House of Commons, December 8, 1856*. North Carolina Collection, University of North Carolina, Chapel Hill.

————. *Speech of Hon. Kenneth Rayner in the House of Commons, on the Bill to Provide for Establishing a Hospital for the Insane*. Raleigh, 1849.

————. *Speeches of Mr. K. Rayner, of North Carolina . . . Prefaced by an Address to His Constituents Declining a Re-Election*. Washington, 1845.

————. *Speech of Mr. Rayner, of North Carolina, on the Question of the Reception of Abolition Petitions . . . June 15, 1841*. N.p., 1841.

Rawick, George P., ed. *The American Slave: A Composite Autobiography*. Westport, 1972.

Smith, R. L. "An Uplifting Negro Cooperative Society: The Farmers' Improvement Society of Texas which Is Substituting Among the Negroes Order and Prosperity for Shiftlessness and Poverty." *The World's Work* 16 (July 1908): 10462–66.

Tindall, George Brown, ed. *A Populist Reader*. New York, 1966.

Valentine, William D., Diaries. Southern Historical Collection, University of North Carolina, Chapel Hill.

War of the Rebellion, Official Records. Series 1. Washington, D.C., 1885.

Wilson, Henry. *History of the Rise and Fall of the Slave Power in America*. 2 vols. Boston, 1872.

Winkler, Ernest William, ed. *Platforms of Political Parties in Texas*. Austin, 1916.

Woodward, C. Vann, ed. *Mary Chesnut's Civil War*. New Haven, 1981.

Newspapers

Austin *Evening News, Statesman*, and *Tribune;* Beeville (Tex.) *Bee* and *Picayune;* Bryan (Tex.) *Eagle;* Calvert (Tex.) *Chronicle, Citizen-Democrat*, and *Vox Populi;* Cameron (Tex.) *Herald;* Cincinnati *Enquirer;* Dallas *Herald, Morning News, Southern Mercury*, and *Texas Advance;* Edna (Tex.) *Jackson County Progress;* El Paso *Times;* Fairfield (Tex.) *Recorder;* Fayetteville *North Carolinian;* Franklin (Tex.) *Central Texan;* Galveston *News;* Greensborough (N.C.) *Patriot;* Hempstead (Tex.) *News;* Hernando (Miss.) *Press;* Houston *Chronicle* and *Post;* Jackson (Miss.) *Clarion;* Jacksonville (Tex.) *Banner;* Jasper (Tex.) *Newsboy;* Kosse (Tex.) *Cyclone;* Livingston (Tex.) *East Texas Pinery;* Lockhart (Tex.) *Register;* Murfreesboro (N.C.) *Albemarle Southron* and *Citizen;* Navasota (Tex.) *Plaindealer;* New York *Times* and *Tribune;* Raleigh *Confederate, Journal of Freedom, News and Observer, Register, North Carolina Standard*, and *Southern Advertiser;* Rockdale (Tex.) *Messenger;* San Antonio *Express* and *New Era;* Smithville (Tex.) *Transcript;* Tarboro (N.C.) *Southerner;* Victoria (Tex.) *Advocate;* Waco (Tex.) *Evening News, Examiner*, and *True Blue;* Washington (D.C.) *Evening Star, Globe, National Era, National Intelligencer, National Republican*, and *Post;* Wills Point (Tex.) *Chronicle;* Wilmington (N.C.) *Daily Journal*

Public Documents

Appendix to the Congressional Globe. 26 Cong., 1st sess. Washington, 1839–40.

Appendix to the Congressional Globe. 26 Cong., 2d sess. Washington, 1841.

Appendix to the Congressional Globe. 27 Cong., 1st sess. Washington, 1841.

Appendix to the Congressional Globe. 27 Cong., 2d sess. Washington, 1842.

Appendix to the Congressional Globe. 28 Cong., 2d sess. Washington, 1845.

Applications and Recommendations for Public Office, Grant Administration, Alabama Claims, Other Posts, 1869–77, General Records of the Department of State, Record Group 59, National Archives, Washington, D.C.

Biennial Report of the Secretary of State of the State of Texas, 1894. Austin, 1895.

Chicot County Land Records. Chicot County Courthouse, Lake Village, Ark.

Chicot County Tax Rolls, 1861. Chicot County Courthouse, Lake Village, Ark.

Edgecombe County Commissioners' Minutes. North Carolina Division of Archives and History, Raleigh.

Edgecombe County Land Records. Edgecombe County Courthouse, Tarboro, N.C.

Edgecombe County Superior Court Records. North Carolina Division of Archives and History, Raleigh.

Eighth Census, 1860. Chicot County, N.C. Agricultural Schedule.

Eighth Census, 1860. Hertford County, N.C. Slave Schedule.

Eighth Census, 1860. Wake County, N. C. Slave Schedule.

Hand-book for County Officers: A Guide For Justices of the Peace. . . . Raleigh, 1869.

Hertford County Wills. North Carolina Division of Archives and History, Raleigh.

Hertford County Land Records. North Carolina Division of Archives and History, Raleigh.

Journal of the Convention, Called by the Freemen of North-Carolina, to Amend the Constitution of the State, which Assembled in the City of Raleigh, on the 4th of June, 1835, and Continued in Session until the 11th Day of July Thereafter. Raleigh, 1835.

Journal of the Convention of the People of North Carolina, Held on the 20th Day of May, A.D., 1861. Raleigh, 1862.

Medical Officers File, Records of the Veterans Administration, Record Group 15, National Archives, Washington, D.C.

Mississippi Wills, Mississipi State Archives, Jackson.

Ninth Census, 1870. Wake County, N.C. Population Schedule.

Proceedings of the Army Board for Correction of Military Records in the Case of Mary Edwards Walker, M.D., May 4, 1877, Records Relating to Corrections to Military Records, Records of the Adjutant General's Office, Record Group 94, National Archives, Washington, D.C.

Records of Boundary and Claims Commissions and Arbitrations, Record Group 76, National Archives, Washington, D.C.

Records of the Assistant Commissioner for the State of North Carolina, Bureau of Refugees, Freedmen, and Abandoned Lands, 1866–70, Record Group 105, National Archives, Washington, D.C.

Records of the Solicitor of the Treasury, Record Group 206, National Archives, Washington, D.C.

Records Relating to Pension and Bounty Land Claims, Records of the Veterans Administration, Record Group 15, National Archives, Washington, D.C.

Robertson County Marriage Records. Robertson County Courthouse, Franklin, Tex.

Robertson County Death Records. Robertson County Courthouse, Franklin, Tex.

Robertson County District Court Records. Robertson County Courthouse, Franklin, Tex.

Sixth Census, 1840. Hertford County, N.C. Population Schedule.

Sixth Census, 1840. Hertford County, N.C. Slave Schedule.

Seventh Census, 1850. Chicot County, Ark. Agricultural Schedule.

Seventh Census, 1850. Chicot County, Ark. Slave Schedule.

Seventh Census, 1850. Hertford County, N.C. Agricultural Schedule.

Seventh Census, 1850. Hertford County, N.C. Slave Schedule.

Seventh Census, 1850. Wake County, N.C. Agricultural Schedule.

Seventh Census, 1850. Wake County, N.C. Slave Schedule.

A Statement of the Number of Votes Given on the 1st and 2nd of April Last, and at the August Elections, in 1833, on the Convention Question; Also, the Number of White Male Persons in Each County, of Twenty Years of Age and Upwards, Agreeably to the Last Census. Raleigh, 1835.

Tenth Census, 1880. Robertson County, Tex. Population Schedule.

Texas Ranger Appointment Papers. Texas Adjutant General's Office. Texas State Library, Austin.

Twelfth Census, 1900. Victoria County, Tex. Population Schedule.

U.S. Census Office. *Compendium of the Tenth Census of the United States, 1880.* Pt. 1. Washington, D.C., 1883.

————. *The Twelfth Census of the United States, 1900, Population.* Pt 1. Washington, D.C., 1902.

U.S. Office of Education. *Negro Education: A Study of the Private and Higher Schools for Colored People in the United States.* 2 vols. Washington, D.C., 1917.

Kenneth Rayner Bankruptcy Papers, U.S. District Court, Tennessee, Western District, 1864–1944, Records of District Courts of the United States, Record Group 21, National Archives Atlanta Branch, Atlanta, Ga.

Wake County Land Records. North Carolina Division of Archives and History, Raleigh.

Wake County Wills. North Carolina Division of Archives and History, Raleigh.

War Department, Collection of Confederate Records, Confederate Papers Relating to Citizens or Business Firms, Record Group 109, National Archives, Washington, D.C.

Books and Articles

Abramowitz, Jack. "John B. Rayner—A Grass-Roots Leader." *Journal of Negro History* 36 (April 1951): 160–93.

————. "The Negro in the Agrarian Revolt." *Agricultural History* 24 (April 1950): 89–95.

————. "The Negro in the Populist Movement." *Journal of Negro History* 37 (July 1953): 257–89.

Alexander, Robert Sue. *North Carolina Faces the Freedmen: Race Relations During Presidential Reconstruction, 1865–67.* Durham, 1985.

Alvord, Wayne. "T. L. Nugent, Texas Populist." *Southwestern Historical Quarterly* 57 (July 1953): 65–81.

Anderson, Eric. *Race and Politics in North Carolina, 1872–1901: The Black Second.* Baton Rouge, 1981.

Appleby, Joyce. *Capitalism and a New Social Order: The Republican Vision of the 1790s.* New York, 1984.

———. "Republicanism and Ideology." *American Quarterly* 37 (Fall 1985): 461–73.

Bailyn, Bernard. *The Ideological Origins of the American Revolution.* Cambridge, Mass., 1967.

Baker, J.W. *A History of Robertson County.* Waco, 1970.

Baker, Jean. "From Belief into Culture: Republicanism in the Antebellum North." *American Quarterly* 37 (Fall 1985): 533–50.

Barnes, Donna A. *Farmers in Rebellion: The Rise and Fall of the Southern Farmers Alliance and People's Party in Texas.* Austin, 1984.

Barr, Alwyn. *Reconstruction to Reform: Texas Politics, 1876–1906.* Austin, 1971.

Barr, Alwyn, and Robert A. Calvert, eds. *Black Leaders: Texans for Their Times.* Austin, 1981.

Barrett, John G. *The Civil War in North Carolina.* Chapel Hill, 1963.

Basler, Roy P., ed., *The Collected Works of Abraham Lincoln.* Springfield, 1955.

Beals, Carleton. *Brass-Knuckle Crusade: The Great Know-Nothing Conspiracy: 1820–1860.* New York, 1960.

Billington, Ray Allen. *The Protestant Crusade, 1800–1860: A Study of the Origins of American Nativism.* New York, 1938.

Bodnar, John, Michael Weber, and Roger Simon. "Migration, Kinship, and Urban Adjustment: Blacks and Poles in Pittsburgh, 1900–1930." *Journal of American History* 66 (December 1979): 548–65.

Boykin, James H. *North Carolina in 1861.* New York, 1961.

Brown, Norman D. *Edward Stanly: Whiggery's Tarheel "Conqueror."* University, Ala., 1974.

Brown, Thomas. *Politics and Statesmanship: Essays on the American Whig Party.* New York, 1985.

Bundy, William Oliver. *Life of William Madison McDonald, Ph.D.* Fort Worth, 1925.

Butts, Donald C. "The 'Irrepressible Conflict': Slave Taxation and North Carolina's Gubernatorial Election of 1860." *North Carolina Historical Review* 58 (January 1981): 44–66.

Cantrell, Gregg, and D. Scott Barton. "Texas Populists and the Failure of Biracial Politics." *Journal of Southern History* 55 (November 1989): 659–92.

Carman, Harry J., and Reinhard Luthin. *Lincoln and the Patronage.* Gloucester, Mass., 1964.

Carmichael, Stokely, and Charles V. Hamilton. *Black Power: The Politics of Liberation in America.* New York, 1967.

Carter, Purvis M. "Robert Lloyd Smith and the Farmers' Improvement Society, a Self-Help Movement in Texas." *Negro History Bulletin* 24 (Fall 1966): 175–90.

Carter, Wilmoth A. *Shaw's Universe: A Monument to Educational Innovation.* Raleigh, 1973.

Casdorph, Paul. *A History of the Republican Party in Texas, 1865–1965.* Austin, 1965.

Cathey, Cornelius Oliver. *Agricultural Developments in North Carolina, 1783–1860.* Chapel Hill, 1956.

Censer, Jane Turner. *North Carolina Planters and Their Children, 1800–1860.* Baton Rouge, 1984.

Chafe, William H. "The Negro and Populism: A Kansas Case Study." *Journal of Southern History* 34 (August 1968): 402–19.

Chitwood, Oliver Perry. *John Tyler: Champion of the Old South*. New York, 1964.

Clinton, Catherine. *The Plantation Mistress: Woman's World in the Old South*. New York, 1982.

Connor, Henry Groves. "The Convention of 1835." *North Carolina Booklet* 8 (October 1908): 89–110.

Cook, Adrian. *The Alabama Claims: American Politics and Anglo-American Relations, 1865–1872*. Ithaca, 1975.

Cooper, William J., Jr. *The South and the Politics of Slavery, 1828–1856*. Baton Rouge, 1978.

Copway, George. *Organization of a New Indian Territory East of the Missouri River*. New York, 1850.

Counihan, Harold J. "The North Carolina Constitutional Convention of 1835: A Study in Jacksonian Democracy." *North Carolina Historical Review* 66 (October 1969): 335–64.

Curran, Thomas J. *Xenophobia and Immigration, 1820–1930*. Boston, 1975.

Cutler, James Elbert. *Lynch-Law: An Investigation into the History of Lynching in the United States*. Rpt. New York, 1969.

Degler, Carl N. *The Other South: Southern Dissenters in the Nineteenth Century*. New York, 1974.

Durden, Robert F. *The Climax of Populism: The Election of 1896*. Lexington, Ky., 1966.

Eaton, Clement. *Henry Clay and the Art of American Politics*. Boston, 1957.

Foner, Eric. *Free Soil, Free Labor, Free Men: The Ideology of the Republican Party before the Civil War*. London, 1970.

Fredrickson, George M. *The Black Image in the White Mind: The Debate on Afro-American Character and Destiny, 1817–1914*. New York, 1971.

Fuller, Henry C. *"A Texas Sheriff."* Nacogdoches, 1931.

Gaither, Gerald H. *Blacks and the Populist Revolt: Ballots and Bigotry in the "New South."* University, Ala., 1977.

Garner, John S. "The Saga of a Railroad Town: Calvert, Texas (1868–1918)." *Southwestern Historical Quarterly* 85 (October 1981): 140–45.

Genovese, Eugene D. *The Political Economy of Slavery: Studies in the Economy and Society of the Slave South*. New York, 1961, 1967.

——— . *Roll, Jordan, Roll: The World the Slaves Made*. New York, 1972.

Gienapp, William E. *The Origins of the Republican Party, 1852–1856*. New York, 1987.

Goodwyn, Lawrence. *Democratic Promise: The Populist Moment in America*. New York, 1976.

——— . "Populist Dreams and Negro Rights: East Texas as a Case Study." *American Historical Review* 76 (December 1971): 1436–56.

Gould, Lewis L. *Progressives and Prohibitionists: Texas Democrats in the Wilson Era*. Austin, 1973.

Grantham, Dewey W. *The Regional Imagination: The South and Recent American History*. Nashville, 1979.

Greven, Philip, Jr. *Four Generations: Population, Land, and Family in Colonial Andover, Massachusetts*. Ithaca, 1970.

Gunderson, Robert Gray. *Old Gentlemen's Convention: The Washington Peace Conference of 1861*. Madison, 1961.

Hackett, Frank W. *The Geneva Award Acts: With Notes, and References to Decisions of the Court of Commissioners of Alabama Claims*. Boston, 1882.

Hackney, Sheldon. *Populism to Progressivism in Alabama*. Princeton, 1969.

Hair, William Ivy. *Bourbonism and Agrarian Protest: Louisiana Politics, 1877–1900*. Baton Rouge, 1969.

Haley, John H. *Charles N. Hunter and Race Relations in North Carolina*. Chapel Hill, 1987.

Haller, Mark H. *Eugenics: Hereditarian Attitudes in American Thought*. New Brunswick, 1963.

Halliburton, Cecil D. *A History of St. Augustine's College, 1867–1937*. Raleigh, 1937.

Hamilton, Holman. *Zachary Taylor: Soldier in the White House*. New York, 1951.

Hamilton, J. G. De Roulhac. *Benjamin Sherwood Hedrick*. Chapel Hill, 1910.

————. *Party Politics in North Carolina, 1835–1860*. Durham, 1916.

————. *Reconstruction in North Carolina*. New York, 1914.

Hamlin, Charles Eugene. *The Life and Times of Hannibal Hamlin*. Cambridge, Mass., 1899.

Hare, Maud Cuney. *Norris Wright Cuney; A Tribune of the Black People*. New York, 1913.

Harlan, Louis R. *Booker T. Washington: The Making of a Black Leader, 1865–1901*. New York, 1972.

Harris, William C. *The Day of the Carpetbagger: Republican Reconstruction in Mississippi*. Baton Rouge, 1979.

————. *William Woods Holden: Firebrand of North Carolina Politics*. Baton Rouge, 1987.

Hart, Roger L. *Redeemers, Bourbons, and Populists: Tennessee, 1870–1896*. Baton Rouge, 1975.

Hartz, Louis. *The Liberal Tradition in America*. New York, 1955.

Hicks, John D. *The Populist Revolt: A History of the Farmers' Alliance and the People's Party*. Minneapolis, 1931.

Hoffmann, William S. *Andrew Jackson and North Carolina Politics*. Chapel Hill, 1958.

Holmes, William F. *The White Chief: James Kimble Vardaman*. Baton Rouge, 1970.

Holt, Michael F. *The Political Crisis of the 1850s*. New York, 1978.

Howe, Daniel Walker. *The Political Culture of the American Whigs*. Chicago, 1979.

Hutchinson, Louise Daniel. *Anna J. Cooper: A Voice from the South*. Washington, D.C., 1981.

Jeffrey, Thomas E. "Internal Improvements and Political Parties in Antebellum North Carolina, 1836–1860." *North Carolina Historical Review* 60 (April 1978): 111–56.

Johnson, Allen, and Dumas Malone, eds. *The Dictionary of American Biography*. 20 vols. New York, 1928–37.

Johnson, Guion Griffis. *Ante-Bellum North Carolina: A Social History*. Chapel Hill, 1937.

Jones, Stanley L. *The Presidential Election of 1896*. Madison, 1964.

Kerber, Linda. "The Republican Ideology of the Revolutionary Generation." *American Quarterly* 37 (Fall 1985): 474–95.

Key, V. O., Jr. *Southern Politics*. New York, 1949.

Kirwan, Albert D. *John J. Crittenden: The Struggle for the Union*. Lexington, Ky., 1962.

————. *Revolt of the Rednecks, Mississippi Politics: 1876–1925.* Lexington, Ky., 1951.

Knobel, Dale T. "Nativists and Indians: Strange Bedfellows?" *The Western Historical Quarterly* 15 (April 1984): 175–98.

————. *Paddy and the Republic: Ethnicity and Nationality in Antebellum America.* Middletown, 1986.

Kousser, J. Morgan. *The Shaping of Southern Politics: Suffrage Restriction and the Establishment of the One-Party South, 1888–1910.* New Haven, 1974.

Kruman, Marc W. *Parties and Politics in North Carolina, 1836–1865.* Baton Rouge, 1983.

Lasswell, Mary. *John Henry Kirby: Prince of the Pines.* Austin, 1967.

Laurie, Bruce. "'Nothing on Compulsion': Life Styles of Philadelphia Artisans, 1820–1850." *Labor History* 15 (Summer 1974): 337–56.

Link, Arthur S. "Theodore Roosevelt and the South in 1912." *North Carolina Historical Review* 23 (July 1946): 313–24.

Martin, Roscoe. "The Greenback Party in Texas." *Southwestern Historical Quarterly* 30 (January 1927): 38–62.

————. *The People's Party in Texas: A Study in Third-Party Politics.* Rpt. Austin, 1970.

Maxwell, Robert S., and Robert D. Baker. *Sawdust Empire: The Texas Lumber Industry, 1830–1940.* College Station, 1983.

McCarver, Norman L., and Norman L. McCarver, Jr. *Hearne on the Brazos.* San Antonio, 1956.

McCormick, Richard P. "New Perspectives on Jacksonian Politics." *American Historical Review* 65 (January 1960): 288–301.

McCoy, Drew. *The Elusive Republic: Political Economy in Jeffersonian America.* Chapel Hill, 1980.

McCulloch, Margaret Callender. "Founding the North Carolina Asylum for the Insane." *North Carolina Historical Review* 13 (July 1936): 185–201.

McLaurin, Melton A. "The Nineteenth-Century North Carolina State Fair as a Social Institution." *North Carolina Historical Review* 59 (July 1982): 213–29.

McMath, Robert C., Jr. *Populist Vanguard: A History of the Southern Farmers' Alliance.* Chapel Hill, 1975.

Meier, August. *Negro Thought in America: Racial Ideologies in the Age of Booker T. Washington.* Ann Arbor, 1963.

Meyers, Marvin. *The Jacksonian Persuasion: Politics and Belief.* Stanford, 1957.

Miller, Worth Robert. "Building a Progressive Coalition in Texas: The Populist-Reform Democrat Rapprochement, 1900–1907." *Journal of Southern History* 52 (May 1986): 163–82.

————. *Oklahoma Populism: A History of the People's Party in the Oklahoma Territory.* Norman, 1987.

Mitchell, Theodore. *Political Education in the Southern Farmers' Alliance, 1887–1900.* Madison, 1987.

Mobley, Joe A. "In the Shadow of White Society: Princeville, a Black Town in North Carolina, 1865–1915." *North Carolina Historical Review* 63 (July 1986): 340–84.

Morgan, George T., Jr. "The Gospel of Wealth Goes South: John Henry Kirby and Labor's Struggle for Self-Determination, 1901–1916." *Southwestern Historical Quarterly* 75 (October 1971): 186–97.

————. "No Compromise—No Recognition: John Henry Kirby, the Southern Lumber Operators' Association, and Unionism in the Piney Woods, 1906–1917." *Labor History* 10 (Spring 1969): 193–204.

Morrill, James R. "The Presidential Election of 1852: Death Knell of the Whig Party in North Carolina." *North Carolina Historical Review* 44 (Autumn 1967): 342–59.

Mowry, George E. "The South and the Progressive Lily White Party of 1912." *Journal of Southern History* 6 (May 1940): 237–47.

Murray, Elizabeth Reid. *Wake: Capital County of North Carolina.* 2 vols. Raleigh, 1983.

National Cyclopaedia of American Biography. 63 vols. New York, 1898–1984.

Nevins, Allan. *Ordeal of the Union.* 8 vols. New York, 1947–71.

Nicolay, John G., and John Hay. *Abraham Lincoln: A History.* New York, 1890.

Nieman, Donald G. "Black Political Power and Criminal Justice: Washington County, Texas, 1868–1884." *Journal of Southern History* 55 (August 1989): 391–420.

Norton, Clarence Clifford. *The Democratic Party in Ante-Bellum North Carolina, 1835–1861.* Chapel Hill, 1930.

Oakes, James. "From Republicanism to Liberalism: Ideological Change and the Crisis of the Old South." *American Quarterly* 37 (Fall 1985): 551–71.

Overdyke, W. Darrell. *The Know-Nothing Party in the South.* Baton Rouge, 1950.

Palmer, Bruce. *"Man Over Money": The Southern Populist Critique of American Capitalism.* Chapel Hill, 1980.

Parker, Richard Denny. *Historical Recollections of Robertson County.* Salado, Tex., 1955.

Parks, Joseph H. *General Leonidas Polk C.S.A.: The Fighting Bishop.* Baton Rouge, 1963.

Parsons, Stanley B., William W. Beach, and Michael J. Dubin. *United States Congressional Districts and Data, 1843–1883.* New York, 1986.

Pegg, Herbert Dale. *The Whig Party in North Carolina.* Chapel Hill, n.d.

Pereyra, Lillian A. *James Lusk Alcorn: Persistent Whig.* Baton Rouge, 1966.

Peterson, Merrill D. *The Great Triumvirate: Webster, Clay, and Calhoun.* New York, 1987.

Pocock, J. G. A. *The Machiavellian Moment: Florentine Political Thought and the Atlantic Republican Tradition.* Princeton, 1975.

Pollack, Norman. *The Just Polity: Populism, Law, and Human Welfare.* Urbana, 1987.

Potter, David M. *The South and the Sectional Conflict.* Baton Rouge, 1968.

Raper, Arthur F. *The Tragedy of Lynching.* Rpt. New York, 1969.

Raper, Horace W. "William W. Holden and the Peace Movement in North Carolina." *North Carolina Historical Review* 31 (October 1954): 493–516.

Rawley, James A. *Race and Politics: "Bleeding Kansas" and the Coming of the Civil War.* Philadelphia, 1969.

Remini, Robert V. *Andrew Jackson.* New York, 1966.

Rice, Lawrence D. *The Negro in Texas, 1874–1900.* Baton Rouge, 1971.

Rothman, David J. *The Discovery of the Asylum: Social Order and Disorder in the New Republic.* Boston, 1971.

Saunders, Robert M. "Southern Populists and the Negro, 1893–1895." *Journal of Negro History* 54 (July 1969): 240–61.

Schurz, Carl. *Henry Clay,* 2 vols. Rpt. New York, 1980.

Scisco, Louis D. *Political Nativism in New York State.* New York, 1901.

Seager, Robert, II. *and Tyler too: A Biography of John & Julia Gardiner Tyler.* New York, 1963.

Seward, Frederick W. *Seward at Washington as Senator and Secretary of State.* New York, 1891.

Shankman, Arnold. *Ambivalent Friends: Afro-Americans View the Immigrant.* Westport, 1982.

Shapiro, Herbert. "The Populists and the Negro: A Reconsideration." In *The Making Of Black America: Essays in Negro Life and History,* ed. August Meier and Elliott Rudwick. 2 vols. New York, 1969.

Shaw, Barton. *The Wool-Hat Boys: Georgia's Populist Party.* Baton Rouge, 1984.

Simms, Henry H. *Emotion at High Tide: Abolition as a Controversial Factor, 1830–1845.* Richmond, 1960.

Simms-Brown, R. Jean. "Populism and Black Americans: Constructive or Destructive?" *Journal of Negro History* 65 (Fall 1980): 349–60.

Simpson, Craig M. *A Good Southerner: The Life of Henry A. Wise of Virginia.* Chapel Hill, 1985.

Sitterson, Joseph Carlyle. *The Secession Movement in North Carolina.* Chapel Hill, 1939.

SoRelle, James M. " 'The Waco Horror': The Lynching of Jesse Washington." *Southwestern Historical Quarterly* 86 (April 1983): 517–36.

Spratt, John Stricklin. *The Road to Spindletop: Economic Change in Texas, 1875–1901.* Rpt. Austin, 1970.

Stampp, Kenneth M. *The Peculiar Institution: Slavery in the Antebellum South.* New York, 1956.

Taylor, R. H. "Humanizing the Slave Code of North Carolina." *North Carolina Historical Review* 2 (July 1925): 323–31.

Thornton, J. Mills, III. *Politics and Power in a Slave Society: Alabama, 1800–1860.* Baton Rouge, 1978.

Tindall, George Brown. *The Emergence of the New South, 1913–1945.* Baton Rouge, 1967.

Turner, Kelly J., and John L. Bridgers, Jr. *History of Edgecombe County, North Carolina.* Raleigh, 1920.

Tyler, Alice Felt. *Freedom's Ferment: Phases of American Social History from the Colonial Period to the Outbreak of the Civil War.* New York, 1944.

van den Berghe, Pierre L. *Race and Racism: A Comparative Perspective.* New York, 1967.

Van Deusen, Glyndon G. *The Jacksonian Era, 1828–1848.* New York, 1959.

Wallace, Wesley H. "North Carolina's Agricultural Journals, 1838–1861: A Crusading Press." *North Carolina Historical Review* 36 (July 1959): 275–306.

Walton, Brian G. "Elections to the United States Senate in North Carolina, 1835–1861." *North Carolina Historical Review* 52 (April 1976): 168–92.

Watson, Alan D. *Edgecombe County: A Brief History.* Raleigh, 1979.

Waugh, Elizabeth Culbertson and Editorial Committee. *North Carolina's Capital, Raleigh.* Chapel Hill, 1967.

Wilson, Charles Reagan. *Baptized in Blood: The Religion of the Lost Cause, 1865–1920.* Athens, 1980.

Winborne, Benjamin B. *The Colonial and State History of Hertford County, North Carolina.* Baltimore, 1976.

Wood, Gordon S. *The Creation of the American Republic, 1776–1787.* Chapel Hill, 1969.
Woodward, C. Vann. *Origins of the New South, 1877–1913.* Baton Rouge, 1951.
———. "The Populist Heritage and the Intellectual." *American Scholar* 29 (Winter 1959–60): 55–72.
———. *Reunion and Reaction: The Compromise of 1877 and the End of Reconstruction.* Boston, 1951.
———. *The Strange Career of Jim Crow.* New York, 1957.
———. *Tom Watson: Agrarian Rebel.* New York, 1938.
Wright, Gavin. *The Political Economy of the Cotton South: Households, Markets, and Wealth in the Nineteenth Century.* New York, 1978.
Wyatt-Brown, Bertram. *Southern Honor: Ethics and Behavior in the Old South.* New York, 1982.

Theses and Dissertations

Banks, Melvin James. "The Pursuit of Equality: The Movement for First Class Citizenship Among Negroes in Texas, 1920–1950." Ph.D. diss. Syracuse University, 1962.
Brophy, William Joseph. "The Black Texan, 1900–1950: A Quantitative History." Ph.D. diss. Vanderbilt University, 1974.
Carroll, Robert. "Robert Lloyd Smith and the Farmers' Improvement Society of Texas." M.A. thesis. Baylor University, 1974.
Glasrud, Bruce. "Black Texans, 1900–1930: A History." Ph.D. diss. Texas Technological College, 1969.
Hazel, Sybal. "Statewide Prohibition Campaigns in Texas." M.A. thesis. Texas Technological College, 1942.
McMillan, Frank Ney, III. "Calvert: An Historical Geography." M.A. thesis. Texas A&M University, 1984.
Ross, John Raymond. "Andrew Jackson Spradley: 'A Texas Sheriff.'" M.A. thesis. Stephen F. Austin State University, 1973.
St. Clair, Lawrence Ward. "History of Robertson County." M.A. thesis. University of Texas, 1931.

Interviews by the Author

Carrington, Arlene. Washington, D.C., April 1987.
Childs, Ann Rayner. Chicago, Ill., January 1987.
Goodwyn, Lawrence. Durham, N.C., March 1987.
Peters, Margaret. Beaumont, Tex., June 1987.
Rayner, A. A. Chicago, Ill., January 1987, College Station, Tex., July 1988.
Rayner, A. A. "Sammie", Jr. Chicago, Ill., January 1987, College Station, Tex., July 1988.
Rayner, Ivan. Chicago, Ill., January 1987.
Williams, Howard. Calvert, Tex., November 1986, June 1987.
Yepp, Jessie. Calvert, Tex., June 1987.

Miscellaneous

I examined Kenneth Rayner's personal library at the Incarnate Word College Library, San Antonio, Tex. The books had been donated to the library by Rayner's great-granddaughter, Ruth Matlock. They were awaiting processing into the library's general collection.

Oil portraits of Colonel William Polk and Susan Polk Rayner and the Rayner Family Bible were examined courtesy of Kenneth Rayner's great-granddaughter, Sallie Savage, Midland, Tex. The 1849 oil portrait of Kenneth Rayner was examined courtesy of his great-grandson, Kenneth Rayner Hyman, Jr., San Antonio, Tex.

Bench and Bar of Memphis, Memorials 3 (1966), Memphis-Shelby County Public Library, Memphis, Tenn.

Captain William H. Bradshaw III, M.D., Brooke Army Medical Center, San Antonio, provided a theoretical diagnosis of John B. Rayner's final illness.

Otis D. Cannon, Houston, furnished a photocopy of a 1931 clipping from the Houston *Press* about his grandfather, Judge O. D. Cannon.

Arlene Carrington, Washington, D.C., furnished copies of the wills of Sarah Hawkins Polk and William Polk as well as a large body of information on Polk-Rayner genealogy. She is a relative of Kenneth Rayner's black daughter, Cornelia Rayner Keeling.

J. P. Daviss, Conroe Normal and Industrial College, Conroe Tex., furnished a copy of a pamphlet, "Program for the Eighteenth Annual William A. Johnson Memorial Institute, held on April 28–30, 1964, at Conroe Normal and Industrial College."

First Baptist Church, Raleigh, N.C. Church Minutes (1856–74), North Carolina Division of Archives and History, Raleigh.

Genie and Hyman H. Kirkpatrick, Weslaco, Tex., furnished a photocopy of a letter from Kenneth Rayner to Sally Rayner, dated June 29, 1866. Hyman Kirkpatrick is a great-grandson of Kenneth Rayner.

Index

Gregg Cantrell received his Ph.D. from Texas A&M University in 1988 and is an assistant professor of history at Sam Houston State University in Huntsville, Texas. He has written several articles on nineteenth-century southern politics and race relations.

Charles Richard Drew: The Man and the Myth
Charles E. Wynes

John Mercer Langston and the Fight for Black Freedom, 1829–65
William Cheek and Aimee Lee Cheek

The Old Village and the Great House: An Archaeological and Historical
Examination of Drax Hall Plantation, St. Ann's Bay, Jamaica
Douglas V. Armstrong

Black Property Owners in the South, 1790–1915
Loren Schweninger

The Sociogenesis of a Race Riot: Springfield, Illinois, in 1908
Roberta Senechal

Coal, Class, and Color: Blacks in Southern West Virginia, 1915–32
Joe William Trotter, Jr.

No Crooked Death: Coatesville, Pennsylvania,
and the Lynching of Zachariah Walker
Dennis B. Downey and Raymond M. Hyser

Black Towns and Profit: Promotion and Development
in the Trans-Appalachian West, 1877–1915
Kenneth Marvin Hamilton

Slaves, Peasants, and Rebels: Reconsidering Brazilian Slavery
Stuart B. Schwartz

Africa in America: Slave Acculturation and Resistance
in the American South and the British Caribbean, 1736–1831
Michael Mullin

The Creation of Jazz: Music, Race, and Culture in Urban America
Burton W. Peretti

Kenneth and John B. Rayner and the Limits of Southern Dissent
Gregg Cantrell

REPRINT EDITIONS
King: A Biography
Second Edition
David Levering Lewis

The Death and Life of Malcolm X
Second Edition
Peter Goldman

Race Relations in the Urban South, 1865–1890
Howard N. Rabinowitz; foreword by C. Vann Woodward

Race Riot at East St. Louis, July 2, 1917
Elliott Rudwick

W. E. B. Du Bois: Voice of the Black Protest Movement
Elliott Rudwick

The Negro's Civil War: How American Negroes Felt and Acted
during the War for the Union
James M. McPherson

Lincoln and Black Freedom: A Study in Presidential Leadership
LaWanda Cox

Slavery and Freedom in the Age of the American Revolution
Edited by Ira Berlin and Ronald Hoffman

Diary of a Sit-In
Second Edition
Merrill Proudfoot; introduction by Michael S. Mayer

They Who Would Be Free: Blacks' Search for Freedom, 1830–61
Jane H. Pease and William H. Pease

The Reshaping of Plantation Society: The Natchez District, 1860–80
Michael Wayne

Rice and Slaves: Ethnicity and the Slave Trade in Colonial South Carolina
Daniel C. Littlefield